MW01712447

Using Microsoft® Works: IBM® Version

Douglas J. Wolf

que® CORPORATION
LEADING COMPUTER KNOWLEDGE

Using Microsoft® Works

IBM® Version

Copyright © 1989 by Que® Corporation.

All rights reserved. Printed in the United States of America. No part of this book may be used or reproduced in any form or by any means, or stored in a database or retrieval system, without prior written permission of the publisher except in the case of brief quotations embodied in critical articles and reviews. Making copies of any part of this book for any purpose other than your own personal use is a violation of United States copyright laws. For information, address Que Corporation, 11711 N. College Ave., Carmel, IN 46032.

Library of Congress Catalog No.: 89-62447

ISBN: 0-88022-467-3

This book is sold *as is*, without warranty of any kind, either express or implied, respecting the contents of this book, including but not limited to implied warranties for the book's quality, performance, merchantability, or fitness for any particular purpose. Neither Que Corporation nor its dealers or distributors shall be liable to the purchaser or any other person or entity with respect to any liability, loss, or damage caused or alleged to be caused directly or indirectly by this book.

92 91 90 8 7 6 5 4 3

Interpretation of the printing code: the rightmost double-digit number is the year of the book's printing; the rightmost single-digit number, the number of the book's printing. For example, a printing code of 89-1 shows that the first printing of the book occurred in 1989.

Using Microsoft Works: IBM Version is based on Microsoft Works IBM Version 2.0 and earlier versions.

Dedication

To my grandmother, Pearl Wolf, who, despite all her setbacks and personal losses, has never lost her basic faith in people and her God. She is surely one of the inheritors of the Earth and a guiding example to me.

Publishing Director

Lloyd J. Short

Acquisitions Editor

Karen A. Bluestein

Product Director

David Maguiness

Production Editor

Sandra Blackthorn

Editors

Luanne Blackburn
Jeannine Freudenberger
Julia Knispel
Jay McNaught
Gregory Robertson
Mary Stansifer

Technical Editor

Cameron Parker

Indexed by

Sherry Massey

Book Design and Production

Dan Armstrong
Brad Chinn
Jodi Jensen
David Kline
Lori A. Lyons
Jennifer Matthews
Cindy L. Phipps
Joe Ramon
Patricia Maupin Riggs
Dennis Sheehan
Louise Shinault
Bruce Steed
Mary Beth Wakefield

Composed in Garamond and Excellent No. 47
by Que Corporation

About the Author

Douglas J. Wolf

Douglas J. Wolf became involved with microcomputing in 1982, when he and a partner founded a software distribution company in Minneapolis. They later sold the company to a larger wholesaler, and Mr. Wolf became the company's sales manager of the software and computer electronics division. He also has held the position of regional sales representative with Business Solutions of Kings Park, NY, and has worked with Via Computer, a company that developed financial modeling tools on mainframe IBMs.

Mr. Wolf holds business and journalism degrees. He is a mortgage banker and has authored several books on a variety of subjects, including Lotus 1-2-3, Quattro, Sprint, Lotus Agenda, and First Choice.

Contents at a Glance

Table of Contents

IV Databases

Trademark Acknowledgments

Que Corporation has made every effort to supply trademark information about company names, products, and services mentioned in this book. Trademarks indicated below were derived from various sources. Que Corporation cannot attest to the accuracy of this information.

1-2-3 and Lotus are registered trademarks of Lotus Development Corporation.

Apple and Macintosh are registered trademarks of Apple Computer, Inc.

CompuServe is a registered trademark of CompuServe, Inc., and H&R Block, Inc.

dBASE is a registered trademark of Ashton-Tate Corporation.

First Choice is a registered trademark of Software Publishing Corporation.

IBM is a registered trademark of International Business Machines.

Microsoft, Microsoft Word, and Microsoft Works are registered trademarks of Microsoft Corporation.

NetWare and Novell are registered trademarks of Novell, Inc.

Quattro and Sprint are registered trademarks of Borland International, Inc.

Telenet is a registered trademark of GTE Telenet Communications Corporation.

Tymnet is a registered trademark of Tymnet, Inc.

Conventions Used in This Book

The conventions used in this book have been established to help you learn to use the program quickly and easily.

Commands and menu names are written with initial capital letters exactly as they appear on-screen. Names of dialog boxes are written with initial capital letters. Options in dialog boxes and on-screen messages are written in a `special typeface` and capitalized exactly as they appear on-screen. Words and letters the user types are written in *italic* or set off on a separate line.

ACKNOWLEDGMENTS

I would like to thank the following people for helping to make this book a reality:

Gloria Wheeler, my wife and favorite editor

Dave Maguiness and Sandy Blackthorn, Que Corporation

William "passing shot" Gladstone, Waterside Productions

Roy Harper, Microsoft Product Support

—D.J.W.

Introduction

Software programs began with epic programs that could do just about anything in a single subject area. Just like the learned professor who knew a lot about very little, the computer program could perform many tasks but only in one area (such as spreadsheets, for example).

Computer programs have now evolved from being specialized to generalized. Computer programs have become *integrated*. Instead of having one program that does everything possible with spreadsheets, you can have one program that does quite a bit with spreadsheets but also has a capable word processor and database.

With Microsoft Works, instead of the learned professor, you have the handyman of software programs. Not only can Microsoft Works produce professional word processing documents, but the program also can create a detailed spreadsheet, create database reports, and communicate with other computers.

Specifically, these are some of the tasks you can perform with Microsoft Works:

Word Processor features

- ❏ Produce letters
- ❏ Produce memos
- ❏ Create reports

Spreadsheet features

- ❏ Create budgets
- ❏ Make forecasts
- ❏ Account for profits and losses

Database features

- ❑ Keep business records
- ❑ Store names and addresses
- ❑ Create mailing lists

Communication features

- ❑ Communicate with CompuServe
- ❑ Communicate with other computers

You have four programs integrated into one. And what's more, these four programs can share information. Your database can talk to your word processor, allowing you to create form letters and mailing labels to match. You can integrate excerpts from your spreadsheet into letters to your board of directors. You can add some research, done through CompuServe, to a staff report.

Microsoft Works is designed to function with the hardware as a complete system so you don't have to spend time transferring files from one program to another. The integration of four programs into one allows you to use the four most common computer applications in one program.

Using the Word Processor

The Microsoft Works word processor lets you easily write and correct letters, memos, proposals, reports, or articles; format them in a way that meets your needs; and print them, either individually or as a batch of personalized documents to your personal customers. The text is stored magnetically on a disk, so you can print the text as many times as you need. You can correct the text or rewrite it without retyping the whole document and then print it again; you also can store different versions of the same text for later use, knowing that each version is available whenever you need it.

Using the Database

A database lets you organize the information you work with in convenient, accessible elements that can be sorted, recalled, and reported in a variety of ways. An example of a database is a list of important names and numbers kept on or near a desktop. This database contains a name, a number, and perhaps a company name and address. In addition, the database may contain notes about specific products with their prices, times when certain individuals are available, or other useful information.

A computerized database lets you keep all this information in a way that allows you to sort, select, and rearrange the information as you need it. As with word processing text, the data is stored magnetically so you can update it, change it, and rearrange it without losing the original information. In addition, you can print the results of each sorting or updating in a separate formatted report without altering the core information in the database.

Using the Spreadsheet

Like the paper item it is named after, a computerized spreadsheet lets you arrange data in rows and columns, and analyze the data using arithmetic functions. Most often, a spreadsheet is used for standard financial reports, such as income statements, balance sheets, and cash-flow statements. Because the computerized spreadsheet is more powerful than its paper predecessor, you can add financial projections, complex calculations, invoices and quotations, and statistical records to your bank of information. The "what if" analysis is done on a spreadsheet with relative ease. Change one piece of data and see the effect on the rest of your calculations. Because you have magnetically stored information, you can store each "what if" analysis in a separate file or print each one for a hard copy of the results of your assumptions.

And you can take raw numbers from the spreadsheet and create charts with Microsoft Works to help you analyze and interpret your information. Charts help make a presentation come alive with graphic representations of numbers. Works provides eight chart types, including bar, line, area, and pie charts.

Communicating with Other Computers and Services

Connect your computer to another computer, an in-line information service, a user service, and many other national and local networks. The Works program dials the phone number and establishes the electronic dialog (referred to as "handshaking") necessary for one computer to talk to another.

Who Should Use This Book?

This book is written for the small-business owner or the department manager who wants to use Microsoft Works to make his or her job easier. Most of the examples used in this book reflect actual business situations. And *Using Microsoft Works: IBM Version* includes quick-start lessons that allow you to be off and running quickly. In the chapters that follow these quick-start lessons, you will find the details you need to do more intricate tasks with Microsoft Works.

How To Use This Book

Using Microsoft Works: IBM Version is a highly visual presentation of Microsoft Works. The book is divided into parts that cover in detail each component of Microsoft Works. You can turn to the part that examines the component you're wanting to use and receive complete, detailed information about that feature.

Included in this book are quick-start chapters designed—as the name implies—to get you started quickly. One quick start covers word processing, another covers spreadsheets, and the third covers databases. If you are using the word processing component, for example, and you want to start typing immediately, turn to the quick-start chapter on word processing. Later, when you find that you need to move text or perform other more advanced procedures, refer to remaining chapters in the word processing section of the book.

How This Book Is Organized

The chapters in *Using Microsoft Works: IBM Version* cover each of the four main components of Microsoft Works: word processing, spreadsheets, databases, and communications. In addition, chapters are included on graphs, macros, and integrating the four components.

Part I covers how to get started. Chapter 1, "Installing Microsoft Works," lists the minimum requirements for using Microsoft Works and covers how to make backups of your new software and how to get into and out of Microsoft Works.

Part II covers the word processing component. You will begin with Quick Start 1, "Creating a Word Processing Document," which briefly examines

Works word processing techniques and gets you started with the word processor.

Chapter 2, "Entering, Editing, and Saving Your Word Processing Document," examines how to use the menu system, open a file, create a document, and edit, format, and work with word processing files.

Chapter 3, "Opening Files and Formatting Text," examines formatting, creating tables with columns, using boldface and italic, and changing fonts.

Chapter 4, "Using Advanced Word Processing Functions and Printing with Works," explains how to search, search and replace, add headers and footers, create form letters by merging documents, and print all or part of a document.

Part III covers the spreadsheet component. You can jump right into the financial aspects of Microsoft Works by working through Quick Start 2, "Creating a Spreadsheet."

Chapter 5, "Creating and Using Spreadsheets," covers how to enter data into a Microsoft Works spreadsheet and how to create a budget. You will enter numbers and labels, move the cursor around the spreadsheet, edit cell entries, and copy formulas and numbers into different cells.

In Chapter 6, "Examining Spreadsheet Basics," you will finish the spreadsheet you began in Chapter 5 and learn more about the basics of using the spreadsheet. Topics include copying cell contents, formatting numbers, creating range names, using relative and absolute formulas, freezing row and column titles, hiding columns, protecting cell contents, and searching the spreadsheet.

Chapter 7, "Using Functions," examines all of Microsoft Works' built-in functions, which can be used with the Works spreadsheet or database. These functions are abbreviations of longer formulas that would be difficult to use in a spreadsheet or database if they were not already part of Microsoft Works.

Chapter 8, "Creating Charts," will help you generate charts from spreadsheet data by using many of the graph options. You can make pie charts, bar charts, x,y charts, and more using Microsoft Works' graphing capabilities.

Part IV examines databases. Quick Start 3, "Creating a Database and Database Report," will help you learn quickly how to keep detailed records necessary in your business.

Chapter 9, "Creating and Using Databases," covers the basics of creating a database. You will learn how to enter field names, enter data into a record, and edit cell contents, as well as enter dates and move fields and records.

Chapter 10, "Creating and Using Database Reports," examines how to make data more useful to you. You will prepare queries and print the data by creating practical reports.

Part V examines the communications component. Chapter 11, "Communicating with Works," covers methods for interacting with CompuServe and other communications tasks available with Works.

Chapter 12, "Creating and Using Macros," covers how to make and use macros for your work.

The real advantage of using a program like Microsoft Works is being able to integrate each of the four aspects of the program. In Part VI, you will learn how to do just that. Chapter 13, "Tying It All Together," covers the many tasks you can complete by using an integrated program. This chapter shows you how to make the best of those features.

Appendix A explains how the Microsoft Works spreadsheet talks to Lotus 1-2-3 and how the Microsoft Works database talks to dBASE. Templates to improve production are examined as well. Transferring Microsoft Works text in and out of ASCII files is included.

Part I

Getting Started

Includes

Installing Microsoft Works

1

Installing Microsoft Works

Microsoft Works is designed to run on IBM personal computers and compatible systems. This chapter takes you through the basic steps for installing and starting the program.

Examining the Minimum Requirements

Following are the minimum system requirements for Microsoft Works:

- ❑ 384K RAM memory
- ❑ DOS 2.0 or higher
- ❑ Either two 360K disk drives, one 720K disk drive, or a hard disk drive
- ❑ CGA, EGA, VGA, or Hercules graphics adapter required for making graphs

An optional peripheral you may want to purchase is a mouse. Microsoft Works takes full advantage of mouse capabilities. With a mouse you can perform all the operations you can with the keyboard, including "point and shoot" menus, select text, and move and extend the cell selector in a spreadsheet. You can generally perform an operation with a mouse much faster than with the arrow keys, particularly if you are not a touch typist.

The mouse enables you to watch the screen rather than the keyboard. Almost any mouse can be used with Microsoft Works. Consult your computer hardware dealer for help in selecting one.

If you intend to use Microsoft Works in a network system, you need the following equipment:

- ❑ DOS 3.1 or higher at each workstation
- ❑ A network system that is compatible with Microsoft networks, such as IBM PC Network, 3Com 3+, AT&T Starlan, Corvus OmniNet, Novell NetWare, Ungermann-Bass Net/One, and others.

If you intend to use the communications options with Microsoft Works, you will need a Hayes-compatible modem.

Installing the Program

After you have established that you have all the equipment you need, you are ready to install Microsoft Works. The installation process is different for floppy disk systems and hard disk systems. Use the appropriate installation procedure for the kind of system you have.

Installation on a Floppy Disk System

The first step in installing Microsoft Works on a floppy disk system is to make backup copies of the original program disks to use as your working disks. You need eight blank, formatted, 5 1/4-inch 360K disks, or four blank, formatted, 3 1/2-inch 720K disks, to copy all the program disks. Make copies of the following:

- ❑ Program Disk
- ❑ Printer Disk 1
- ❑ Printer Disk 2
- ❑ Spell/Help Disk
- ❑ Setup/Utilities Disk

You do not need to copy the Learning disks, although you may want to use them at some point. If you think you will want to use the tutorial, you should make backup copies of the Learning disks also.

To copy the contents of your Microsoft Works disks onto the blank disks, follow these steps:

1. Turn on your computer. Put the Program Disk into drive A and a blank, formatted disk into drive B.

2. Type *copy a:*.* b:* and press Enter.
3. After a few moments, the following message appears:

   ```
   Copy complete, Copy another (Y/N)
   ```

   Press Y for yes.
4. Replace the Program Disk in drive A with Printer Disk 1 and replace the disk in drive B with a new, blank formatted disk. Repeat this procedure until all the disks are copied.

Important: Remember to label the disks as you copy them.

Now that you have created a set of working disks, store the original program disks in a safe place. If one of the working disks becomes damaged, you can replace it by making a new working disk from your original.

To complete the installation process, insert the Utilities/Setup Disk into drive A. At the DOS prompt (`A:\>`), type *a:setup* and press Enter. The setup program begins and leads you through the installation process. The key to installing Microsoft Works correctly is to read the screen messages and to follow carefully the instructions given. Microsoft, to its credit, has done an outstanding job in developing this setup program. You need only do what the screen tells you, and you are on your way.

Microsoft Works estimates almost all your equipment capabilities, but you need to know the brand name and model number of your printer. In most cases, when you see a screen prompt regarding your equipment, simply press Enter to confirm the selections Works has made. If Works is incorrect, choose the correct option and press Enter.

Installation on a Hard Disk System

To install Microsoft Works on a hard disk system, follow these steps:

1. Turn on your computer. After the `C:\>` prompt appears, insert the Utilities/Setup Disk into drive A.
2. Type *a:setup* and press Enter. The setup program begins and leads you through the installation process.

Starting Microsoft Works on a Floppy Disk System

To start Microsoft Works on a floppy disk system, first turn on the computer. Insert your backup copy of the Program Disk into drive A. Insert a blank, formatted disk into drive B to store your work. At the DOS prompt, type *works* and then press Enter. You see the opening screen (see fig. 1.1).

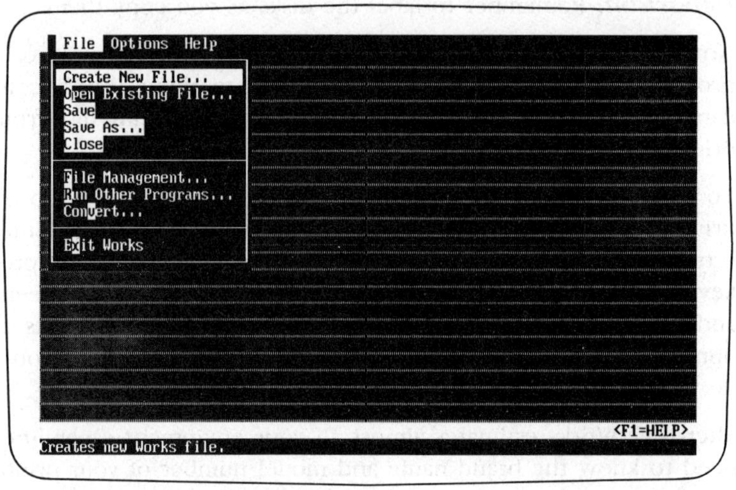

Fig. 1.1.

The Microsoft Works opening screen.

The bold letters on the File menu indicate the method for selecting the tool you want from the menu. Press O when you want to open an existing file, for instance; press S when you want to save a file; and so on. If you choose the option Create New File, Microsoft Works enables you to choose one of the program's four main components: word processor, spreadsheet, database, or communications. These four components are called *tools.*

Starting Microsoft Works on a Hard Disk System

To start Microsoft Works on a hard disk system, first turn on the computer. At the DOS prompt, change to the directory in which you installed Works when you used the setup program (the default name is WORKS). Go to the WORKS directory by typing *cd\works* and pressing Enter. If you put the program in a directory with a different name, type *cd* followed by the name of the directory.

Another DOS prompt (C:\WORKS>) appears on-screen. Type *works* again and press Enter. The Microsoft Works opening screen appears.

Select the File menu's Create New File option, because you have not created any files yet. The Create New File menu appears. Select the type of new file you want to create. Do you want to create a word processing, spreadsheet, database, or communications file? Move your cursor to the appropriate selection by using the up- and down-arrow keys and then press Enter. The opening screen appears for the Microsoft Works tool you select.

Exiting Microsoft Works

To exit Microsoft Works from any one of its four tools, press Alt to access the menu bar and then F for the File menu.

The word processing File menu is shown in figure 1.2. Notice the menu choices (called *commands*). You can execute commands in either of the following two ways:

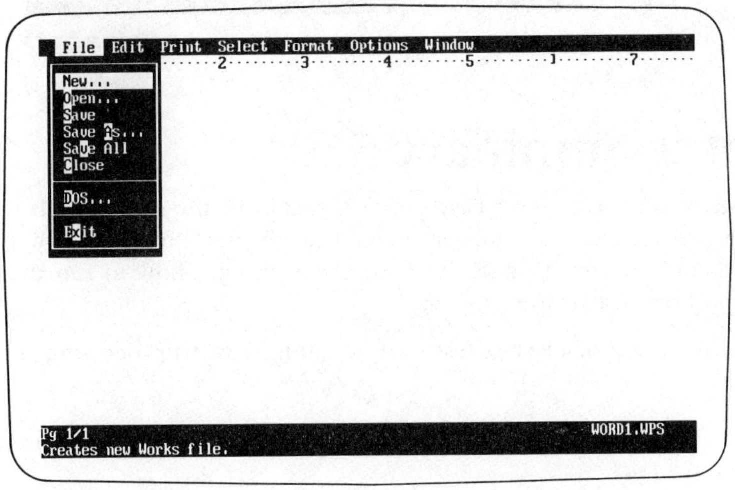

Fig. 1.2.
The word processing File menu.

- ❑ You can move the highlight to the desired command by using the up- and down-arrow keys and then pressing Enter. The highlighted command is executed. If you want to exit the program, highlight the command Exit.

- ❑ Look closely at the commands listed. Each command has a letter that is either underlined or displayed in reverse video, depending on your type of screen. In the Exit command, for example, the letter x is underlined or in reverse video. Press X to exit Microsoft Works and return to the operating system.

If you try to exit Microsoft Works and have not saved all your files, Microsoft Works asks whether you want to save your files (see fig. 1.3).

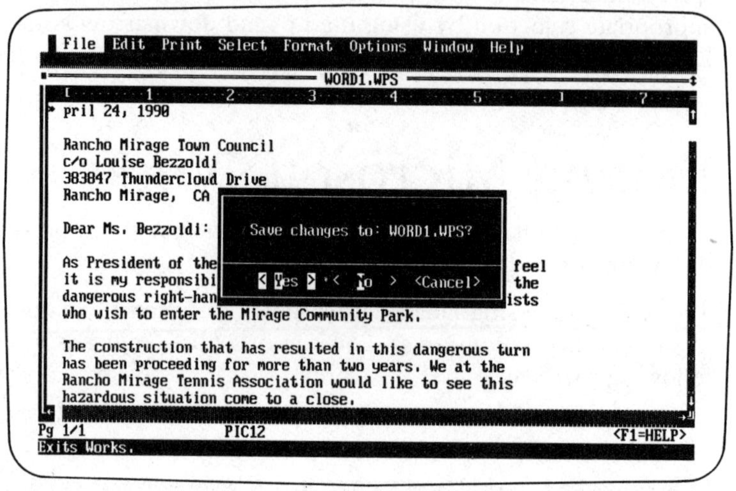

Fig. 1.3.
The Save File warning screen.

Chapter Summary

Installing Microsoft Works is an easy process, thanks to the step-by-step instructions provided in the setup program. This chapter explained how to install Works on both floppy disk and hard drive systems, how to run the program, and how to exit the program.

The next chapter is a quick-start lesson on creating a word processing document.

Part II

Word Processing

Includes

Quick Start 1

Creating a Word Processing Document

This quick-start lesson briefly examines the Works word processing feature. You will follow step-by-step instructions for opening a file; entering, editing, inserting, selecting, copying, and moving text; using the spelling-checking program; and saving, printing, and closing the file. In Chapters 2, 3, and 4, you will examine these word processing features in detail.

Opening a File with Works

When you start Works, the File menu appears. Open a new file by doing the following:

1. Select the Create New File option from the File menu and press Enter.

2. Select the New Word Processor option from the menu that appears and press Enter. A blank word processing screen appears.

Entering Text

Type text on the word processing screen just the same as you type on a piece of paper using a typewriter. Works automatically wraps words by starting a new line when the line you're typing on is filled. You can force the end of a line by pressing the Enter key. The cursor moves to the next line for you to begin typing. The screen shows 24 lines; after you fill the screen, Works scrolls the text down as you continue to type.

Follow these steps to enter a short memo (you can use the Backspace key to correct any errors you make):

1. Type *To:* and press the Tab key twice.
2. Type *Management Staff* and press Enter twice.
3. Type *From:* and press Tab twice.
4. Type *Executive Director* and press Enter twice.
5. Type *Re:* and press Tab twice.
6. Type *Annual Bonus* and press Enter twice.

Your screen should look like the one shown in figure QS1.1.

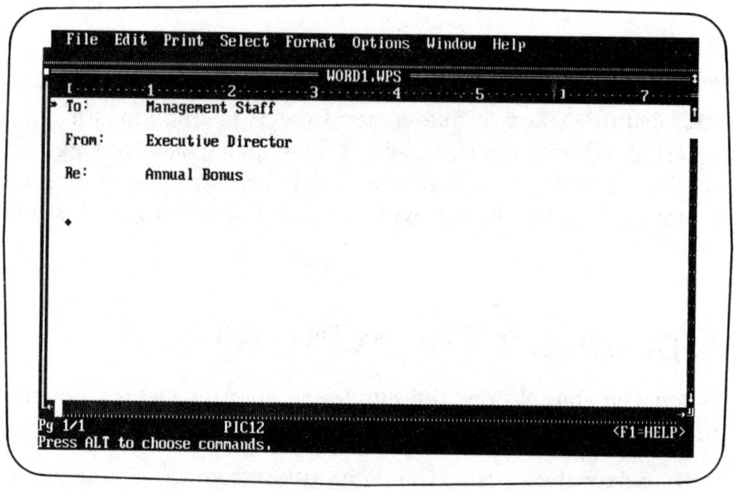

Fig. QS1.1.
The first part of the memo.

Note that you forced the end of each line by pressing Enter. Pressing Enter is similar to pressing Return on a typewriter. The action brings you to the left margin of the next line.

Add a paragraph of text to the memo by typing the following:

> Look for the annual bonuses for each department in the interoffice mail on December 21. Happy Winter Solstoce!

(One typing error was made intentionally in the preceding paragraph. You will correct the error in the next section.)

Notice how Works moved the word *interoffice* to a new line when no more room was available on the line. This feature is called *word wrapping* and is standard in word processing. You do not have to press Enter to end every line.

Editing Text

In this memo, the word *Solstice* was misspelled. Do the following steps to correct the misspelling (if you made other typing errors, you can correct them with this same procedure):

1. Use the left-arrow key to move the cursor to the left until it is under the letter c in the word *Solstoce.*
2. Press the Backspace key one time to delete the letter o.
3. Press the letter i. The word *Solstice* is now spelled correctly.

Inserting Text

Whether you want to insert text between other words, sentences, or paragraphs, the steps are the same:

1. Move the cursor to the position in the text where you want to insert more text.
2. Type the text. The text that was already in the file automatically moves to the right and down to accommodate the inserted text.

Selecting Text

You need to select text before you move or copy it. Works doesn't know which text to move unless it has been selected previously. With Works, you can select text in two ways. Use this first method when you want to select small blocks of text:

1. Move the cursor to the beginning of the text you want to select.
2. Press the Shift key and hold it down.
3. Press the cursor-movement keys (the arrow keys) until the text you want selected is highlighted on-screen.

If you are using a mouse, click at the beginning of the text you want to select and then drag to continue selecting text. Release the mouse button when you are done selecting text.

You can turn the selection off by pressing any cursor-movement key. Then the screen highlighting no longer appears over the text just selected.

The second method involves selecting text after you press the F8 function key a certain number of times. Press F8 one time, and `EXT` appears on the status line indicating that the selection mode is turned on. After `EXT` appears on the status line, highlight blocks of text by continuing to press F8; use the following formula:

Text to be selected	*Number of times to press F8*
The word the cursor is in	One time
The sentence the cursor is in	Two times
The paragraph the cursor is in	Three times
The entire file	Four times

When using the F8-key method of selecting text, turn off the selection by pressing the Esc key to leave the EXT mode and then pressing a cursor-movement key to remove the highlighting.

Copying Selected Text

When you copy text, you leave the selected text in its original location and then move a duplicate of that text to a new location. Here is the procedure for copying text:

1. Select the text you want to copy by pressing F8 or holding down the Shift key while pressing the cursor-movement keys.
2. Press Shift-F3 (press Shift and hold it down while you press F3). Alternatively, select Copy from the Edit menu by pressing Alt to activate the menu bar, E for Edit, and C for Copy. `COPY` now appears on the status line.
3. Move the cursor to the location where the selected text should be inserted.
4. Press Enter and the selected text is inserted at the cursor position.

If you insert text between text that is already entered, the existing text is moved down and to the right automatically to accommodate the inserted text.

Moving Selected Text

Just as with copying text, to move text you must select it first. The text you select to move is removed from one location and then inserted in another location. You can use this feature, for example, when your boss tells you to remove a large section of text from a document. Be safe and move that large section to another file. If your boss changes his or her mind, you still have the text on disk and can move the text back to the document electronically.

Follow these steps to move text:

1. Select the text you want to copy by pressing F8 or holding down the Shift key while pressing the cursor-movement keys.
2. Press F3. Alternatively, select Move from the Edit menu by pressing Alt to activate the menu bar, E for Edit, and then M for Move. `MOVE` now appears on the status line.
3. Move the cursor to the location where you want the selected text to be inserted.
4. Press Enter and the selected text is moved from the original location to the cursor position.

Any existing text is automatically moved to the right and down to make room for the new block of text.

Using the Spelling-Checking Program

With Works checking spelling is easy, and you have many options from which to choose. You can do any of the following with a misspelled word, depending on the situation:

- ❑ Replace the misspelled word with a correctly spelled word (press Enter with the correct word highlighted).
- ❑ Change all occurrences of the misspelled word (press Alt-H).
- ❑ Ignore this instance of the word (press Alt-I).
- ❑ Ignore the word each time it is found in the file (press Alt-G).
- ❑ Ask Works to suggest other spellings of the word (press Alt-S).
- ❑ Select a word from the list of suggestions and then press Alt-C to change the word.
- ❑ Add the word to the Works dictionary (press Alt-A).

All these options are on the Works Check Spelling dialog box. Check the spelling in your Works file by doing the following:

1. Press Alt to activate the menu bar. Press O to select the Options menu. Press S for the Check Spelling option.
2. As Works finds words in the file that it does not recognize, the words appear on the Check Spelling dialog box. Choose which response you want for each misspelled or unrecognized word.

Saving a Works File

You should save text at 15-minute intervals and before you stop for an interruption (such as a phone call or lunch). A simple way to save a Works file follows: Press Alt to activate the menu bar. Press F to select the File menu. Press S for the Save option. If you haven't previously saved the file, the Save As dialog box appears. Works writes the file's text to disk.

The file of information is now at your disposal anytime you want to see it again.

Printing a Works File

Assuming that you want to print only one copy of the entire file in which you are working, the steps for printing are simple. Do the following:

1. Press Alt to activate the menu bar. Press P to select the Print menu. Press P for the Print option.
2. Check to see that the printer is on and that paper is ready to be fed through the printer.
3. Leave all the Print dialog box's default settings and press Enter.

Works sends a message to the printer to print one copy of the text in that file.

Closing a Works File

Closing a file takes that file off the screen. If you have already saved the file, it is on disk but is just not visible anymore. Close a file when you will not be working on it or will not need to access it during the present work session. Press Alt to activate the menu bar. Then press F for the File menu and press C to close the file.

The file is removed from the screen. If you haven't already saved the file, you are asked to save it before closing. If you do not save the file and then you close it, the text in that file is lost. Choose to save the document before closing the file.

2

Entering, Editing, and Saving Your Word Processing Document

Word processing has become popular with business users, creative writers, and personal letter writers because it is such a convenient way to process text. You can type at your own speed and not be concerned about mistakes that are entered. Editing the document is quick and easy. The document is recorded on magnetic media, not on paper. Instead of typing and then retyping an entire document so that it is, in the end, perfect, you can word process the document: type it on the screen, edit it, and then print a finished document. You have saved a great deal of paper and hours of frustration. As with most new technology, a little time invested in the beginning saves you hours in the future.

In this chapter, you will see how the Microsoft Works word processor can help you use the menu system and open a file; then you will create a document by typing and printing a letter. After your document is on the screen, you will learn the specifics of editing, formatting, and working with word processing files, as well as advanced word processing techniques.

Getting Started

Starting Works on a floppy disk system is different from starting it on a hard disk system. To start Microsoft Works on a floppy disk system, follow these steps:

1. Before turning on your computer, put your backup DOS disk into drive A. Then turn on the computer.
2. Replace the DOS disk in drive A with the Microsoft Works Program Disk. At the `A:\>` prompt, type *works*.
3. Press Enter.

If you are using a hard disk, follow these steps:

1. Turn on your computer. At the DOS prompt, type *cd\works* and press Enter.
2. Type *works*.
3. Press Enter.

The Works opening screen appears, as shown in figure 2.1. On this screen, you see the File menu and the Microsoft Works copyright information.

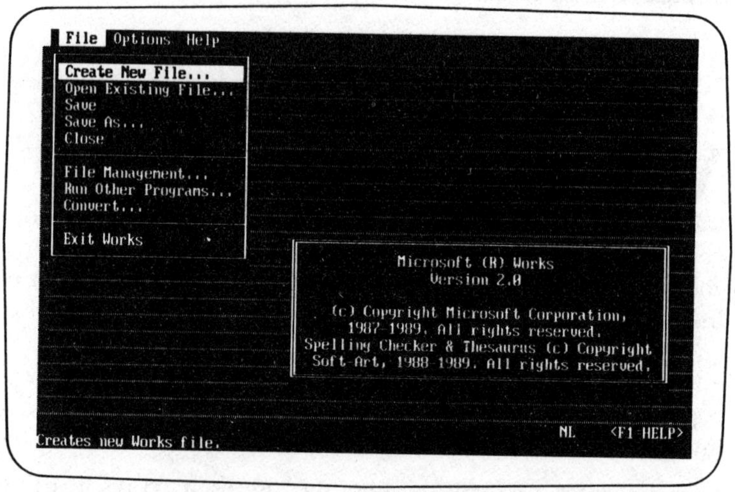

Fig. 2.1.

The Microsoft Works opening screen.

On the upper portion of the File menu, you are given the following options: Create New File, Open Existing File, Save, Save As, and Close. Your cursor is already positioned on the Create New File option. To start a new document, select this option by pressing Enter (it is already highlighted) or by pressing N. After you select this option, you see the screen shown in figure 2.2.

You must tell Works whether the new file you are creating is for the word processor, the spreadsheet, the database, or the communications module. Choose the word processor by placing the cursor on the New Word

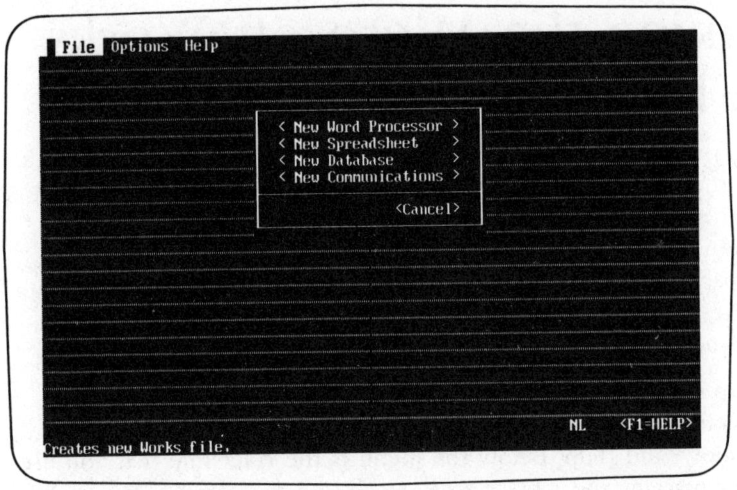

Fig. 2.2.

The screen for creating a new file.

Processor option and pressing Enter. The word processor opening screen appears (see fig. 2.3).

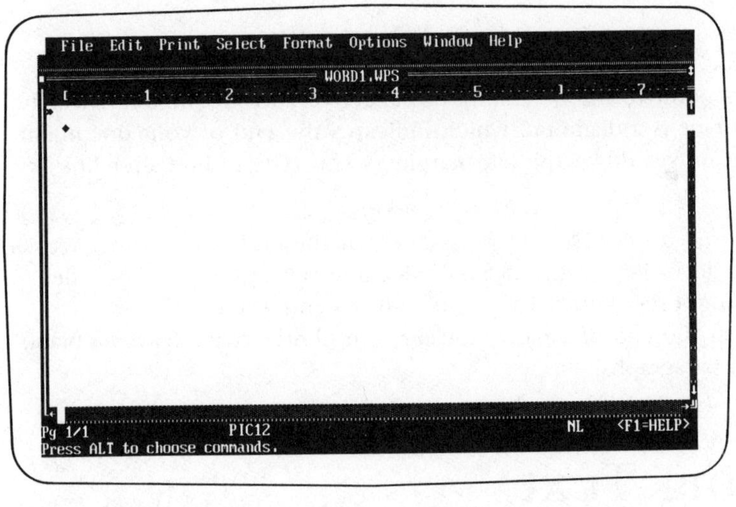

Fig. 2.3.

The opening word processing screen.

If your system has a mouse, you can open menus by moving the arrow to the menu name and clicking the mouse. The menu opens, and you can move the arrow to the command you want to select. Again, click the mouse and the command is executed.

Examining the Microsoft Works Word Processing Screen

On the word processor opening screen, the *cursor*, a blinking line, is at the upper left corner of the work space. The cursor indicates where the next character you type will be entered. As a character is typed, the cursor moves to the next character position. A *character* is any letter, number, symbol, or space. The *work space* is where your document appears when you enter text. Text you enter on this work space appears as it would if you were typing on paper.

Across the top of the word processing screen is the menu bar that is available to you. The menu items are File, Edit, Print, Select, Format, Options, Window, and Help. Below the menu is the ruler line that you use to set up your margins and tabs.

The ruler line has default (automatic) margins established for standard 8 1/2-by-11-inch paper. The default margins are 1 inch for both the top and bottom margins, 1.3 inches for the left margin, and 1.2 inches for the right margin. You will learn how to change margins and paper size in Chapter 3.

On your work space to the left of the cursor are two arrows facing right. These arrows point to the beginning of page 1 of your document. Directly below the cursor is a diamond, which indicates the end of your document. The diamond moves down the left margin as you type in line after line of text.

As you type, you do not have to press Enter at the end of each line. Works ends the line according to the default ruler line settings, a process called *word wrapping*. Press Enter when you want to end a line without wrapping or at the end of a paragraph. Pressing Enter twice leaves a blank line between paragraphs.

Entering Text

With your cursor in the upper left corner, begin by typing the following sample letter. This typing is called entering text. Don't worry about making mistakes. Correcting mistakes and editing are covered later in this chapter.

April 24, 1990

Rancho Mirage Town Council
c/o Louise Bezoldi
383847 Thundercloud Drive
Rancho Mirage, CA 92128

Dear Ms. Bezoldi:

As President of the Rancho Mirage Tennis Association, I feel it is my responsibility to voice a complaint regarding the dangerous right-hand turn that has to be made by motorists who wish to enter the Mirage Community Park.

The construction that has resulted in this dangerous turn has been proceeding for more than two years. We at the Rancho Mirage Tennis Association would like to see this hazardous situation come to a close.

To alleviate some of the danger, a warning light could be placed before the park entrance to encourage motorists to slow down before reaching the park entrance. While we are concerned about motorists, we are even more concerned about the thousands of children who frequent the park. It is for their safety that we express this concern.

Sincerely,

Arnold P. Schwarzkraut
President
Rancho Mirage Tennis Association

The beginning of your letter can be seen on the screen shown in figure 2.4.

Scrolling

The letter you typed has more than 24 lines; therefore, the entire letter cannot be seen on the screen at one time. As you type more than 24 lines, Works scrolls the text up half a screen; that is, the top lines move up and off the screen as new lines are added at the bottom. The first lines you typed are still there and stored. View the text that has scrolled out of view by pressing the PgUp key.

Conceptually, the screen display covers only a small area of available electronic paper. Imagine a piece of paper that is 8 1/2 inches wide but is hundreds of feet long. This imaginary long page is what you have to work with in a word processor. Microsoft Works takes care of deciding where to

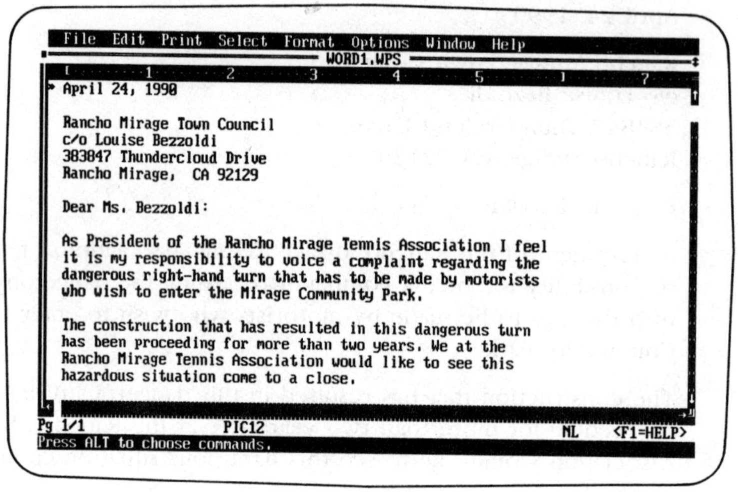

Fig. 2.4.

The letter on the screen.

break pages when you print your work. So, as you type more than 24 lines, the electronic paper is simply pushed up to make room for more characters.

Moving the Cursor with the Keyboard

Before you can perform editing functions, you have to know how to move the cursor around your Microsoft Works document. Table 2.1 lists how to move the cursor to the error you want to change, the spot where text is to be inserted, or the beginning of text you want to delete.

Table 2.1
Keystrokes Used for Editing in Works Word Processor

Function	*Keystroke*
Right one character	Right-arrow key
Left one character	Left-arrow key
Up one line	Up-arrow key
Down one line	Down-arrow key
Right one word	Ctrl-right-arrow key
Left one word	Ctrl-left-arrow key
Up one paragraph	Ctrl-up-arrow key
Down one paragraph	Ctrl-down-arrow key
To the beginning of the line	Home key
To the end of the line	End key
To the beginning of the file	Ctrl-Home key

To the end of the file	Ctrl-End key
Up one window	PgUp key
Down one window	PgDn key
To the beginning of the window	Ctrl-PgUp key
To the end of the window	Ctrl-PgDn key

As you can see, special keys allow you to move one character, line, word, paragraph, screen, or file at a time. With practice, you will be able to get around your documents quickly.

Moving the Cursor with a Mouse

If your system is equipped with a mouse, a large arrow or a rectangle appears on the screen when you start the program (an arrow appears if you are in Graphics mode, and a rectangle appears if you are in Text mode). This arrow or rectangle is where the mouse selector is at that moment. Your mouse has two or more buttons that can be pressed and released, or pressed and held. Pressing and releasing is called "clicking" because most mouse devices make an audible click when a button is pressed. Pressing and holding is called "clicking and dragging." This process causes the highlight to be extended and is explained later in this chapter. With a mouse attached to Microsoft Works, you can move the cursor to any specific character by simply moving the mouse. With the mouse arrow on any character in your text, click the mouse. The cursor appears under the character you have selected.

Editing a Document

If you find that you have made a typing error in the letter you typed earlier in this chapter, you can quickly go back and edit the mistake. Press the up-arrow key until you are on the line of the error. Use the right- and left-arrow keys to get you to the exact location of the error.

To replace a character, start by moving the cursor to the character to the right of the one you want to replace. Suppose, for example, that your document contains the misspelled word *danferous*. Place the cursor under the letter *e*. Then press the Backspace key one time, erasing the letter *f*. Now *danerous* appears on the screen. Type the letter *g* to correct the text; the word *dangerous* is corrected.

You can correct this same example another way: Move the cursor to the letter *f* and press the Del key; then type the letter *g*. You can use your mouse to assist in either of these types of corrections.

Printing

This section presents a brief introduction to printing. More options are covered in Chapter 4.

When you have entered the letter presented earlier in this chapter (see fig. 2.4), you can print it by following these steps:

1. Press Alt. This action activates the menu bar, highlighting the letters you press to choose a menu.
2. Press P to select the Print menu, which is then displayed by Works (see fig. 2.5).
3. Press P. A dialog box appears (see fig. 2.6). A dialog box is different from a menu in that it offers choices to make about a specific task.
4. Following the selection screen, decide on the print parameters you want, such as how many copies you want to print, what pages you want printed, whether you want the printer to stop between pages, whether the file is to be printed on paper (also called a *hard copy*) or on a disk, and the quality of print for the hard copy. For this exercise, press Enter to accept the default values in the dialog box. Your letter is printed.

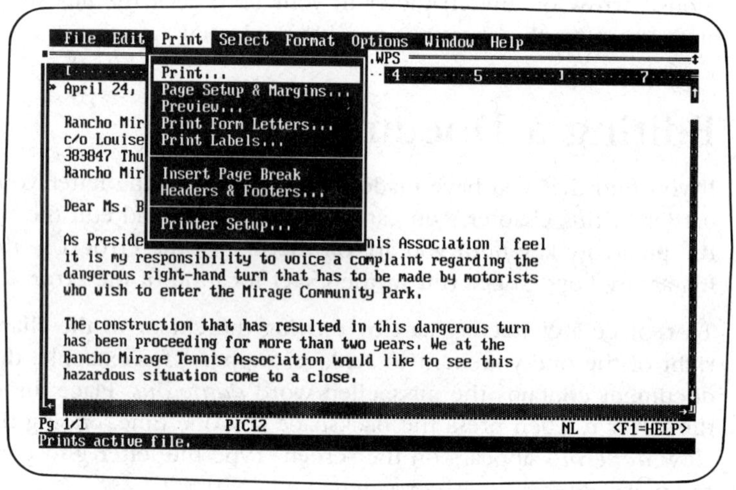

Fig. 2.5.

The Print menu.

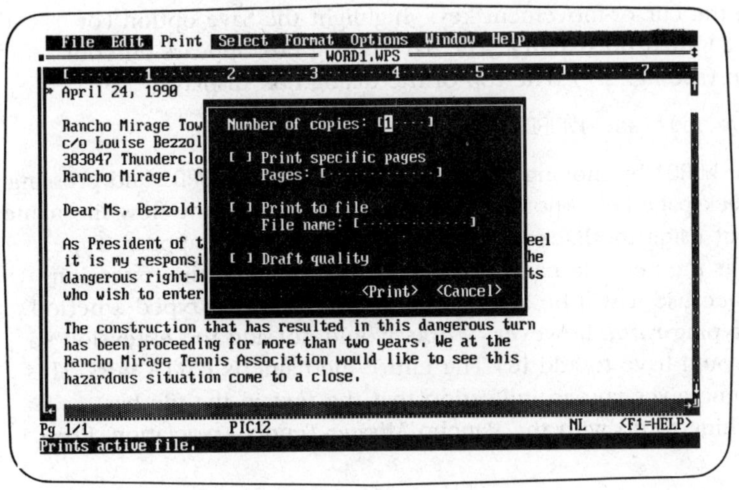

Fig. 2.6.

The Print dialog box.

Tip: If Microsoft Works doesn't print your document after you follow the preceding instructions, you may have entered the wrong printer or port when you installed the program. Return to the setup program, install a different printer or port, and try again. Consult your printer manual to make sure that you select the appropriate model number. If your printer is not listed, select the Works print.file Driver. Ports also can be adjusted in the Printer Setup dialog box.

Saving a Document

Saving a document creates a copy of your text on either your hard drive or floppy drive. If you don't need to use a document again and have no need to keep a record of it, you do not have to save it. However, you can keep a copy that can be called up at any time.

Floppy disk users need to have a blank formatted disk in the floppy drive on which to copy the file. Place this disk in drive B. With your cursor on the letter you just printed, do the following:

1. Press Alt. This action activates the menu bar, highlighting the letters you press to choose a menu.

2. Press F and the File menu appears on the screen.

3. Using the cursor-movement keys, highlight the Save option (or press S); then press Enter. The Save dialog box appears on your screen (see fig. 2.7). The top of the dialog box displays

   ```
   Save file as: [WORD1.WPS.......]
   ```

4. Delete `WORD1` by moving the cursor to the end of `WORD1` and pressing the Backspace key. Another method is just to type the new file name without using the Backspace key; `WORD1.WPS` will disappear. Type *rmta* as the new file name. You don't need to type the extension WPS because it will be added automatically. (If you typed a period after typing *rmta*, however, Works would not add the extension so you would have to add it.) The entire file name is RMTA.WPS. This file name gives you an indication that the text in the file has something to do with the Rancho Mirage Tennis Association. Press Enter.

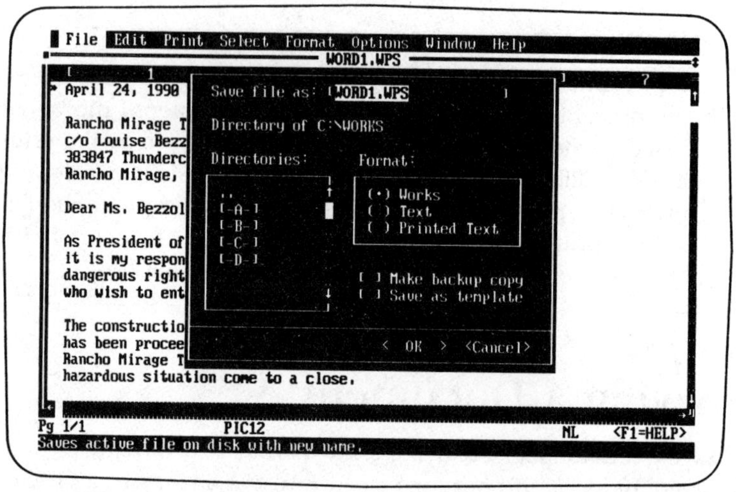

Fig. 2.7.
The Save dialog box.

After you follow the outlined procedure, Microsoft Works saves the file for you. All word processing documents are given the file extension WPS, which tells you that the file was created on the word processing component of Works.

You have just typed, printed, and saved your first document with Microsoft Works. This portion of the chapter covered the basics of getting a document into print. Your printed document can be seen in figure 2.8.

April 24, 1990

Rancho Mirage Town Council
c/o Louise Bezzoldi
383847 Thundercloud Drive
Rancho Mirage, CA 92129

Dear Ms. Bezzoldi:

As President of the Rancho Mirage Tennis Association I feel it is my responsibility to voice a complaint regarding the dangerous right-hand turn that has to be made by motorists who wish to enter the Mirage Community Park.

The construction that has resulted in this dangerous turn has been proceeding for more than two years. We at the Rancho Mirage Tennis Association would like to see this hazardous situation come to a close.

Our attorney is being notified of our concern. We hope legal action will not be necessary. To protect our members, we will take any action necessary.

To alleviate some of the danger, a warning light could be placed before the park entrance to encourage motorists to slow down before reaching the park entrance. While we are concerned about motorists, we are even more concerned about the thousands of children who frequent the park. It is for their safety that we express this concern.

Sincerely,

Arnold P. Schwarzkraut
President
Rancho Mirage Tennis Association

Fig. 2.8.
The printed letter.

Editing Text

You have printed your first document and have found how easy using a word processor is. But what if errors had been in that first document? What if you had typed the same paragraph twice? What if you wanted to change the order of the paragraphs or insert or delete text? These are all editing functions, and you will learn to do them in the following sections.

Using the Go To Command

Earlier in this chapter, you practiced moving the cursor. When you have created a long document, use the Go To command to get to the required page without moving line by line or screen by screen. Press Alt for the menu bar and then S for the Select menu. The Select menu appears (see fig. 2.9). Select the Go To command and press Enter.

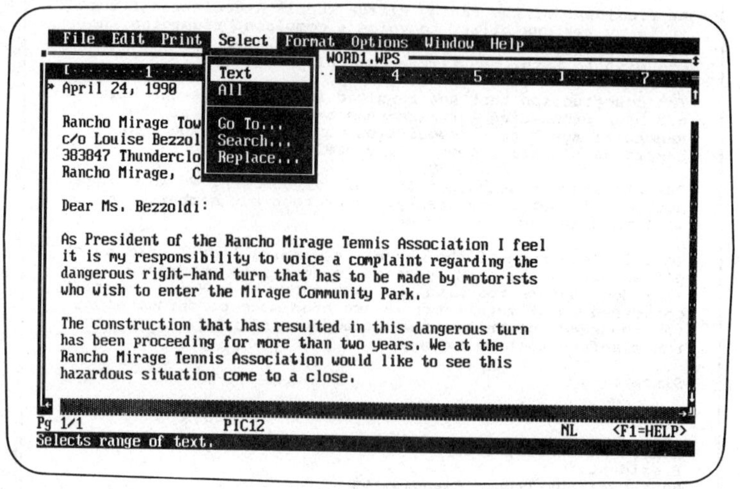

Fig. 2.9.

The Select menu.

A dialog box appears (see fig. 2.10). Type in the desired page number and press Enter. Microsoft Works moves your cursor to the first character on that page.

If you type a page number greater than the number of pages in your document when using the Go To command, you get a warning saying that you have entered an invalid page number (see fig. 2.11). Press Enter to type in another page number, and Microsoft Works moves you to that page.

Tip: Instead of pressing Alt, S, and then Enter to get to the Go To option, use a command key, or *hot key*. Press the F5 function key, and you bypass the Select menu and go directly to the Go To dialog box shown in figure 2.10. Many commands in Microsoft Works have hot keys. Other hot keys will be pointed out to you in future chapters. Remember them to save keystrokes.

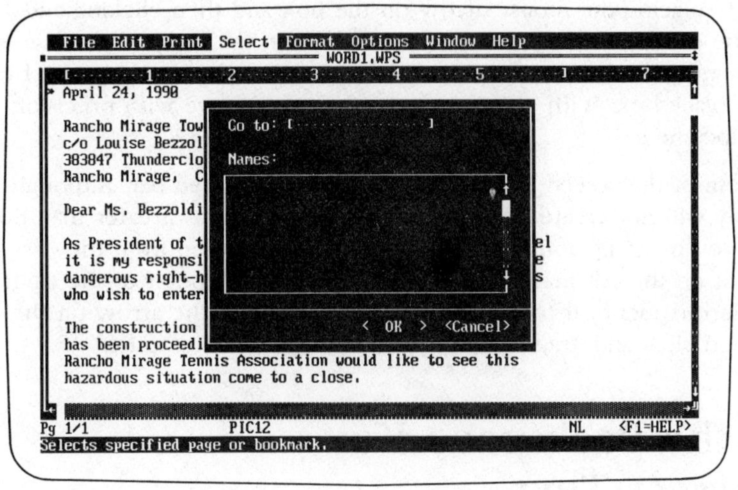

Fig. 2.10.

The Go To dialog box.

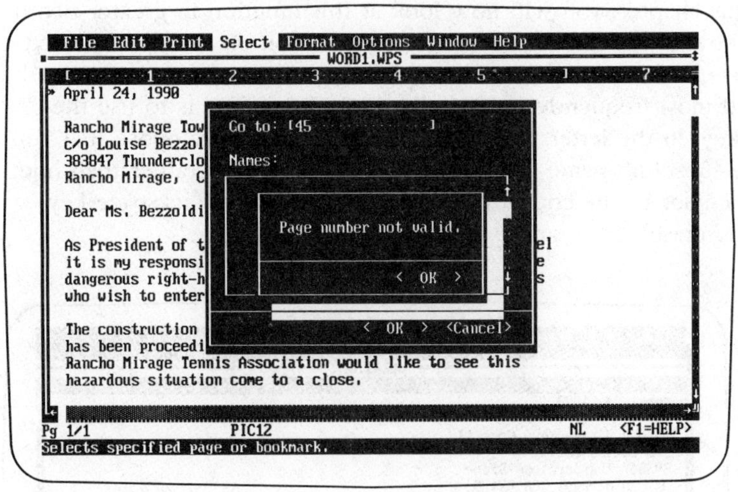

Fig. 2.11.

The Invalid Page Number screen.

Using the Mouse To Move through a Document

On the far right side of the screen is a border area that is a dotted bar in which a black box (or reverse video box) is located. This bar represents the entire length of the document. When the cursor is at the very top of the screen, the box is at the top of the dotted bar just below an arrow that points up. By placing the mouse arrow on the box and then clicking and dragging, you can move the black box up and down the dotted bar. In a long document, you can move rapidly from top to bottom or vice-versa by moving the black box. With a little practice, you can move with precision through a document.

At the bottom of the screen is a small black box and dotted bar. Although you probably will not create documents with right margins greater than 80 characters, you have the ability to move the cursor location from the farthest point on the left margin of the document to any point to the right. The procedure is identical to moving vertically. Position the arrow on the black box and click and drag to where you want the cursor to be.

Using the Backspace Key To Correct Text

Correcting text was discussed briefly in the "Editing a Document" section earlier in this chapter; you will now look at this function in greater depth. You know how to move your cursor to any location on the screen. Next you want to erase misspelled words or delete certain information. The simplest and most frequently used method of editing text is to use the Backspace key. In the letter you just typed, for example, suppose that you checked Ms. Bezoldi's name and found that it has two z's rather than one. Move your cursor to the end of her name and press the Backspace key four times to erase i, d, l, and o (see fig. 2.12).

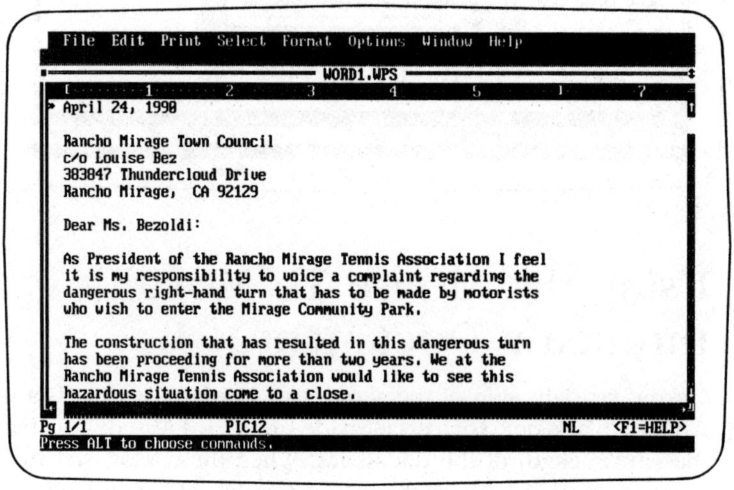

Fig. 2.12.

*The cursor located just after the letter z, with **oldi** erased.*

Type *zoldi*. Her name is spelled correctly as shown in figure 2.13.

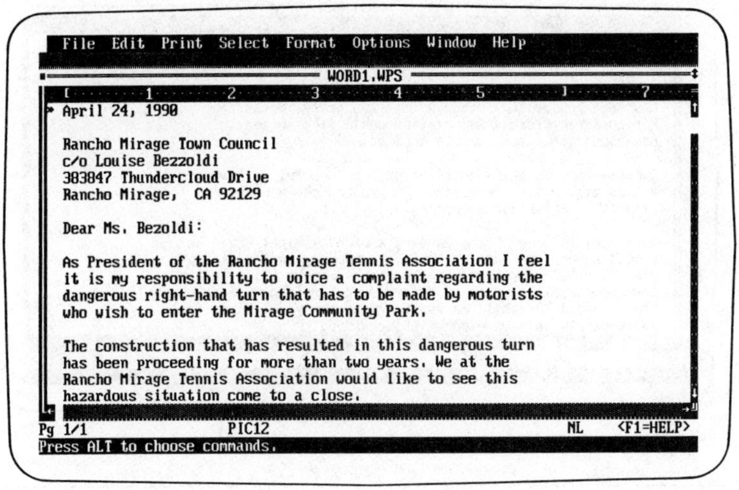

Fig. 2.13.

*The letters **zoldi** typed and the name spelled correctly.*

Tip: Make sure that you find the incorrect word every time it occurs so all occurrences can be corrected. Only one other occurrence of *Bezzoldi* is in this letter. In a longer document, you will want to do a search and replace (see Chapter 4 for instructions on how to search for a specific word and then replace it).

No white-out, correcting tape, or fancy maneuvering are needed to edit text. Just backspace over the incorrect text, and the information stored in the computer is gone. Type in new text, and new information replaces the old. The electronic typing page is easy and quick to use.

Inserting Text

Suppose that you decide to add a threatening paragraph in this letter you have typed. To insert the paragraph, move your cursor to the line between the second and third paragraphs; then press Enter. Type the following:

> Our attorney is being notified of our concern. We hope legal action will not be necessary. To protect our members, we will take any action necessary.

Press Enter. Figure 2.14 shows how the inserted paragraph appears on your screen.

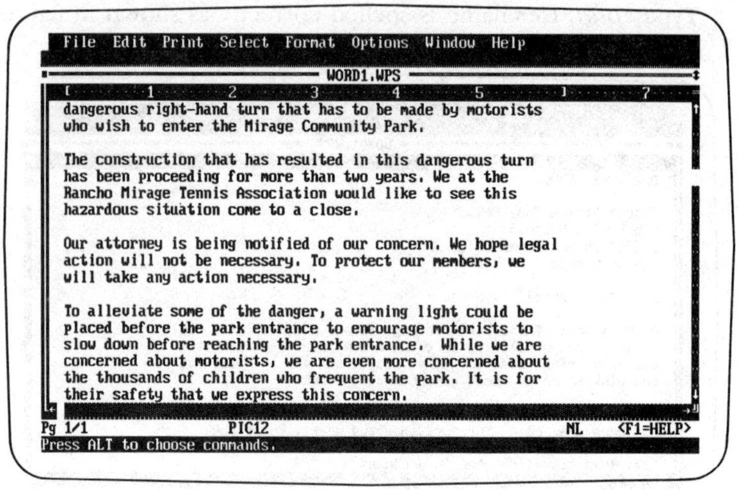

Fig. 2.14.

The inserted paragraph on-screen.

Tip: Pressing Enter before and after you type the paragraph leaves a blank line before and after the inserted text, making it a separate paragraph. If you do not want this material to be a separate paragraph, simply start typing at the end of the preceding paragraph (after the word *close*).

Notice that when new text is inserted, the text that already appears on the screen moves to accommodate the addition. The last paragraph and closing scroll down automatically. All the information still exists even though it doesn't appear on your screen. The screen always shows you the cursor location. Move your cursor, and the remaining text appears on the screen.

Selecting Text

Before you can do major editing jobs, such as moving paragraphs around or deleting large blocks of text, you must know how to select the text you want to delete, copy, or move. When you select text, that text is highlighted on the screen. The next command you choose affects the text that is highlighted.

You can select text that consists of just one character or an entire file. You may want to select one paragraph, one sentence, or one section. In a longer document, you may decide that Chapter 2 really should be Chapter

5. In that case, you can select Chapter 2 and move it to the Chapter 5 location.

Remember, all these editing tasks are done with keystrokes. You don't have to print out something, cut and paste, and then retype it. All the editing is done on an electronic screen. You arrange the text to your liking and then print it!

With Microsoft Works, you can select text in more than one way. You can select text by using the Shift key; this method is more convenient when you are selecting small sections of text, such as a character, word, or group of words. Here is the procedure:

1. Move your cursor to the location of text you want to select, using the cursor-movement keys.
2. Press and hold down the Shift key.
3. Press the cursor-movement keys to highlight the text you want to select.

Tip: Keep the Shift key pressed down the entire time you are selecting text.

Going back to the example letter you have typed, move your cursor to the beginning of the fourth paragraph, under the letter T (see fig. 2.15).

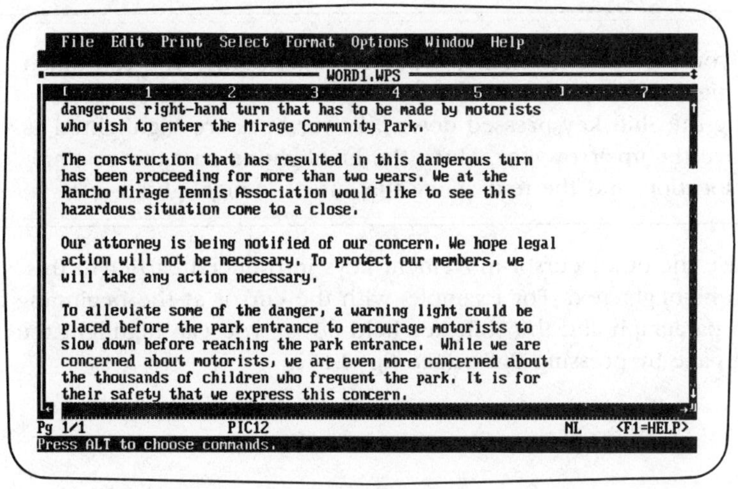

Fig. 2.15.

Preparing to select the fourth paragraph.

You are going to select this paragraph for editing. Press the Shift key and hold it down. Press the down-arrow key until the entire paragraph is highlighted (see fig. 2.16).

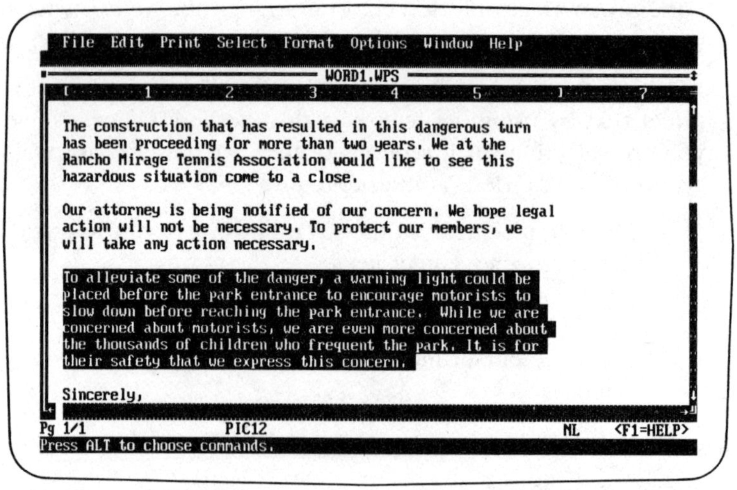

Fig. 2.16.

The fourth paragraph, highlighted for editing.

As you move the arrow keys, you see how the highlighting moves. Press the right-arrow key and highlight one character at a time, moving right across your screen. By pressing the down-arrow key, you highlight one line at a time.

Tip: If you press the down-arrow key too many times and too much text is highlighted, press the up-arrow key to reverse the process (keeping the Shift key pressed down). Fewer lines are highlighted as you move the up-arrow key. Move the highlighting past the original cursor location, and the text above the cursor is highlighted.

You can use the other cursor-movement keys introduced earlier in this chapter to highlight text. For example, with the cursor at the beginning of the fourth paragraph and the Shift key held down, you can highlight the remaining page by pressing PgDn (see fig. 2.17).

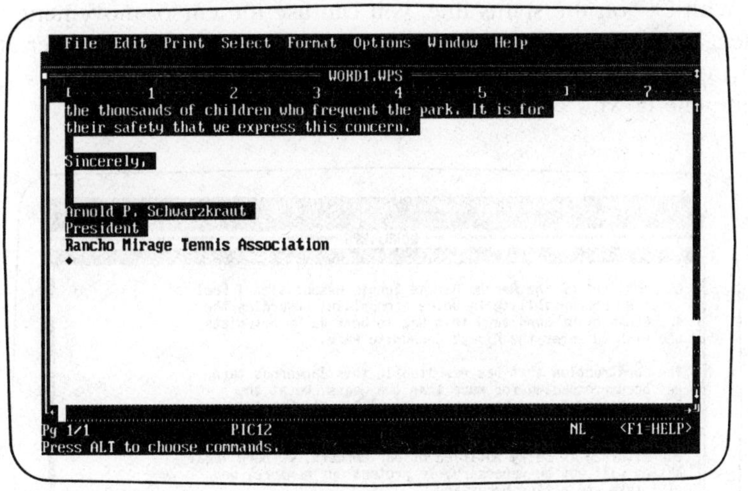

Fig. 2.17.
Highlighting with the Shift key and the PgDn key.

Note: The last line of the closing is not highlighted. The reason is that you highlighted one page down from the original cursor location, which does not include the last line of the closing. If you want to highlight the remainder of the file, see the following tip.

Tip: To highlight an entire file, place your cursor at the beginning of the file, press and hold down the Shift key, and press Ctrl-End.

Unselecting Text

You have selected the fourth paragraph of the example letter. Suppose that you decide you don't want to edit that paragraph. To unselect selected text, press any cursor-movement key. *Do not* press the Shift key. Pressing a cursor-movement key turns the highlighting off.

Selecting Text by Using F8

Just as you do when using the Shift key, move your cursor to the beginning of the text you want to be selected; then press F8. EXT appears on the status line (see fig. 2.18). EXT is the abbreviation for the Extend command. With EXT on the status line, you can use the cursor-movement keys to select text. Press the right-arrow key and highlight one character at a time, moving right across your screen. Press the down-arrow key and highlight one line down.

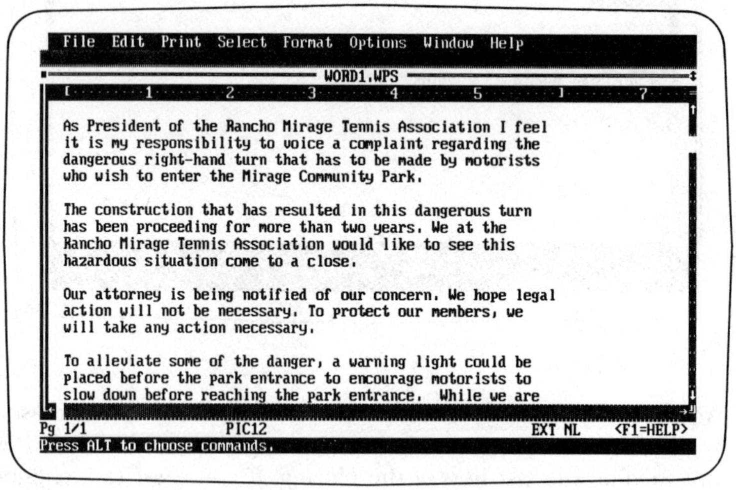

Fig. 2.18.

EXT *on the status line.*

An added feature of using the F8 key for selecting text is that it selects specific amounts of text in sequence. As you continue to press F8, more text is selected. Move your cursor to the beginning of the second paragraph in the example letter, starting with the word *The*. The following chart shows which text is selected, in sequence, after you press F8 one time and EXT appears on the status line:

Select	*Press F8*	*As seen in*
The word the cursor is in	one time	figure 2.19
The sentence the cursor is in	two times	figure 2.20
The paragraph the cursor is in	three times	figure 2.21
The entire file	four times	figure 2.22

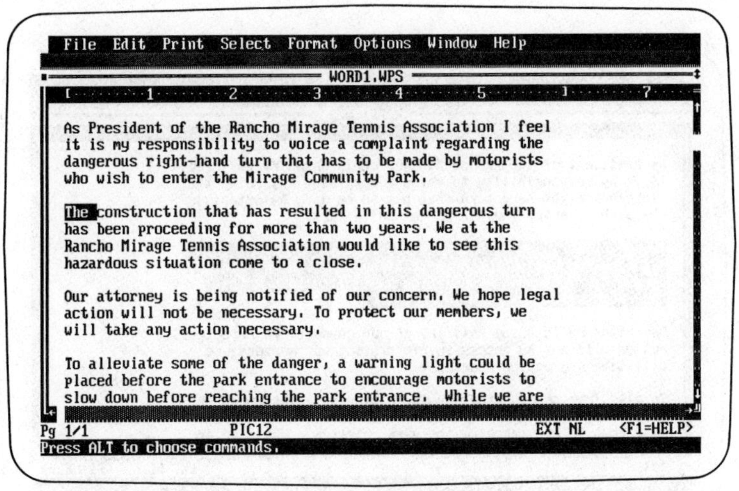

Fig. 2.19.

The word selected.

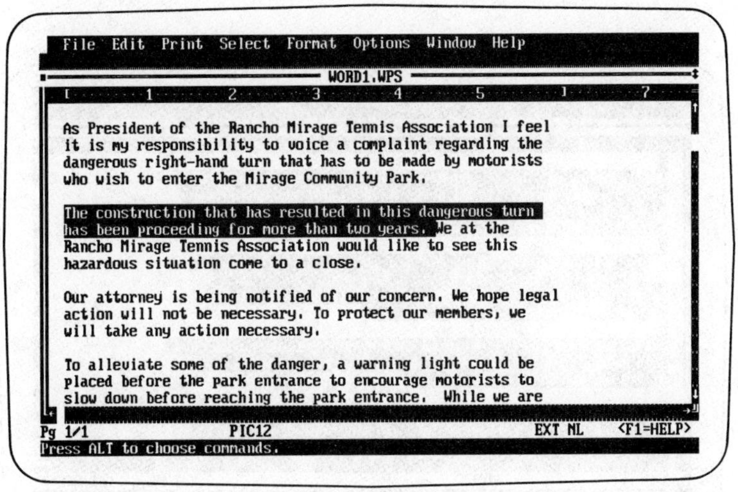

Fig. 2.20.

The sentence selected.

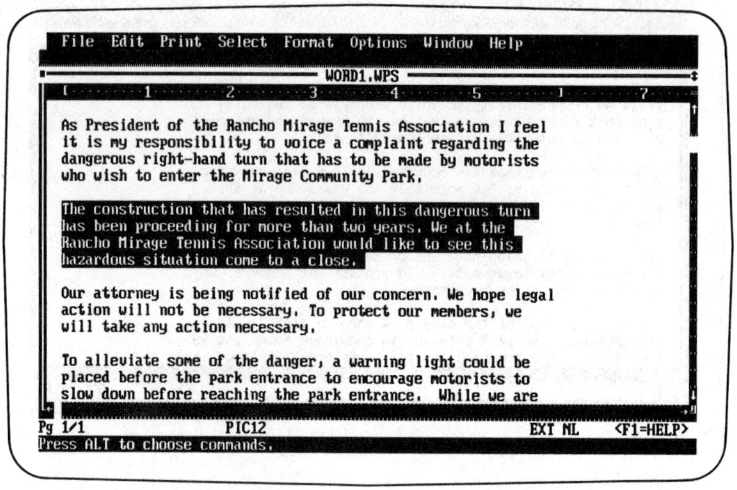

Fig. 2.21.

The paragraph selected.

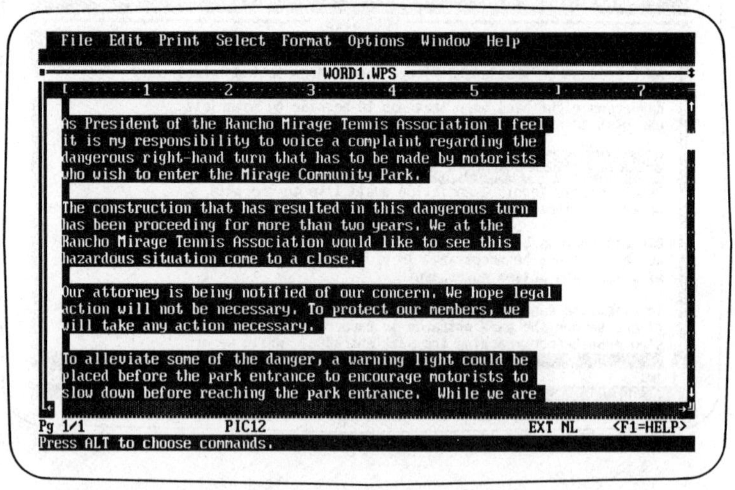

Fig. 2.22.

The entire file selected.

Tip: The F8 Extend command works in conjunction with the Go To command on the Select menu. After you press F8 one time and EXT appears on the status line, press F5. The Go To dialog box appears. Figure 2.23 shows the Go To dialog box with EXT on the status line. Specify a page number, and the text between the cursor and the beginning of that page is selected. Turn this highlighting off by pressing a cursor-movement key.

In the same way, you can select text for a specific word. Press F8 so EXT appears on the status line. Press Alt and then S for the Search menu; press S to search. When the Search dialog box appears, type a word. The text between your cursor and the next occurrence of the word you typed is selected. Turn this highlighting off by pressing a cursor-movement key.

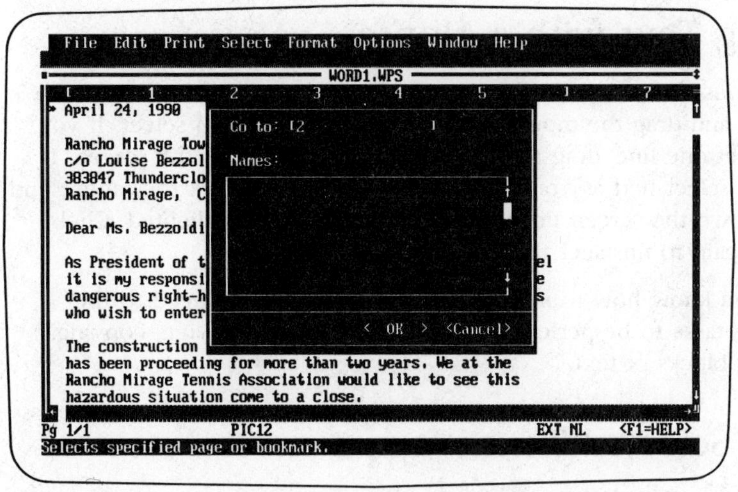

Fig. 2.23.

The Go To dialog box with EXT *on the status line.*

Unselecting Text When You Have Used F8

You pressed F8 four times after EXT appeared on the status line. The entire file is selected. Press Shift-F8 and text is unselected in the same increments as it was selected. With the entire file selected, press Shift-F8 and the paragraph your cursor was in is highlighted; the remainder of the file is no longer selected.

After EXT appears on the status line, you cannot press a cursor-movement key to turn the highlighting off. Pressing a cursor-movement key only selects more text; pressing F8 selects more text. Turn the F8 selection process off by pressing the Esc key. EXT no longer appears on the status line, and you can continue editing functions.

Selecting More Than One Paragraph

With your cursor at the beginning of the second paragraph in the example letter, press F8 and EXT appears on the status line. Press F8 three more times, and the paragraph is selected. If you press F8 again, the entire file is selected. If, instead, you want the next two paragraphs selected, press Ctrl-down-arrow key and the highlighting extends to the next paragraph. Press Ctrl-down-arrow key twice to select the next paragraph in the example letter. You have to press Ctrl-down-arrow key once for the blank line and once for the next paragraph.

Selecting Text with a Mouse

Place the mouse arrow on the character that begins the text you want to select. Click and drag the mouse over the text you want to select. If you want to select one line, drag the mouse to the right across the screen. If you want to select text as you move down the screen, click the mouse and then drag down the screen until the necessary text is highlighted. Click the mouse again to unselect the text.

Now that you know how to select text, you will be introduced to the basic editing tasks to be performed with selected text: moving, copying, and deleting blocks of text.

Moving Selected Text

When you want to move text from one place to another, the text must be selected first. Use the skills you have just learned to select text for moving. In the letter to the Rancho Mirage Tennis Association, move the third paragraph to the end of the body of the letter, making it the fourth paragraph:

1. Select the third paragraph, which begins with *Our*.
2. With your cursor under the letter O in *Our*, press F8 three times; the entire paragraph is highlighted on your screen.
3. Press Alt to activate menu bar.

4. Press E and the Edit menu appears on your screen, as you see in figure 2.24. The second option on the Edit menu is the Move option.
5. Highlight the Move option either by using the down-arrow key or by pressing M for Move (see fig. 2.24).

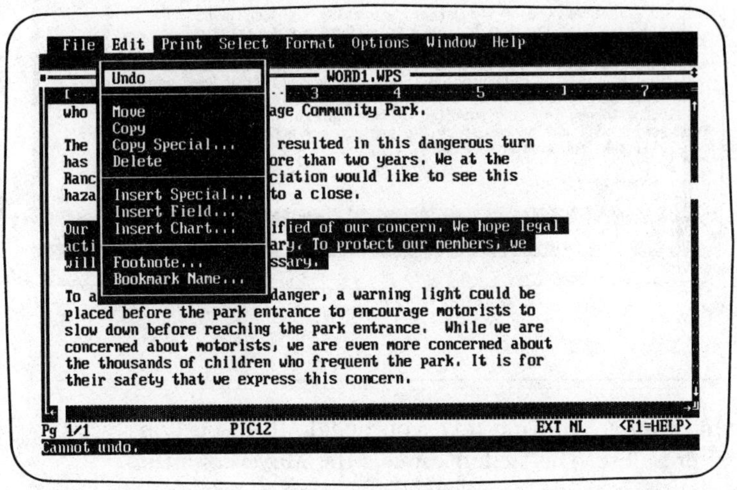

Fig. 2.24.

The Edit menu.

6. Press Enter. The Edit menu disappears from the screen; the paragraph remains highlighted.
7. Move the cursor below the last paragraph by using the down-arrow key.
8. Press Enter. The highlighted paragraph is moved to the new location (see fig. 2.25).

You can see from this screen that you have to make a few minor adjustments to clean up the letter. First, move your cursor to the word *concern*, which ends the paragraph preceding the one you just moved. Press Enter to put a blank line between the two paragraphs. Now move the cursor above the letter T in what is now the third paragraph. Press the Backspace key one time to eliminate an extra blank line between these two paragraphs. Your letter is now neat and consistent.

The hot-key method for moving text is to press F3. Highlight your text and press F3; MOVE appears on the status line, indicating that you are in the Move mode. Move the cursor to the new location for this text and press Enter. The same text move is accomplished.

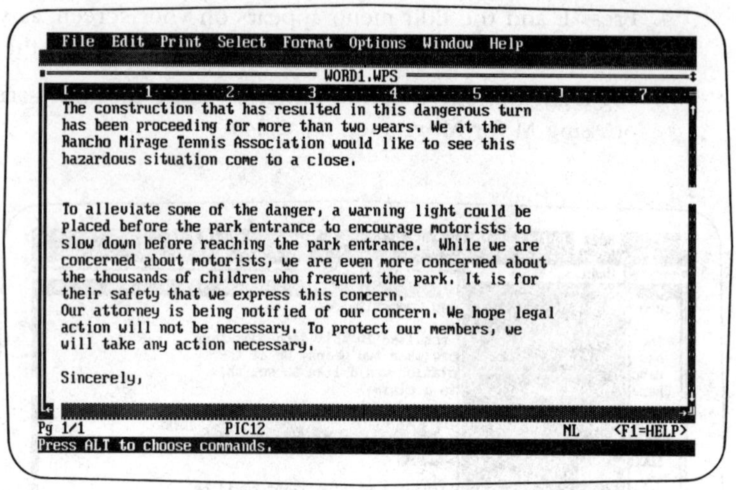

Fig. 2.25.

The selected paragraph moved to the end of the letter.

Tip: If, while you are moving text, you decide that you don't want to move text, press Esc. This action cancels the Move command.

Character styles and paragraph formats are moved with the text that is moved. Moving text from file to file is covered later in this chapter.

Replacing Selected Text

You can use the Edit Move command to replace text in another location with selected text. For example, if you select a paragraph to be moved, press Alt, E, and then M; move your cursor to the new location and highlight a second paragraph; press Enter and the first highlighted paragraph replaces the second paragraph. This feature saves you the steps of deleting one paragraph before you move another paragraph to that location.

Copying Selected Text

Suppose that you are preparing four documents for various staff members. Each of these documents, though different, has the same introduction. Save yourself time and potential errors by copying the introduction to each document. When you copy text, you duplicate the selected text without altering the original document. You then insert or "paste" that text into a new location. With the four documents, each with the same introduction, you type the introduction one time and then copy that text to the three other copies of the document.

Practice copying text in the letter you have on-screen. With your cursor under the letter O in *Our* in the last paragraph of the body of the letter, follow these steps to copy text:

1. Select the last paragraph by pressing F8 three times.
2. Press Shift-F3. Alternatively, press Alt to activate the menu bar, press E for Edit, and press C for Copy; then press Enter. COPY now appears on the status line.
3. Move the cursor up to the line between the second and third paragraphs of the letter (after the word *close* and before the word *To*).
4. Press Enter and the last paragraph is inserted at the position of the cursor (see fig. 2.26).

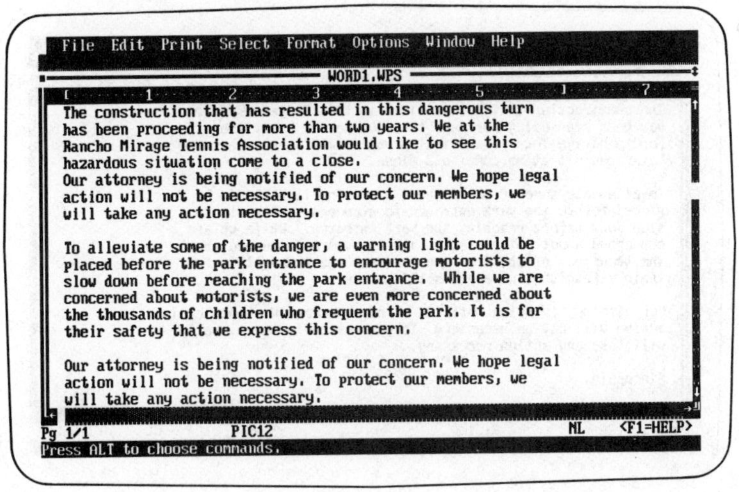

Fig. 2.26.
The paragraph inserted in the letter.

You also can use the Edit Copy command to replace text. Select text at the new cursor location and, with the Typing Replaces Selection command on, press Enter. Works replaces the selected text with the copied text. Access this toggle option by pressing Alt, O, and then Y.

Deleting Selected Text

As you see on your screen, now two paragraphs in the letter begin with *Our attorney*. The next step is to decide which to keep and which to delete, and then to delete the unwanted paragraph. As with the copy and move functions, you can delete any amount of text you can select, from one character to an entire file. Do the following to delete the unwanted text:

1. Move the cursor to the letter O in the word *Our* in the paragraph you want to delete.
2. Press F8 three times to select the entire paragraph.
3. Press Alt to activate the menu bar, press E for the Edit menu, and then press D for the Delete command. Or bypass the menus by pressing the Del key. For this example, the paragraph just copied was deleted. Figure 2.27 shows the body of the letter with one of the repetitive paragraphs deleted.

Fig. 2.27.

The paragraph deleted.

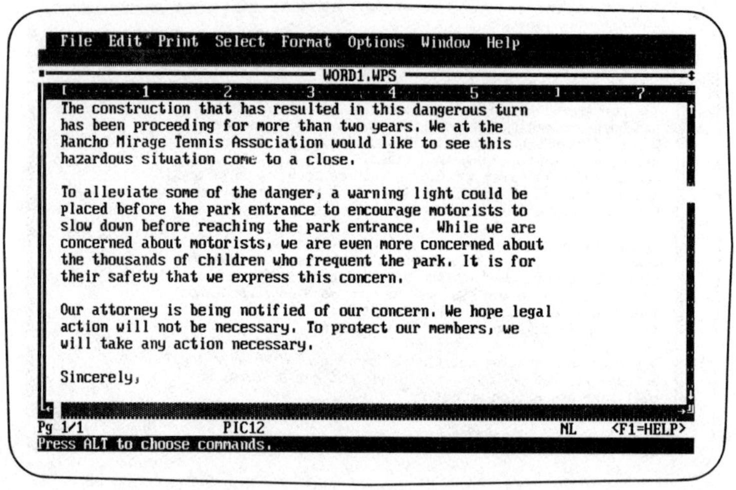

Using the Edit Undo Command

The first option on the Edit menu is Undo. This is a valuable feature that helps prevent major mistakes from happening. Imagine what would happen if you selected an entire chapter from a book you had written and pressed Del. Reproducing the prose you had lost might take considerable effort. With the Microsoft Works word processor, all is not lost. Immediately after you press the Del key, press Alt, E and then U. You undo the deletion. The text you have just deleted is restored.

Note: The Undo command must be used immediately after deleting. If any new deletions occur between the mistaken deletion and the Undo command, the deleted text is lost.

Undo reverses many of your most recent editing and formatting actions. Other examples of commands you may want to undo are

- ❑ All commands on the Format menu
- ❑ All commands on the Edit menu (except Bookmark Name and Undo because you cannot undo an Undo command)
- ❑ The Check Spelling command by undoing all the corrected words

When you delete text, Microsoft Works stores the deleted text in RAM (random-access memory) in a temporary file that holds only one occurrence of deleted text. If you delete more text, the first deleted text is replaced in the temporary file with the newly deleted text. Therefore, in order to retrieve deleted text, you must retrieve it immediately, or the temporary file may no longer be holding the deleted text you want.

Moving and Copying Text between Documents

Now that you have worked with moving and copying, you can distinguish the difference between the function of each. When you move text, it is removed from its original location and inserted in a new location. When you copy text, it remains in the original location and is inserted in the new location.

Before you move and copy from one file to another, another file has to be available to receive text. Start by opening a new file. Press Alt for the menu bar and then F for the File menu. Select Create New File. Four options appear on your screen, one for each component of Works. Highlight the New Word Processor option and press Enter.

The default name of this new file (assigned by Works) is WORD2.WPS. You want to rename the new file. Press Alt, F, and then S. The Save dialog box appears with `WORD2.WPS` at the top. Change the name of the file to COPY.WPS (see fig. 2.28) and press Enter.

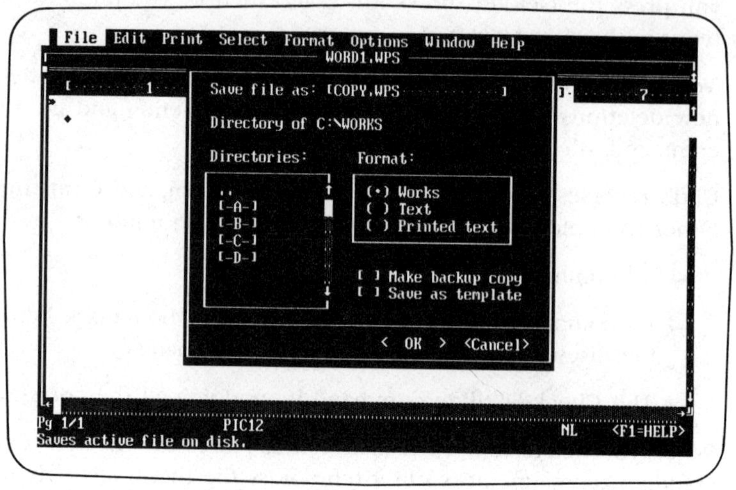

Fig. 2.28.

The new file named COPY.WPS.

To copy to the file, do the following:

1. First make sure that the cursor is back in RMTA.WPS. (Do so by pressing Alt to activate the menu bar, F for the File menu, and O to open a file that already exists; when the dialog box appears, move the cursor to `RMTA.WPS` and press Enter.) Then move the cursor to the beginning of the text you want to copy. In this case, you want to copy the name and address at the beginning of the letter. The cursor should be under the letter R in *Rancho*.
2. Hold down the Shift key and move the down-arrow key until the inside address is highlighted.
3. Press Shift-F3 so that `COPY` appears on the status line. You are in Copy mode.
4. Open the new file and copy the text to it. Press Alt to activate the menu bar, press F for the File menu, and press O to open an existing file.
5. When the dialog box appears, highlight `COPY.WPS`; then press Enter. The new file is superimposed on the second file, which is still open. You can see how your screen looks in figure 2.29.
6. Press Enter and the highlighted text from RMTA.WPS is inserted into COPY.WPS (see fig. 2.30).

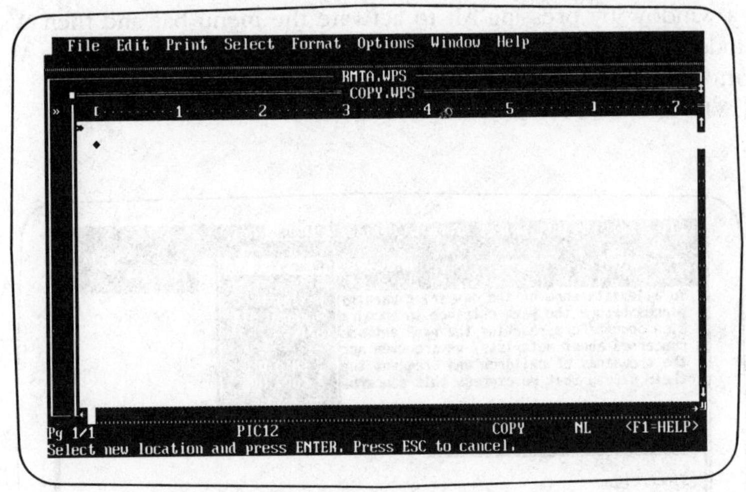

Fig. 2.29.
COPY.WPS appearing over RMTA.WPS.

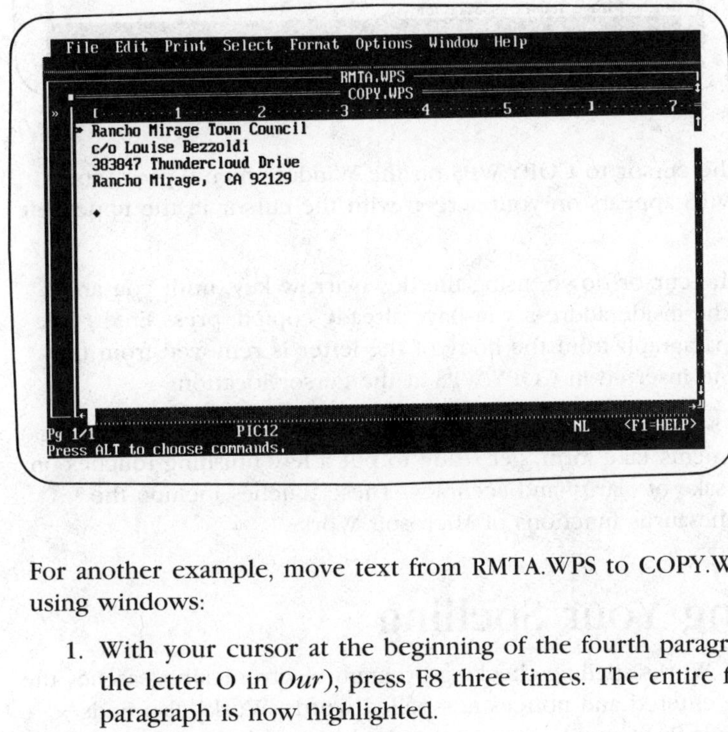

Fig. 2.30.
Copied text in COPY.WPS.

For another example, move text from RMTA.WPS to COPY.WPS, this time using windows:

1. With your cursor at the beginning of the fourth paragraph (under the letter O in *Our*), press F8 three times. The entire fourth paragraph is now highlighted.
2. Press F3; MOVE appears on the status line, indicating that you are in the Move mode.

3. Open a window by pressing Alt to activate the menu bar and then W for Window. The Window menu appears as you see in figure 2.31. At the bottom of the menu are the names of the two open files: RMTA.WPS and COPY.WPS.

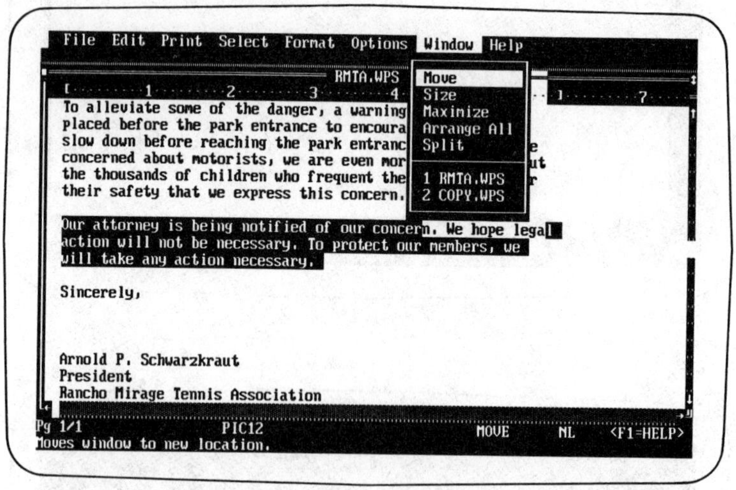

Fig. 2.31.
The Window menu.

4. Move the cursor to COPY.WPS on the Window menu; press Enter. COPY.WPS appears on your screen with the cursor in the upper left corner.

5. Move the cursor down, using the down-arrow key, until you are below the inside address you have already copied; press Enter. The fourth paragraph from the body of the letter is removed from the letter and inserted in COPY.WPS at the cursor location.

Your skills at selecting, moving, copying, and deleting text are improving. As your documents take form, get ready to put a few finishing touches on them for the sake of clarity and accuracy. These touches include the spelling and thesaurus functions of Microsoft Works.

Checking Your Spelling

The Microsoft Works spelling-checking program electronically searches the text you have entered and notices misspelled words. Works also finds incorrectly capitalized words such as *WOrks*, incorrectly hyphenated words such as *hyp-henated*, and repeated words such as *and and*.

For practice, look through the letter you have in the file RMTA.WPS. If no spelling errors exist, you may want to create some to see how well the spelling-checking program works. A few spelling mistakes have been added for this exercise:

1. Move the cursor to the upper left corner of the word processing document (press Ctrl-Home). In a longer document, you may choose to move the cursor to where you want to begin checking the spelling. Works moves forward when checking spelling, starting with the cursor location to the end of the file.

2. Press Alt to activate the menu bar. Press O for the Options menu. Highlight the Check Spelling option and press Enter, or press S.

3. Works starts searching through the text for words it does not recognize. When such a word is found, the Spelling dialog box appears. Figure 2.32 shows the first word that Works does not recognize, which is *Louise*.

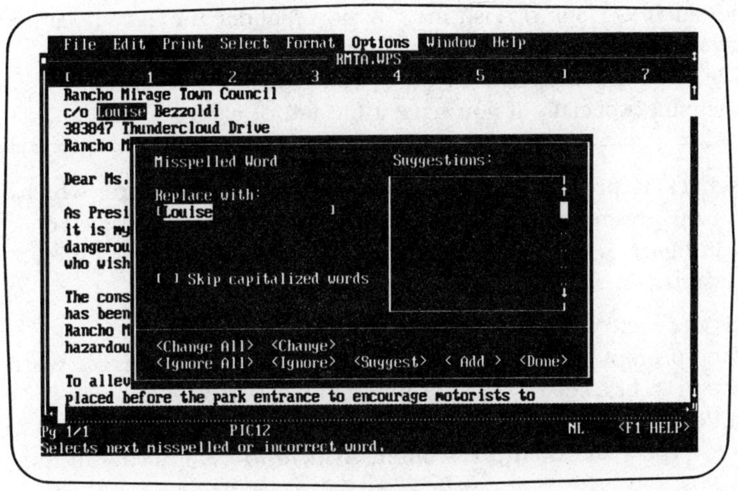

Fig. 2.32.
The Spelling dialog box.

When a word is not recognized, you have many options:

- ❑ Replace the word with a correctly spelled word
- ❑ Change all occurrences of the misspelled word (press Alt-H)
- ❑ Ignore this instance of the word (press Alt-I)
- ❑ Ignore the word each time it is found in the file (press Alt-G)

- ❑ Ask Works to suggest some other spellings of the word (press Alt-S)
- ❑ Select a word from the list of suggestions and then press Alt-C to change the word
- ❑ Add the word to the Works dictionary (press Alt-A)

When you have made a decision on the word Works does not recognize, Works then searches for the next questionable word. Notice that with each word Works finds, a brief description of the problem appears in the upper left corner of the Spelling dialog box. In this case, *Louise* is considered to be a misspelled word.

Because Louise spells her name this way, the best option here is to ignore all occurrences of *Louise* in the file. Press Alt-G. The next word Works finds is *Bezzoldi.* Press Alt-G again.

Tip: You can see a pattern developing here. Most names are not recognized by Works unless those such as Cook or Fish are used. Even names such as Cook or Fish may be noted under the `Irregular Capitalization` prompt. Prevent this interruption by selecting the `Skip capitalized words` option on the Spelling dialog box. This option is helpful, especially if you have a file full of names.

The spelling-checking program highlights the next misspelled word, which is *Presibent* in this example. Ask Works for suggestions, and you receive those shown in figure 2.33. Highlight the correct option and press Enter. *President* is inserted in the text.

ASsociation is the next word highlighted with the `Irregular Capitalization` prompt. The cursor starts at the end of the incorrect word in the `Replace with` brackets. Using the left- and right-arrow keys, move the cursor under the lowercase s. Press the Backspace key to delete the capital letter S. Type *s* and then press Enter. *Association* is inserted in the text.

The next error found in this example is *to to* in the second-to-the-last paragraph of the body of the letter. Press the Backspace key, which eliminates the *to to* between the brackets. Type *to* and press Enter. The *to to* in the body of the letter is replaced with *to.*

Works finds *Arnold* and *Schwarzkraut* in the closing of the letter. Because this is the name of the person writing the letter, add these words to the dictionary. Press Alt-A for both of these additions.

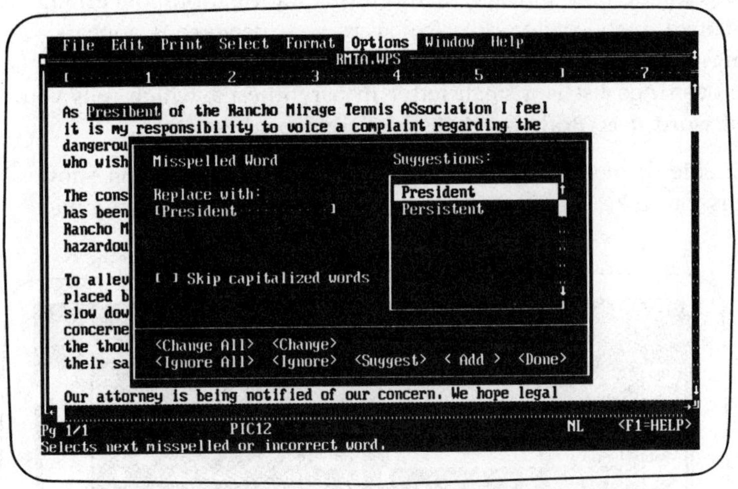

Fig. 2.33.

Suggestions for correcting the spelling of ***Presibent.***

If you didn't start checking the spelling at the beginning of the file, when Works reaches the end of the file, a prompt appears and asks whether you want to continue to check spelling from the start of the file. Choose `OK` and Works starts checking spelling. Move the cursor to the right using the right-arrow key to select `Cancel`. This action stops the spelling checking. You also can press Esc to cancel the spelling checking.

Tip: Press Esc anytime during the process of spelling checking to stop the procedure. Pressing Alt-D also stops the process.

Using the Thesaurus

Use the Microsoft Works thesaurus to improve your clarity and style when writing. The thesaurus helps you find the word that is just right or interject a little variety in your choice of words.

In the second paragraph of the letter in RMTA.WPS, the writer has used the word *dangerous* after using the same word in the first paragraph. Move the cursor to the letter d in *dangerous* in the second paragraph. Press Shift and move the right-arrow key until the word is selected. Press Alt for the menu bar and then O for the Options menu; select Thesaurus and press Enter.

The Thesaurus dialog box appears. At the top is information concerning what is contained in the dialog box. Synonyms for: dangerous appears. Two meanings for *dangerous* are listed: risky and menacing. After each word in the Meanings list is a small letter in parentheses, which tells you what kind of word it is. Both words listed here are adjectives.

On the right side of the dialog box are the synonyms. Figure 2.34 shows the synonyms for *risky*. Figure 2.35 shows the synonyms for *menacing*.

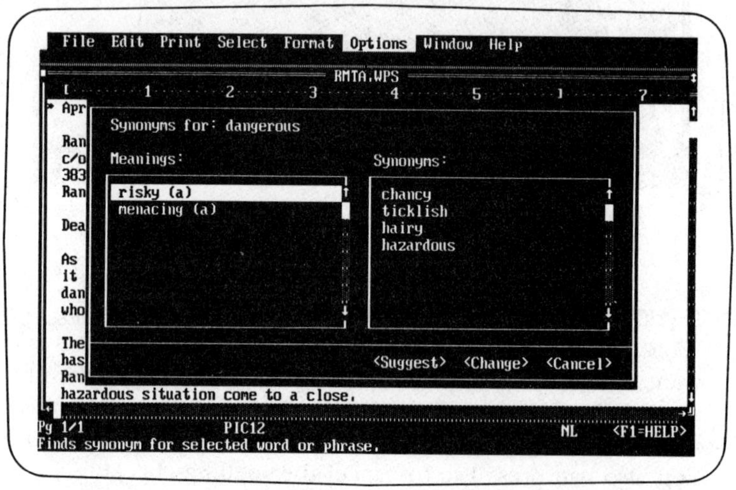

Fig. 2.34.

*Synonyms for **risky**.*

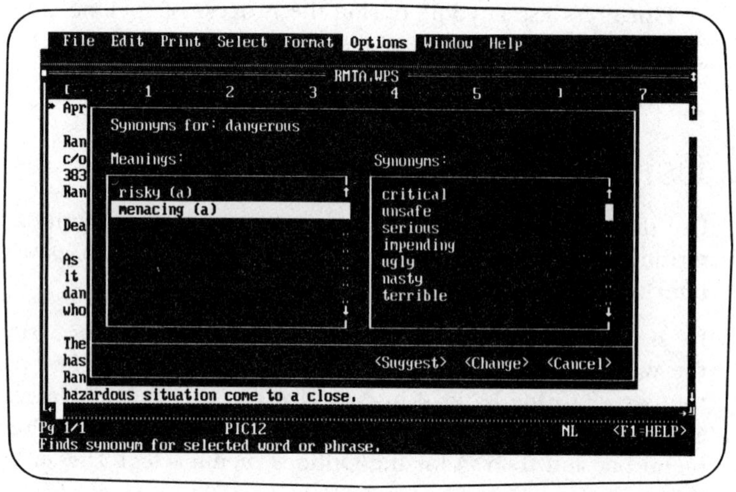

Fig. 2.35.

*Synonyms for **menacing**.*

Use the right-arrow key to move the cursor to the `Synonyms` box. Highlight the word you want to use instead of *dangerous*. In this example, move the cursor to the word `hazardous` and press Alt-C. *Hazardous* is inserted in the text in place of *dangerous*.

Tip: You can search for the synonym of a synonym. With one synonym highlighted, press Alt-S. Works lists any synonyms for the selected word, from which you can make a choice.

Saving Your Document

Now that your letter has been edited, save this revised version by pressing Alt and then F. The two options you can use to save text are Save and Save As. If you exit Works without saving or if a power loss occurs, you lose all your work. Many computer users make a habit of saving their files about every 15 minutes.

Most of the time, you will use the Save command. Press Alt, F, and then S, and press Enter. The text in your file is saved to your hard disk or floppy disk.

At times you will want to use other saving options. For example, you can save files in other file formats, making them compatible with other word processors. You can send a file to a communications device. You can give a file a new file name.

Some of the Save As options are covered here. First, look at the Save As dialog box shown in figure 2.36.

As you saw earlier, Works names your files for you in the following manner: WORD1.WPS, WORD2.WPS, and so on. Because these names aren't descriptive, you renamed the first document you created as RMTA.WPS, which told you the document was a letter regarding the Rancho Mirage Tennis Association. The next file was one where you practiced copying and moving text, so it was named COPY.WPS. Names of files can be eight characters in length with a one- to three-character extension. Works automatically adds the following extensions if you don't add one yourself:

Word Processor	WPS
Spreadsheet	WKS
Database	WDB
Communications	WCM

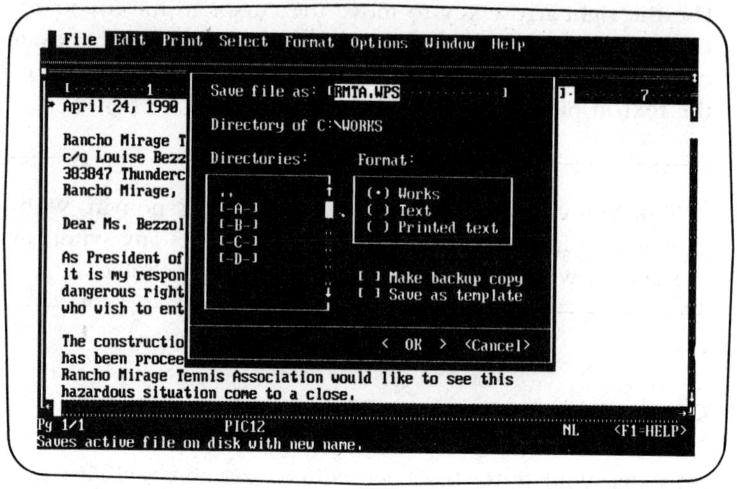

Fig. 2.36.

The Save As dialog box.

Add your own extensions if you want to identify your files even further. For example, if the name of your company is Hot Cross Buns, you may want to use HCB as a file extension for everything that has to do with your business.

The Save As dialog box shows the name you have given the file. The directory is listed—in this case, C:\WORKS, which tells you the file is to be saved on drive C in the WORKS subdirectory. Below that, four other directories are listed with a list of the formats for saving text.

Saving to Another Directory

Highlight the directory you want to use while you are in the Save dialog box. The A directory is the next highest directory, the B directory is the subdirectory, and the C and D directories (D directories will not appear with most computers) are used for other drives. Select the directory you want and press Enter. In the `File Name` text box, type the name for the file in the new directory and press Enter. When you use this method, the drive or directory you select becomes the new current drive and directory.

Save the file to another drive or directory without changing the current directory by choosing Save As from the File menu. When you are prompted with `Save file as: [A.....]`, type the complete path name and file name. Type the following, for example:

D:\WORKS\RMTA.WPS

Press Enter and the file is saved to drive D.

Saving Files in ASCII Format

When you save files in Works, the files are saved in Works format. Use ASCII format to save files that you may want to use with other word processing programs (ASCII files are also called text files). ASCII files contain only the text and numbers from the file without Works formatting.

While in the Save dialog box, move the cursor to the `Text` option and press Enter. That file is saved to the current directory, or any other directory you have specified, in ASCII format.

Closing Files

You now have two open files that you have created for the word processor. The first, RMTA.WPS, contains a letter. The second, COPY.WPS, contains some text you copied or moved from the letter. Both of these files have been saved. You now can close the files to clear the screen. Usually you close a file when you are finished working with it.

With your cursor in RMTA.WPS, open the File menu by pressing Alt and then F. Select the Close option. The file RMTA.WPS is removed from the screen (and from RAM), and the cursor is in COPY.WPS. Press Alt, F, and C to close that file. Only the File menu appears on the screen now.

Even though these files are closed, they are saved on disk and you can retrieve them by using the Open Existing File option. If you did not already save these two files, you are prompted with a dialog box. `Save changes to` appears in the box. Select `Yes` and press Enter. The files are saved and then closed.

Choose `No` in this dialog box, and your file is closed without being saved, which means you will not have a permanent copy of the file. Select `Cancel` and the procedure to close the file is terminated.

Exiting Microsoft Works

With the two files closed and the File menu on the screen, press X to exit Microsoft Works. You are taken to the `C:\>` prompt if you have a hard disk or to the `A:\>` prompt if you have a floppy disk system. You now can safely turn off the computer. Relax and take a break; you have worked hard.

Chapter Summary

Your skills at editing, including moving around in your text; correcting, inserting, selecting, moving, and copying text; and saving your document, have been improved. If the electronic page is new to you, you are learning about the convenience and ease with which you can create documents. If you are an experienced word processor, you can see how the Works word processor can help you create professional documents.

If you are looking for different ways to format your text, look at Chapter 3. You will find information on formatting, creating tables with columns, using boldface and italic, and changing fonts.

Chapter 4 takes you through the advanced word processing features of Works. You will learn to search, search and replace, add headers and footers, create form letters by merging documents, and print all or part of a document.

3

Opening Files and Formatting Text

Your word processing prowess is improving! You are now able to edit your documents for accuracy and style and are ready to add the finishing touches to your documents' appearance. The Microsoft Works formatting options allow you to center and justify text, vary type styles, change margins, and, in many other ways, enhance the look of your finished document. As always, remember to save the documents to disk so that you do not lose your formatting changes.

Opening Works Files

You already opened a file when you created the one in which you typed a letter called RMTA.WPS. You created another new file, which you named COPY.WPS. At the end of the last chapter, you closed the two files. In this section, you will practice opening files already closed.

If the computer is turned off, turn it on and wait for the `C:\>` prompt. If you have a floppy disk system, you will receive an `A:\>` prompt. In this case, put your program disk into drive A and proceed.

For a hard disk system, at the prompt, type

CD\WORKS

At the next prompt, type

WORKS

The Works' opening screen appears with the File menu in the upper left corner.

Now follow these steps:

1. Move the cursor down, using the arrow keys to highlight Open Existing File. Press Enter. (Or simply press O.)
2. The Open dialog box appears (see fig. 3.1).
3. Press the down-arrow key until `RMTA.WPS` is highlighted.
4. Press Enter, and that file is displayed.

You now have a file, easily opened, with which to work. You may have up to eight files open at the same time. You are able to open Works files any time; however, if you have eight files open already, you must close one before opening another. A file remains open until you either close it or exit Works.

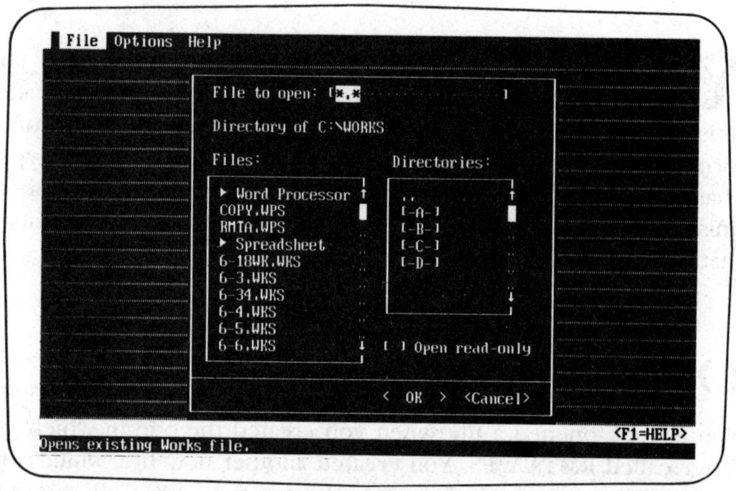

Fig. 3.1.
The Open dialog box.

Understanding What You See On-Screen

At the top of your screen, the message `File to open:[*.*.....]` appears. In this space, you can type the name of the file you want to open. Typing *.* opens all files.

The next line tells you the disk and the directory in which you are working. In this case, you see `Directory of C:\WORKS`.

The box on the left lists the two word processing files you have already created. The remaining files are listed in the space below in alphabetical order, by type, such as word processing or spreadsheet files.

The box on the right lists options [-A-], [-B-], [-C-], and [-D-]. (Not all screens display four options here. The drives and directories available on your system are listed.) From here you can choose to open files from other drives or directories.

The Open read-only option is for use on a network. It protects files when more than one person is allowed to use the same file at the same time.

Opening a File from Another Drive

Suppose that you have just purchased a template that works with Microsoft Works. (A *template* is a file created to do repetitive jobs so that you don't have to reinvent formats or documents.) You have a hard disk drive and want to load a template file into Works. To do so, place the template disk into drive A and close the drive, press Alt to activate the menu bar, and press F for the File menu. Then press O (for Open Existing File), and the Open dialog box appears.

Using the down- and right-arrow keys, position your cursor on the [-A-] in the Directories box, which allows you to access the disk in drive A.

Press Enter. The disk light for drive A goes on, and the disk is read. After Directory of, you see A:\, indicating which drive is reading the files. The Files box in the dialog box lists the files found on the disk in drive A (see fig. 3.2).

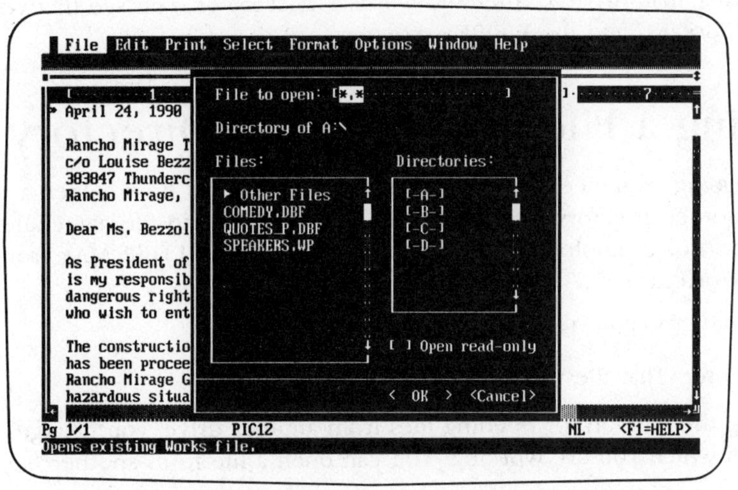

Fig. 3.2.

List of files found on the Template Disk in drive A.

Highlight the file you want to open—in this case, SPEAKERS.WP. Press Enter. That file is read from drive A and appears on your screen (see fig. 3.3).

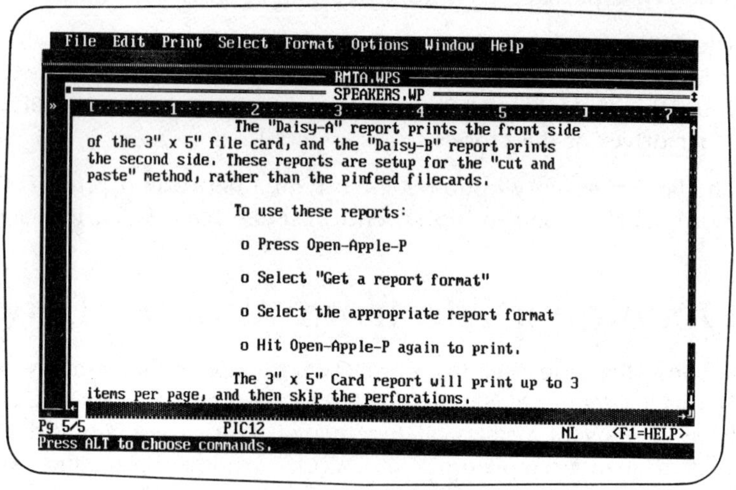

Fig. 3.3.

The file from drive A on-screen.

Repeat the steps up to this point to continue opening files from drive A. If you are done copying files from drive A, follow the remaining steps to return to drive C.

Follow the same procedures until the Open dialog box appears again. Press Alt for the menu bar, F for the File menu, and then O to reach the Open dialog box.

Using the down- and right-arrow keys, place your cursor over the [-C-] under Directories and press Enter. Now you are working with files from drive C rather than drive A. After the words Directory of, you see that you are back in drive C and the WORKS directory.

Opening a File from Another Directory

In the foregoing sequence, you opened a file from another drive. Open a file from another directory by typing the complete path and file name after File to open. For example, if you want to open the file LETTERS.MAY from Microsoft Word in the WORD directory, type

C:\WORD\LETTERS.MAY

and press Enter. That file will appear on your screen.

Note: Using the method for opening files from another drive, you change the drive in which you are working. You can open a file from another drive without moving out of drive C. For example, suppose that you are looking for BOS_AUTO.WP. Type

\BOS_AUTO.WP

after `File to open` and then press Enter. That file will be read from drive A while you continue to work in drive C. This method saves the step of having to return to the Open dialog box and change the drive back to C. The method described in the preceding section is more useful if you don't remember or don't know what is on the disk in drive A. By changing to drive A, you get a list of all the files.

With your cursor in the file you copied from the template in drive A, press Alt to activate the menu bar and F for the File menu; then close the file by pressing C.

RMTA.WPS is on your screen. The next step is to prepare a document to test the formatting options available with Microsoft Works.

Creating a New File

Now you will practice formatting options in a new file. Open one to hold the text for your next catalog advertisement. This file will hold a one-page advertisement with various formatting styles, including boldfaced and italicized text, to draw attention to specific sections of the advertisement.

Press Alt to activate the menu bar, F for the File menu, and then N. Select which type of file you want. In this case, the cursor is already on New Word Processor, so press Enter.

A blank work space appears, ready for your input. Type the advertisement printed here, and then you can experiment with some of Works' formatting functions:

Double Data Announces the

Easy Printer

A Printer Sharing Device just made for your needs at a great price!

This special price of $249.95 is only available through September 30.

The Easy Printer has all the high-tech features of our other printer sharing devices, but it is economically packaged on an interface card. The Easy Printer Controller Card resides in a host computer, allowing up to five computers to share one or more printers automatically, with no waiting. Standard equipment is a 64K memory buffer that can be expanded to 256K. The Easy Printer has room for high-speed, simultaneous storage of each print job from each computer. Fantastic features are

Simultaneous inputting

Built-in, high-speed memory buffer

Automatic action

Parallel output port

Eighteen-month limited warranty

Examining the Options on the Font & Style Dialog Box

Take a look at the Font & Style dialog box by pressing Alt to activate the menu bar, T for the Format menu, and then F for the Font & Style option. The screen shown in figure 3.4 appears.

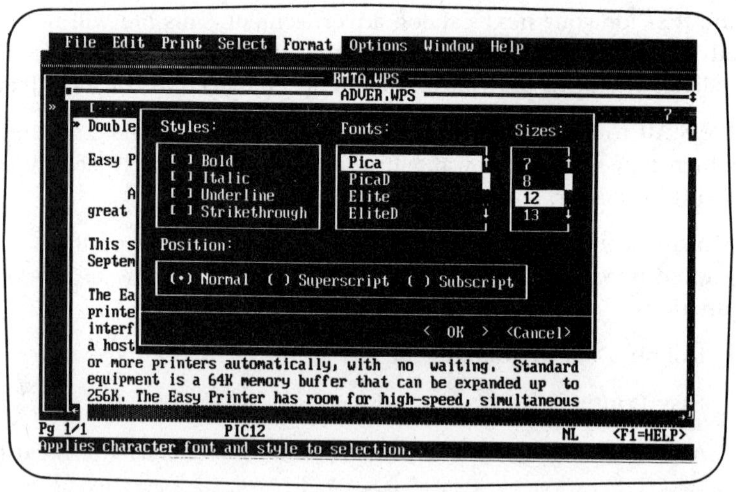

Fig. 3.4.

The Font & Style dialog box.

The style of text refers to the way the characters look compared with the surrounding text. A variety of styles are available with Microsoft Works, including those listed here:

- ❑ Plain
- ❑ Bold

- ❑ Underline
- ❑ Italic
- ❑ Strikethrough

Some styles of text are commonly used for specific reasons. Words are sometimes emphasized with boldfaced text, foreign words and phrases are usually italicized, and book titles are underlined. The Strikethrough option is often used in legal documents.

Fonts, also called typefaces, are analogous characters in various sizes and styles, which you can use to change the look or length of your document. Several fonts are listed here:

- ❑ Courier
- ❑ Helvetica
- ❑ Roman
- ❑ Times
- ❑ Gatsby
- ❑ Western

The fonts available to you depend on the capabilities of your printer. Some printers may be able to print one basic font in pica, elite, large type, double wide, and other variations. Other printers may offer as many as 50 different fonts. Find out what fonts are available to you by pressing Alt to activate the menu bar, T for the Format menu, and then F for the Font & Style dialog box. The fonts available to you are listed in the box under Fonts.

Note: If your printer's fonts are not listed, you may have set up Works with the wrong printer. Go back to the Printer Setup dialog box and select another model or printer.

Another characteristic of type is its position. At the bottom of the Font & Style dialog box are Position options. The Superscript option places the text above the normal line level, as you would see in a footnote reference number. Choosing Subscript places the text below the normal line level; subscript is often used for technical or scientific references, such as H_2O.

The last choice available to you on the Font & Style dialog box is the type size. Type size is measured in points; 1 point is 1/72 inch. Most text appears in 12-point text. You will find that 6-point text is very small, sometimes called "the fine print." Point sizes of 14 or 18 are generally used for headings or titles.

Some printers measure the size of text in *pitch*, or the number of characters per horizontal inch. A value of 10 pitch is roughly equivalent to 12 points.

Changing the Style of Text

Now that you are familiar with the options featured in the Font & Style dialog box, you are ready to make some changes to your text. You can determine the style before typing the text or after, but because you already have typed the text, the second method will be used here.

Many options are available for style, font, size, and position. You can combine any of these options to form almost endless permutations of typefaces. For example, you can have a portion of your text italicized, underlined, and in an 8-point Times font. You can have text boldfaced and in a 12-point Courier font. You even can have italicized superscript.

Style changes are most often used when you want to emphasize a particular item. When sending out letters with the names of your products, for example, you may want to have the names appear in italic or boldface. In business reports, you can emphasize headings and titles with different styles or fonts so that the readers will easily recognize them.

Tip: Be careful not to overdo the font and style changes. You do not want to have so many different fonts and styles that the reader has difficulty reading the text.

To begin experimenting with fonts and styles, start with the advertisement you just typed. First, make *Double Data* appear in boldface text. With your cursor at the beginning of the file, follow these instructions to change the style of text:

1. Select the text you want to change by holding down the Shift key and moving the cursor to the right until `Double Data` is highlighted.

2. Press Alt to activate the menu bar. Press T for the Format menu. Press F for the Font & Style option.

3. Press the space bar while your cursor is on the `Bold` option (or press Alt-B). When an `X` appears in the box next to the option, press Enter.

When you return to the text on the screen, `Double Data` is still highlighted. Press the down-arrow key, and the highlighting is removed. You can see that the text you selected appears bold on the screen.

Selecting Text Using a Mouse

You can use a mouse to select text. Point to the `D` in `Double Data`. Click and drag the arrow until `Double Data` is highlighted. Move the point to Format on the menu bar and click the mouse. The Format menu appears. From there, point to the Bold option and click, and the selected text becomes boldfaced. You are returned to the text on-screen with `Double Data` highlighted. Press any cursor-movement key to turn off the highlighting.

Changing Styles Using the Format Menu

For a quicker way to change a style, use the Format menu. Although this method saves time, you can use it to select only one style for text. (Choosing two styles for text is covered later in this chapter.) In this example, italicize the sentence that talks about the great price of Easy Printer:

1. Move the cursor to the beginning of the text you want to italicize. The cursor should be under the `T` in `This special price`.

2. Press F8 two times to highlight the entire sentence.

3. Press Alt to activate the menu bar. Press T for the Format menu (see fig. 3.5). From the Format menu, select the Italic option.

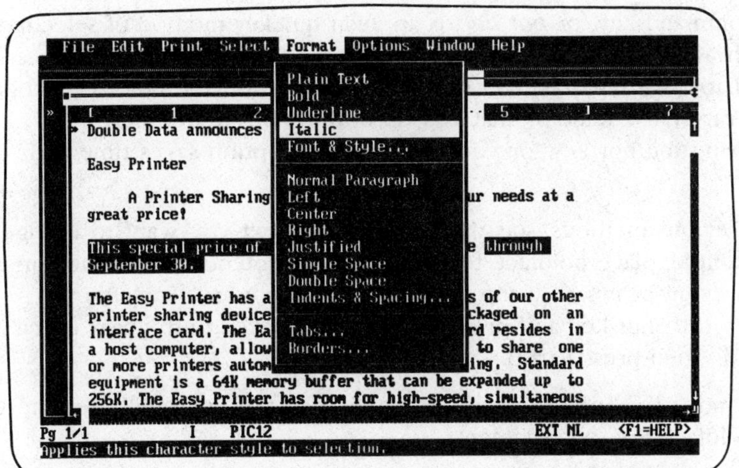

Fig. 3.5. *The Format menu.*

4. You are now back in the text with the sentence still highlighted. Press a cursor-movement key to turn off the highlighting.

The text you want italicized may appear boldfaced on-screen, but it will be printed in italic.

Note: If your printer cannot italicize, it will underline instead.

Tip: Some screens display styles differently. Like the variability in printers, you will see differences in screens, too. Some may be able to show underlined text; others may simply boldface every type style that is not plain text. Some color monitors show different styles in different colors. You will quickly become familiar with how your screen and printer handle these options.

Tip: In the Works Settings dialog box (press Alt, O, and then W to reach this dialog box), you may be able to choose between a graphic or text screen, depending on the options available with your hardware. In Graphics mode, the different character styles appear boldfaced, underlined, or italicized on-screen, and Text mode displays the different styles in different colors.

Changing the Styles Using Command Keys

Using a command key, or *hot key*, is an even quicker method of selecting styles with Microsoft Works. When you become familiar with the different styles available with Works, you may find that you use the boldface option often but rarely use italic or that you do nothing but underline. Remembering the hot key for your favorite style option saves time and energy.

As with previous methods, start by selecting the text you want to change. In this example, place boldface text in part of a sentence. Move the cursor to the words `great price` in the sentence after the words `Easy Printer`. Hold down the Shift key and press the right-arrow key until `great price` is highlighted. Then press Ctrl-B.

After you move the cursor out of the highlighted text, you will see that it appears boldfaced on your screen.

Tip: The command keys (hot keys) for the style options are

Bold	Ctrl-B
Italic	Ctrl-I
Underline	Ctrl-U

Inserting Text after Choosing the Style

At times you may add a quote to your text or may want to make specific letters or words stand out from the rest. You can choose the style you want and then enter the text. In this example, you will insert a phone number and underline it at the end of the advertisement you are formatting. Start by moving the cursor to the end of the document by pressing Ctrl-End.

Press Alt to activate the menu bar, T for the Format menu, and U for Underline. U appears on the status line. Now type the text you want to underline:

Call now to order Easy Printer at 1-800-EZPRINT.

When you are done typing the sentence with the telephone number, press Alt to activate the menu bar. Press T for the Format menu and then select the Plain Text option. The U disappears from the status line.

Tip: When you use this method, always remember to turn the type style off or you will continue to insert text in the style you have selected.

Choosing Two Styles for Text

When you use the menu method of turning on the options you want, you can choose more than one. For the words *Easy Printer*, choose the boldface and underline options.

1. With the cursor under the E in Easy, hold down the Shift key and press the right-arrow key until Easy Printer is selected.

2. Press Alt to activate the menu bar, T for the Format menu, and then F for the Font & Style option.

3. In the dialog box, with the cursor to the left of the Bold option, press the space bar or Alt-B.

4. Use the down-arrow key to move the cursor to the left of the Underline option. Press the space bar to turn on that option, as well.

5. Now press Enter. You return to the text with the words Easy Printer still highlighted.

Use a cursor-movement key, and the highlighting disappears; the words Easy Printer appear in boldface on-screen. Although the text isn't underlined on the screen, it will be when printed.

Removing Styles

You decide that you like the words *Easy Printer* boldfaced and underlined; however, you are not happy with *Double Data* in boldface. To remove the style changes to *Double Data*, begin by selecting it. Now move the cursor to the D in Double, hold down the Shift key, and press the cursor-movement keys until Double Data is highlighted.

Press Alt to activate the menu bar, T for the Format menu, and P for Plain Text. Once more, you are back in the text with Double Data highlighted. Press a cursor-movement key, and the highlighting disappears. Double Data no longer appears in boldface on your screen (see fig. 3.6).

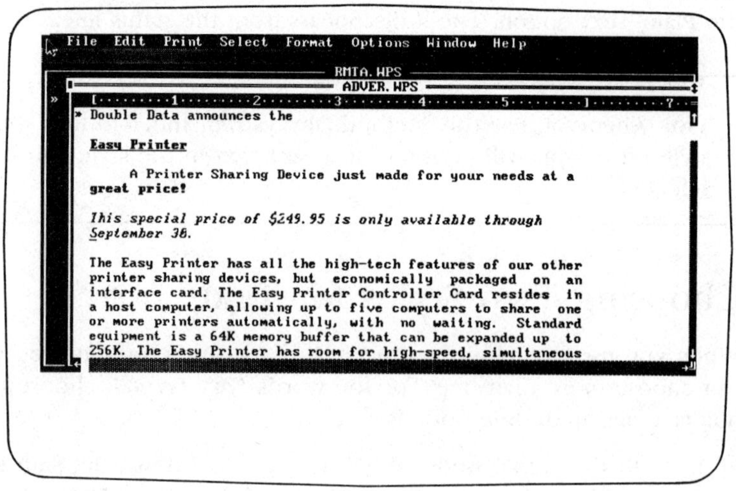

Fig. 3.6.

Easy Printer *bold and underlined on-screen and* Double Data *in plain text.*

Tip: How do you tell which style you are using? Because some screens will not show you the exact style changes you have made, you have to read the secret code, which appears on the status line. Move the cursor to `Double Data` at the top of the screen. Use an arrow key to move down one line at a time. When you come to the line with `Easy Printer` on it, `BU` appears on the status line to the left of `PIC12`. `BU` stands for boldfaced, underlined text. Continue moving the cursor down, and you will see the codes change to `B` when the cursor is in `price` and to `I` when the cursor is in `This`. `B` tells you that the cursor is in boldface text, and `I` tells you the text is italicized. Watch the status line for information on text styles. Figure 3.7 shows the `BU` on the status line.

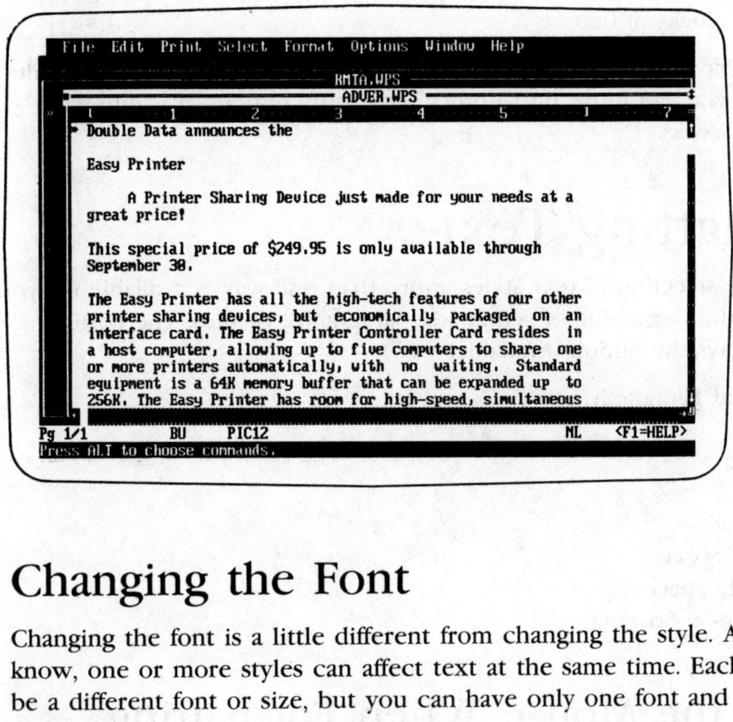

Fig. 3.7. `BU` *(for bold underlined text) on the status line.*

Changing the Font

Changing the font is a little different from changing the style. As you now know, one or more styles can affect text at the same time. Each letter can be a different font or size, but you can have only one font and one size per character.

Font names and sizes direct a dot-matrix or laser printer to print in different modes. If you used different fonts on a daisywheel printer, you would select the corresponding print wheel.

Up to this point, you have changed style in relatively small blocks of text. Change the font for the entire file by following these steps:

1. Move the cursor to the beginning of the file (in this case, under the `D` in `Double Data`).
2. Highlight the entire file by pressing F8 four times.
3. Press Alt to activate the menu bar, T for the Format menu, and F for the Font & Style option.
4. Press the right-arrow key to move the cursor to the `Fonts` box. Press Enter with the cursor on `Pica` (or choose any font available with your printer).

The entire file is now converted to the font you selected. Use this same method to change fonts in smaller blocks of text by highlighting them. In the same way, you can change the point size for the document or for individual blocks of text.

After you have accented the appropriate words and the text is in the file you want, you can move on to other formatting options available with Microsoft Works.

Formatting Text

As with the selection of text styles, more than one way is available for you to change the formatting of sentences, paragraphs, or files. The Format menu displays the options available:

- ❑ Normal Paragraph
- ❑ Left
- ❑ Center
- ❑ Right
- ❑ Justified
- ❑ Single Space
- ❑ Double Space
- ❑ Indents & Spacing

Using the Mouse When Formatting

After using the mouse to select text for formatting, use the mouse to point to the menu and menu options you want and click. For example, select the text you want centered—`Easy Printer`—by pointing to the `E`, clicking, and dragging to the right until both words are highlighted.

Point to Format on the menu bar and click. The Format menu appears. Point to the Center option and click. `Easy Printer` is centered on the page.

With the mouse, you have to go through the same steps as described in the rest of this chapter, but you don't need to use the keyboard for all the input. At times, you will have to type a number, such as *2″* for a left-margin setting. With all formatting options, you will not be able to use the mouse exclusively. Use it to save keystrokes when you do not have to enter a specific number in a dialog box.

Centering Text

Move to the line `Easy Printer` in your text. This line is already boldfaced and underlined. Because this advertisement is announcing a new product, the name of the product should be centered:

1. With the cursor under the `E` in `Easy`, press the Shift key and hold it down.
2. Move the right-arrow key until `Easy Printer` is highlighted.
3. Press Alt to activate the menu bar. Press T for the Format menu and C for Center. `Easy Printer` moves to the center of the screen between the right and left margins.

Using the Centering Command Key

After text is selected, use the centering command key (hot key). Press Ctrl-C and highlighted text is centered without the need for accessing the Format menu.

Tip: The formatting command keys (hot keys) are

Left justified	Ctrl-L
Centered	Ctrl-C
Right justified	Ctrl-R
Both margins justified	Ctrl-J

Justifying Text

Use the same procedures for justifying as you would to center text. With both margins justified, the lines of text are evenly aligned between the right and left margins.

You will find that left-justified text is commonly used on all kinds of word processors (the left margin is aligned, and the right margin is not). Use the left-justify command when you want to undo justification or right-justified text.

Right-justified text is used only in special situations (the right margin is aligned, and the left margin is not). Right justification is occasionally used for headers or for aligning columns in tables.

To justify the paragraph in the sample advertisement, select the entire text. With the cursor under the `T` in `The` at the beginning of the paragraph, press F8 four times to highlight the entire paragraph. Press Ctrl-J. The text will shift, especially on the right margin, so that the right margin is straight and aligned.

Changing the Spacing

To determine whether your document will be single- or double-spaced, simply choose the preferred option from the Format menu.

Follow these steps to double-space the justified paragraph of text:

1. Move the cursor so it is under the `T` in `The` at the beginning of the paragraph.
2. Press F8 four times until the entire paragraph is highlighted.
3. Press Alt to activate the menu bar, T for the Format menu, and D for the Double Space option.

The selected text appears justified and double-spaced on-screen (see fig. 3.8).

Examining the Spacing Options

Beyond single- and double-spacing, you can specify triple-spacing. Press Alt to activate the menu bar and T for the Format menu. Select A and the Indents & Spacing dialog box appears (see fig. 3.9).

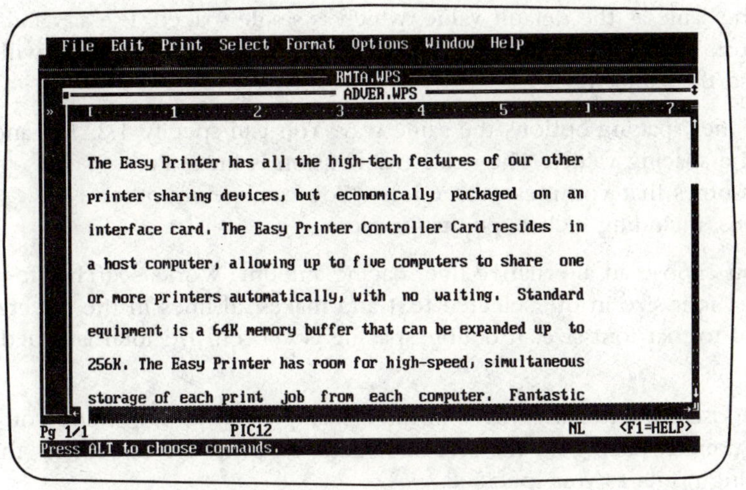

Fig. 3.8.

Text justified and double-spaced on-screen.

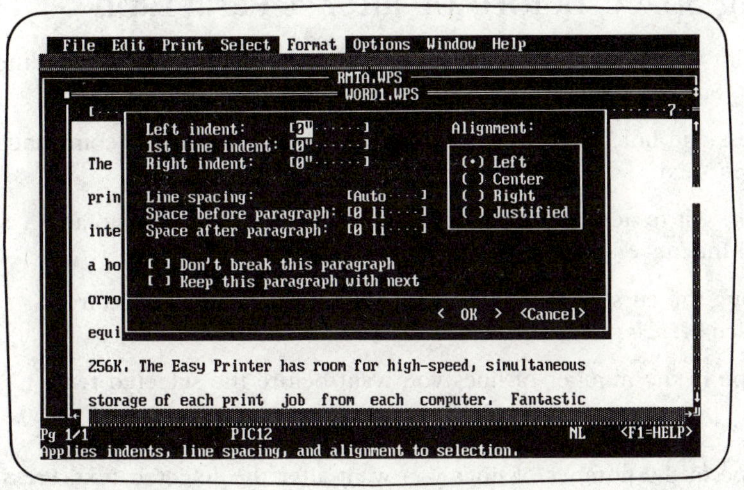

Fig. 3.9.

The Indents & Spacing dialog box.

Select the text you want to print triple-spaced. Press and hold down Shift while pressing the cursor-movement keys or press F8 for the Extend command.

Press Alt to activate the menu bar and T for the Format menu. Select A and the Indents & Spacing dialog box appears. Now move the cursor, using the cursor-movement keys, until it is beside the line `Line spacing: [Auto....]`.

`Auto` is the same as the default value, which is single-spaced. Press 3 and press Enter. The text you selected is triple-spaced on the screen and will be printed the same way.

Choose other spacing options the same way. You can specify 1.2, 1.8, and 2.33 as the spacing values. The default dimension is lines. Press 3 and Works assumes that you mean three lines. You can specify other dimensions, including inches, points, or picas.

When you choose an alternative line-spacing amount, Works searches for the largest font size in the selected text and makes all lines in the selected text equal to that font size. If double-spacing is chosen, 1/6 inch is added between lines.

If you choose a fractional amount of line spacing, such as 2.33 lines, you see only double-spacing on the screen. When you print the document, the line spacing prints as you specified.

Adding Space before or after a Paragraph

If you want to set off a paragraph or heading, select it and then go to the Indents & Spacing dialog box. Do the following:

1. Press and hold down the Shift key or use the F8 Extend command to select text.
2. Press Alt to activate the menu bar, T for the Format menu, and A for the Indents & Spacing dialog box.
3. Using the cursor-movement keys, place your cursor across from `Space before paragraph: [0 li....]`.
4. Type in the number of lines you want before the selected text.
5. Move the cursor across from `Space after paragraph: [0 li....]`.
6. Type in the number of lines you want after the selected text. Press Enter.

Works will add the designated amount of space before and after the selected text.

Indenting Paragraphs

Several options are available for indenting paragraphs. You can indent the first line of a paragraph, indent levels in an outline, create numbered and bulleted lists, or create a hanging indent.

Normally, paragraphs appear on your screen and are printed in left-justified format with a ragged-right edge. The paragraph is set off by one blank line above and below it. This default format can be changed within the Format menu.

Start by indenting the line that starts with `A Printer Sharing Device` in the text on your screen. Using this method will indent only the first line in a paragraph:

1. With the cursor under the `A` for `A Printer Sharing Device`, press F8 two times to highlight the sentence.

Tip: If you have a long document and want the first line of every paragraph indented, press F8 two more times to highlight or select the entire file. Every paragraph will have an indented first line, providing that you follow the remaining steps for indenting the first line of a paragraph.

---

2. Press Alt to activate the menu bar, T for the Format menu, and A for the Indents & Spacing dialog box.

3. Using the down-arrow key, move the cursor across from `1st line indent: [0"......].`

4. Type *.5"* and press Enter. The dimension is inches, so you have chosen to indent 1/2 inch. (You can enter any number of inches to indent.)

Back in your text, the line remains highlighted, and it is indented five spaces (see fig. 3.10).

You may want to indent all the lines in a paragraph to set the block of text apart from the others. Often, this format is used for quotations, which distinguishes them from the remaining text. To try this format, follow these steps:

1. Select the paragraph(s) to be indented.

2. Press Alt to activate the menu bar, T for the Format menu, and A for the Indents & Spacing dialog box.

3. Press 1 across from `Left indent: [0"......].`

All lines of the selected text should now be indented 1 inch.

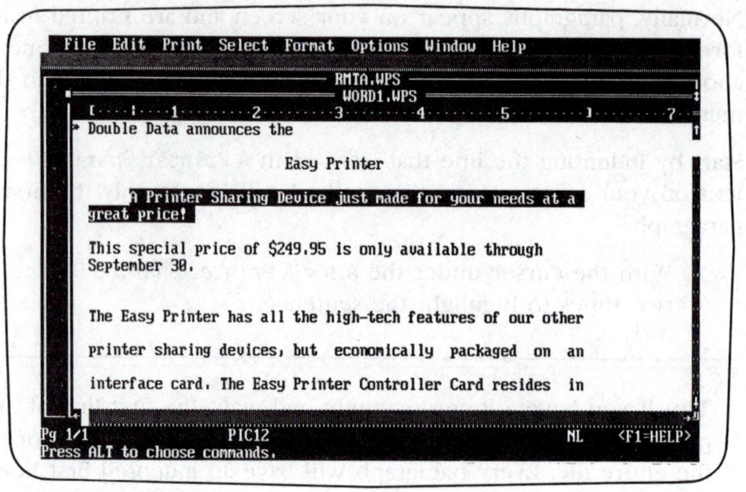

Fig. 3.10.

Text on-screen indented 0.5 inch.

Removing Indents

To remove indents, you use the same procedure as each of the indent steps. Instead of typing in the number of inches to indent text, however, press 0 at each field:

```
Left indent: [0"......]
1st line indent: [0"......]
```

When the value in either slot is 0 inches, the indenting is removed.

Creating a Hanging Indent

The text at the end of the advertisement you typed lists the fantastic features of Easy Printer. Use a hanging indent to draw attention to these features. A *hanging indent* starts the paragraph on the left margin, and the lines that follow the first line have an indentation. Usually this feature is used when a statement about a topic is followed by a descriptive list.

Move the cursor to the text for which you plan to implement a hanging indent. For this example, place the cursor under the S in Simultaneous. Type an asterisk (*). Press the Tab key to leave space between the asterisk and the beginning of the text. The asterisk and the hanging indent together draw attention to each item on the list.

With the cursor still under the S, hold down the Shift key. Press the right-arrow key so the remainder of the sentence is highlighted. Press Ctrl-H.

(The H stands for the hanging indent formatting option.) Works automatically creates a hanging indent with this selected text.

Repeat these steps with every item on the list. You will end up with a list headed by asterisks.

Note: When you are making indentations, notice the *ruler line*, the scale above the work space. With indenting, you see the scale shown here:

```
[....|...1.........2
```

The bracket ([) shows the left margin. The indent mark (|) shows where the indent occurs. With a hanging indent, you see a different ruler line:

```
|....[....1.........2
```

The indent mark (|) is to the left of the bracket ([), which shows the text indentation.

Making Tab Stops with Works

You can select custom tab stops, or you can use the Works default tab stops. Press the Tab key, and Works moves your cursor to the next tab stop. The tab stops appear on your screen when the Show All Characters option is on. At the beginning of the example text, the Tab key was pressed four times. You can see the small arrows pointing to the right in figure 3.11.

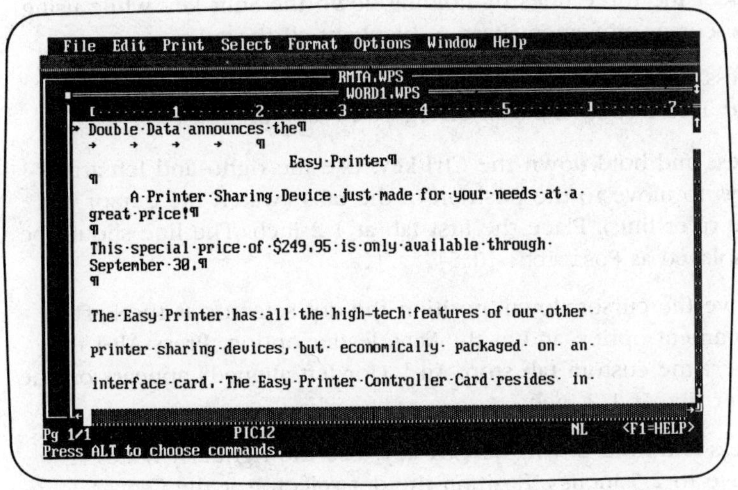

Fig. 3.11.
Tab marks visible with Show All Characters turned on.

Tip: You can show all characters by pressing Alt to activate the menu bar, O to see the Options menu, and L to toggle on the Show All Characters option. Repeat the procedure to turn this option off. With Show All Characters on, your screen displays paragraph marks, tab marks, spaces between typed characters, and so on.

The default Works tabs are 1/2 inch apart. Most of the time, you can use these default tab stops to line up columns or indent text. For custom tables and indentations, customize your tab stops. Set custom tab stops in this example at the end of the file in which you are working.

Add some additional products at the end of the file with their stock numbers and prices. You will see how well Works can create tables.

Follow these steps:

1. Type the following three lines at the end of your draft advertisement (use the Tab and Enter keys):

Disk Notcher (tab)	DN8845 (tab)	$5.95 (Enter)
Ribbons (tab)	R7633 (tab)	3.99 (Enter)
Keyboards (tab)	K89900 (tab)	100.25 (Enter)

   The table you are setting up is not aligned properly at this time. Do not add extra tabs to line it up now. You are going to line up the table later.

2. Select the three lines by holding down the Shift key while using the cursor-movement keys to highlight all three lines.

3. Press Alt to activate the menu bar, T to see the Format menu, and T to display the Tab dialog box (see fig. 3.12).

4. Press and hold down the Ctrl key. Use the right- and left-arrow keys to move to the position of the tabs (watch the cursor on the ruler line). Place the first tab at 1/2 inch. The line should be displayed as `Position: [0.5"....]`.

5. Move the cursor down, position the dot selector at the `Left` alignment option and at the `None` leader option. Press Alt-I to insert the custom tab stop. An `L` (for left aligned) appears on the ruler line at 1/2 inch.

6. Press and hold down the Ctrl key. Use the right-arrow key to move to 2.5 inches. Position the dot selector at the `Center` alignment option (press Alt-C) and at the `None` leader option.

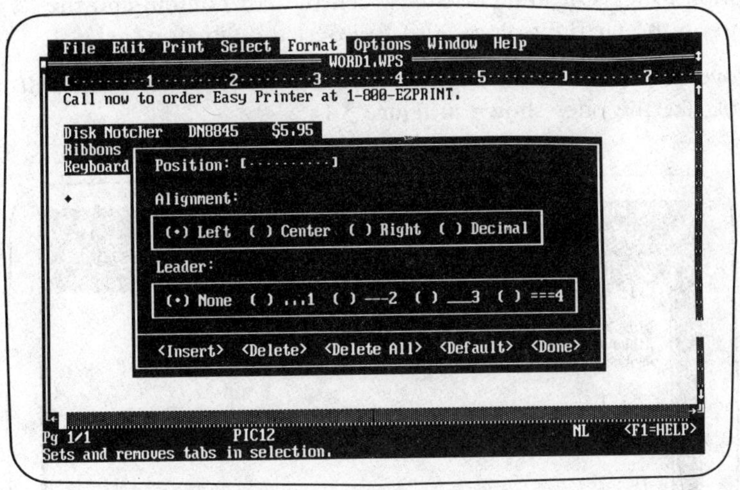

Fig. 3.12.

The Tab dialog box.

7. Press Alt-I to insert the custom tab stop. A `C` (for centered) appears on the ruler line at 2.5 inches. The Tab dialog box appears as shown in figure 3.13.

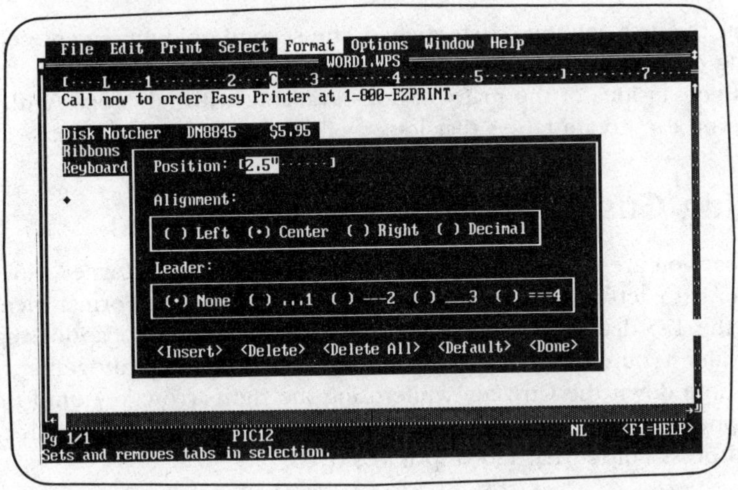

Fig. 3.13.

The Tab dialog box for 2.5 inches.

8. Press and hold down the Ctrl key. Use the right-arrow key to move to 4.5 inches.

9. Move the cursor to position the dot selector at the `Right` alignment option. Position the dot selector at the `...1` leader

option to leave leading dots between the last column and the one on the far right. Press Alt-I to insert the tab stop.

10. Move the cursor to `Done` and press Enter. Your custom tabs will look like the ones shown in figure 3.14.

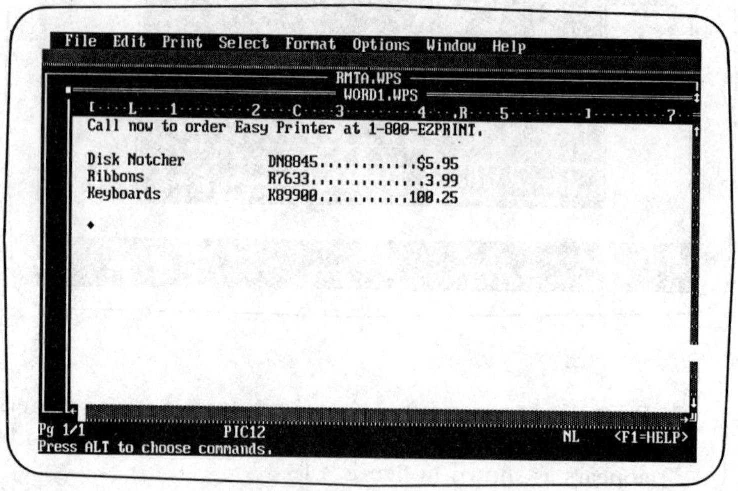

Fig. 3.14.
Custom tabs on-screen.

Notice that the first column is left aligned, the second column is centered, and leading dots bring you to the third column, which is right aligned. This gives you an idea of the many options available with tab stops. With tab stops, you can create tables that look well crafted and professional.

Changing Custom Tab Stops

Suppose that you are not quite happy with the way this table turned out. First press Alt to activate the menu bar. Then press T for the Format menu and T for the Tab dialog box. Move your cursor to the same locations and reset the values you chose before. If you don't like a tab stop altogether, press and hold down the Ctrl key while using the right-arrow key until the tab stop appears in the `Position` box. Then move the cursor to the `Delete` option and press Enter. That tab stop is removed.

Removing Custom Tab Stops

Go back to the Tab dialog box. Move your cursor to the `Delete All` option and press Enter (or press Alt-A). All custom tab stops are removed.

To remove one or more tab stops, but not all of them, keep the cursor in the `Position` box. Press and hold down the Ctrl key. Use the right- or left-arrow key until you stop on the tab stop you want to remove.

Move the cursor to `Delete` and press Enter (or press Alt-T). The letter that represents the alignment of that tab stop is removed, removing the tab stop. Press Esc or move the cursor to the `Done` option and press Enter. The tab stop you want or the one that wasn't quite correct is easily removed.

Changing Margins

The default values for the Works page can be seen in figure 3.15. Works has the page and margins already established for 8 1/2-by-11-inch paper. The top and bottom margins are 1 inch, the left margin is 1.3 inches, and the right margin is 1.2 inches. If you create a header or footer, it is placed 1/2 inch inside the top and bottom margins, respectively. For more information about creating headers and footers, see Chapter 4.

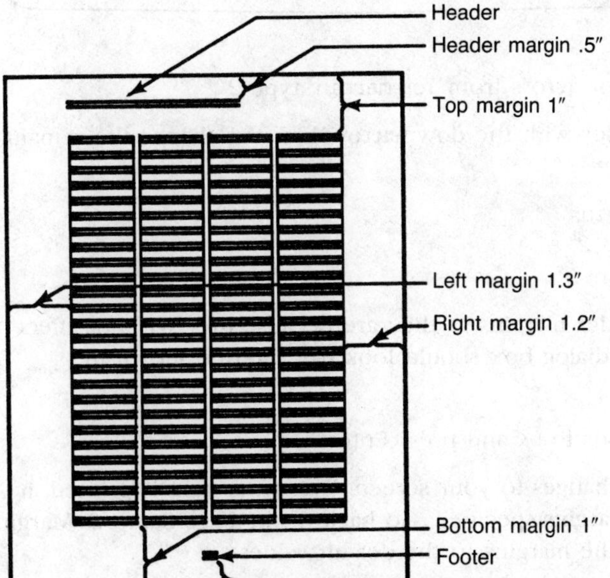

Fig. 3.15.
The Works default margins.

When you want to change margins for the printed page, you will see these values again. This time they will appear on the Page Setup & Margins dialog box. Reset the advertisement's margins for a smaller piece of paper:

1. Press Alt to activate the menu bar, P for the Print menu, and M for the Page Setup & Margins dialog box (see fig. 3.16).

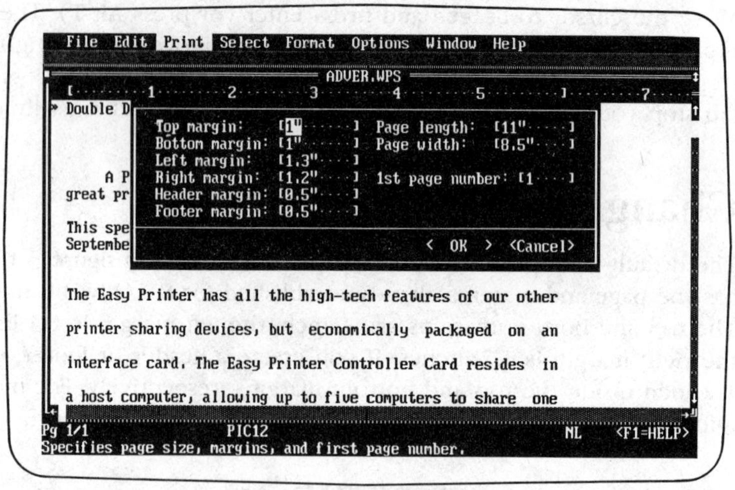

Fig. 3.16.

The Page Setup & Margins dialog box.

2. With the cursor across from `Top margin`, type *2"*.
3. Move the cursor with the down-arrow key and change the remaining values as follows:

   `Bottom margin:` *2"*
   `Left margin:` *2"*
   `Right margin:` *2"*

   Leave the header margins as they are because they will not affect this text. The dialog box should look like the one shown in figure 3.17.

4. Move the cursor to `OK` and press Enter.

You will see some changes to your screen. When this text is printed, it will fit within the margins specified. Go back to the Page Setup & Margins dialog box to reset the margins to the default values.

Tip: If you plan to bind the text you are printing, consider increasing the left margin. A left margin of 2 inches will ensure that the binding does not interfere with the left margin of the text.

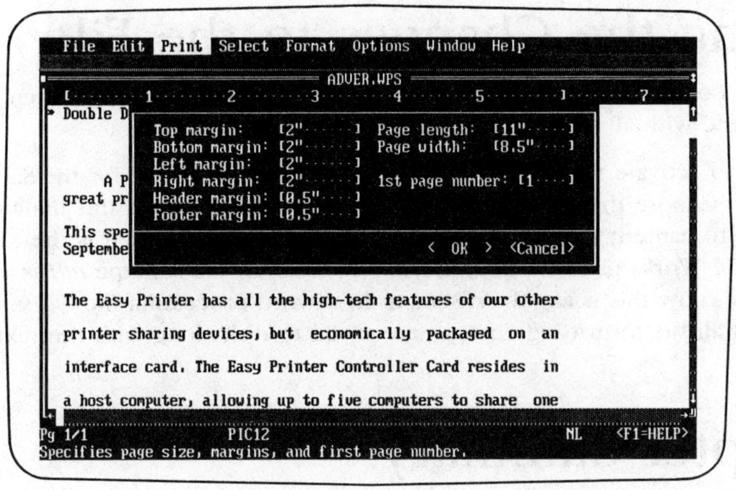

Fig. 3.17.

The Page Setup & Margins dialog box with new values.

Changing Paper Size

Using the Page Setup & Margins dialog box, change the paper size. Picture yourself sending out an invitation on specially ordered paper. You are going to use your office printer to invite business customers to an open house. You have prepared the text on-screen and need to change the page size. Press Alt to activate the menu bar, P for the Print menu, and M for the Page Setup & Margins dialog box. Using the cursor-movement keys, move the cursor across from the `Page length` option (or press Alt-L) and type *6"*. Move the cursor across from `Page width` and type *4.5"*. Now move the cursor to `OK` and press Enter.

The text on-screen will change to fit the page size you have established. The text will be printed with the Works' default margins. Even though the paper is smaller, there will still be 1-inch top and bottom margins just like you would have on an 8 1/2-by-11-inch piece of paper. When you change the paper size, consider changing the margins as well. A 1-inch margin may be unreasonable for such a small piece of paper, allowing little room for text. With paper that is only 4.5 inches wide, for example, a 1.2-inch and 1.3-inch margin takes up 2.5 inches of room. You are left with only 2 inches of space to print text. Right and left margins of 0.6 inch or 0.75 inch may be more reasonable. In contrast, you may want to increase the margins for larger paper.

Go back to the Page Setup & Margins dialog box to set the page size back to the default values. You will have to type in *8 1/2"* and *11"* in their respective places.

Saving the Changes to the File

You have completed a great deal of formatting in the text on the screen. Save the file with all the formatting changes.

Press Alt to activate the menu bar, F for the File menu, and A for the Save As option. Choose this option because you have not yet saved this file and you want to name it something other than WORD3.WPS (which is the default title Works gives the file). Across from `Save file as`, type *adver.wps* to let you know this is an advertisement in a word processing file. Press Enter and all the formatting changes are saved to disk along with the text.

Chapter Summary

You have had practice in this chapter opening and creating word processing files. Take advantage of the formatting options available with Works, including justification, single- and double-spacing, and indentation. Create tables with Works' tab stops. Adjust the margins to print text on various sizes of paper. You now have the skills to prepare your own advertisements, mailers, and announcements with the variety of styles and fonts available on your equipment and Works.

In Chapter 4, look for advanced formatting and editing techniques. You will learn to search your document using the search and replace features, create headers and footers, and merge documents for form letters and mailing labels.

4

Using Advanced Word Processing Functions and Printing with Works

The most commonly used editing and formatting functions in Works were introduced to you in Chapters 2 and 3. Many more options are available, including search functions, headers and footers, page breaks, and printing. As you create longer and more complicated documents, you will find that these advanced functions help streamline your work.

You will learn to find characters and words in your text using the search functions. You will replace characters, words, or expressions globally or selectively by using the search and replace option. You will use bookmarks with Works to find specific subject areas in longer documents.

Advanced formatting options covered in this chapter include adding headers and footers to a document and forcing page breaks. After you have fine-tuned your document with these advanced editing and formatting functions, you will review the many printing options available with Works.

The last major section in this chapter covers preparing form letters. This task involves merging a Works database file with a Works word processing file, which results in letters personalized with database information. Similarly, techniques for creating mailing labels are included. These are some of the many ways Works makes a big job seem smaller.

Examining the Search Function

The longer your document is, the more useful the search function is. You may want to search a document when you have overused a word. Suppose, for example, that you decide you do not want to use the word *business* too often in a report. Use the search function to find the word *business*; then use the thesaurus to find suitable synonyms for business. Works comes up with *exchange*, *trade*, *industry*, *production*, *interest*, *concern*, *corporation*, *firm*, *syndicate*, *operation*, and so on. Use a variety of these terms to make the report more colorful.

Another reason that you may want to use the search function is to make a reference to a specific location in your text. Suppose that on the 10th page of your document, you make a reference to taxes. You already covered the subject of taxes earlier in the document, but you are not sure where. Move the cursor to the beginning of the file by pressing Ctrl-Home (press and hold down the Ctrl key and press Home) and search the document for the word *taxes*. You find it on the third page. Now you can move your cursor back to the location of the reference to taxes and type *See page 3 for more information on taxes*. You can do this procedure with a few keystrokes. The word processor enhances your speed and efficiency by assisting in finding the exact location of any topic.

You can search for specific words and character strings in your document. When you activate the search function, Works begins searching at the location of the cursor to the end of the document. Search an entire document by moving the cursor to the beginning of the document and then activating the search function. If text is selected, Works begins the search at the end of the selected text and then goes to the end of the document. When Works finds the text you are looking for, the program selects the text with highlighting.

Using the Search Function

To start searching for text, load the RMTA.WPS file. Open the file by pressing Alt to activate the menu bar, F for the File menu, and O for the Open Existing File option. At the `File to open: [......]` prompt, type

RMTA.WPS

and press Enter.

As an example, search for the word *President* in the text:

1. With the cursor at the beginning of the file RMTA.WPS (press Ctrl-Home), press Alt to activate the menu bar, S for the Select menu, and then S for the Search option. The Search dialog box appears (see fig. 4.1).

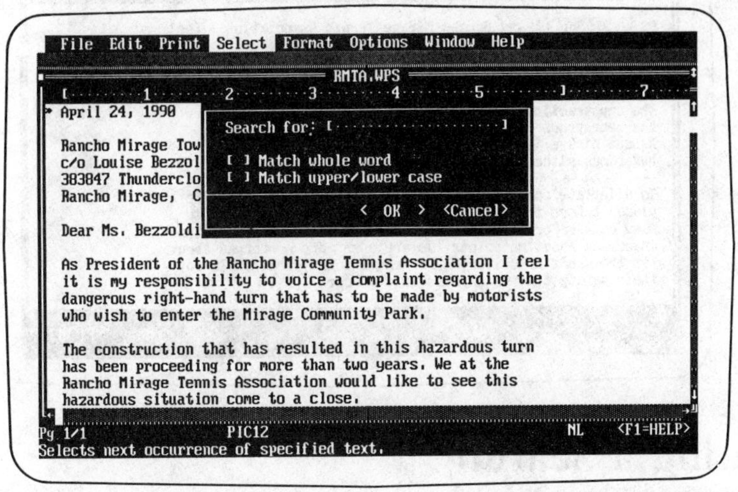

Fig. 4.1.

The Search dialog box.

2. Type *President* at the `Search for` field. Your screen should look like the one shown in figure 4.2.

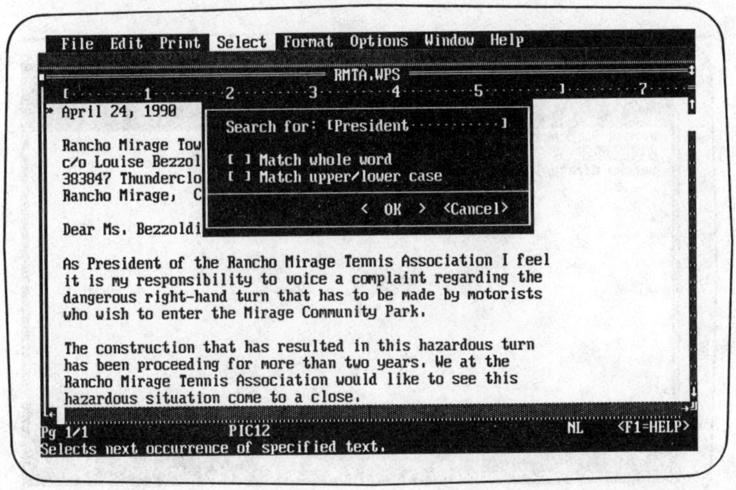

Fig. 4.2.

The word ***President*** *in the* `Search for` *field.*

3. Move the cursor to OK and press Enter. Immediately, the first occurrence of *President* in the document is highlighted (see fig. 4.3). You have found the topic you are looking for in a split second.

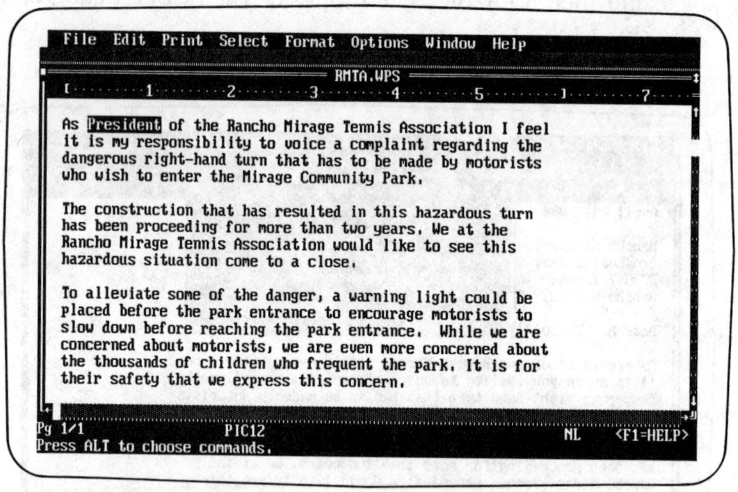

Fig. 4.3.
President *highlighted in the search procedure.*

Repeating a Search

After you have designated a character string for Works to find, you do not have to reenter that word for the next search. If you want to change the word, repeat the preceding steps. If you want to continue searching for *President*, press F7. Works immediately finds the next occurrence of *President* in the text (see fig. 4.4).

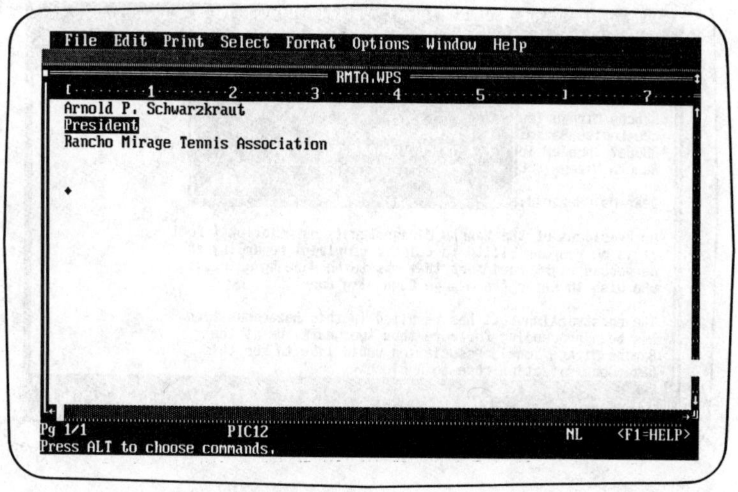

Fig. 4.4.
President *highlighted in the repeat search.*

When your search reaches the end of the document, Works informs you that it can no longer find a match to the word entered in the Search dialog box (see fig. 4.5). With the cursor on OK, press Enter and the search is canceled.

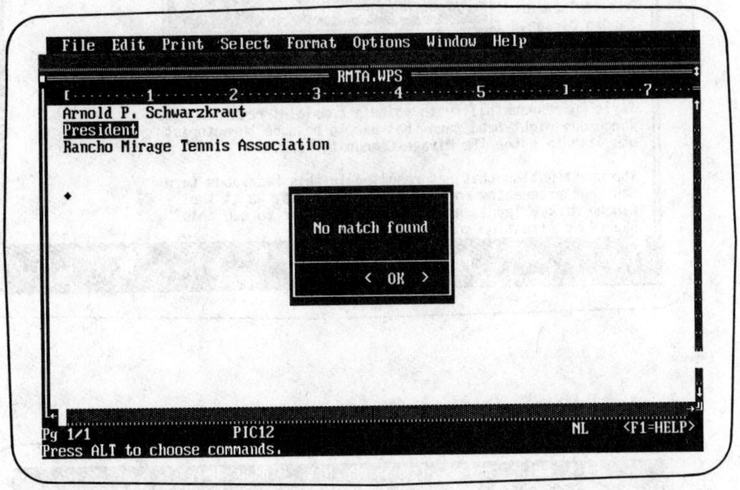

Fig. 4.5.
No match found *prompt.*

Canceling a Search

If you decide to cancel the search before the end of the document is reached, press the Esc key. The search is canceled, and the F7 repeat no longer functions for the previous word.

Using the Match Whole Word Option

Use the Match whole word option in the Search dialog box when you want Works to search for whole words only. For example, with the cursor at the beginning of the file RMTA.WPS (press Ctrl-Home), press Alt to activate the menu bar, S for the Select menu, and then S for the Search option. In the Search dialog box, type *and* (see fig. 4.6).

Move the cursor to OK and press Enter. Look what happens! Works finds *and* in *hand* (see fig. 4.7). Press F7 and Works finds *and* in *thousands* (see fig. 4.8).

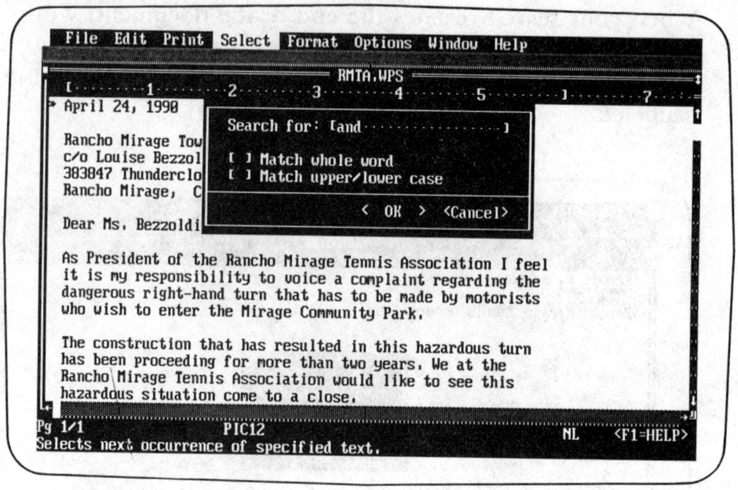

Fig. 4.6.

*The word **and** in the Search dialog box.*

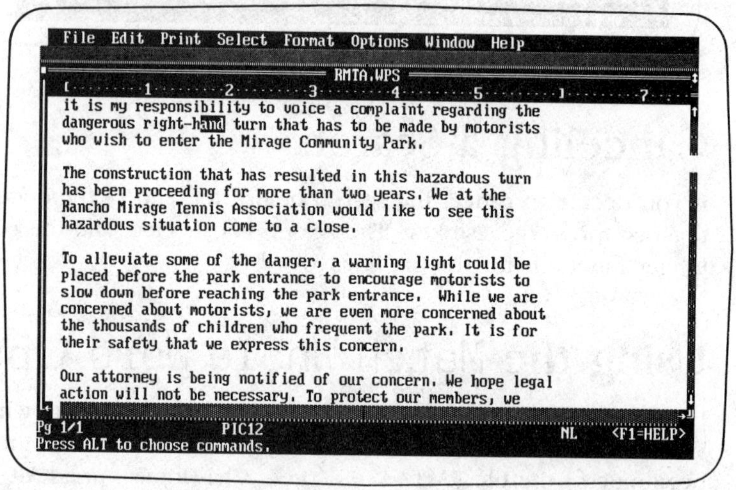

Fig. 4.7.

*The **and** in **hand** highlighted.*

Another example is with the word *the*. Search for *the*, and the program stops at *together*, *their*, *there*, *Thesaurus*, *theory*, and so on. You can see that in a lengthy document, this search would become bothersome if you were looking for a whole word and were being prompted when the word showed up within other words. Using the `Match whole word` option can be beneficial. Use this option as follows:

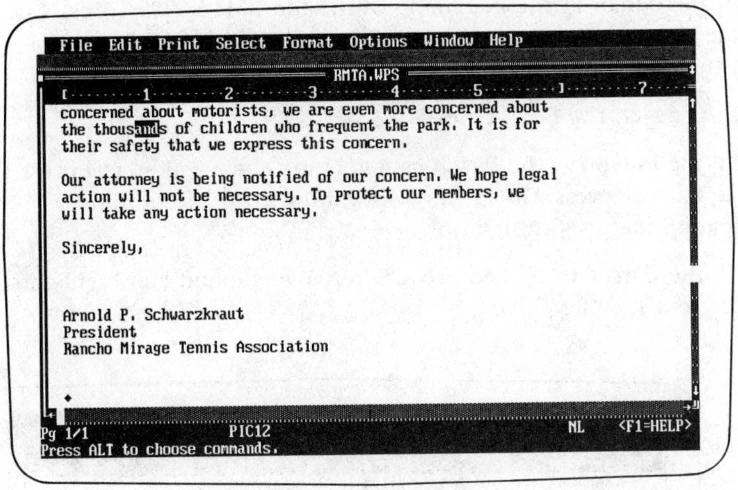

Fig. 4.8.

*The **and** in **thousands** highlighted.*

1. With the cursor at the beginning of the file RMTA.WPS (press Ctrl-Home), press Alt to activate the menu bar, S for the Select menu, and then S for the Search option. The Search dialog box appears.

2. Type *and*.

3. Move the cursor to the Match whole word option. Press the space bar or press Alt-M. An X is inserted in the box, indicating that the option is turned on.

4. Move the cursor to OK and press Enter. In this case, you are told that no match has been found. The word *and* does not appear alone in this letter.

The Match whole word option is a toggle. Pressing Alt-M again turns off the option.

Matching Upper- and Lowercase

While searching through documents, sometimes you will want to find a capitalized version of a word only—not the lowercase version. For example, you may want to find the occurrence of the word *Works* when referring to a product name but not *works* when referring to whether a task works. To do this search, use the Match upper/lower case option in the Search dialog box. In the file RMTA.WPS, to search for the word *We* but not *we*, do the following:

1. With the cursor at the beginning of the file RMTA.WPS (press Ctrl-Home), press Alt to activate the menu bar, S for the Select menu, and then S for the Search option. The Search dialog box appears.
2. At the `Search for` field, type *We*.
3. Move the cursor to the `Match upper/lower case` option and press the space bar (or press Alt-U). An `X` appears next to the option, indicating that it is turned on.
4. Move the cursor to `OK` and press Enter. *We* is found and highlighted in the text (see fig. 4.9).

Fig. 4.9.

***We** found using the* `Match upper/lower case` *option.*

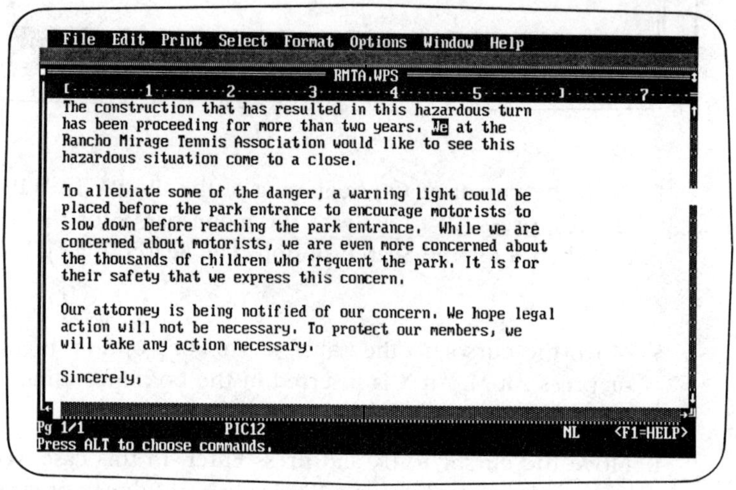

Continue the search by pressing F7. The `No match found` announcement appears. The word *we* occurs later in the letter, but the *w* is lowercase and no match occurs.

Using Wild Cards in Searches

If you are not sure how a word is spelled or how it appears in the text, use wild cards to find the word. A question mark (?) is a Works wild card that represents any single character. Search for *f?x* and Works finds *fix*, *fax*, and *fox*. Substitute the question mark for any character when you type the word in the Search dialog box.

Using Search and Replace

The search and replace function goes one step beyond the search function. The search and replace function finds the character sequence you enter and then replaces it with another character sequence of your choice. You can match whole words in the search, use wild cards, and match upper- and lowercase letters.

Use a search and replace function when you want to change the occurrence of a word some of the time, or every time, it appears in a file.

Suppose, for example, that prior to making a bid you specify that you need 3/4-inch pipe. You find out just before the bid is submitted that you're really supposed to get 1/2-inch pipe. Use the search and replace function to search for each occurrence of *3/4* and replace it with *1/2*.

Another possible use of the search and replace function is when you are not sure of some information as you write a report. If you are not sure whether you are going to need 3/4- or 1/2-inch pipe, place a symbol in the position where the value will be. For example, type ***#-inch pipe***. When you find that you need 3/4-inch pipe, search for the # symbol and replace it with *3/4*.

The search and replace feature allows for efficient management of many business functions. Suppose that the president of the Rancho Mirage Tennis Association shares his letter with a friend, the president of the Rancho Mirage Golf Association. The golf association president decides to send the same letter to the Rancho Mirage Town Council. A search and replace can change the letter appropriately:

1. Move the cursor to the beginning of the file (press Ctrl-Home).
2. Press Alt to activate the menu bar, S for the Select menu, and then R for the Replace option. The Search & Replace dialog box appears (see fig. 4.10).
3. At the `Search for` prompt, type ***Tennis***.
4. Use the down-arrow key to move to the `Replace with` prompt. Type ***Golf***.
5. Because you want to find ***Tennis***, not ***tennis***, press Alt-U to turn on the `Match upper/lower case` option (see fig. 4.11).
6. Move the cursor to the `Replace` option by pressing Alt-R. By selecting this option, you can view and decide on each replacement. Press Enter. The prompt `Replace this occurrence?` appears (see fig. 4.12).

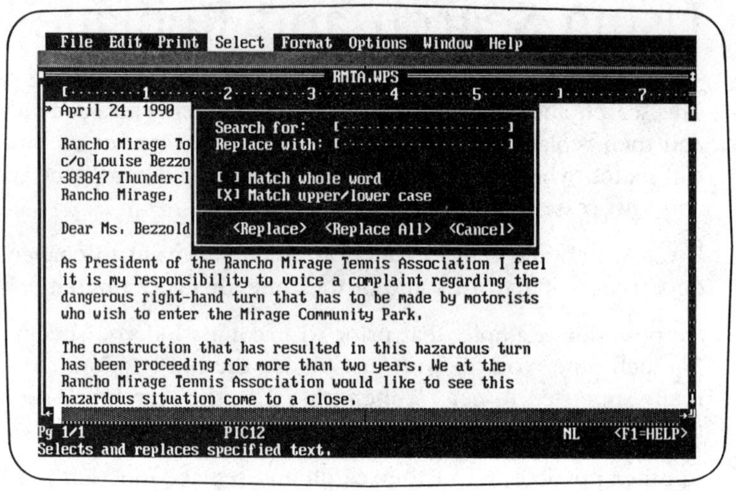

Fig. 4.10.

The Search & Replace dialog box.

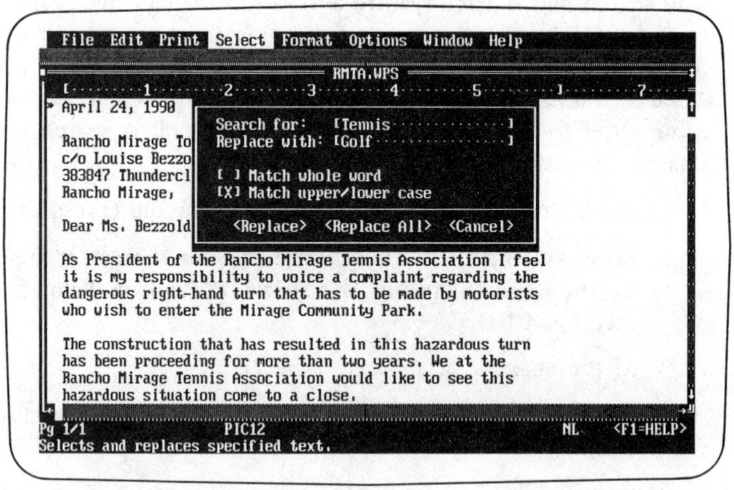

Fig. 4.11.

The Search & Replace dialog box filled in.

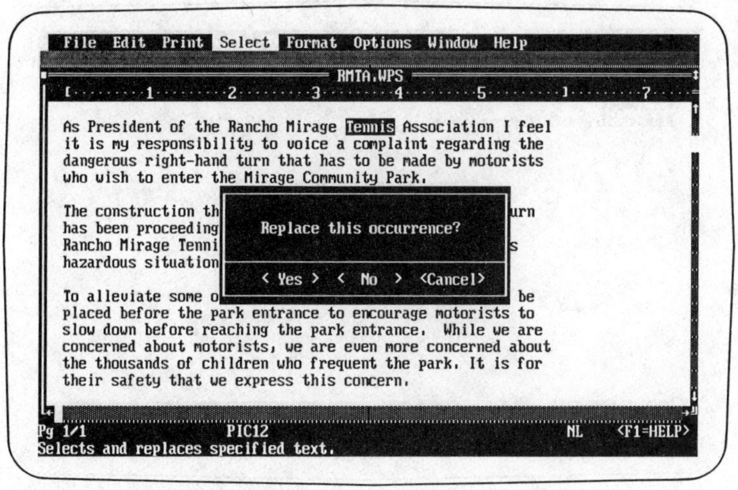

Fig. 4.12.

The Replace this occurrence *prompt.*

7. With the cursor on Yes, press Enter. Works moves to the next occurrence of *Tennis* and prompts you again. Select Yes and press Enter. The last occurrence is shown in figure 4.13.

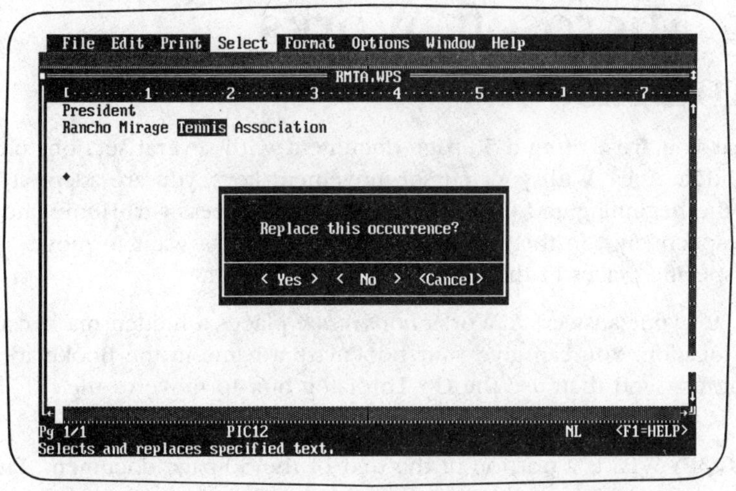

Fig. 4.13.

The last occurrence of ***Tennis****.*

8. After you select Yes and replace the last occurrence, a No more occurrences message appears (see fig. 4.14). Press Enter.

You have successfully replaced every occurrence of *Tennis* with *Golf.* To finish the letter, replace the name *Arnold P. Schwarzkraut* with the name of the president of the golf association. Replacing three occurrences of a

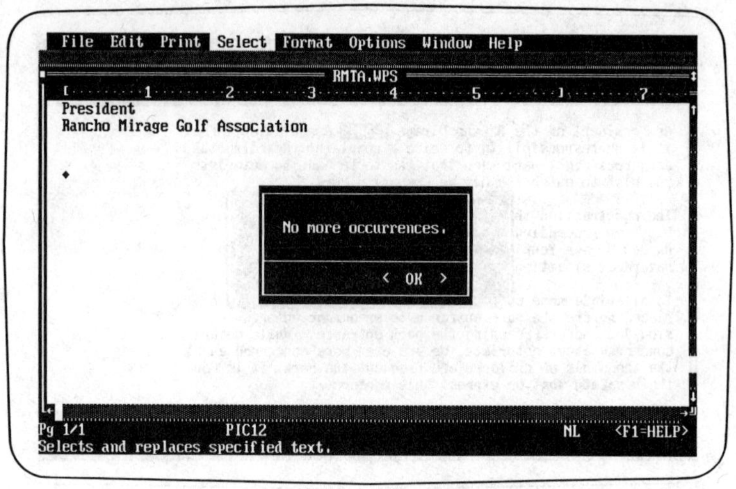

Fig. 4.14.
The No more occurrences *box.*

text string may not seem like such an overwhelming task, but imagine how easy replacing the text would be if you had many more than that.

Using Microsoft Works Bookmarks

Suppose that you are writing a 50-page document with several sections on the High Middle Ages. With your cursor-movement keys, you are adept at moving to the beginning and end of your document (press Ctrl-Home and Ctrl-End, respectively). In this longer document, you also want to move quickly to specific places in the middle of the document.

Bookmarks are your answer! A Works *bookmark* places a hidden marker at the cursor location. You can give your bookmark a name in the Bookmark Name dialog box and then use the Go To dialog box to move to the bookmark.

In the file COPY.WPS is a portion of the text of the 50-page document. Put a bookmark in the middle of this sample document by following these steps:

1. Move the cursor to the location where you want the first bookmark—in this example, under the M in Many in the second paragraph (see fig. 4.15).

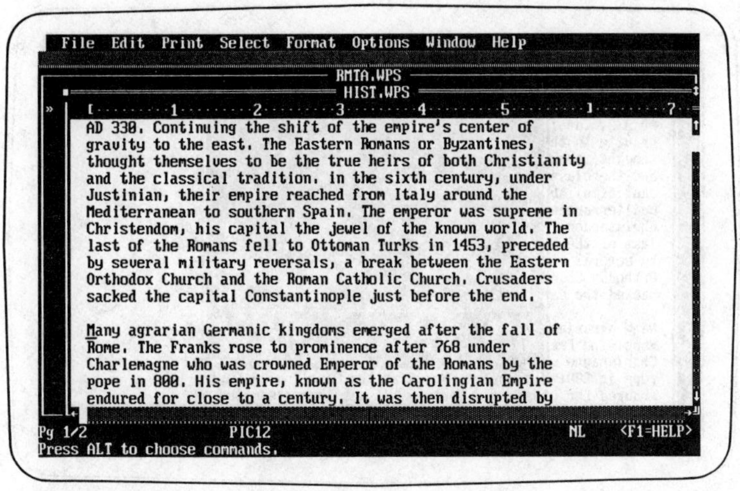

Fig. 4.15.

The cursor location for the first bookmark.

2. Press Alt to activate the menu bar, E for the Edit menu, and then N for the Bookmark Name option. The Bookmark Name dialog box appears (see fig. 4.16).

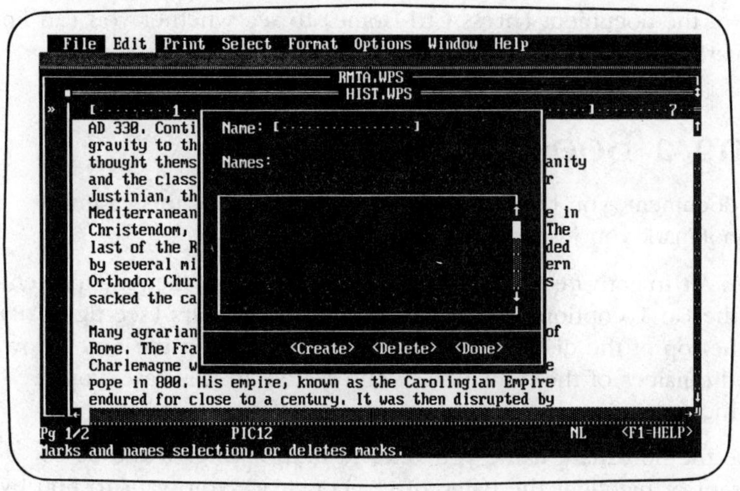

Fig. 4.16.

The Bookmark Name dialog box.

3. At the `Name` prompt, type the name of the first bookmark. Choose a name that reflects the subject matter so you can easily recognize the marker at a later time. In this example, type ***Viking***.

4. Move the cursor to the `Create` option in the dialog box by pressing Alt-C (see fig. 4.17).

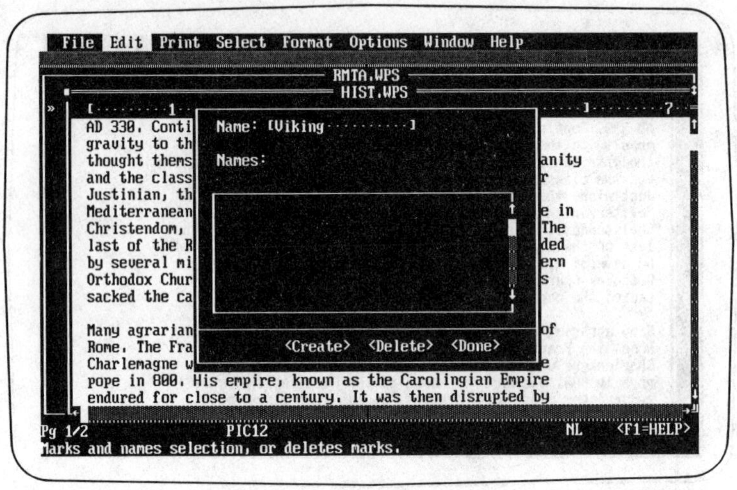

Fig. 4.17.

Viking *in the Bookmark Name dialog box.*

5. Below the status line you see `Marks and names selection, or deletes marks.` Press Enter and nothing appears to happen. The mark in your text is invisible, but it is there.

You have created a bookmark in your text. Move the cursor to the beginning of the document (press Ctrl-Home) to see whether you can find the bookmark again.

Finding a Bookmark

In a long document, you may have several bookmarks. In this example, find the bookmark you just created:

1. Press Alt to activate the menu bar, S for the Select menu, and then G for the Go To option. The Go To dialog box appears (see fig. 4.18). At the top of the dialog box is the prompt `Go to`. In the box below are the names of the bookmarks you created. In this case, you see `Viking`.
2. Type the bookmark name you want to find, *Viking*, at the `Go to` prompt or highlight the name of the bookmark you want to find by using the down-arrow key (see fig. 4.19).
3. Press Enter. The cursor is moved to the location of the hidden bookmark in your text.

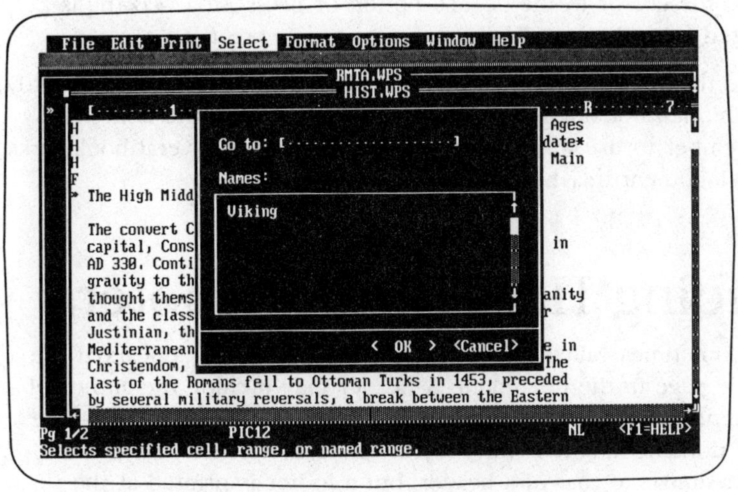

Fig. 4.18.

The Go To dialog box.

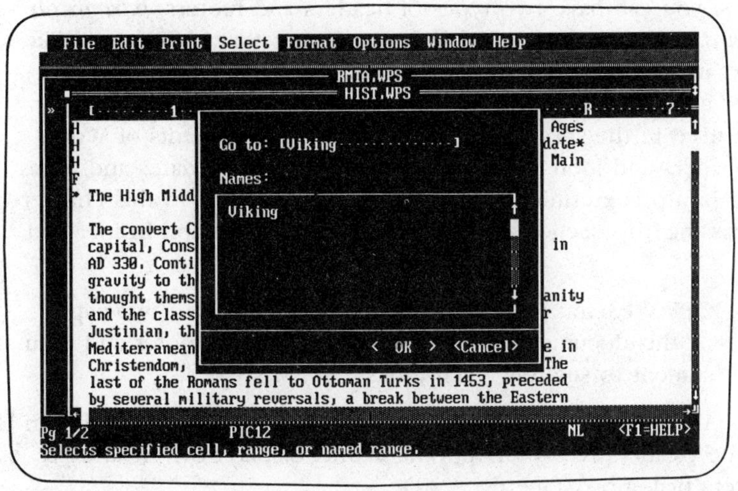

Fig. 4.19.

***Viking** typed in the Go To dialog box.*

Deleting a Bookmark

If you want to eliminate a hidden bookmark, do the following:

1. Press Alt to activate the menu bar, E for the Edit menu, and then N for the Bookmark Name option. The Bookmark Name dialog box appears.

2. In the Names box, type in the name of the bookmark you want to delete. In this case, type *Viking*.

3. Move the cursor to the `Delete` option or press Alt-T. `Viking` is deleted from the list of bookmarks you have created.

4. Move the cursor to the `Done` option and press Enter (or press Alt-D). The hidden bookmark code is now removed from the text. Remember to use this option if you end up with several bookmarks in a document that have become useless.

Including Headers and Footers

A *header*, sometimes called a running header, is text that appears at the top of every page in the document. A header may include the author of the document, the date the document was prepared, page numbers, the title of the document, and/or the subject covered. A *footer* can contain information similar to that of a header, but a footer is printed at the bottom of every page of a document.

With Works, you can have two types of headers and footers: *paragraph* and *standard*. A paragraph header or footer is text that is formatted like regular text including tab marks and multiple lines. This text can be centered or aligned at the right margin. A standard header or footer is most often used in the spreadsheet and database components of Works. Standard headers and footers are automatically centered; dates and times are printed in a predetermined format. Because the focus in this chapter is word processing, this section concentrates on the paragraph header and footer.

In the file COPY.WPS, more text has been added to make a two-page document. For this document, create both a header and footer and then print the document to see how each looks:

1. Press Alt to activate the menu bar, P for the Print menu, and then H for the Headers & Footers option. Works displays the Headers & Footers dialog box (see fig. 4.20).

2. Move the cursor to the `Use header & footer paragraphs` option. Press Alt-U to turn the option on. An `X` appears in the box next to the option.

3. Move the cursor to `OK` and press Enter. Your screen should look like the one shown in figure 4.21.

4. Move the cursor up to the `H` to type text for the header. Type *The Middle Ages* and press the Tab key.

5. To insert the date, press Alt to activate the menu bar, E for the Edit menu, and then P for the Insert Special option.

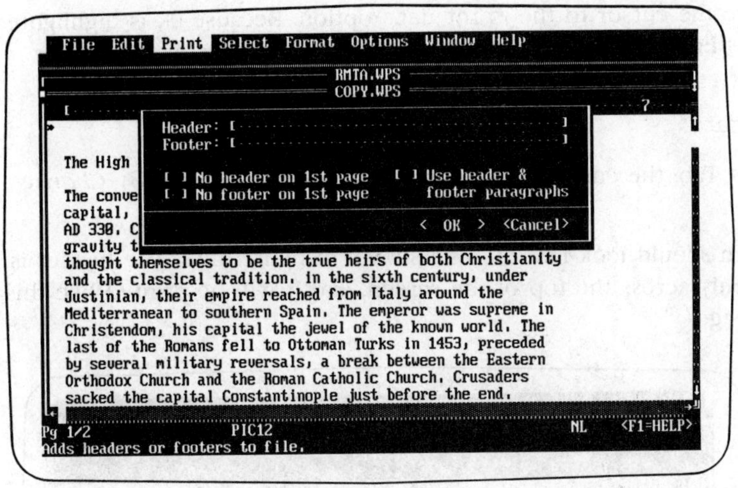

Fig. 4.20.

The Headers & Footers dialog box.

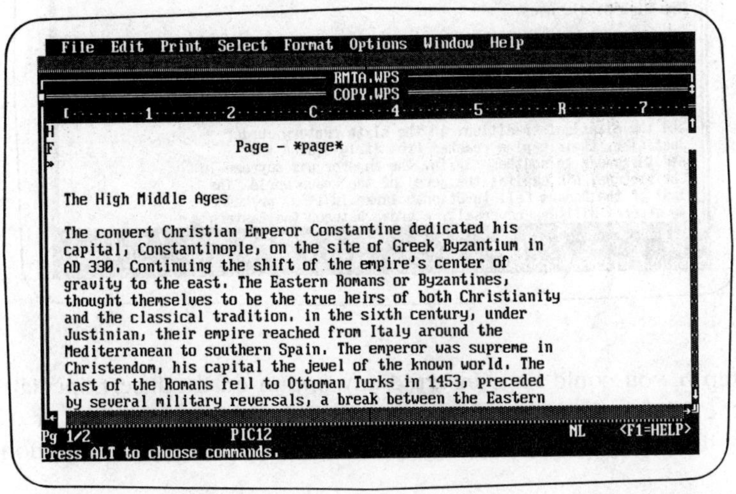

Fig. 4.21.

The Header and footer paragraph commands on-screen.

Tip: The date is inserted in the MM/DD/YY format. The date is especially useful if you have a document that is being revised frequently. If you are printing several revisions a day, you may want to add the time the document is printed to the header. You always will know which copy is the most recent revision.

---

6. Move the cursor to the Print date option. Because OK is highlighted, press Enter. The date symbol appears in the center of the header line:

   date

7. Press Tab; the cursor is now on the right margin. Type *By Charlie Main.*

Your screen should look like the one shown in figure 4.22. The header is spaced evenly across the top of the screen, and it will be printed like this on every page.

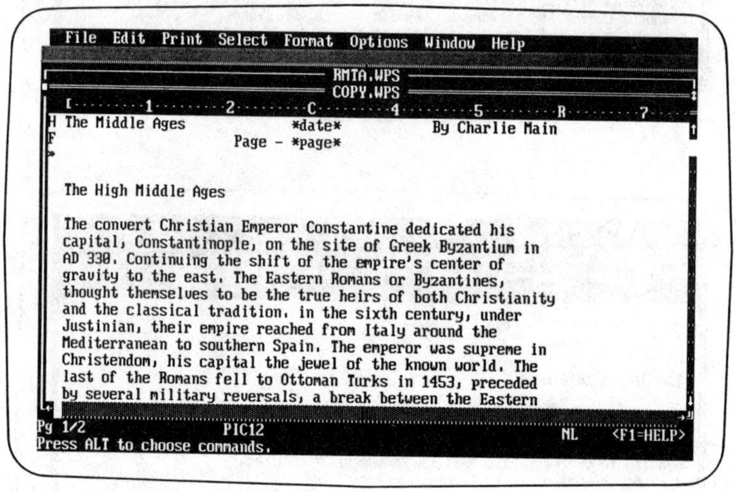

Fig. 4.22.

The header on-screen.

Note: In step 6, you could have inserted any option on the Insert Special option of the Edit menu. You may want to include the page number or time in any header. Do so by following steps 5 and 6, selecting the option you want.

The header is entered. The footer line is still on the screen with Page - *page* in the center. Add more text by simply typing it on the footer line. In this case, leave the footer as it is. A page number will be printed in the document at the bottom center of every page. Figure 4.23 shows the printed document with header and footer.

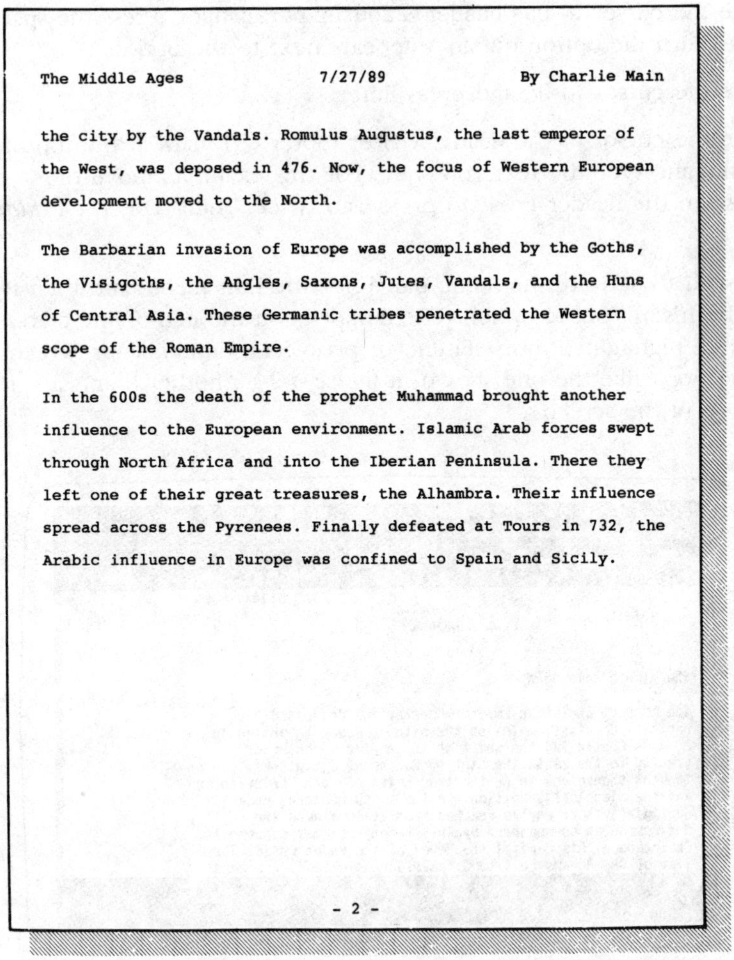

The Middle Ages 7/27/89 By Charlie Main

the city by the Vandals. Romulus Augustus, the last emperor of the West, was deposed in 476. Now, the focus of Western European development moved to the North.

The Barbarian invasion of Europe was accomplished by the Goths, the Visigoths, the Angles, Saxons, Jutes, Vandals, and the Huns of Central Asia. These Germanic tribes penetrated the Western scope of the Roman Empire.

In the 600s the death of the prophet Muhammad brought another influence to the European environment. Islamic Arab forces swept through North Africa and into the Iberian Peninsula. There they left one of their great treasures, the Alhambra. Their influence spread across the Pyrenees. Finally defeated at Tours in 732, the Arabic influence in Europe was confined to Spain and Sicily.

\- 2 -

Fig. 4.23.

The printed page with header and footer added.

Adding More Lines to a Header or Footer

Instead of having the header spread across the page, you can have all the header information at the right or left margin. Here are the steps for making a multiple-line, right-justified header in your Works document:

1. Press Alt to activate the menu bar, P for the Print menu, and then H for the Headers & Footers option. Works displays the Headers & Footers dialog box.

2. Move the cursor to `Use header & footer paragraphs`. Press the space bar to turn the option on; an `X` appears next to the option.

3. Move the cursor to `OK` and press Enter.

4. Move the cursor to the header (`H`) or footer (`F`) mark at the top of the file and type the text you want. For this example, move the cursor to the header line and press Tab twice. Then type *The Middle Ages*.

5. Press Alt to activate the menu bar, E for the Edit menu, and then P for the Insert Special option. The cursor is on the end-of-line mark. With `OK` highlighted, press Enter (or press Shift-Enter). Your screen should look like the one shown in figure 4.24. Another `H` appears at the top of the screen.

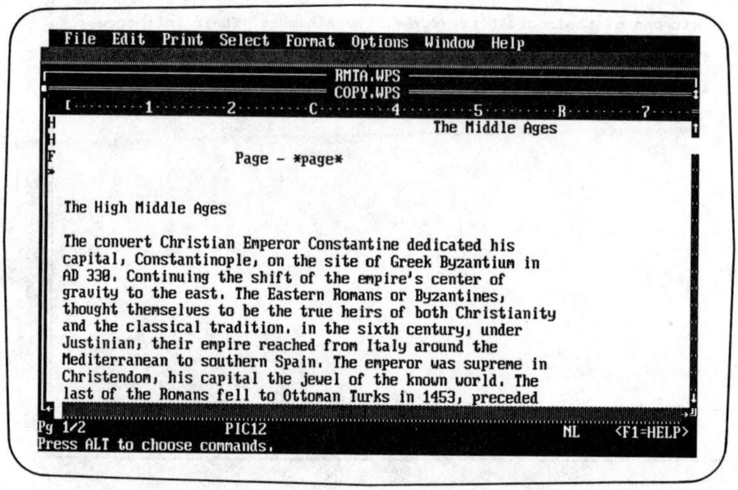

Fig. 4.24.

Two-line header.

6. Now add the next line to the header. Press Tab twice. Then press Alt to activate the menu bar, E for the Edit menu, and then P for the Insert Special option.

7. Move the cursor to the `Print date` option and press Enter. A `*date*` symbol appears under `The Middle Ages`.

8. Press Alt to activate the menu bar, E for the Edit menu, and then P for the Insert Special option. With the cursor at the end-of-line mark, press Enter. Another header (`H`) line is added at the top of the file.

9. Press the Tab key twice. Type *By Charlie Main*. The screen should look like the one shown in figure 4.25 with a three-line, right-justified header.

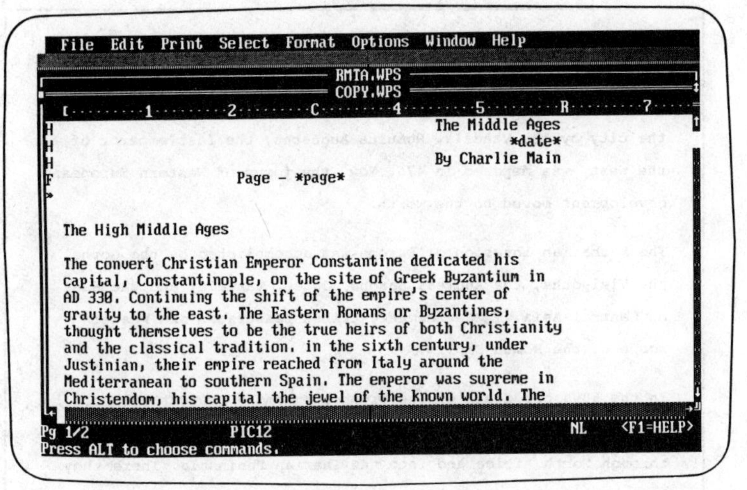

Fig. 4.25.

Three-line, right-justified header on-screen.

10. Move the cursor out of the header area and continue typing or editing text.

Print this file and see how your header looks on the printed page. Press Alt to activate the menu bar and P for the Print menu. Press Enter for the Print dialog box and then press Enter again to print. Figure 4.26 shows the right-justified header when the file is printed.

Notice that only two lines of the header are printed. The next section explains how to fix this problem.

Adding Space When the Header Is Too Large

The standard margin setting for headers is only 0.5 inch. In order to print a header or footer with three or more lines, you need to increase the header and footer margins:

1. Press Alt to activate the menu bar, P for the Print menu, and then M for the Page Setup & Margins option. The Page Setup & Margins dialog box appears.

2. Move the cursor to the `Header margin` option. Type *.2"* (see fig. 4.27).

3. With `OK` highlighted, press Enter.

Fig. 4.26.

The right-justified header in print.

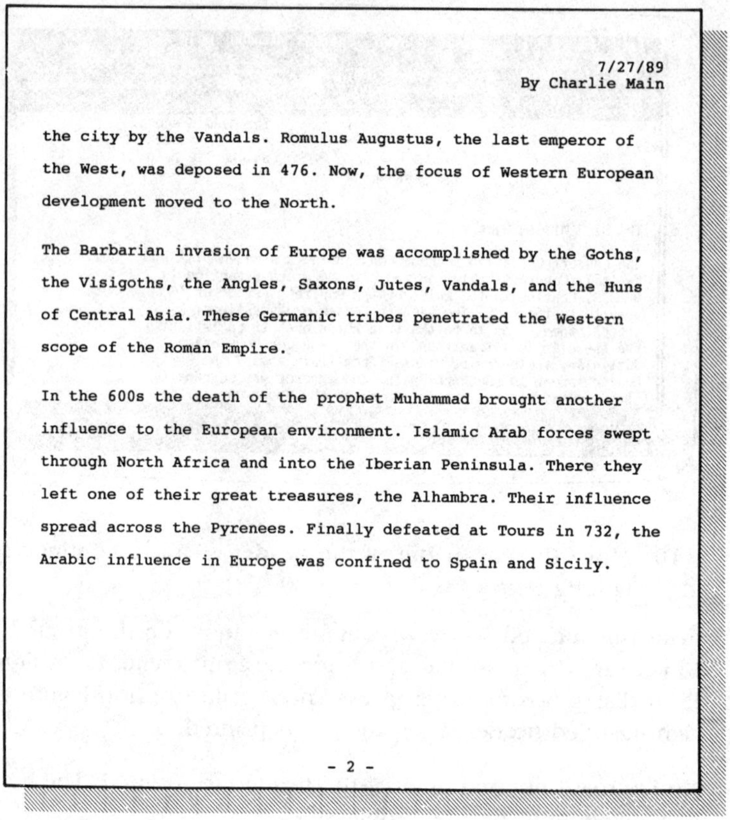
7/27/89
By Charlie Main

the city by the Vandals. Romulus Augustus, the last emperor of the West, was deposed in 476. Now, the focus of Western European development moved to the North.

The Barbarian invasion of Europe was accomplished by the Goths, the Visigoths, the Angles, Saxons, Jutes, Vandals, and the Huns of Central Asia. These Germanic tribes penetrated the Western scope of the Roman Empire.

In the 600s the death of the prophet Muhammad brought another influence to the European environment. Islamic Arab forces swept through North Africa and into the Iberian Peninsula. There they left one of their great treasures, the Alhambra. Their influence spread across the Pyrenees. Finally defeated at Tours in 732, the Arabic influence in Europe was confined to Spain and Sicily.

- 2 -

Fig. 4.27.

The Page Setup & Margins dialog box with a new header value.

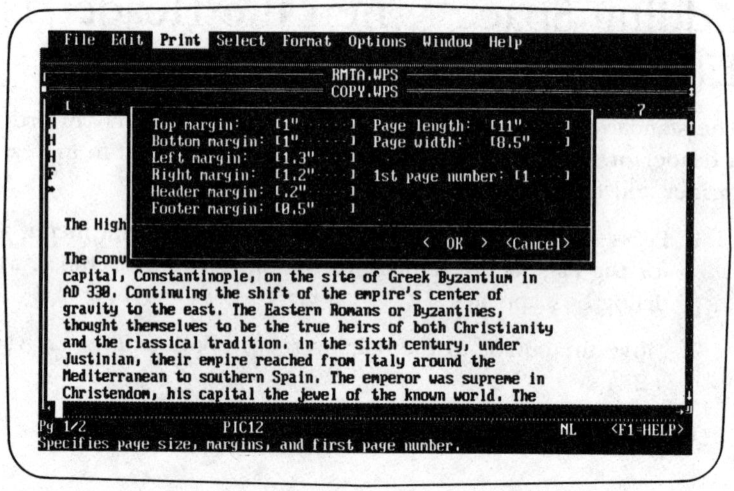

Tip: You may think that you should make the header margin larger by typing *.8"* or *1.0"*. Instead, you want to make the header margin smaller to make room for the extra line of text. If you type *.8"*, only one line of the three-line header is printed. If you type *1.0"*, none of the three-line header is printed. By typing *.2"*, you are allowing the printing to start higher on the page, making room for the three lines of the header.

Now when you print the document, you have a three-line, right-justified header. Figure 4.28 shows how the printed header looks now that you have made room for the extra line.

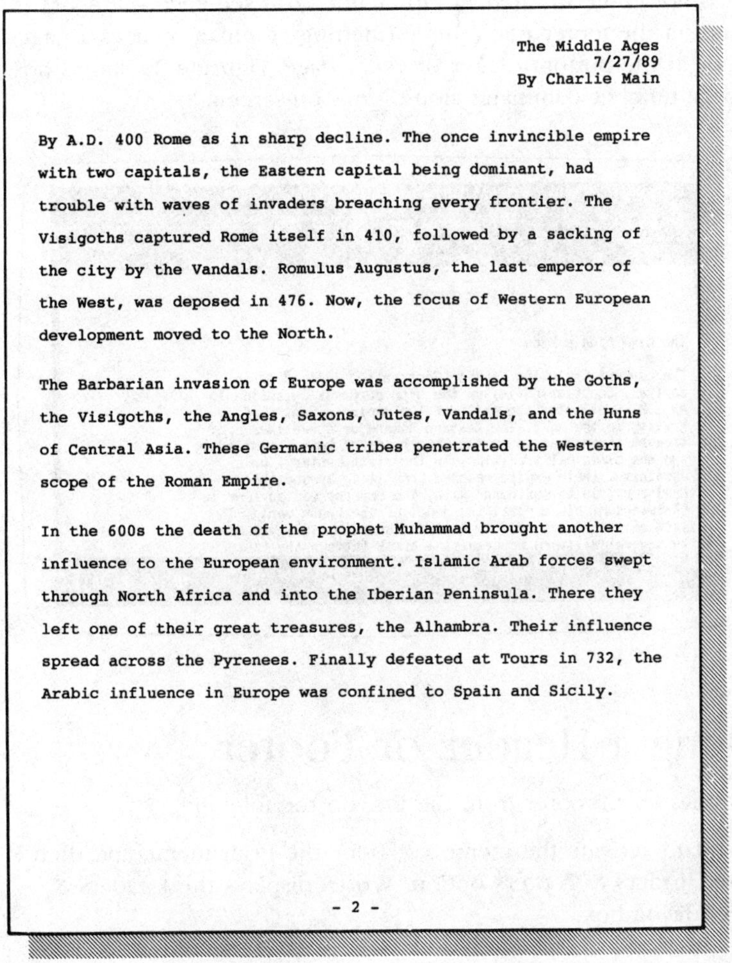

The Middle Ages
7/27/89
By Charlie Main

By A.D. 400 Rome as in sharp decline. The once invincible empire with two capitals, the Eastern capital being dominant, had trouble with waves of invaders breaching every frontier. The Visigoths captured Rome itself in 410, followed by a sacking of the city by the Vandals. Romulus Augustus, the last emperor of the West, was deposed in 476. Now, the focus of Western European development moved to the North.

The Barbarian invasion of Europe was accomplished by the Goths, the Visigoths, the Angles, Saxons, Jutes, Vandals, and the Huns of Central Asia. These Germanic tribes penetrated the Western scope of the Roman Empire.

In the 600s the death of the prophet Muhammad brought another influence to the European environment. Islamic Arab forces swept through North Africa and into the Iberian Peninsula. There they left one of their great treasures, the Alhambra. Their influence spread across the Pyrenees. Finally defeated at Tours in 732, the Arabic influence in Europe was confined to Spain and Sicily.

- 2 -

Fig. 4.28.

The three-line right-justified header.

Adding a Page Number

If you want to have page numbers typed on the pages but don't want any other text in the header or footer, follow these steps for a document that does not already have a header or footer:

1. Press Alt to activate the menu bar, P for the Print menu, and then H for the Headers & Footers option. Works displays the Headers & Footers dialog box.
2. Move the cursor to the Use header & footer paragraphs option and press the space bar to turn it on.
3. With OK highlighted, press Enter.
4. The header (H) and footer (F) lines are inserted at the top of the file. Do not enter any text in either line. You see Page - *page* printed on the footer line. This formatting command places a page number at the bottom center of every page. Figure 4.29 shows how the page number command alone looks on-screen.

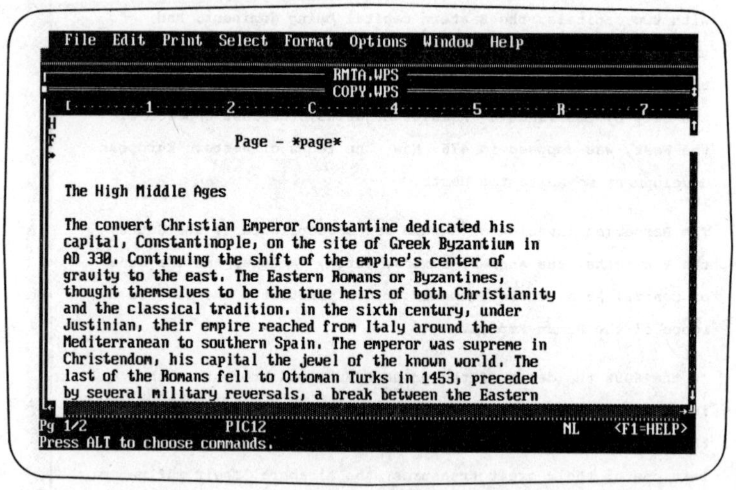

Fig. 4.29.

The page number command in the footer.

Removing a Header or Footer

To remove a header of footer from the file, do the following:

1. Press Alt to activate the menu bar, P for the Print menu, and then H for the Headers & Footers option. Works displays the Headers & Footers dialog box.

2. Move the cursor to Use header & footer paragraphs. Press the space bar to turn the option off. The X no longer appears next to the option.
3. Move the cursor to OK and press Enter. The header (H) and footer (F) lines are removed from the top of the file.

Showing All Characters

When you create a header, you select an end-of-line mark for the right-justified header. A hidden symbol is inserted in that location. In this example, Works inserts a down arrow at the end of the line. You can see this symbol by pressing Alt to activate the menu bar, O for the Options menu, and then L for the Show All Characters option. On-screen, you see the down arrows at the end of the header lines. You also see the arrows facing right, which show tabs.

Use the Show All Characters option when you want to see exactly what you have done to format your text. Repeat the preceding procedures to turn off the option (press Alt, O, and then L, and the formatting characters are removed from the screen).

Forcing Page Breaks

The default margins established in Works tell the printer when to stop one page and then start another. This is done automatically with the values you see on the Page Setup & Margins dialog box. If you insert paragraphs or pages of text, or delete pages of text, the page break is automatically adjusted according to the amount of text on the screen.

You can force a page break in places where you want to control what text is on a page. For example, you may want to force a page break just before a section heading. You then can be sure that the heading is on the top of the page, not on the bottom of one page with the text that follows it on the next page.

On the two-page document now in COPY.WPS, move toward the end of the document. When you see a double right-facing arrow (») to the left of the text, you can see where the page break occurs. Instead of having the page break divide the paragraph, force a page break between the paragraphs. Follow these steps:

1. Move the cursor to the location in the document where you want a page break to occur. In this example, move the cursor between the previous paragraph and one in which the page break now occurs.

2. Press Alt to activate the menu bar, P for the Print menu, and then I for the Insert Page Break option. A dotted line is inserted on the screen above the cursor location. To the left of the cursor is the double right-facing arrow (») that symbolizes the page break. Notice these changes on the screen (see fig. 4.30).

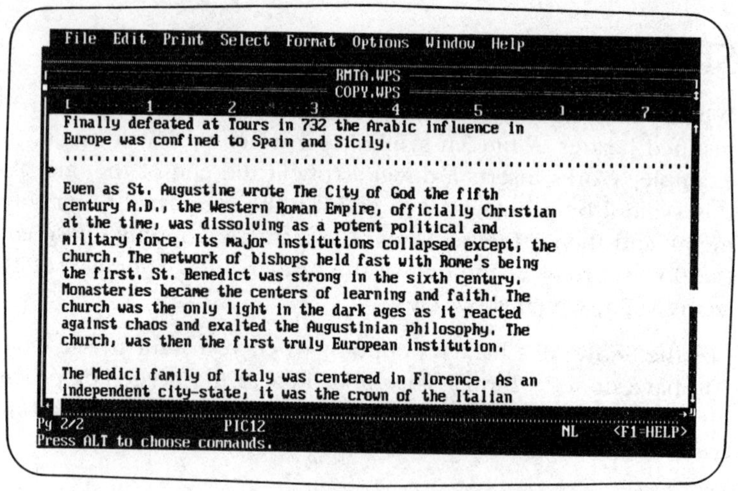

Fig. 4.30.

An inserted page break on-screen.

Print this document now, and the last two paragraphs are printed on the second page. No paragraphs are divided.

Removing a Forced Page Break

If you change your mind about the location of forced page breaks, you can delete them. Move the cursor to the forced page break, placing the cursor directly on the dotted line, and press Shift-End. You have selected the page break. Press Del; the dotted line symbolizing the page break disappears, as do the page break arrows (»).

Printing Your Document

You have printed several documents by pressing Alt to activate the menu bar and pressing P for the Print menu. Because the cursor starts on the Print option, press Enter. If you do not want to make any other choices, press Enter again and the document is printed.

In this section, the printing options available with Works are reviewed. Look at the Print dialog box in figure 4.31. These printing options give you greater control over the printed output.

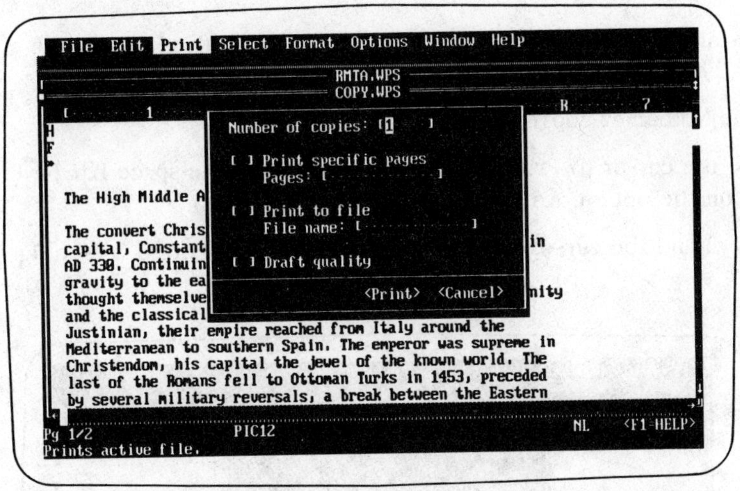

Fig. 4.31.

The Print dialog box.

Examining Printing Options

The `Number of copies` prompt allows you to choose the number of copies you want to print of this document; the default value is 1. Enter a new number when you want to print multiple copies of any document.

The `Print specific pages` prompt lets you select which pages of a document to print. The default prints from the beginning of the file to the end. As an example, instead of printing an entire 50-page document, you can specify printing to begin with page 20 and end with page 35. You can tell works to print this range of pages by typing either *20-35* or *20.35*.

Works also prints a series of pages that are not continuous. Type *20, 28, 32, 35*. Works will print only pages 20, 28, 32, and 35. The program will not print pages between these numbers.

The `Print to file` option lets you save your file to be used by other software or lets you send a file to another computer using the communications system. When you choose this option, a file is created with all the printer commands in it. Therefore, you can print it without starting or using Microsoft Works.

The print `quality` option lets you select the quality of your printed document. The `Draft quality` option may allow for quicker printing, but it will not print charts, it will not allow you to use microspacing, and it will have little effect on daisywheel printers.

With the text in COPY.WPS, print two copies of the second page by adjusting the Print dialog box:

1. Press Alt to activate the menu bar and then P for the Print menu. Press Enter and the Print dialog box appears.
2. At the `Number of copies` prompt, press 2.
3. Move the cursor to `Print specific pages`. Press the space bar to turn on the option. An `X` appears next to the option.
4. Press G and the cursor moves to the `Pages` option; press 2 (see fig. 4.32).

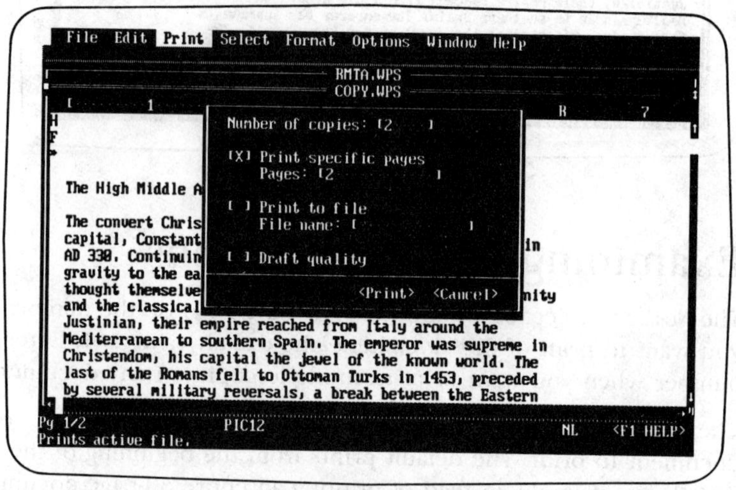

Fig. 4.32.

The Print dialog box filled in.

5. Move the cursor to `Print` by pressing Alt-P and press Enter. You get two copies of page 2 of your document.

Previewing a Document

In Chapter 3, you worked primarily in ADVER.WPS. This was a one-page advertisement with bold, underlined, justified, tabbed, and italicized text. In this file or a comparable file with many formatting options used, you may want to look at the file on-screen before you print it. This is called previewing a document.

Previewing gives you a chance to see how your document looks on-screen before you print it. You may find that you want to make some last-minute changes before you actually print your document. As with many word processing features, this one may not seem like too much of a timesaver with a one-page document. However, with a lengthy document and a slow printer, you can get an electronic picture of how the finished product looks before taking the time necessary to print the document.

Open ADVER.WPS by pressing Alt to activate the menu bar, F for the File menu, and then O for the Open Existing File option. Highlight `ADVER.WPS` on the list of files and press Enter. To preview ADVER.WPS on the screen, follow these steps:

1. Press Alt to activate the menu bar, P for the Print menu, and then V for the Preview option.
2. The Preview dialog box appears, which is almost identical to the Print dialog box. You can preview specific pages, several copies, or an entire document.
3. Move the cursor to `Preview` and press Enter (or press Alt-P). The document you are previewing is on the right side of the screen (see fig. 4.33).

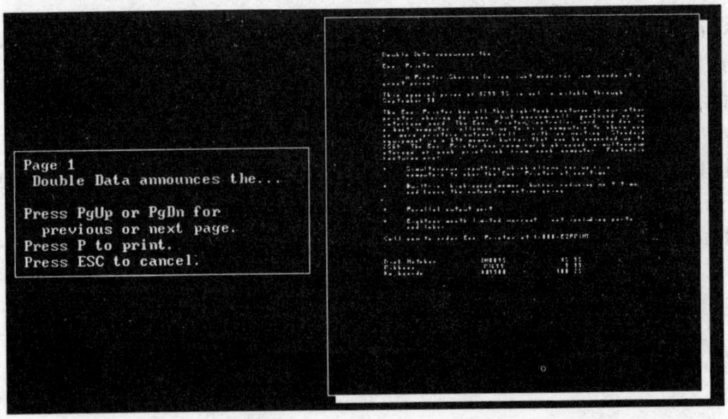

Fig. 4.33.
ADVER.WPS previewed to the screen.

You get an idea of how a whole page looks with the formatting adjustments you have made. The first line of the document appears in the box at the left. You are also instructed how to view additional pages. Press Esc to cancel the preview.

Using the Works Merge Feature

Use Microsoft Works' merge feature to print form letters when you need to send the same letter to many different people. Using the form letter allows you to personalize the letter for each individual on your list. Use form letters when you are sending letters to those who owe you money. In each letter, you can specify the amount owed. Send form letters when you want to remind several people of their next appointment with you. In the example for this chapter, Rancho Mirage Tennis Association is sending renewal notices to members who are due to renew in May.

In order to print form letters, you need two things:

- ❑ A database file that contains records from which you retrieve information that you insert into the form letter
- ❑ A word processing document into which you insert information from the database file

In this section, you will create the word processing document. In Part IV, you will create one or more databases. In Part VI, you will learn more about integrating the different components of Works.

Creating a Form Letter

The membership chairperson for the Rancho Mirage Tennis Association (RMTA) is sending letters to the members who need to renew in May. Create the form letter by typing a letter in the word processor. In this letter, insert *fields* that will later be filled in with information from the database. Each field in the typed form letter will hold a place for a single piece of information, and each field in the database holds one piece of information. The RMTA membership database includes information such as

First Name
Last Name
Address
City
State
Zip
Phone
Member Since (date)
Updated
Renewal Fee

When you want the first name of the person listed in the database to be printed in the form letter, insert a field as a place holder in the text of the letter. A short database of three members has been created for this example. It is in the file RMTA.WDB. For more information on fields and creating databases, see Part IV. To create a form letter, do the following:

1. Create a new file by pressing Alt to activate the menu bar, F for the File menu, and N for the Create New File option. Then press Enter for the New Word Processor option.

2. Type *May 1990* and press Enter two times.

3. Start adding field names for the inside address. Press Alt to activate the menu bar, E for the Edit menu, and then F for the Insert Field option. You see the Insert Field dialog box (see fig. 4.34).

Tip: The database file you want to use as the source for field names has to be open and listed in the Insert Field dialog box. Open the file by pressing Alt, F, and then O. Highlight the database file you want to open and press Enter.

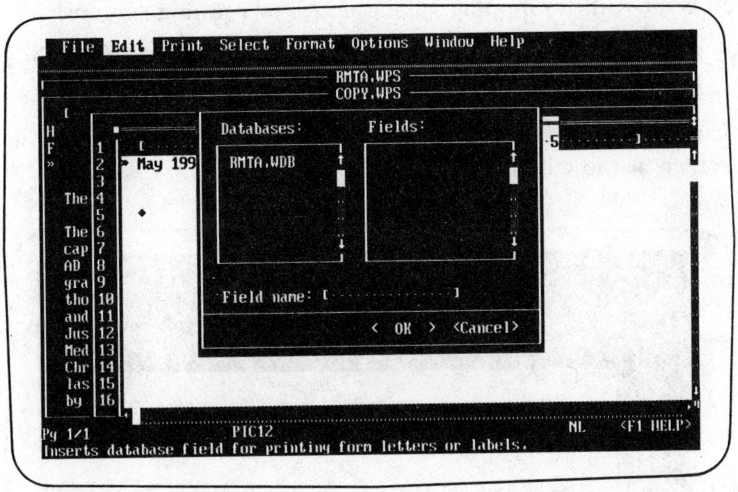

Fig. 4.34.
The Insert Field dialog box.

4. In the `Databases` box, you see the list of open database files. Move the cursor to `RMTA.WDB`, the database you want to use for this letter. The fields available in that database are displayed in the `Fields` box (see fig. 4.35).

Note: With many databases, remembering the exact names of all the fields can be difficult. (For example, is a particular field named *Zip* or *Zip*

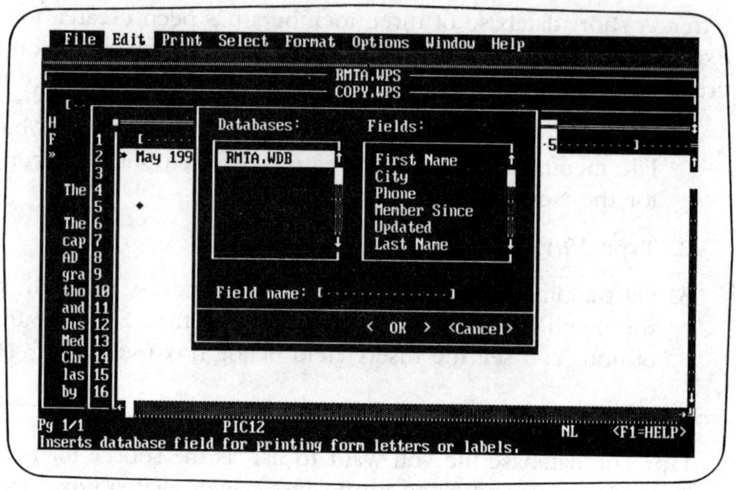

Fig. 4.35.
RMTA.WDB *highlighted with fields listed.*

Code?) You have to make a list of the fields by writing them down or print a copy of the database form with the names of the fields. With Works, the field names unique to each database file are displayed. You simply select the one you want with no flipping, taking notes, or printing screens!

5. Move the cursor to the Fields box and select the field you want to insert in the form letter.

6. The cursor is on First Name. Press Enter. «First Name» appears on the screen at the cursor location (see fig. 4.36).

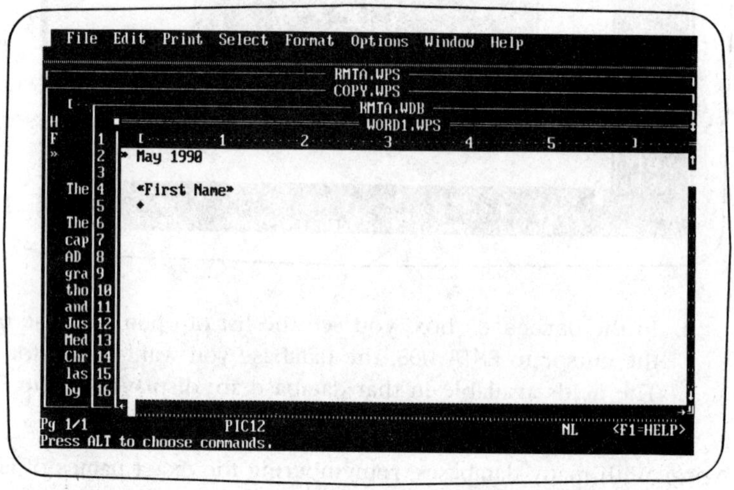

Fig. 4.36.
«First Name» *on the screen.*

Tip: All punctuation and spacing has to be added to the word processing document.

---

7. Press the space bar once. Press Alt to activate the menu bar, E for the Edit menu, and then F for Insert Field.
8. Move the cursor to `Last Name` in the `Fields` box. Press Enter.
9. Press Enter to move to a new line in the letter. Press Alt to activate the menu bar, E for the Edit menu, and then F for Insert Field.
10. Move the cursor to `Address` and press Enter.
11. Press Enter to move to a new line in the letter. Press Alt to activate the menu bar, E for the Edit menu, and then F for Insert Field. Move the cursor to `City` and press Enter.
12. Type a comma (,) and press the space bar to insert a blank. Press Alt to activate the menu bar, E for the Edit menu, and then F for Insert Field. Move the cursor to `State` in the `Fields` box and press Enter.
13. Press the space bar twice. Press Alt to activate the menu bar, E for the Edit menu, and then F for Insert Field. Move the cursor to `Zip` and press Enter. The inside address is now complete (see fig. 4.37).

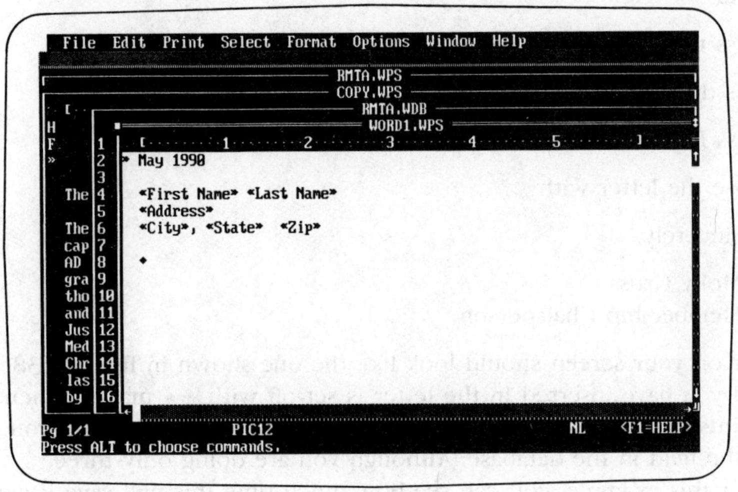

Fig. 4.37.
Fields entered in the inside address.

14. Press Enter twice. Type *Dear* and press the space bar.

15. Press Alt to activate the menu bar, E for the Edit menu, and then F for Insert Field. Move the cursor to `First Name` because this is a friendly letter. Press Enter.

16. Type a colon (:) and press Enter two times.

17. Type

    You have been a member with our Association since

    and press the space bar. Press Alt to activate the menu bar, E for the Edit menu, and then F for Insert Field.

18. Move the cursor to `Member Since` in the `Fields` box and press Enter. Type a period (.).

19. Press the space bar. Type

    We sincerely hope you have enjoyed the Rancho Mirage Tennis Club.

20. Press Enter two times to begin the next paragraph. Type

    As of May 1, 1990, your renewal fee of $

21. Press Alt to activate the menu bar, E for the Edit menu, and then F for Insert Field. Move the cursor to the `Renewal Fee` field and press Enter.

22. Press the space bar to insert a space; type

    is due. We appreciate your prompt payment.

    Press Enter two times.

23. Close the letter with

    Sincerely,

    Molly Gross
    Membership Chairperson

The letter on your screen should look like the one shown in figure 4.38. Each field you have inserted in the letter is set off with « » marks. When Works prints the letter, it reads the field name and inserts the value you have for the field in the database. Although you are doing only three records for this example, you can see how much time this will save if you have to type many letters.

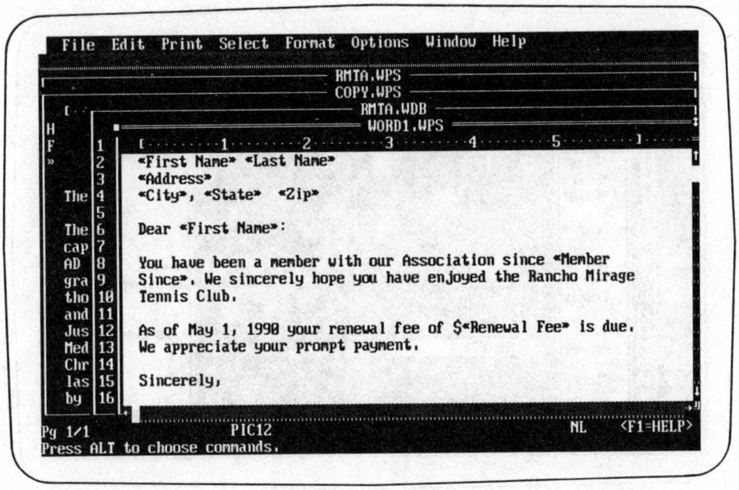

Fig. 4.38.

The form letter on-screen.

Saving the Form Letter

Save this file by pressing Alt to activate the menu bar, F for the File menu, and then A for the Save As option. Instead of calling the file WORD1.WPS, rename it as RENEW.WPS and press Enter. The new name is inserted at the top center of the work space.

Printing the Form Letter

One letter is printed for each record you have entered in the database. Follow these steps to print the example form letter:

1. Open the database file that holds the records you want to use, if you have not already done so. Press Alt to activate the menu bar, F for the File menu, and then O for the Open Existing File option. Move the cursor to `RMTA.WDB` (see fig. 4.39) and press Enter.

2. Press Alt to activate the menu bar and then W for the Window menu. Highlight `RENEW.WPS` and press Enter. The form letter in RENEW.WPS appears on the screen.

Tip: Now is the time to prepare your printer. Make sure that it has enough paper for the number of letters you are printing and that it is ready to print. Insert special forms or paper if needed.

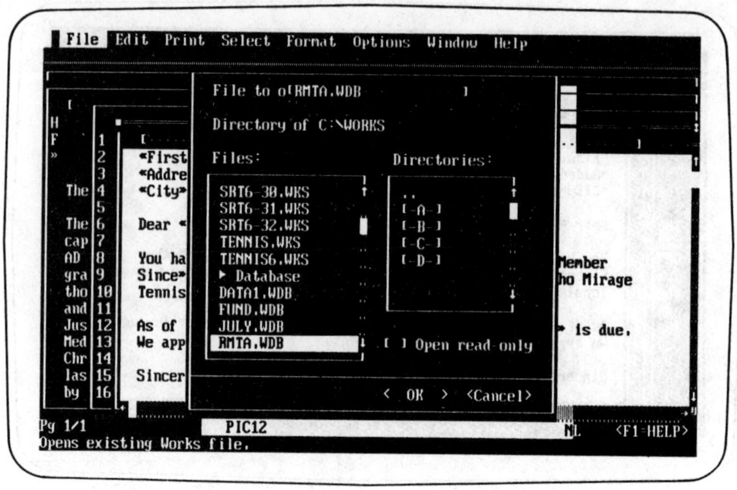

Fig. 4.39.
RMTA.WDB *highlighted for opening.*

3. Press Alt to activate the menu bar, P for the Print menu, and then F for the Print Form Letters option.
4. Move the cursor to the database you want to use for the form letter. In this example, highlight RMTA.WDB and press Enter.
5. The Print dialog box appears. Press Enter.

The form letter you have created is printed. An example of one of the letters can be seen in figure 4.40. The information from the fields in the database is inserted into the letter. The name, address, membership date, and member's renewal fee are inserted into the letter automatically. What a breeze! The membership chairperson, Molly Gross, is playing tennis rather than typing hundreds of letters.

Tip: Press Esc to stop the printing process at any time. If you start printing your form letters and find an error, press Esc; the printer finishes the current page and then stops.

Testing the Form Letter

If you are in a situation where you are planning to print many letters, you can test your form letter for accuracy. This process gives you an example letter for proofreading and review:

May 1990

Moette Champagne
9306 Twin Trail
San Pedro, CA 92929

Dear Moette:

You have been a member with our Association since 5/10/86.
We sincerely hope you have enjoyed the Rancho Mirage Tennis
Club.

As of May 1, 1990 your renewal fee of $180 is due. We
appreciate your prompt payment.

Sincerely,

Molly Gross
Membership Chairperson CB

Fig. 4.40.
A printed form letter.

1. Open the database file that holds the records you want to use. Press Alt to activate the menu bar, F for the File menu, and then O for the Open Existing File option. Move the cursor to `RMTA.WDB` and press Enter.

2. Press Alt to activate the menu bar and press W for the Window menu. Highlight `RENEW.WPS` and press Enter. The form letter in RENEW.WPS appears on the screen.

3. Press Alt to activate the menu bar and then press P for the Print menu. With the cursor on Print, press Enter. Press Enter after the Print dialog box appears.

One copy of the letter is printed on the screen. This letter is shown in figure 4.41. Instead of the values from the fields being placed in the letter, the field names are inserted. From this printed form letter, you can make any necessary changes or additions to the letter without having to spend time printing incorrect letters.

Fig. 4.41.

A test form letter.

```
May 1990

<<First Name>> <<Last Name>>
<<Address>>
<<City>>, <<State>>  <<Zip>>

Dear <<First Name>>:

You have been a member with our Association since <<Member
Since>>. We sincerely hope you have enjoyed the Rancho Mirage
Tennis Club.

As of May 1, 1990 your renewal fee of <<Renewal Fee>> is due. We
appreciate your prompt payment.

Sincerely,


Molly Gross
Membership Chairperson
```

Printing Mailing Labels

As with form letters, to print mailing labels, you need a database file with information in records that can be inserted into fields of the label form prepared in the word processor. This includes information such as first and last name and address. Other information may be included, such as an invoice number or order number.

In the steps that follow, the database file continues to be RMTA.WDB. Open a new word processing file with the specific purpose of holding mailing labels.

Tip: One word processing file made for mailing labels can be used with many database files, as long as the fields and field names required by the word processing file are used consistently among the databases.

Do the following:

1. Create a new word processing file. Press Alt to activate menu bar, F for the File menu, and then N for Create New File. With the cursor on New Word Processor, press Enter.

2. With the cursor at the top of the file, press Alt to activate the menu bar, E for the Edit menu, and then F for Insert Field.
3. Highlight the database file you want to use with this mailing list. Move the cursor to the `Fields` box by pressing the right-arrow key.
4. With `First Name` highlighted, press Enter. Press the space bar to enter a space.
5. Press Alt to activate the menu bar, E for the Edit menu, and then F for Insert Field. In the `Fields` box, move the cursor to `Last Name` and press Enter.
6. In the word processing document, press Enter to move to the next line. Press Alt to activate the menu bar, E for the Edit menu, and then F for Insert Field. Highlight `Address` and press Enter.
7. Press Enter to move to a new line. Press Alt to activate the menu bar, E for the Edit menu, and then F for Insert Field. Highlight `City` and press Enter.
8. Type a comma (,) and press the space bar. Press Alt to activate the menu bar, E for the Edit menu, and then F for Insert Field. Highlight `State` and press Enter.
9. Press the space bar two times. Press Alt to activate the menu bar, E for the Edit menu, and then F for Insert Field. Highlight `Zip` and press Enter.
10. Press Enter to move the cursor to the next line in the word processing file.

The place holders are in place for one label. Save the file by pressing Alt for the menu bar, F for the File menu, and then A for Save As. Call the file LABEL.WPS. Press Enter.

Setting Up Margins for Labels

You have the word processing file ready to go and a database file with records in it. Before you print the labels, set the page size and margins:

1. With the cursor in the word processing file (LABEL.WPS), press Alt to activate the menu bar, P for the Print menu, and then M for the Page Setup & Margins option. The Page Setup & Margins dialog box appears.
2. Move the cursor to the `Page length` option. Type *12"*, which is the length of one sheet of labels (the length of one sheet, perforation to perforation, of tractor-feed labels).

3. At the `Page width` option, type *3.5"*, which is the width of the labels for one-across labels. Some labels are three across a page. Measure the width from the left side of the left label to the right side of the right label.

4. Move the cursor to the `Top margin` option. If you are using continuous, tractor-feed labels, press 0.

Tip: If you are printing on individual label sheets, set the top and bottom margins equal to the width of one label. You get better results if you do not try to print on the top and bottom labels.

---

5. Move the cursor to the `Bottom margin` option. For continuous, tractor-feed labels, press 0.

6. At the `Right margin` and `Left margin` options, press 0 if no space exists between the left and right edges of the label and the left and right edges of the paper. With tractor-feed paper, do not count the tractor portion as part of the page. If space exists between the label and the edge of the paper, on either side, type that amount at the right and left margin options.

The Page Setup & Margins dialog box should look like the one shown in figure 4.42 for tractor-feed labels with one row of labels across the page.

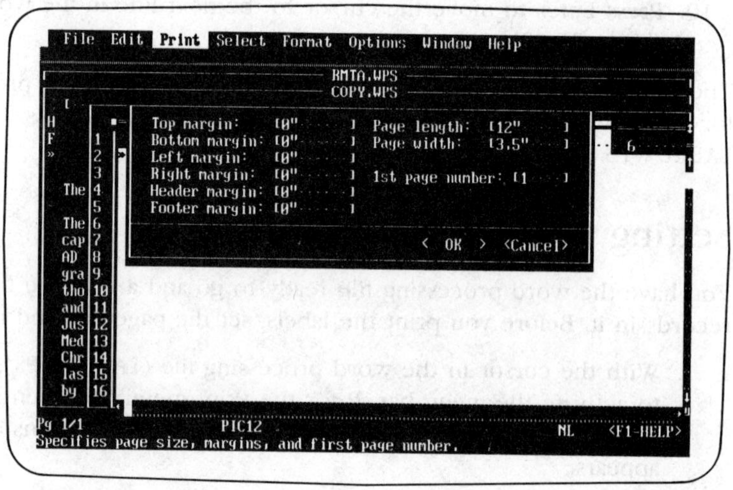

Fig. 4.42.

The Page Setup & Margins dialog box tractor-feed label settings.

Printing the Labels

With the margins set and the word processing file ready to go, you are ready to print the mailing labels. Open the appropriate database file if it is not already open. (Press Alt, F, and then O to open an existing file. Move the cursor to `RMTA.WDB` and press Enter.) With the cursor in the word processing file, get ready to print. (Go back to the word processing file by pressing Alt and then W. Move the cursor to `LABEL.WPS` and press Enter.) Do the following:

1. Set up the printer for labels by inserting the labels and making any necessary adjustments.
2. Press Alt to activate the menu bar, P for the Print menu, and then L for the Print Labels option. The Labels dialog box appears on the screen.
3. Highlight `RMTA.WDB`, the database you want to use.
4. At the `Vertical` option, type the distance from the top of one label to the top of the next label. In this case, leave the value at `1"`.
5. At the `Horizontal` option, type *3"*, which is the width of a single label in this example. If you are printing with more than one label in the horizontal position, type the distance between the left edge of one label to the left edge of the next label.
6. Leave the value for `Number of labels across page` at 1. Type the number of labels across the page if it is different from 1.
7. Press Alt-T to run a two-label test. The Page Setup & Margins dialog box appears. You already set these values in the preceding steps, so press Enter.
8. The Print dialog box appears. Press Enter for the test. One label is printed. (Note that you can change the setting for the number of labels to print.)
9. On the screen, you see the prompt `Print all labels or reprint test labels?`

If you are satisfied with the test, highlight `Print` and press Enter. The Print dialog box appears again. Choose any options you want. From here you can print duplicate copies of the mailing labels or print specific pages of labels. When you have made the selections you want, highlight `Print` and press Enter. The remaining labels for the database RMTA.WDB are printed.

If you need to make some adjustments, highlight `Test` and press Enter. Works prints another test label for you.

Note: The test label is the first label in your database. When you print the entire list of labels, the first label is printed again with any adjustments you have made.

Chapter Summary

You started this chapter by practicing the search functions in Works; these functions included searching text for specific characters, searching text for bookmarks you have placed, and using the search and replace functions.

You learned that headers and footers can be placed easily in Works documents and that they can be centered, right or left aligned, and used with or without page numbers. In addition, you learned that you can make the header and footer margins larger or smaller as needed to accommodate your headers and footers.

You reviewed more printing details, including printing multiple documents and portions of a document. You learned that you can insert page breaks and preview a document to the screen to get a look at the overall layout of the pages.

Integration of the word processor and database is used for creating and printing form letters and mailing labels. Instead of spending *hours* typing many nearly identical letters, you have the ability to merge files and relax while Works does all the work.

Part III

Spreadsheets

Includes

Quick Start 2

Creating a Spreadsheet

In this quick-start lesson, you will learn to enter numbers into a spreadsheet. Then you will perform calculations with the numbers, format the spreadsheet to represent the numbers accurately, and edit the numbers.

Opening a Spreadsheet File

To begin creating a spreadsheet file, select the Create New File option from the Microsoft Works opening screen. You can select this option by highlighting it and then pressing Enter or by moving the mouse arrow to click the option. Next, select New Spreadsheet from the menu that appears. The next screen you see is the spreadsheet with the file label `SHEET1.WKS` shown at the top.

A spreadsheet can contain three types of data: labels, numbers, and formulas. *Labels* are text entries you use to describe and explain the information entered into the spreadsheet. *Numbers* are the values used in spreadsheet calculations. *Formulas* tell Microsoft Works what to do with the values that have been entered. Formulas contain operators that act on the values—divide, multiply, or add the values, for example. Works also has sophisticated built-in formulas called *functions* that relieve you of the task of creating complex formulas.

The following sections introduce you to the steps involved in entering numbers, labels, and formulas into the spreadsheet.

Entering Labels

Any entry beginning with an alphabetic character is considered to be a label by Works. In addition, an entry containing a mixture of numbers and alphabetic characters (such as 123 Elm Street) is also considered to be a label. The only exception is with the use of scientific notation—12.34E, for example—which is still considered to be a number. To enter a number as a label, you must precede the entry with a quotation mark (").

Now you will enter some labels in a Works spreadsheet. Open a spreadsheet file. Notice the highlight in cell A1. This highlight is the *cell selector*, which is your navigation tool in the spreadsheet. To enter labels in your spreadsheet, do the following:

1. Use the down-arrow key or the mouse to make the cell A3 the active cell.
2. Press the Caps Lock key and type *SALES*.
3. Press the down-arrow key. Notice that the label is entered in cell A3, and now cell A4 is the active cell. (You could have pressed Enter, but you saved a step by pressing the down-arrow key.)
4. Type *EUROPE* in cell A4 and press the down-arrow key.
5. Type *ASIA* in cell A5 and press the down-arrow key.
6. Type *JAPAN* in cell A6 and press the down-arrow key twice.
7. Now type *TOTAL SALES* in cell A8.

Your spreadsheet should look like the one shown in figure QS2.1.

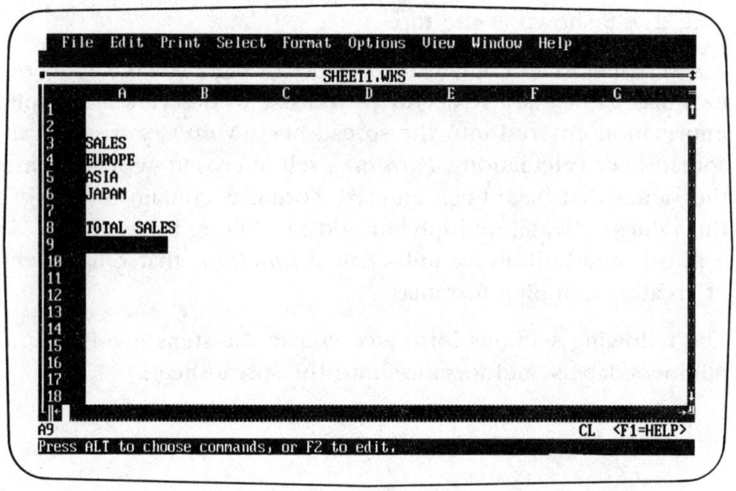

Fig. QS2.1.

Cells with labels.

To finish entering the labels, type *Q1 Actual*, *Q2 Actual*, *Q3 Plan*, *Q4 Plan*, and *Total* in cells B2 through F2, respectively (see fig. QS2.2). Use the right-arrow key to move the active cell after every entry.

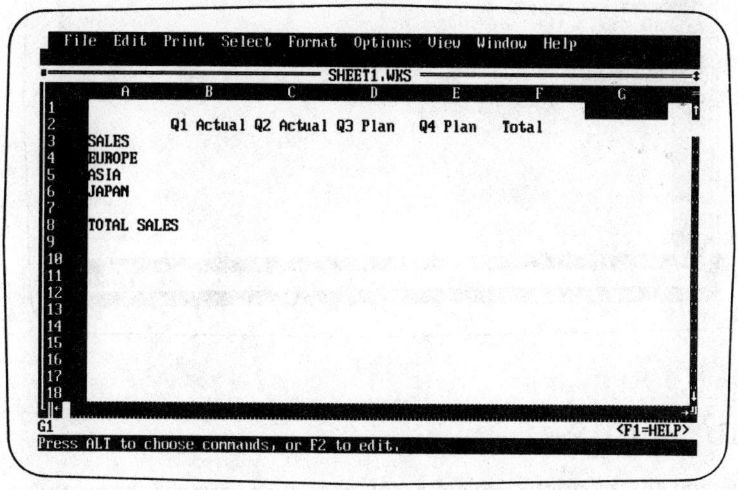

Fig. QS2.2.
The spreadsheet with column headings added.

Entering Numbers

Numeric entries can contain the digits 0 through 9, the minus sign, and the decimal point. Your entries must be in the appropriate form to be interpreted as numbers.

Other characters may be entered, but Works either ignores them or performs appropriate conversions. (Remember that the exception is with the letter E for exponentiation.) Dollar signs are ignored, and commas are deleted if not correct. An entry with a percent sign (%) is converted to a percent. When you enter *4567%* into the cell, for example, the formula bar displays `45.67`, without the percent sign.

To enter numbers into the spreadsheet, try these steps:

1. Make B4 the active cell either by moving the mouse pointer and clicking or by using the arrow keys.
2. Type *123456* and press the down-arrow key. The number appears in cell B4, and cell B5 is now active.
3. Repeat the preceding steps, entering *113456* and *488765* in cells B5 and B6, respectively.

Figure QS2.3 shows the result.

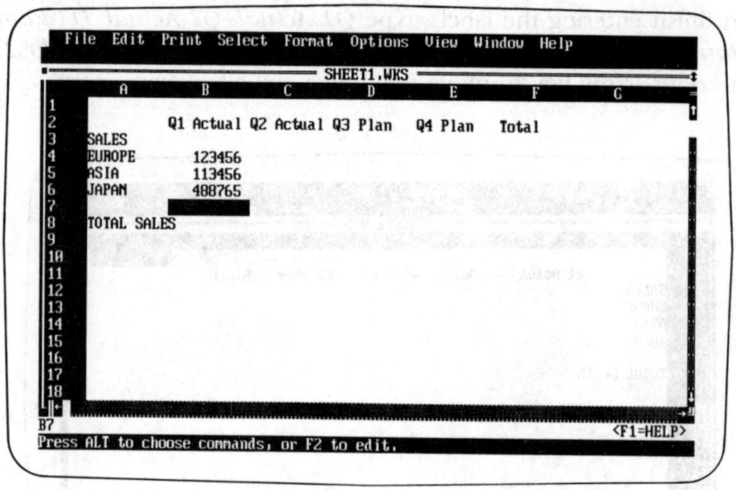

Fig. QS2.3.

Numeric entries.

Copying Cells

To work through the examples given as this lesson progresses, enter the numbers that follow. Performing these steps will give you access to an easy way of making entries into a range of cells:

1. Make C4 the active cell.
2. Enter *107232* in cell C4, *110785* in cell C5, and *101867* in cell C6.
3. In cell D4, type *140000* and press Enter.
4. Press and hold down the Shift key while you press the right- and down-arrow keys until the pointer is in cell E6. Alternatively, with a mouse, point to cell C4, click and hold the button, and drag the pointer to cell E6.
5. Release the Shift key and arrow key, or release the mouse button. As you can see, the entire area is now displayed in a different color from the rest of the spreadsheet. (Or the area is in reverse video.)
6. Press the Alt key to activate the menu bar and then select Edit either by pressing the letter E or by using the mouse to point to and click the Edit option.
7. The pull-down menu contains the option Fill Down. Select this option and press Enter. The number 140000 is copied to cells D5 and D6.

8. Press the Alt key to access the Edit menu again. This time select the option Fill Right. The number 140000 is entered into the cells E4 to E6 (see fig. QS2.4).

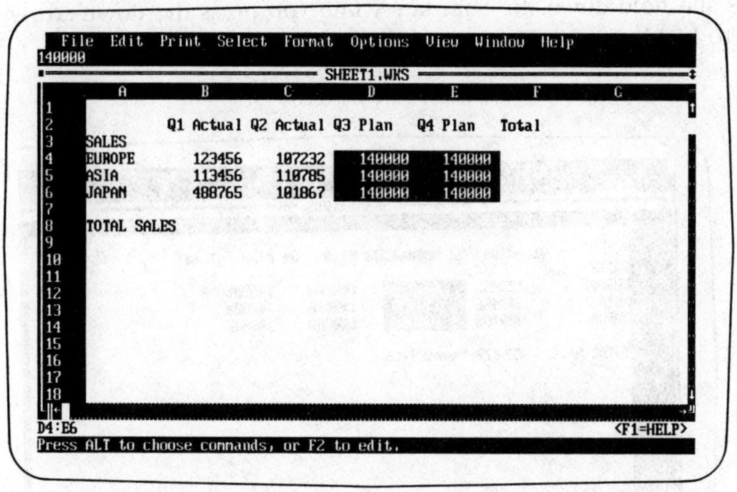

Fig. QS2.4.
Entering numbers in a range of cells.

Entering Formulas

Formulas are at the heart of an electronic spreadsheet. Without the capability for performing calculations automatically, spreadsheets would be little more than expensive alternatives to using pencils, paper, and erasers.

Every Works formula begins with an equal sign (=). The equal sign is followed by either a function name or cell address. You can use a formula in this spreadsheet example. Make cell B8 the active cell. Type the following formula and then press Enter:

=B4+B5+B6

When you have entered such an equation, the results are displayed immediately in cell B8. If you make a change in any of the cells in the equation, a new value is calculated by the formula.

Entering formulas in this way works, but the task is tedious and can lead to typing errors. Works allows you to point to the cells you want to add, which is a faster and more accurate method.

Follow these steps to point formulas:

1. Make cell C8 the active cell.

2. Type an equal sign (=).

3. Type *SUM(* after the equal sign. Your screen should display =SUM(.

4. Move the cell selector to cell C4. Works inserts the C4 into the formula.

5. Press and hold down the Shift key while you press the down-arrow key, to highlight cells C5 and C6 (see fig. QS2.5).

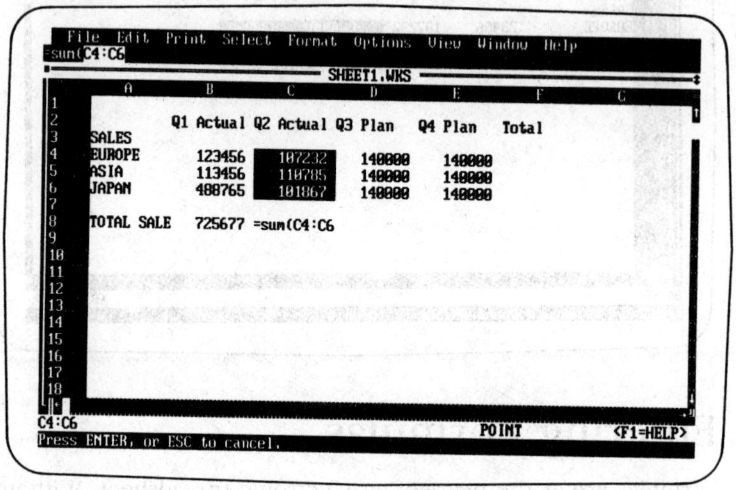

Fig. QS2.5.
Highlighting the rest of the cells to be included in the formula.

6. Type *)* and press Enter.

The total is entered into cell C8. Repeat the procedure with columns D and E.

To subtotal the sales areas in column F, type formulas in cells F4, F5, and F6. The total should reflect the numbers in cells B, C, D, and E in each respective row. Cell F4 sums the values in cells B4, C4, and D4. The last formula, in cell F8, is of the total sales row and reflects the sales for every area (see fig. QS2.6).

Formatting the Spreadsheet

In this section, you will change the appearance of the spreadsheet by adding boldface, underlining, and other enhancements. Microsoft Works allows you to change a single cell, an entire column or row, or the entire spreadsheet.

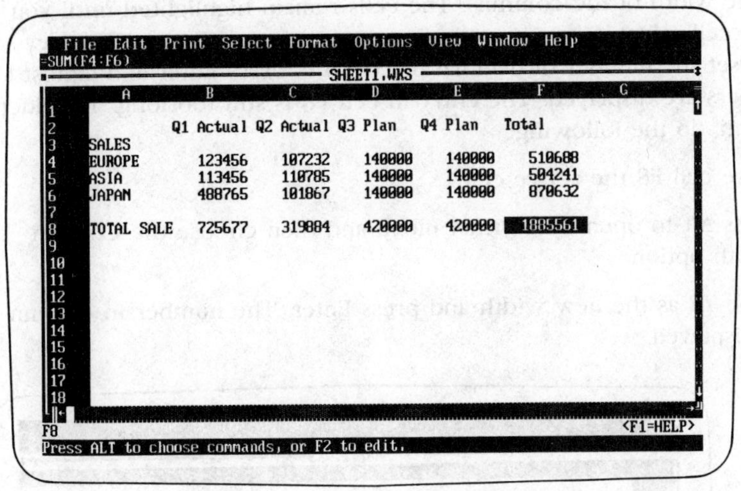

Fig. QS2.6.
The total sales for every area.

The procedure for making format changes follows:

1. Move the cell selector to column A, row 1. (With a mouse, you can click the column letter to highlight the entire column.)

2. Press Shift-down arrow to highlight all the label entries in column A (A3 through A8).

3. Open the Format menu by pressing Alt for the menu bar and then T. The Format menu contains the option Style. Select Style and the Style dialog box appears.

   You can choose options from this dialog box in two ways. You can press and hold down the Alt key while you type the letter that is underlined in the format you desire. Or you can use the Tab key to move from style to style and press the space bar when you arrive at the desired style. For this example, choose `Bold` and press Enter.

4. Select the cells in row 2 (B2 through F2). Open the Format menu and select Style. When the Style dialog box appears, choose `Underline`.

5. Now select the range of cells B4 to F8 (all the numeric entries) and open the Format menu. For the currency format, you do not have to open the Style dialog box. Choose Currency and leave the setting at two decimals. Press Enter.

The entire screen is filled with number signs (see fig. QS2.7), which indicates that the entries in the cells are longer than 10 characters, the default width of the cells. You have two options: change the format or change the width of the columns. The cells remain highlighted until you move the cell selector, so open the Format menu and choose Currency and then set the number of decimal places to 0. Press Enter and almost all the numbers are displayed. The entry in cell F8 is still too long. To widen the column, do the following:

1. Make cell F8 the active cell.

2. Press Alt to open the Format menu and then choose the Column Width option.

3. Type *12* as the new width and press Enter. The number in column F is displayed.

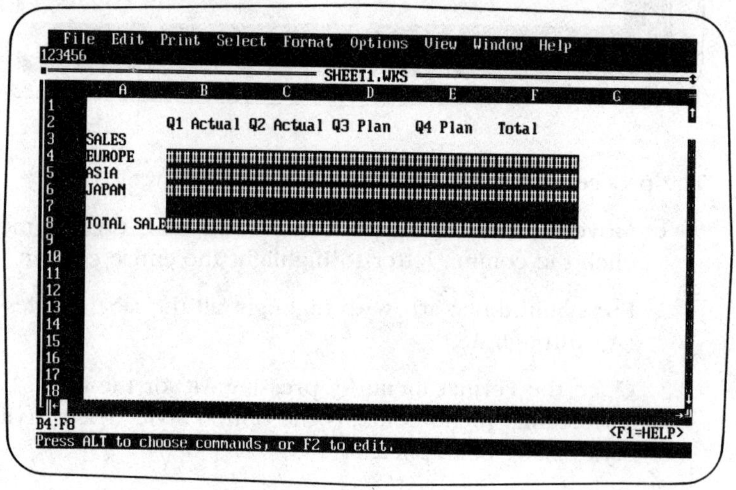

Fig. QS2.7.

The screen filled with number signs, indicating that the entries are longer than the default width of the cells.

Printing the Spreadsheet

The next logical step is to print your work. Follow these steps:

1. Press Alt and select Print from the menu bar. Many options appear. You can set margins or preview the printing, for example. Because the example spreadsheet is rather small, the default settings should work. You do not need to change them.

2. To start printing, press Enter.

Microsoft Works prints only the area that has entries. You must specify for anything else to be printed. The resulting printout is shown in figure QS2.8.

	Q1 Actual	Q2 Actual	Q3 Plan	Q4 Plan	Total
SALES					
EUROPE	$123,456	$107,232	$140,000	$140,000	$510,688
ASIA	$113,456	$110,785	$140,000	$140,000	$504,241
JAPAN	$488,765	$101,867	$140,000	$140,000	$870,632
TOTAL SALE	$725,677	$319,884	$420,000	$420,000	$1,885,561

Fig. QS2.8.

The printed spreadsheet.

Saving the Spreadsheet

To save the spreadsheet, press Alt to activate the menu bar, select File, and then select Save. The first time you save a spreadsheet file, the Save As dialog box appears (see fig. QS2.9).

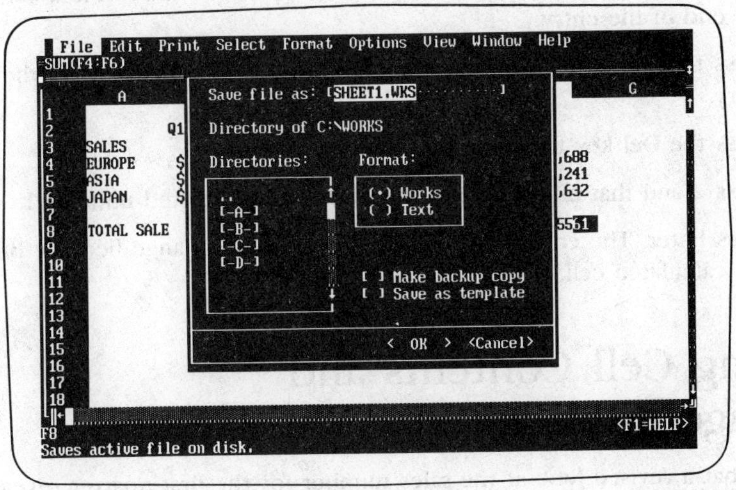

Fig. QS2.9.

The Save As dialog box.

Works supplies the default file name for any new spreadsheet, which is SHEET1.WKS, but that name is not very descriptive. Try typing a more specific name, up to eight characters long, with no spaces. Works will add the WKS extension to the name you type. If you want, you can save the file to a specific disk drive other than the default.

Editing the Spreadsheet

Suppose that after you print your spreadsheet and look it over, you decide that some changes need to be made. Editing the spreadsheet is relatively easy if you follow some simple safeguards prior to making any changes. The best thing you can do is make a backup copy of the spreadsheet before editing. Select the Save As option from the File menu to save the file under a different name. Another way to make a backup copy is to select Save As from the File menu and then select the `Make backup copy` option from the dialog box that appears. Works makes a second file with the extension BKS. Then if you make a major error while editing, you have a backup copy to refer to. When you use the File menu's Save As option, the spreadsheet file is saved and your changes are made on the file with a different name.

The procedure for making changes to text, numbers, and formulas is the same. For practice in fundamental editing techniques, follow these steps:

1. Make cell B4 the active cell.
2. Press the F2 function key. An underline appears in the formula bar at the end of the entry.
3. Press the Home key to move the underline to the beginning of the entry.
4. Press the Del key to delete the number 1.
5. Press 2 and that number takes the place of the deleted number 1.
6. Press Enter. The entries in cells B4 and B8 both change because B8 is a calculated cell.

Erasing Cell Contents and a Range of Cells

Suppose that a revised look at the sales number for the first quarter reveals an increase in the sales for ASIA. The best way to enter the new number is to move the cell selector to cell B5 and delete the current entry in its entirety. Do the following:

1. Move the cell selector to cell B5 and press Del. Works asks you to confirm the deletion by pressing Enter. If you have made a mistake and don't want the contents deleted, press Esc and the contents are returned. In this example, you want to delete the contents, so press Del and then Enter.

2. Now enter the new number, *120000*.

Alternatively, you can simply type over the old entry. If you use the type-over method, be certain the entire entry is overwritten.

You cannot erase a range of cells without using the menu system. To erase a range, select the cells with the Shift and arrow keys and then open the Edit menu. From that menu, choose the Clear option. With this method of deletion, you have no second chance. After you choose Clear, the cells are emptied.

Moving Cells

For an example of moving cells, you will take the cells in column F and move them to a location underneath the four quarters. Follow these steps:

1. Select the range of cells F2 to F8.

2. Press Alt and then select Edit.

3. From the Edit menu, select Move. Works displays the message `Select new location and press ENTER. Press ESC to cancel.`

4. Move the cell selector to cell C10 and press Enter. The cells are relocated (see fig. QS2.10).

Although the cells were moved, column C is not wide enough for the grand total. The formulas all calculate correctly. Because you used the Move command, Works did not adjust them relative to their new location except for the entry in cell C16. The number in cell C16 is larger than the column width.

Inserting Rows and Columns

Because the spreadsheet is electronic, it is malleable. Rows or columns can be inserted as needed. In your example spreadsheet, a good place to insert a row would be above the SALES label entry so the entries would read more clearly. Do the following:

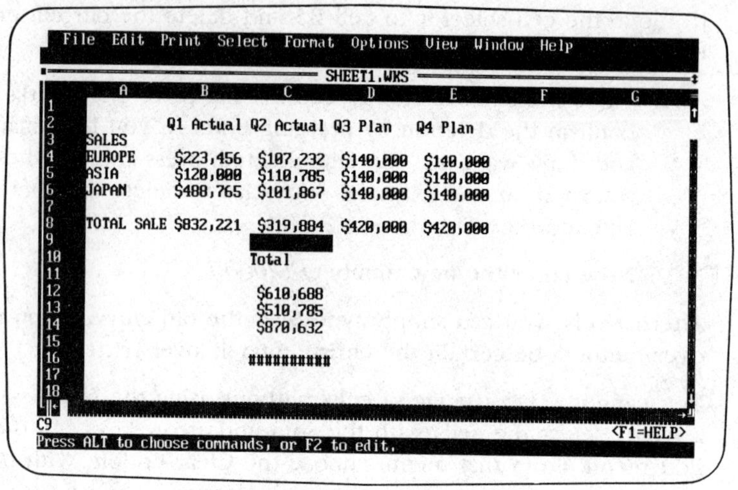

Fig. QS2.10.

The moved cells.

1. Move the cell selector to cell A3.
2. Press Alt to activate the menu bar and open the Edit menu.
3. Select the option Insert Row/Column. A dialog box opens and asks for the type of insertion you want (a row or column).
4. Select the Row option and press Enter. The row is inserted above SALES (see fig. QS2.11).

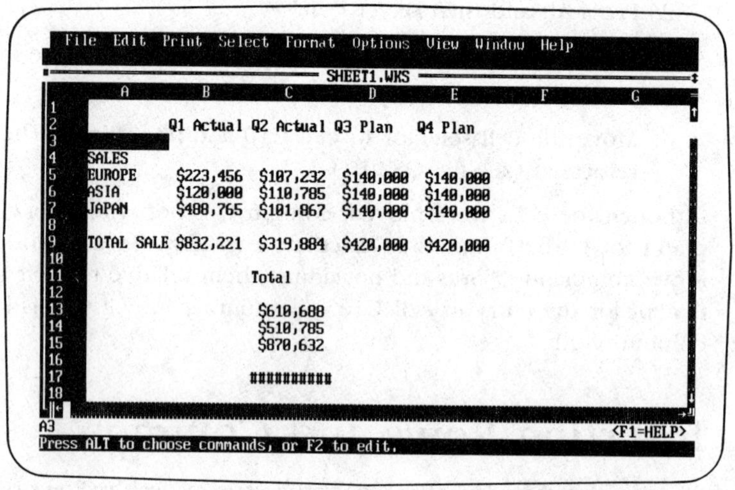

Fig. QS2.11.

The new row above SALES.

When inserting a column, remember that the new column will be inserted to the right of the location of the cell selector. The cell selector can be located in any cell of the column, or you can use the mouse to click the column letter and then insert the column.

Warning: When you insert a row or column, the old formulas will adjust to their new location but will not extend to cells that may have been moved out of a range. Always test your spreadsheet for accuracy after making such an adjustment.

Closing the Spreadsheet

Closing the spreadsheet involves using the File menu. Press Alt, select the File menu, and choose Close. If you have made any changes since the last save or close, Works asks whether you want to save those changes or discard them.

Because Works allows for more than one open file, you also can use the mouse to squeeze down the display of the spreadsheet and then switch to another file using the Window menu. For more on this procedure, see Chapter 13, "Tying It All Together."

[illegible]

Closing the Spreadsheet

[illegible]

5

Creating and Using Spreadsheets

In this chapter, you will be entering data into a Microsoft Works spreadsheet and creating a budget for a tennis club. To create the spreadsheet, you will enter numbers and labels, move the cursor around the spreadsheet, edit cell entries, and copy formulas and numbers into different cells.

Opening a Spreadsheet File

Getting started with a spreadsheet file requires that you access the same menu you use to begin a word processing file. After starting Works, the opening screen appears (see fig. 5.1).

Because you are starting a new task, the logical choice is to select the Create New File option from the menu. Select the option in one of two ways: either highlight the Create New File option and press Enter, or press N, which is highlighted or in reverse video (depending on the type of monitor you are using) in Create New File. The Create New File menu appears, as shown in figure 5.2.

You want to begin working with a spreadsheet, so move the cursor to New Spreadsheet and press Enter. The spreadsheet appears as in figure 5.3.

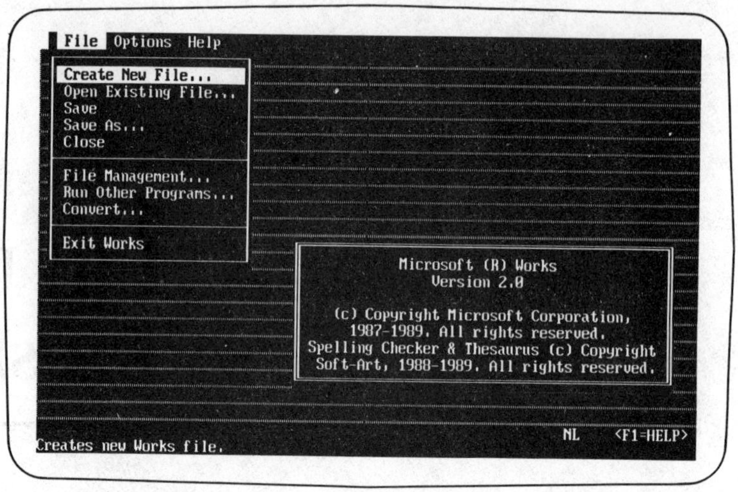

Fig. 5.1.

The opening Works screen.

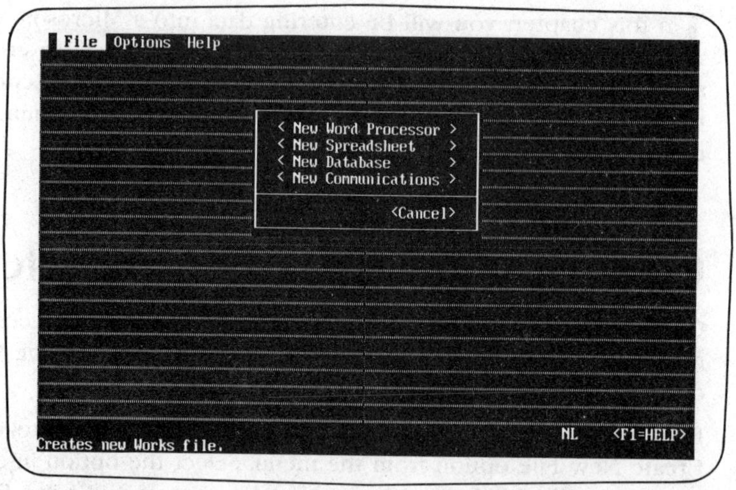

Fig. 5.2.

The Create New File screen.

Looking at the Spreadsheet Screen

If you are new to spreadsheets, it is important that you grasp the concept of the way labels, numbers, and formulas interact to create a financial model. A *financial model* is a combination of labels, numbers, and formulas in chart form, such as a budget, a profit-and-loss statement, or a cost estimate.

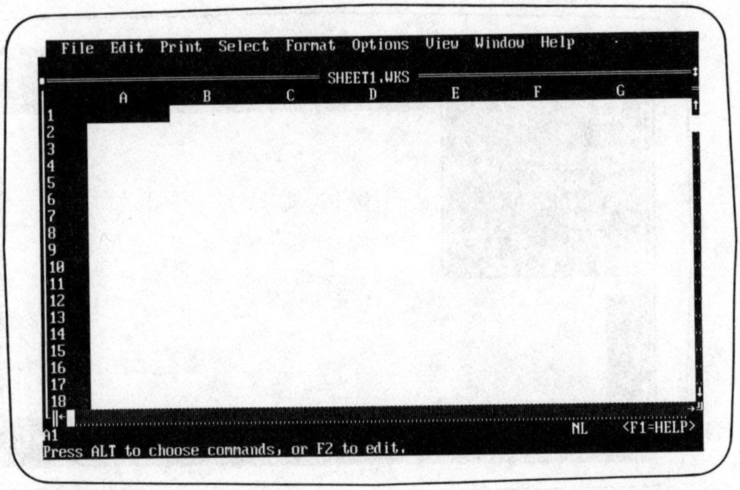

Fig. 5.3.
The spreadsheet screen.

A *label* is any cell entry that begins with a letter or any entry that has as its precedent an apostrophe (') or quotation mark (").

A *number* is just that. Numbers come in many forms, but as long as the first character Works encounters is a number or an arithmetic operator such as a plus sign (+) or minus sign (−), it is considered to be a number.

A *formula* always begins with either an equal sign (=) or a plus sign (+). The formula itself follows the leading equal sign or plus sign.

Across the top of the screen is the list of menus you can access by pressing the Alt key, which activates the menu bar.

Press Alt and look at each command and the letter that is in reverse video or underlined in the command. To open any menu, you press the highlighted letter. As an example, you can access the File menu by pressing F because it is highlighted. Press the letter F now to open the menu, as shown in figure 5.4.

The spreadsheet File menu is similar to the File menu found in the word processor component of Microsoft Works. If you select Create New File from this menu, you have the same file options that you have on the File menu in the word processor. Microsoft Works is consistent in this respect: you can move easily between Works applications because all have similar menus. Switching from the spreadsheet to the word processor and back again is easy.

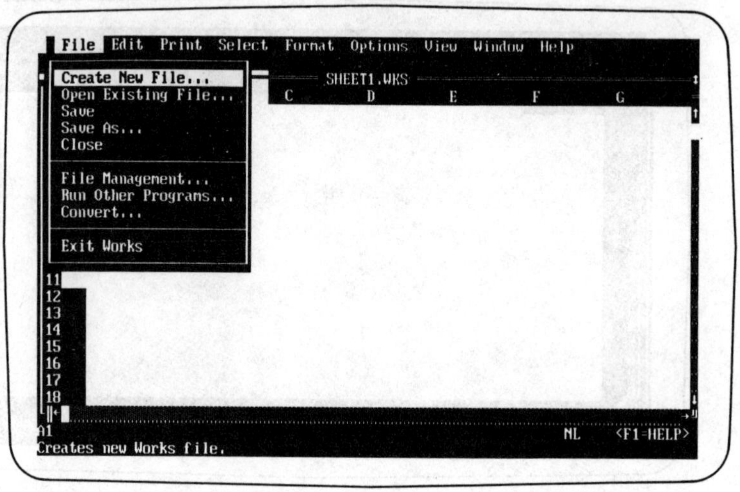

Fig. 5.4.

The spreadsheet File menu.

Access the other menus by pressing the right-arrow key to highlight the menu name you want to use and pressing Enter. As you move across the screen to the right, you see other menus that are specific to using spreadsheets. For example, the Format menu contains options controlling the manner in which data entered into cells is displayed (see fig. 5.5).

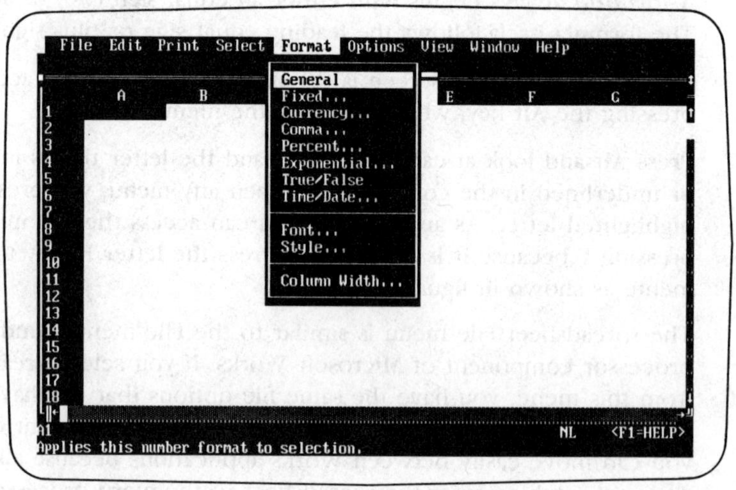

Fig. 5.5.

The spreadsheet Format menu.

Press Esc to close the menus.

Now that you are becoming familiar with the menus, move down to the next line on the screen, the formula bar. When you type information into a spreadsheet cell, the information is displayed simultaneously in the cell and in the formula bar. This display allows you to edit the entry before entering it into the cell. Also, as you move the cursor around the spreadsheet, entries of the cells you move to are displayed in the formula bar.

The next line down is the active file bar. When you first open a new spreadsheet file, Microsoft Works automatically assigns a name to the new spreadsheet, such as SHEET1.WKS, SHEET2.WKS, and so on. All spreadsheet files end with the extension WKS in Microsoft Works.

Moving Around in the Spreadsheet

The next line across the top of the working area is lettered A, B, C, and continues to IV. The letters run from A to Z and then begin repeating, AA, AB, AC, and so on, until the letters reach IV, a total of 256 columns. These are the column letters. When you open a new spreadsheet, the cell selector, which is the reverse video, or highlight, is located in cell A1 (it is in cell address column A, row 1). You can learn the location of the cursor at any time by looking in the lower left corner of the screen.

Take a quick tour of the spreadsheet to see how large it is.

To move the cursor to the end of the columns, press the Ctrl key and the right-arrow key together. Almost instantly, the cursor appears under the IV column heading, as shown in figure 5.6.

Down the left side of the screen are the row numbers, 1, 2, 3, and so on. You have yet to move the cursor out of row 1. To move the cursor to the bottom of the spreadsheet while still in column IV, press the Ctrl key and the down-arrow key together. The cursor jumps to cell IV4096. Microsoft Works has 4,096 rows! This figure means that the Works spreadsheet has a total of 1,212,416 cells (256 columns × 4096 rows).

Press the Ctrl key and the left-arrow key together. The cursor moves to A4096 (column A and row 4,096). To move the cursor back to cell A1, press Ctrl-up arrow or Ctrl-Home.

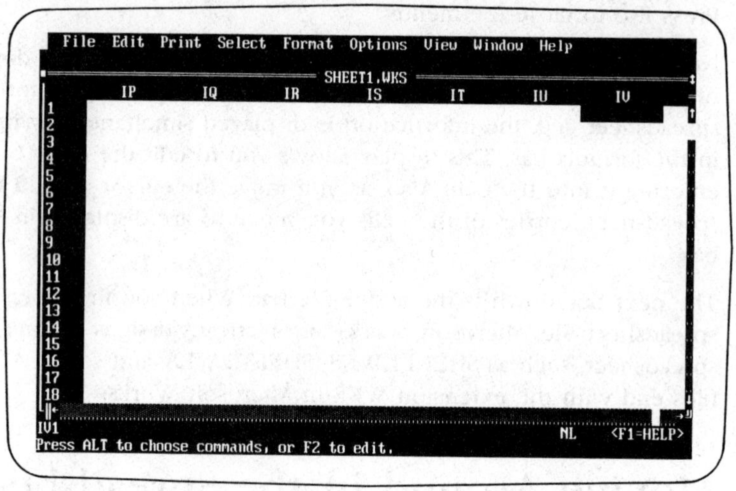

Fig. 5.6.

The cursor in cell IV1.

Looking at the Spreadsheet Window

As you move the cursor to the four corners of the spreadsheet, only a small portion of the available cells are visible at any one time. In fact, only 18 rows and 7 columns are normally seen. Therefore, the screen you see is only a small opening on a large electronic grid of rows and columns.

Looking at Cells

In preparing a spreadsheet, you enter all information into the cells. A *cell* is an area at the intersection of a row and a column. With the cursor in cell A1, you can see the size of an individual cell by the length and height of the cursor. A cell is designated by its cell address. If you have been typing along with the text, the cursor is currently in cell A1.

The size of the cells can be changed as needed, but that topic is covered in the next chapter. For now, begin entering information relating to the tennis club budget.

Entering Information into Cells

The spreadsheet needs identifying information at the top; and because a spreadsheet has the form of a chart, column headings and row labels need to be added so that the contents can be easily understood.

Begin by entering the month and year for the proposed budget, as follows:

1. Use the right-arrow key to move the cursor to cell C1. Check that you are positioned correctly by looking at the cell indicator in the lower left corner of the screen.

2. Type

   Budget June 1990

Notice as you type that the information is being displayed in two places: in cell C1 and in the formula bar at the upper left of the screen. Because this entry is longer than the width of the cell, the text scrolls through the cell, allowing you to see only a portion of the entry at any time. In the formula bar, the entire entry is visible (see fig. 5.7).

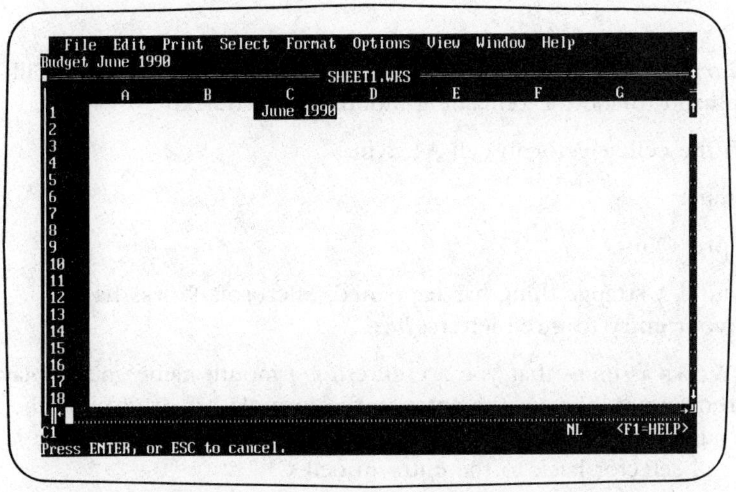

Fig. 5.7.
The entry in the formula bar.

3. Press Enter to insert the information into the cell. As you can see in figure 5.8, the entire entry now appears in the spreadsheet.

Although you can see the entire entry, if you make an entry in cell D1, the new entry overwrites the C1 entry. The entry in cell C1 is not changed if overwriting occurs; the entry in C1 is only in cell C1, even though Microsoft Works displays a long entry across cell boundaries when the spreadsheet has the room to do so.

With the spreadsheet title entered, move the cell selector to cell A4. Because a budget is a statement of income and expenses over a specific period of time, you need to add the months of the year as column heads.

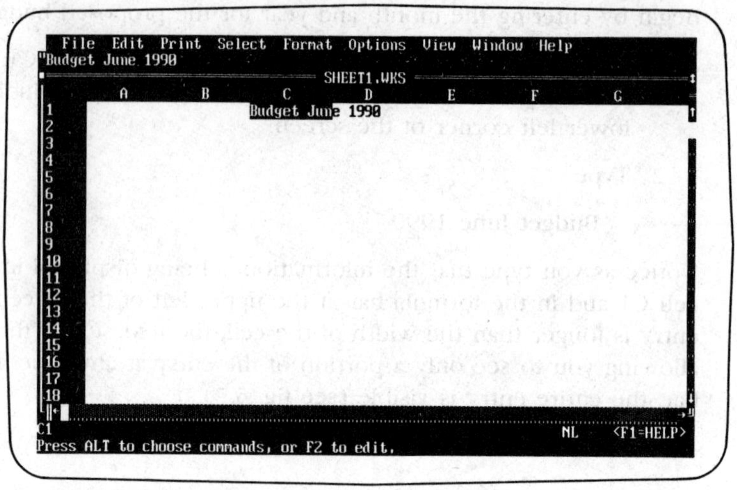

Fig. 5.8.

The entry in the cell.

Type *January* and *February* as you do normally; then use the special Fill Series command to add the remaining month names quickly:

1. With the cell selector in cell A4, type

   January

   and press Enter.

Wait a minute! A strange thing has happened. Microsoft Works has shortened your entry to three letters: *Jan*.

Microsoft Works assumes that you are entering a month name and displays the preferred format. Look at the entry in the formula bar. It displays the shortened name also. Notice, too, that no character precedes the letter *J*. Move the cell selector back to the entry in cell C1.

With the cell selector in C1, take a close look at the formula bar: the word *Budget* is preceded by a quotation mark. Works automatically adds the quotation mark when the program detects a label entry. This method is Microsoft Works' way of designating the entry in the cell as a label. Works' manner of handling *January* allows you to enter month names quickly, substituting the entire name with three-letter abbreviations.

2. Move the cell selector to cell B4.

3. Type

   Feb

4. This time, don't press Enter to insert the name in the cell. Instead, press the right-arrow key. When you do so, the month name *Feb* is entered into the cell, and the cell selector moves to the next logical cell for an entry, cell C4.

Tip: Using the arrow keys to make entries is much faster than pressing Enter, because this technique simultaneously enters information into a cell and moves the cell selector to the next cell.

Using Microsoft Works' Series Fill Command

You can easily move across the columns and type the remaining months of the year. But Microsoft Works has a feature for entering the months of the year with fewer keystrokes.

Using the Series Fill method requires that you know how many entries you have to enter. In this case, you have 10 more entries, because you already have *January* and *February* in place. Follow these steps, and you will be delighted with the result:

1. Move the cell selector into cell B4, the one containing the *Feb* entry.
2. Press Alt to activate the menu bar.
3. To select the cells in which you want to enter the remaining months of the year, press S to pull down the Select menu (see fig. 5.9). The menu has a list of command options that you can select. Select the cells to the right of cell B4.
4. Choose the Cells option either by pressing E or highlighting Cells and pressing Enter. The menu closes.
5. On the lower right of the screen, EXT appears. This notation indicates that the cell selector is in Extend mode, meaning that the cell selector will stretch across or down cells as directed. Press the right-arrow key once. As you can see, the cell selector now covers cells B4 and C4; it is extended.
6. You have 10 months left to enter, so you need to move the cell selector a total of 10 cells to the right. You have already moved the cell selector one cell, so press the right-arrow key 9 more times so that the cell selector extends to column L.

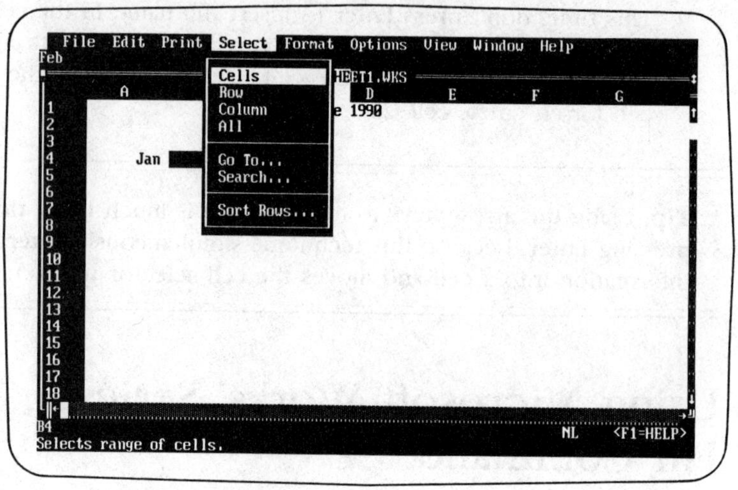

Fig. 5.9.

The Select menu.

You have now selected the cells into which you want to insert the month names. But did you make a mistake by including the B4 cell, which had the *Feb* entry?

In this instance, Microsoft Works needs to know what kind of information you want to fill into the rest of the cells. In order to determine that, the first cell selected must contain the first entry in the series. *February* works well as the first entry because Microsoft Works is smart enough to know that the rest of the entries should be the months after February, even though it is not the first month of the year.

7. To finish the entries, press Alt to activate the menu bar and then press E to choose the Edit menu (or highlight Edit and press Enter). Figure 5.10 shows the Edit menu.

8. Highlight the Fill Series command and press Enter, or press L, to display the Fill Series dialog box (see fig. 5.11).

Microsoft Works now needs two pieces of information: the type of data you want to have inserted and the size of the increment. You are inserting months.

9. With the up- or down-arrow key, move to the Month option.

10. With the Tab key, move to the Step by option. Because you want every month to be inserted, choose the default option of 1 step. If you were entering only the names of the months of the year by quarter, the step value would be 3.

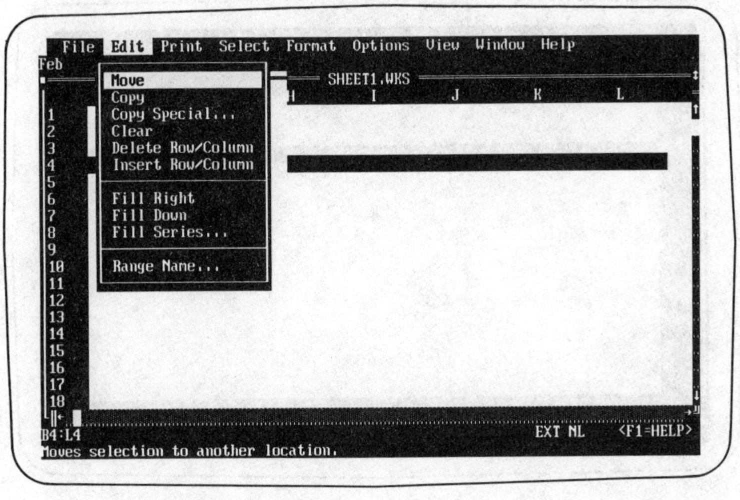

Fig. 5.10.

The Edit menu.

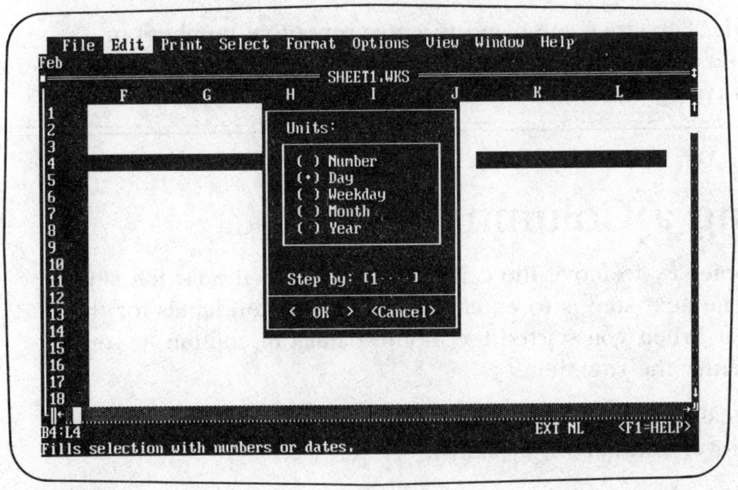

Fig. 5.11.

The Fill Series dialog box.

11. Press the Tab key to select the OK option and then press Enter (see fig. 5.12).

You have just completed an exercise in Microsoft Works: selecting cells and then filling them with sequential data.

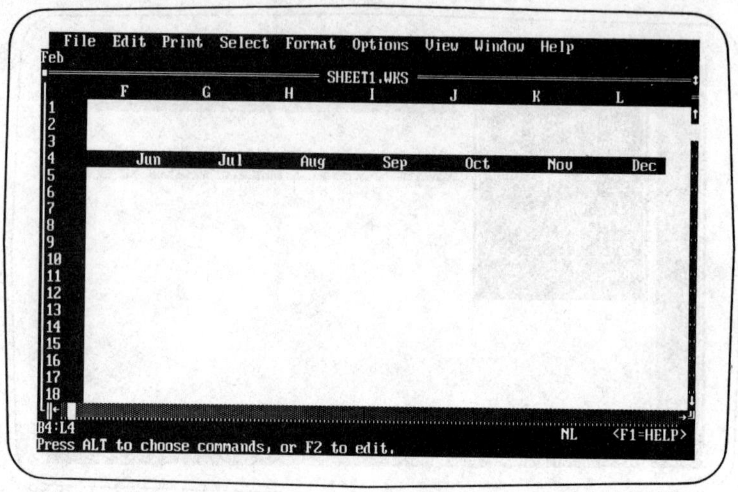

Fig. 5.12.

The month names entered.

Tip: Use the Fill Series command to enter repetitive numbers or labels into a series of cells. This method involves less work and eliminates typing errors.

Inserting a Column

Press the Home key to move the cell selector back to the far left side of the screen. The next step is to enter the income section labels for the club. However, when you started the month names in column A, you left no room to enter the row items.

This lack is really not a problem. With Microsoft Works, inserting a new column wherever you need it is simple:

1. With the cell selector in column A, press Alt to activate the menu bar and then press E for the Edit menu.
2. Select the Insert Row/Column option.
3. Choose to insert either a row or column. Select Column and press Enter.

The new column is inserted, and, if you move the cell selector to the right, you see that all the month names have been shifted over one column to accommodate the new column (see fig. 5.13).

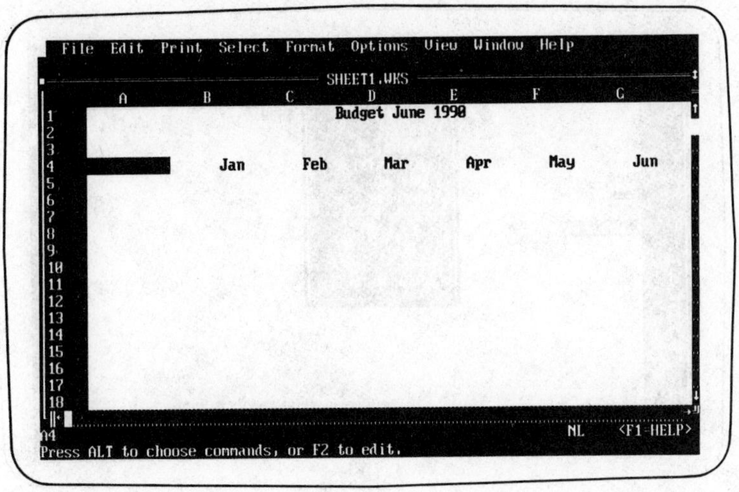

Fig. 5.13.

The new column inserted.

Tip: To move the cell selector to the right edge of the spreadsheet, press the End key. Microsoft Works moves the cell selector to the farthest right entry in the current row.

You now have room for labels. Move the cell selector to cell A5 and type

Dues

Press the down-arrow key to enter the *Dues* label. The next source of income is a fee charged to a local professional tennis player who gives lessons on the club courts. In cell A6 type

Fees

Then press the down arrow.

Dues and fees are the sources of income. Move the cell selector to cell A8. *Expenses* is the next label; enter this label and set off the labels for this section of the spreadsheet by underlining the section head, *Expenses*. Type the label

Expenses

and press Enter; this command enters the label but leaves the cell selector on cell A8.

To underline this label, follow these steps:

1. Press Alt to activate the menu bar and press T for the Format menu (see fig. 5.14).

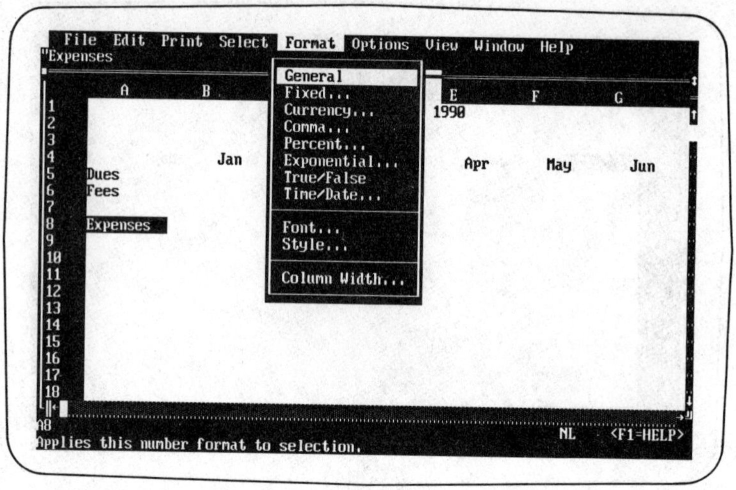

Fig. 5.14.

The Format menu.

2. Select the Style option, which lets you change the appearance of the label in this cell (see fig. 5.15).

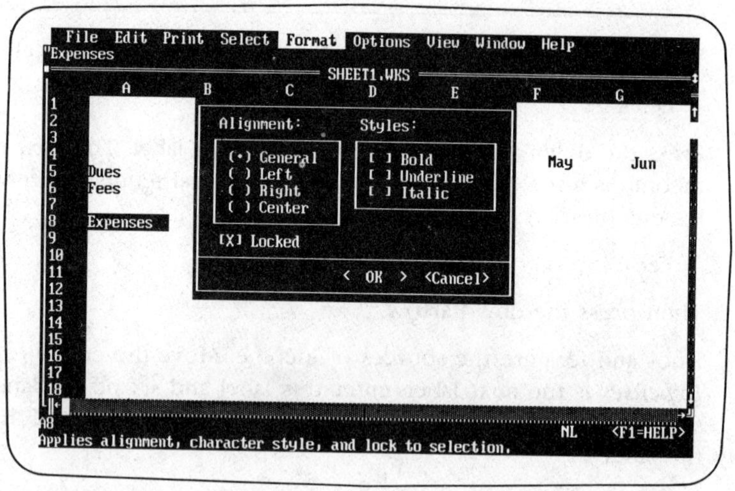

Fig. 5.15.

The Format Style dialog box.

Style choices fall into three categories: cell entry alignment, the style of the entry, and the `Locked` option—whether or not the information in the cell is locked. If the `Locked` option is selected, the information in the cell(s) cannot be edited unless you come back to this menu and unlock the cell(s).

3. Select the Styles option; then press U, which turns on the Underline prompt.

Leave this dialog box now by pressing Enter.

The label *Expenses* is underlined, and you can begin to enter expense subheadings. Type the following in the cells as indicated to finish the column:

In cell A10, type *Salaries*.
In cell A11, type *Trailer Rental*.
In cell A12, type *Electric*.
In cell A13, type *Telephone*.
In cell A14, type *Supplies*.
In cell A15, type *Postage*.
In cell A16, type *Printing*.
In cell A17, type *Tournaments*.
In cell A18, type *Accounting*.
In cell A19, type *Misc exp*.

Your spreadsheet should resemble figure 5.16.

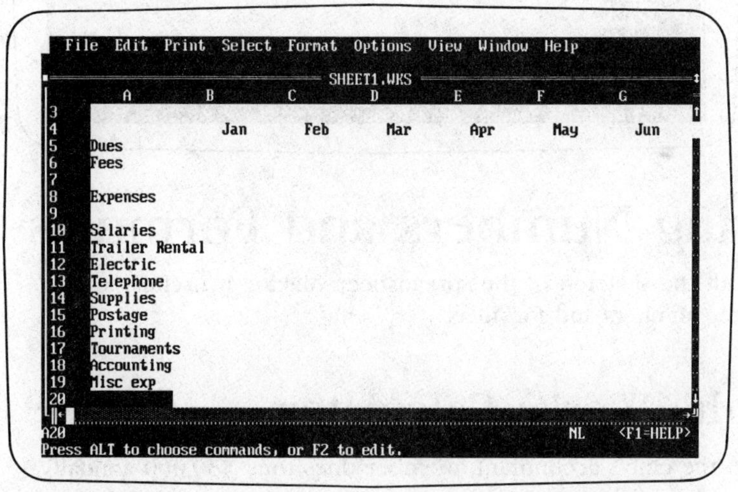

Fig. 5.16.
The completed expenses section.

Inserting a Row

Looking at the two items set out as income items in cells A5 and A6, notice that no section head was entered. To be consistent, make that entry by following these steps:

1. Move the cell selector to cell A5.
2. Press Alt to activate the menu bar and select the Edit menu.
3. From the Edit menu, choose the Insert Row/Column option; then press R to select Row and press Enter.

The new row is inserted above the location of the cell selector. Now enter the label *Income* in cell A5. Finish the entry by adding the Underline option from the Format and Style menus.

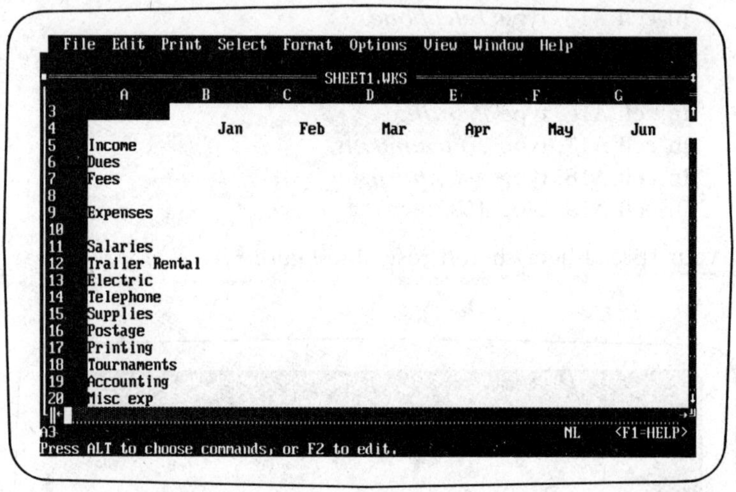

Fig. 5.17.

*The **Income** label entered.*

Entering Numbers and Formulas

You have built the skeleton of the spreadsheet. Making it useful requires that you enter numbers and formulas.

Using the Works Calculator

According to the club's accountant, member dues total $30,000 annually. This total is helpful, but you need a monthly figure for your budget. You will find that 30,000 divided by 12 months is easy to calculate with Microsoft Works' pop-up calculator. Follow these steps:

1. Move to cell B6, the cell that will have the first entry for dues.
2. Press Alt to activate the menu bar.
3. Press O to select the Options menu (see fig. 5.18).

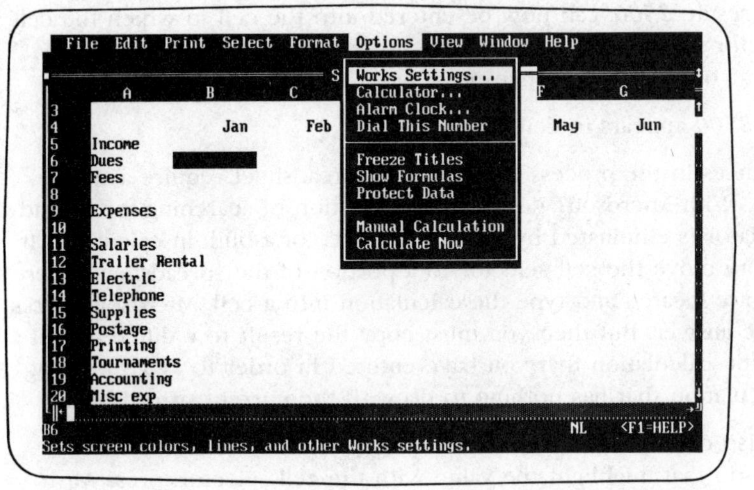

Fig. 5.18.

The Options menu.

4. Select the Calculator option (see fig. 5.19).

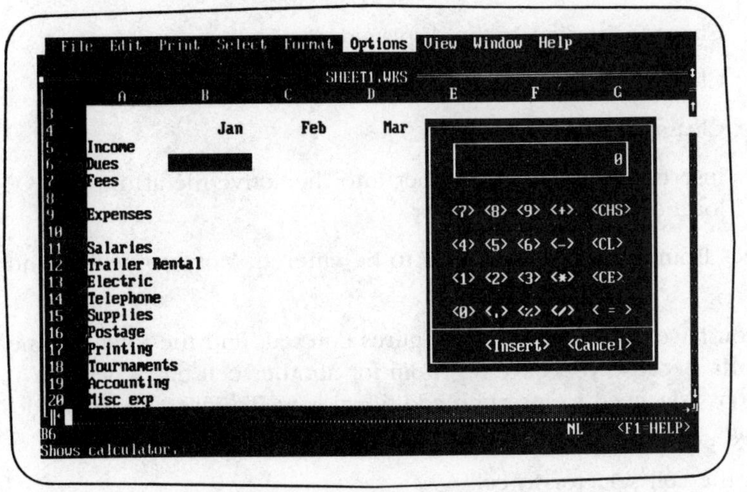

Fig. 5.19.

The Calculator.

5. The calculator works as any desktop calculator does. Use the number keys to enter the value *30000*. (Don't include a comma.) Press the forward-slash key (/) to indicate a division operation and then type the number *12*. Press Enter.

6. The result, *2500*, can now be entered into the cell in which the cell selector is positioned. To do that, either press Tab to highlight `Insert` or press I, and then press Enter.

The value *2500* appears in cell B6.

Many instances in the process of building a spreadsheet require a simple calculation. With Microsoft Works, the aggravation of searching for a hand-held calculator is eliminated by the convenience of a built-in calculator. It is possible to move the cell selector to a portion of the spreadsheet where no entries are located and type the calculation into a cell. Microsoft Works delivers the answer. But then you must copy the result to a different cell and erase the calculation that you have entered in order to avoid printing a stray calculation that has nothing to do with the current spreadsheet.

You may also display a value from the spreadsheet in the calculator display. To do that, highlight the value with the cell selector; press Alt to activate the menu bar, select the Edit menu, and select the Copy command. Then open the Options menu and choose Calculator. The number is copied to the display.

The special keys on the calculator, and their functions, are:

CHS	Changes the sign of the displayed number
CL	Clears all calculator entries
CE	Clears only the last entry
Insert	Inserts the displayed number into the active file at the location of the cell selector

Next the fees from the tennis pro need to be entered. Move to cell B7 and enter *450*.

Now that you have the initial income figures entered, find the total income for the month. Because you have no room for another cell entry beneath the *Fees* entry, you need to insert an additional row. To insert this row, do the following:

1. Move the cell selector to cell A9.
2. Press Alt to activate the menu bar, select the Edit menu, and then select the Insert Row/Column option.
3. Choose Row as the insertion and press Enter.

The spreadsheet still looks a little crowded, so repeat the steps to insert a second row, a blank row to give a neater appearance. To shorten the process, press the Alt, E, I, and R keys in sequence, and then press Enter.

In cell A9, enter the label

Total Income

Entering a Formula

Entering formulas in the Microsoft Works spreadsheet requires that you understand this simple concept: formulas are calculated based on the information in the cells using the cell addresses.

In the example, *2500* is entered in cell B6 and *450* is entered in cell B7. The cell selector is in cell B9, which is where you want the total of *2500* and *450* to appear. Therefore, the formula you enter in cell B9 is

=B6+B7

The formula is based on the cell addresses (B6 and B7), not the values in those cells.

If you were to read aloud the formula, it would read "cell B9 equals (=) the sum of the values entered in cells B6 and B7."

Enter the formula now and see what happens:

1. Type the equal sign (=) to begin the formula. All formulas begin with an equal sign (=).
2. Type the cell address containing the first value you want to include in the formula: *B6*.
3. Type the mathematical operator, in this case the addition sign: +.
4. Finish with the cell address containing the second value you want in the formula: *B7*.
5. Press Enter. Your spreadsheet should resemble figure 5.20.

That was easy, wasn't it? Notice that the text from cell A9 has been overwritten by the entry in cell B9.

All formulas in Microsoft Works use the same principle. The cell addresses in the formula determine what values are going to be acted on, and the mathematical operator determines the result of that action.

To illustrate the power this concept provides, move the cell selector to cell B6 and change the value there. Type *1000* and press Enter.

Instantaneously, Microsoft Works recalculates the total of the values in cells B6 and B7 and displays the result, *1450*, in cell B9.

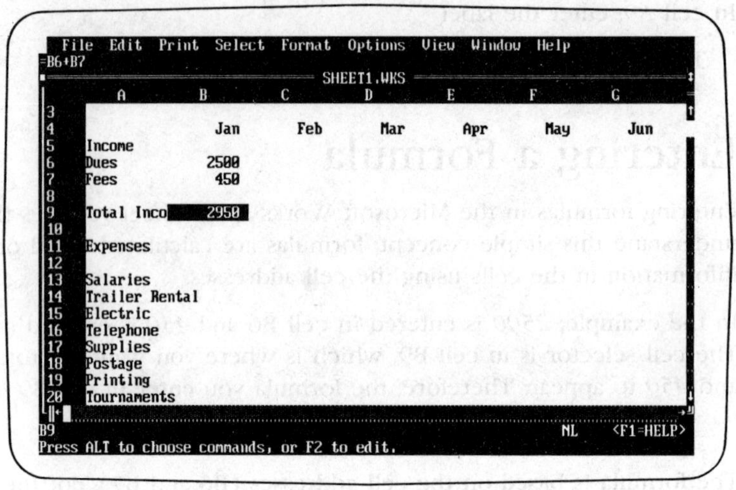

Fig. 5.20.

The formula entered into cell B9.

Editing Cell Entries

You have just edited a cell by replacing one entry with another. With the cell selector in the cell you want to change, editing cell entries can be accomplished in either of two ways: one is simply to type the new entry; the other is to press the F2 function key and use the arrow keys to move through the cell entry to make changes. Using the F2 key to edit is helpful if you have a long or complex cell entry, such as a long title or a formula.

As an example, look at the title for this spreadsheet, *Budget June 1990*. You have left out an important word: *Proposed*. This budget is not yet final, and to make that fact clear, you need to edit the title:

1. Move to cell D1.

2. Press the F2 key.

At the lower left of the screen is the message `Press ENTER, or ESC to cancel` (see fig. 5.21). This message tells you that when you have finished correcting the cell contents, pressing Enter inserts the correction into the cell. If you decide not to make any edits, or make them and then decide the original entry was better, pressing Esc leaves the cell as it was before the edit.

3. The word *Proposed* has to be inserted at the beginning of the title. The cursor is the small underline at the end of the title. Use the left-arrow key to move the cursor to the *B* in the word *Budget*.

4. Type

   Proposed

   Press the space bar to insert a space and press Enter (see fig. 5.22).

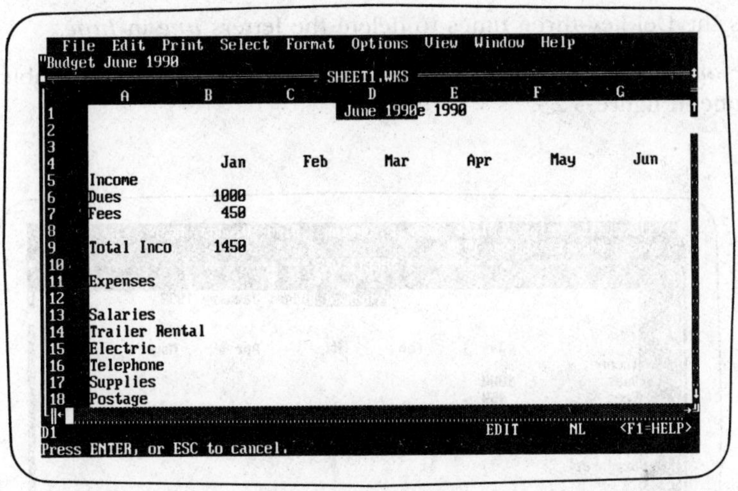

Fig. 5.21.
The Edit messages.

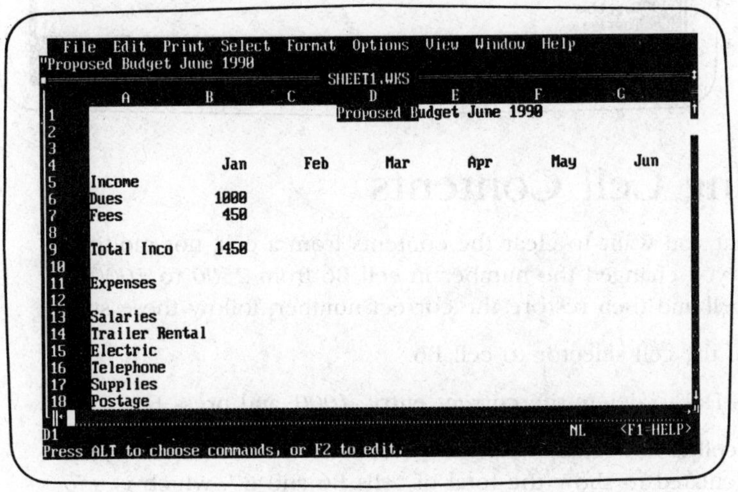

Fig. 5.22.
Proposed *added to the title.*

Something else is amiss. The title says that this proposed budget is for June 1990, not January, as the spreadsheet reads. As long as you are making changes, go back and change that, too:

1. With the cell selector in D1, press F2 to go into Edit mode.
2. Move the cursor to the *u* in the word *June*.
3. Press the Del key three times to delete the letters *une* in *June*.
4. Type *anuary* and press Enter. The spreadsheet title should resemble the one in figure 5.23.

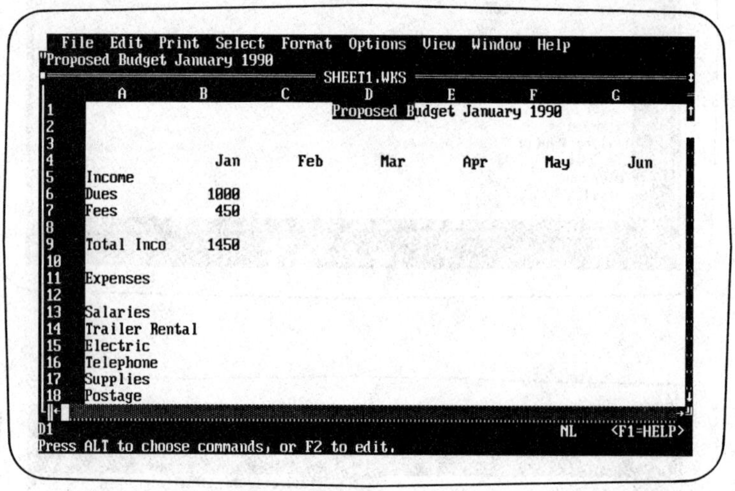

Fig. 5.23.

The new title completed.

Clearing Cell Contents

Suppose that you want to clear the contents from a cell, not modify it. Previously, you changed the number in cell B6 from *2500* to *1000*. To clear this cell and then restore the correct number, follow these steps:

1. Move the cell selector to cell B6.
2. Press Del to delete the current entry, *1000*, and press Enter.
3. The cell is now blank, and the formula in cell B9 has correctly recalculated to show the total of cells B6 and B7, which is *450* (0+450).
4. Type *2500* and press Enter.

The formula is recalculated, and the correct value of *2950* is now in cell B9.

Table 5.1 identifies the keys to press for Works' editing functions in the formula bar.

Table 5.1
Formula Bar Editing Keys

Key	*Action*
Home	Moves cursor to beginning of entry
End	Moves cursor to end of entry
Left arrow	Moves cursor left one character
Right arrow	Moves cursor right one character
Backspace	Deletes character to left of cursor
Delete	Deletes character on cursor
Shift-left arrow	Selects character(s) left
Shift-right arrow	Selects character(s) right
Enter	Accepts edits
Up/down arrow	Accepts edits
Esc	No change

Aligning Cell Entries

Microsoft Works automatically aligns labels and numbers when they are entered into a cell. The default is that labels are left-justified in the cell and numbers are right-justified.

Changing the alignment for labels is accomplished with the Format Style command. In the Proposed Budget spreadsheet, you have already set off the section heads, *Income and Expenses*, by underlining them. Now move the *Income* head to the right side of cell A5:

1. Move the cell selector to cell A5.
2. Press Alt to activate the menu bar.
3. Select the Format menu and then select the Style option. A dialog box appears (see fig. 5.24).

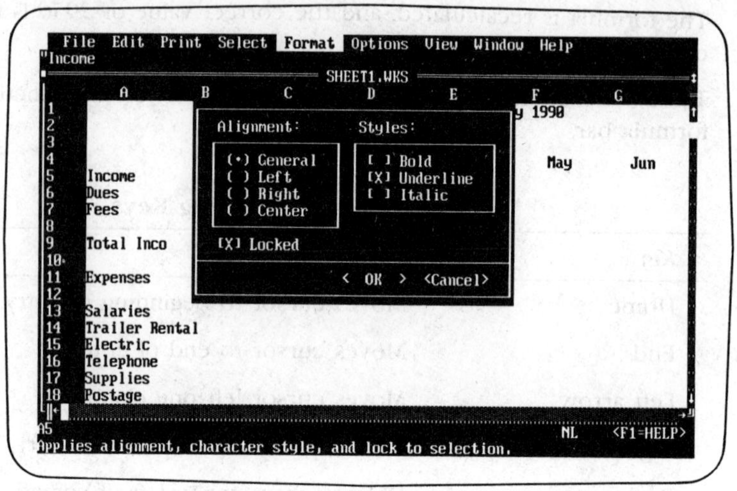

Fig. 5.24. *The Format Style dialog box.*

4. Because you have already underlined this cell, an `X` precedes that choice. To change the alignment, press R or move the cursor to `Right`.
5. Press Enter, or move the cursor to the `OK` option and then press Enter.

Income is now right-justified (see fig. 5.25).

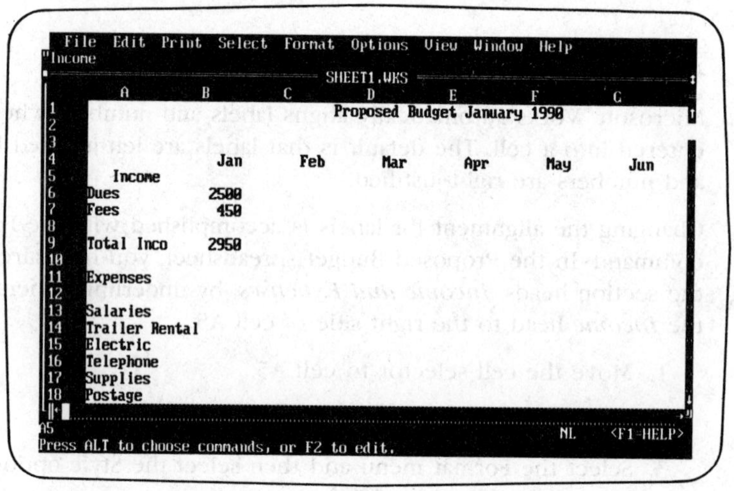

Fig. 5.25. Income *right-aligned.*

Entering Values into Cells

To determine the budget for the month of January, you need to insert the numbers related to the expense section items.

Enter the following numbers:

In cell B13, type *1250*.
In cell B14, type *150*.
In cell B15, type *120*.
In cell B16, type *35*.
In cell B17, type *175*.
In cell B18, type *75*.
In cell B19, type *75*.
In cell B20, type *100*.
In cell B21, type *100*.
In cell B22, type *25*.

With these expenses entered, you can calculate whether the club made money. When you calculated the income section of the spreadsheet, the formula (=B6+B7) involved only two cells.

In the *Income* section, having only two cells to total makes it easy to enter the formula. You also can add every cell individually in a long formula, like =B13+B14+B15+B16....

That method works, but the complexity of the process and the possibility of typing errors render this method impractical. Of course, Microsoft Works provides a better way.

Summing a Range of Cells

You want to add the values in a range of cells. A *range* is any contiguous group of cells. In this example, the range is B13 to B22, the cells that contain the values relating to expenses.

Earlier, you used the Series Fill command to insert the names of the months of the year into a selected range of cells. This time, select the cells to be included in the range to be totaled. Follow these steps:

1. Move the cell selector to cell B24, where the expenses will be totaled.
2. Start the formula with the equal sign: =.

3. Add a function name. Microsoft Works has many functions with which you can construct formulas. The SUM function totals a range of values. Type *SUM* after the equal sign so that the formula bar displays =SUM.

4. Because you are going to sum a range of cells, this range in the formula needs to be surrounded by parentheses. Type the opening parenthesis *(*. The formula now looks like =SUM(.

5. Add the range of cells. You can use the menu commands, but Microsoft Works provides an easier way. First, move the cell selector to cell B13, as shown in figure 5.26.

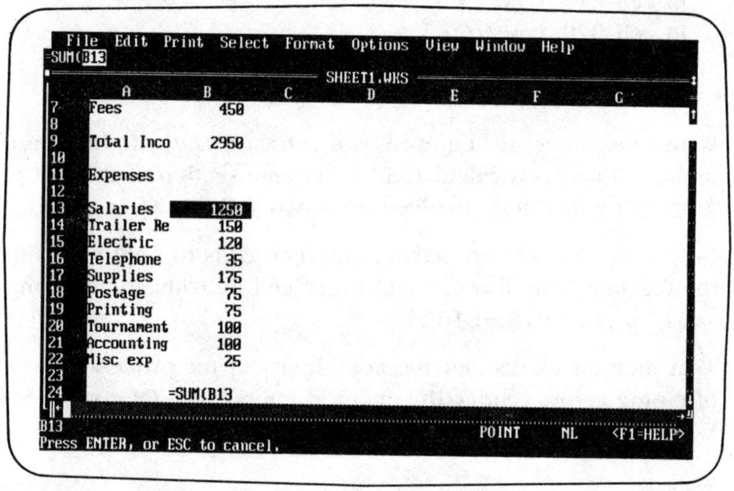

Fig. 5.26.

The cell selector in B13.

Cell address B13 is displayed in the formula. Also, near the lower right corner of the spreadsheet, a screen message appears indicating that you are in Point mode, which means that you are going to point to the range of cells desired.

6. Hold down the Shift key and then press the down-arrow key. The cell selector goes into the Extend mode and stretches as you continue pressing the down-arrow key.

7. When the cell selector is on cell B22, stop pressing the Shift and down-arrow keys. The range B13 through B22 is highlighted (see fig. 5.27).

8. Type the closing parentheses, *)*, and press Enter to finish the formula.

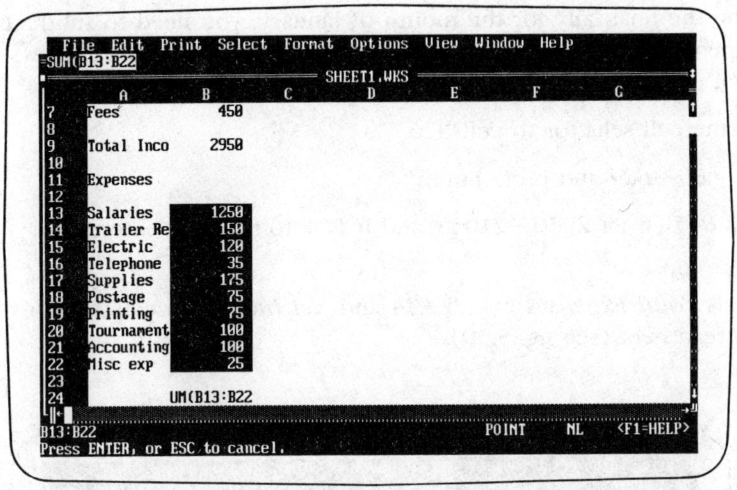

Fig. 5.27.

The range B13 to B22 selected.

If you followed the steps closely, your screen should resemble figure 5.28.

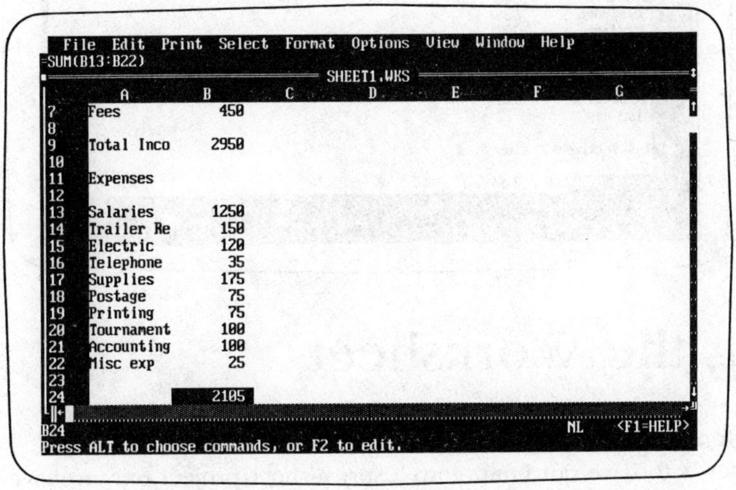

Fig. 5.28.

Completed expense sum formula.

You have taken a big step toward mastering one of the key concepts of working with the Microsoft Works spreadsheet. You can use a function and then select a range of cells on which the function operates. This technique opens a wide range of formulas to you. In Chapter 7, all the built-in functions are illustrated with working examples.

To determine the final tally for the month of January, you need to subtract the total expenses from the total income. You already know those figures; include a cell for that result:

1. Move the cell selector to cell B26.
2. Type *=B9−B24* and press Enter.

The result is *845* (from 2950−2105), and it is automatically entered in this cell.

Add the labels *Total Expenses* in cell A24 and *Net Income* in cell A26 to finish this spreadsheet (see fig. 5.29).

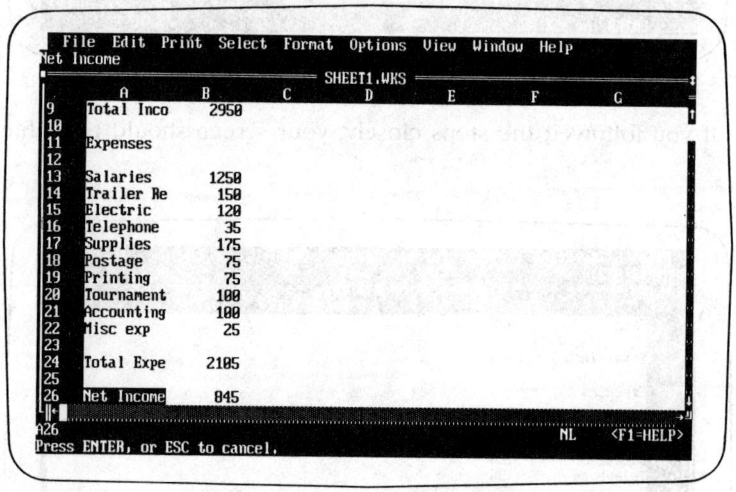

Fig. 5.29.

Columns A and B completed.

Saving the Worksheet

You have put a great deal of work into the spreadsheet, and you want to save your efforts. One of the worst experiences you can have as a computer user is to have put hours into a spreadsheet project only to have a power surge or failure destroy your spreadsheet. So take a moment to save the spreadsheet:

1. Press the Alt key to activate the menu bar.
2. Select File from the menu.

If you choose the Save option, Microsoft Works saves the spreadsheet in a file called SHEET1.WKS. A more descriptive name is better to use so that in the future you will remember the contents of the spreadsheet from its name.

3. Select the Save As option (see fig. 5.30).

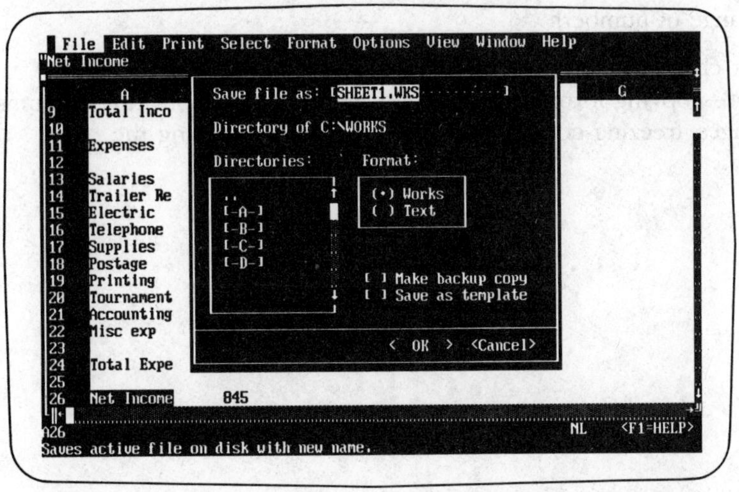

Fig. 5.30.
The Save As dialog box.

Take a look at this dialog box. At the top is the spreadsheet file name Microsoft Works thinks you want to use. Next is the `Directory` option. Microsoft Works lets you see what files are in other subdirectories (assuming that you have a hard disk) or switch directories to save the file where you choose.

Under the `Format` section, you have the opportunity to save the spreadsheet as a Works file or as a text file. Saving the spreadsheet as a text file is an option that allows the spreadsheet to be sent via electronic transfer to another computer or exported to other software programs. For more information on how this transfer can be done, see Appendix A.

One other option is to turn on the `Make backup copy` option. This file name has the extension BKS rather than WKS. Every time you save the main file, Works makes a backup unless you turn off this option.

4. Type *tennis* and press Enter.

The spreadsheet file is saved as TENNIS.WKS, and you are returned to the spreadsheet screen. The new name for the spreadsheet is displayed in the title line.

Chapter Summary

In this chapter, you have learned how to enter labels, numbers, and formulas into the cells of the spreadsheet. In addition, you have used the Series Fill command to insert the names of the months of the year, edited text, formatted and aligned label entries, and used a function in a formula to sum a range of numbers.

In the next chapter, you do more work with the TENNIS.WKS spreadsheet—copying formulas and data, using fonts, manipulating columns, naming ranges, freezing column and row titles, and searching the spreadsheet.

6

Examining Spreadsheet Basics

In the preceding chapter, you began entering into the spreadsheet cells the basic elements that make up a spreadsheet: the labels that describe the information that is contained in the spreadsheet, the numbers associated with the labels, and the formulas that make the numbers useful.

In this chapter, you finish the TENNIS.WKS spreadsheet and, in doing so, learn more about the basics of using the Microsoft Works spreadsheet. The topics covered are copying cell contents, formatting numbers, creating range names, using relative and absolute formulas, freezing row and column titles, hiding a column, using the Go To command, protecting cell contents, and searching the spreadsheet.

Opening a Saved Spreadsheet File

At the end of Chapter 5, you saved the proposed budget for the tennis club in a file called TENNIS.WKS. To access the file, follow these steps:

1. From the Microsoft Works opening menu, select Open Existing File (see fig. 6.1).

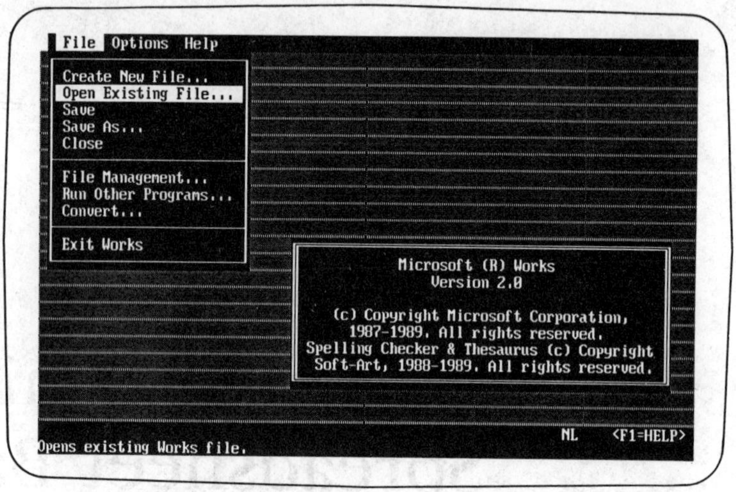

Fig. 6.1.

The File menu.

2. The Open dialog box appears (see fig. 6.2).

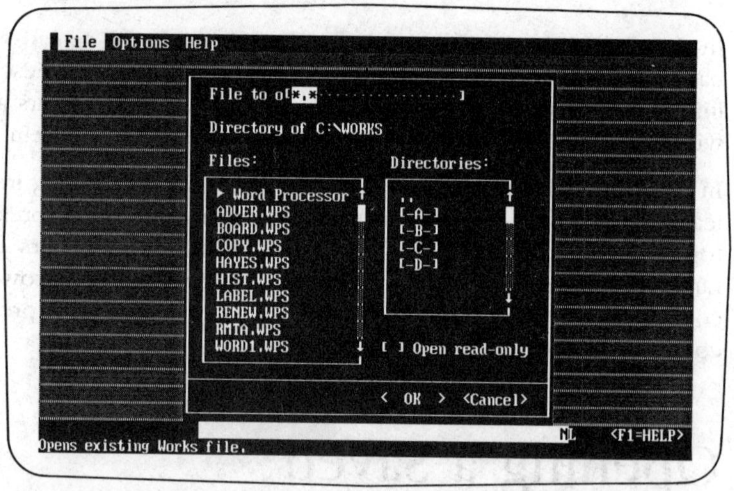

Fig. 6.2.

The Open dialog box.

As shown in figure 6.2, Microsoft Works displays the available disk drives and the files already saved in the C:\WORKS subdirectory. Works determines which disk drives your computer has and displays them in the box on the right. In figure 6.2, Works detects four drives: A, B, C, and D. If you had saved the TENNIS.WKS spreadsheet on a floppy disk, and not in the C:\WORKS subdirectory, and then wanted to retrieve the spreadsheet, you would first need to use the Directories box to switch to drive A, assuming that is the disk drive in which you have inserted your files disk. Once you switch drives, Works displays in the Files box the files on the disk in that drive. (If you need more information on files, check the end of Chapter 3 in the word processing section.)

Works is currently displaying *.* as the suggested file to open. This notation is a shorthand method used by DOS to select all files to open, but this method is not necessary here.

3. Press the down-arrow key to move the highlight down into the Files box. The files are separated by the types of information they contain: word processing, spreadsheet, database, or other files. As you highlight file names, they are inserted into the File to open area at the top of the screen.
4. Move the highlight until the file TENNIS.WKS is highlighted and inserted into the File to open area.
5. Press Enter. The spreadsheet appears (see fig. 6.3).

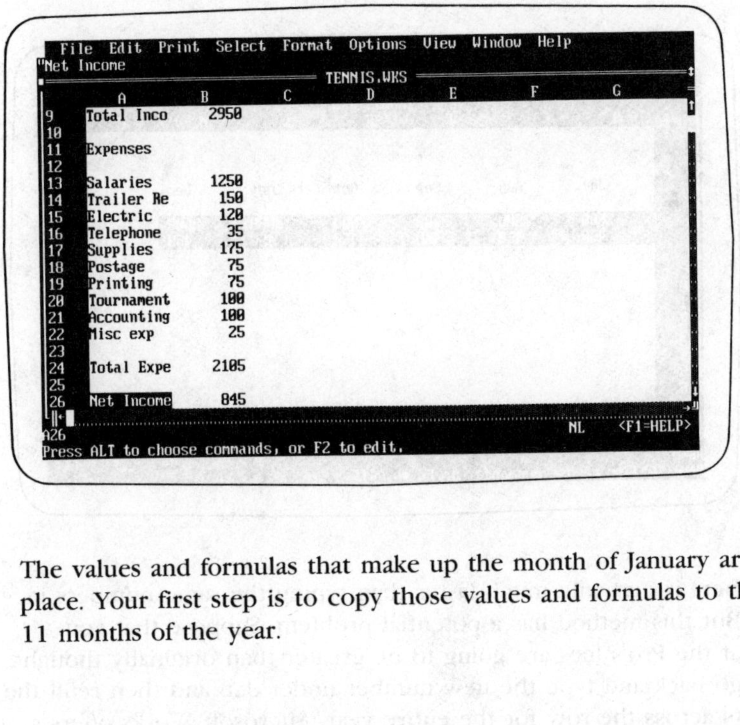

Fig. 6.3.

The TENNIS.WKS file.

The values and formulas that make up the month of January are already in place. Your first step is to copy those values and formulas to the remaining 11 months of the year.

Copying Cell Contents

To copy cell contents, start in the `Income` section:

1. Move the cell selector to cell B6.
2. Press the Shift key and hold it while also pressing the down-arrow key until cells B6 and B7 are selected. You want to copy the values in these cells to the right through column M.
3. Use the cell selector to highlight those cells across the row where you are inserting the income figures. With the Shift and right-arrow keys pressed, stretch the cell selector across to column M, which is the `Dec` column. Press Alt to activate the menu bar and press E to begin an edit.
4. From the Edit menu, highlight the Fill Right option. Notice at the bottom of the screen the effect choosing this command has. You see the prompt `Copies leftmost cell(s) to rest of selection.`

Instantly, Microsoft Works copies the information (see fig. 6.4).

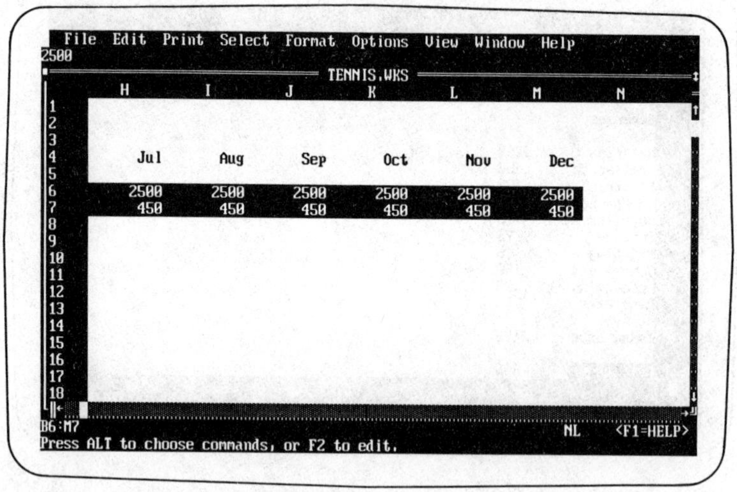

Fig. 6.4.
The `Income` *numbers filled across the months.*

Filling numbers is certainly much faster than typing the same numbers in every cell. But this method has a potential problem. Suppose that you discover that the Pro's fees are going to be greater than originally thought. You could go back and type the new number under `Jan` and then refill the cell contents across the row for the entire year. Microsoft Works offers a faster method as shown in the following section.

Making Dependent Cell Entries

Move the cell selector to cell B7, the cell containing the initial entry for Fees. Type *500* in the cell. The number is inserted, but the rest of the months remain the same at 450.

Enter a short formula in cell C7 and then copy the formula across the row, as follows:

1. With the cell selector in cell C7, type

   =B7

   Press Enter. Works interprets the formula as "This cell (C7) equals the contents in cell B7," and so the value 500 is now also in cell C7.

2. Move the cell selector to cell C7 and then press the Shift and End keys together. This command stretches the cell selector across the spreadsheet. Press Alt, select the Edit menu, and select the Fill Right option.

The new value 500 is entered in every cell in row 7. These entries, however, are different from those where you simply entered numeric values. Move the cell selector back to cell B7. Now, enter the old value for Fees, 450, and press Enter.

All the cells in row 7 now contain the value 450. Look at the contents of cell E7 by moving the cell selector there. The cell displays 450, but the formula bar displays the formula =D7.

Because you copied the formula =B7 in cell C7, why does the formula bar show =D7 as the contents? Microsoft Works has automatically adjusted the copied formula to be relative to its column position.

Relative versus Absolute Copying

Microsoft Works assumes, as the default, that copied formulas are to be adjusted to their new location in the spreadsheet. If you scroll the cell selector across row 7, you see that every formula has been adjusted to copy the cell just to its left, not to copy the original cell copied, C7.

To see an example of this principle at work, move the cursor to cell E7 again. Do the following:

1. Change the entry in cell E7 to 600.

2. Press Enter. The cells to the right of E7 also change value because they contain relative copies of cell contents.

3. Change the entry in E7 back to the relative formula =D7.
4. Move the cell selector to cell C7, the address where this formula originates.

Microsoft Works has a special key just for this situation: the F4 function key. To use this key, you must activate it *as* the formula is entered, not after the formula is entered.

5. To use the relative/absolute key, you must first erase the formulas in the cells in row 7. With the cursor in cell C7, press the Shift and End keys to stretch the highlight across the entire row. Press Alt and select the Edit menu.
6. From the Edit menu, select the Clear command. All the contents of the cells will be cleared.
7. Move the cursor to C7 and type an equal sign (=) to begin the formula.
8. Move the cursor to cell B7. Works will insert the B7 cell address in the formula bar.
9. Press the F4 key once. As you can see, dollar signs are inserted in front of the B and the 7 (see fig. 6.5).

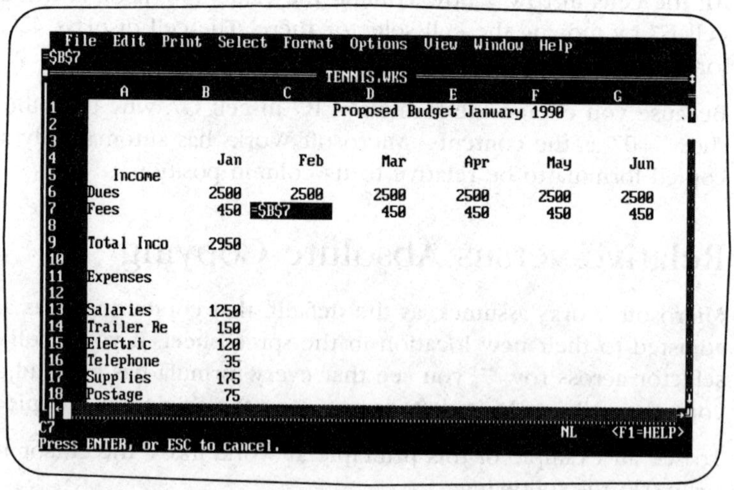

Fig. 6.5.
The formula with dollar signs inserted.

An *absolute reference* is an address for a specific cell; an absolute address does not adjust to the relative cell location. In the preceding example, the cells adjusted across the row, =D7, =E7, and so on. In most instances when you copy formulas or numbers, you want them to be relative to their location. The dollar signs indicate that no matter where the formula is copied in the spreadsheet, only the contents of that specific referenced cell are used.

If you press the F4 key again, the dollar sign in front of the B disappears, but the one in front of the 7 remains.

This reference is called a *mixed reference*. If you copy the cell contents now, only the row reference remains constant, not the column reference. Pressing the F4 key again reverses the situation, and the column reference is constant while the row reference is relative. The F4 function key cycles through the choices of absolute and relative references.

10. Press the F4 key until both the column and row are absolute references.
11. Press Enter to insert the new formula into C7.
12. Use the Fill Right command to insert the formula into cells D7 through M7.

If you scroll across the cells in row 7, you see that the formulas are now absolute. The absolute formula gives you new flexibility. Suppose that in the month of July, the teaching pro takes a month off. In that month, the `Fees` revenue is 0. By having the formulas absolute, you can adjust one month without disturbing the formulas for all the months following July.

Later in this chapter, you will use percentage formulas that require mixed references in order to work properly.

Finish the `Income` section by copying the formula in cell B9 to cells C9 through M9:

1. Move the cell selector to cell B9.
2. Press and hold the Shift key and then press the End key. The cell selector is extended to column M.
3. Press the Alt key, press E, and then select the Fill Right option. The formula is entered across the row relative to its position.

Copying Contents of a Range of Cells to a Different Range

The bottom section of the TENNIS spreadsheet is not completed; the expenses are not yet copied across the columns. Follow these steps:

1. Move the cell selector to cell B13.

2. Press and hold down the Shift key and press the down-arrow key until the cell selector stretches to the end of the entries in column B, row 26.

3. Still holding the Shift key, press the End key. The entire range from C13 to M26 is selected.

4. Press the Alt key, press E to select Edit, and select the Fill Right option.

As shown in figure 6.6, Microsoft Works quickly fills in the cell contents over many cells. This technique is quite fast and has the advantage that fewer errors are made.

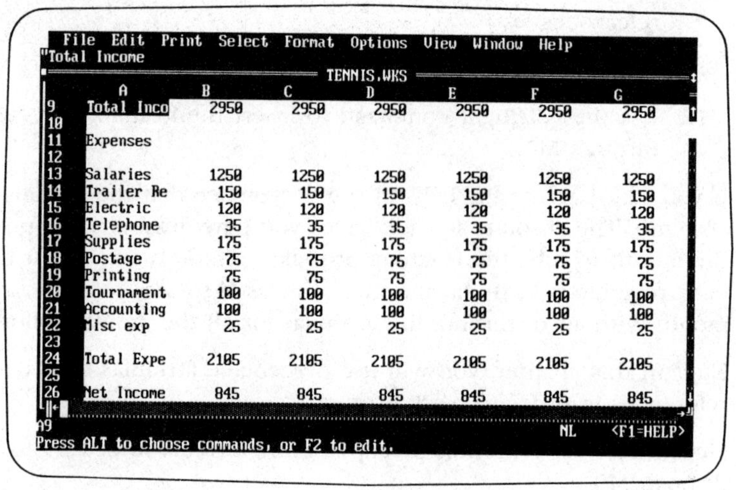

Fig. 6.6.

The TENNIS budget filled in.

You now have a complete TENNIS budget, which is flexible in that you can change assorted numbers and immediately find the effect on net income.

Remember, there are significant differences in the manner in which you copy information across the cells. In the example of the Expenses section, every cell is independent, not dependent, because you copied the contents of column B without regard to what occurs if the entry in column B changes. When you are creating a spreadsheet, the best policy usually is to make the cells to the right dependent on the cells preceding them. By doing this as a habit, you can avoid errors when playing what-if scenarios.

Combining Relative and Absolute Addresses

To try different economic assumptions easily, make the Expenses section depend on the entries in cells B13 to B26:

1. Move the cell selector to C13 and press the Shift key and down-arrow key together. This command highlights the cells in the range C13 to C26. The active cell is still cell C13, and you enter the formula, =*$B13*, into that cell.

2. Press F2 to edit.

3. Press the Backspace key to delete the characters 1250.

4. Type =*$B13* and press Enter.

When you copy this formula, the column reference remains absolute, but the rows change to reflect their positions.

By making the entries absolute, you can make changes in midyear numbers without disturbing the entire spreadsheet.

The next step is to copy the cell contents in C13 to the other cells in column C, through cell C26. Press the Alt key and select the Edit menu. From the Edit menu, highlight the Fill Down option (see fig. 6.7).

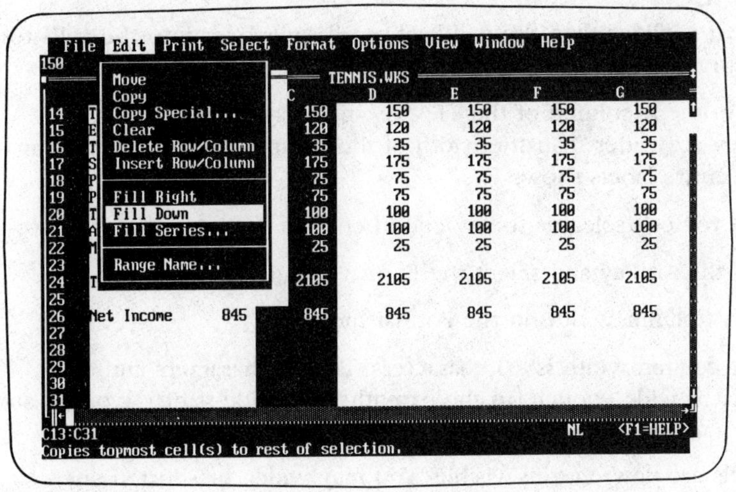

Fig. 6.7.

The Fill Down menu option highlighted.

Microsoft Works displays the message `Copies topmost cell(s) to rest of selection`. Because you want to have all the cells dependent on the entries in column B, this choice is correct. Press Enter to confirm.

Check to see whether the cells have the correct entries by moving the cell selector down the C column. The entries in the formula bar reflect the cell addresses from column B. Cells C23 and C25 display zero values. The zeros are logical because no entries in the B column have been copied to those cells. For cosmetic reasons, you can clear the entries in those two cells, either by using the Del key or by selecting the Edit menu and choosing the Clear option.

The final step in preparing the spreadsheet is to copy the formulas in column C to the rows for the rest of the year. Use the Shift and arrow keys to highlight cells C13 through M26. Press the Alt key, select the Edit menu, and choose the Fill Right option. The entire `Expenses` section is now dependent on the entries in column B.

Before making any more changes to the spreadsheet, save it so that you can retrieve a copy of the work you have done, just in case you make a mistake.

To save the file, press Alt, select File, and choose Save.

Setting the Width of a Column

An entry that is wider than the width of a cell spills over into the cells to the right if no entries are in the adjoining cells.

The labels in the A column of the TENNIS spreadsheet cannot be read because they are wider than the width of the column. Widen the column so that the entire labels show:

1. Move the cell selector to any cell in column A.
2. Press the Alt key and select the Format menu (see fig. 6.8).
3. Select Column Width on the Format menu.

The default column width is 10 characters. Try 15 characters and see whether that is wide enough. In the parentheses beside `Width`, type *15* and press Enter (see fig. 6.9).

All the labels are now entirely visible. You may widen or shorten any column on the spreadsheet. Shortening columns allows more columns to be visible on the display; the action does not affect the contents of the cells.

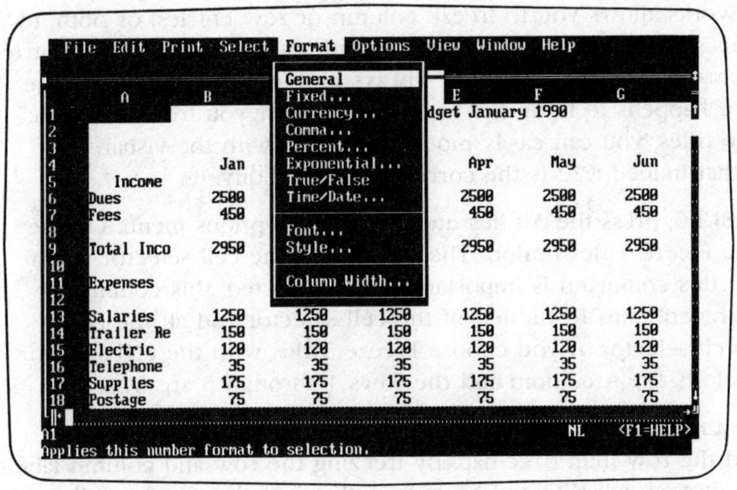

Fig. 6.8.

The Format menu.

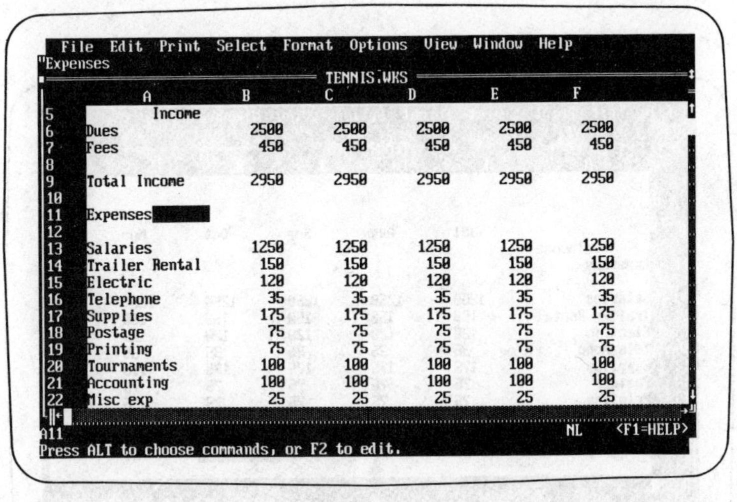

Fig. 6.9.

A column expanded to 15 characters.

Freezing Row and Column Titles

Suppose that you learn that in the month of October an extraordinary expense will be incurred relating to item `Misc exp`. The cell affected by this change is cell K22. You have no easy way to identify this cell as the correct cell because scrolling to the left in the spreadsheet removes the entries in column A from the screen. In addition, the month names can also disappear from view. The scrolling of the screen makes correctly editing the proper cell difficult.

Microsoft Works allows you to freeze column or row entries, or both, to alleviate this situation. The titles for the month names and the label entries for the `Income` and `Expense` lines are always visible no matter where the cell selector happens to be in the spreadsheet. After you freeze the row and column titles, you can easily modify cell K22, with the visual assurance that indeed K22 is the correct cell to modify.

Move to cell B6; press the Alt key and select the Options menu. On the menu is the Freeze Titles option. The location of the cell selector when you choose this command is important. When selected, this command freezes all the columns to the left of the cell selector and all the rows above the cell selector. If you choose Freeze Titles with the cell selector in B6, therefore, the A column and the rows 1 through 5 are frozen.

Next move the cell selector to the cell at the intersection of the `Oct` column and the row item `Misc exp`. By freezing the row and column labels, you can easily find cell K22 and be certain that it is the correct cell to edit. Figure 6.10 displays the screen as it looks with the frozen rows and column.

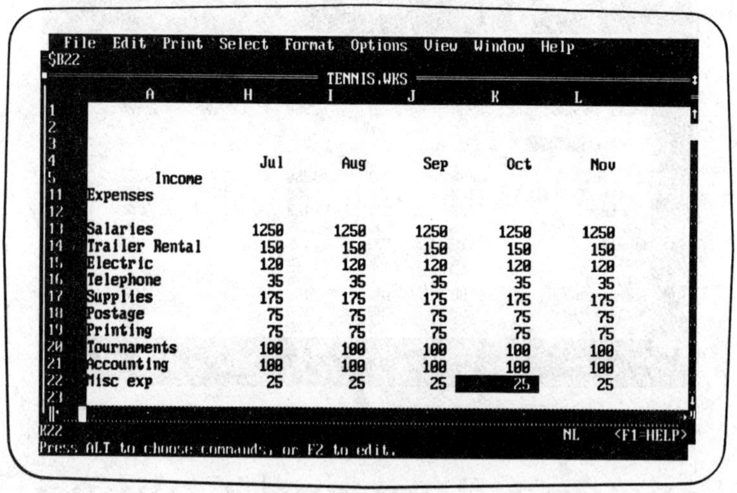

Fig. 6.10.

The Titles frozen.

To eliminate frozen titles and return the spreadsheet display to its original form, press Alt and select Options. The menu now has a selection Unfreeze Titles. Microsoft Works knows that you had previously frozen either columns or rows. Selecting the Unfreeze Titles option returns the display to normal.

Splitting the Screen Display into Several Windows

When you have finished a spreadsheet in terms of the numbers, labels, and formulas, you can begin entering numbers or modifying formulas in order to see the effects of the changes.

One of the problems with spreadsheets is that they are larger than the screen display of the computer. Consequently, when you make changes in the numbers that affect important calculations, you may not be able to see the results without moving the cell selector to the cell with the modified result.

For instance, if you change the entry in cell G6, the `Dues` income for June, the effect on the `Total Income` is displayed in cell G9, but the effect on the `Net Income` is not visible unless you move to cell G26. Seeing both cells at the same time would be better.

Remember that the display is electronic and therefore can be manipulated according to your needs. Microsoft Works allows you to split the screen display into windows; each window can display the same or different areas of a spreadsheet. Think of these displays as window panes overlaid on a single large window, the spreadsheet as a whole.

To see both the `Income` section of the TENNIS spreadsheet and the `Net Income` entry, split the screen into two windows. Move the cell selector to cell B9; press Alt and then select the Window menu (see fig. 6.11).

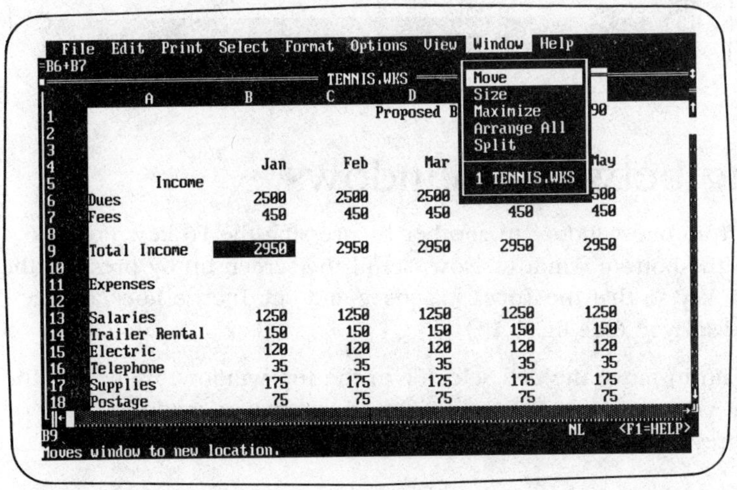

Fig. 6.11.

The Window menu.

The bottom of the menu displays the name of the current window, 1 TENNIS.WKS. Highlight the Split command; at the bottom of the screen, Microsoft Works describes the Split command. The Split command creates the individual window panes to display the different parts of the spreadsheet file.

When you select the Split command, Works responds with two additional double lines on the screen: the vertical line to the left of the A column and the horizontal one just below the name of the spreadsheet file. Pressing the right- or left-arrow key moves the vertical line across the screen. In this case, you want to move the line down from the top of the screen with the down-arrow key to row 10.

The location of the line determines the window border. Press Enter when the line is at row 10 (see fig. 6.12).

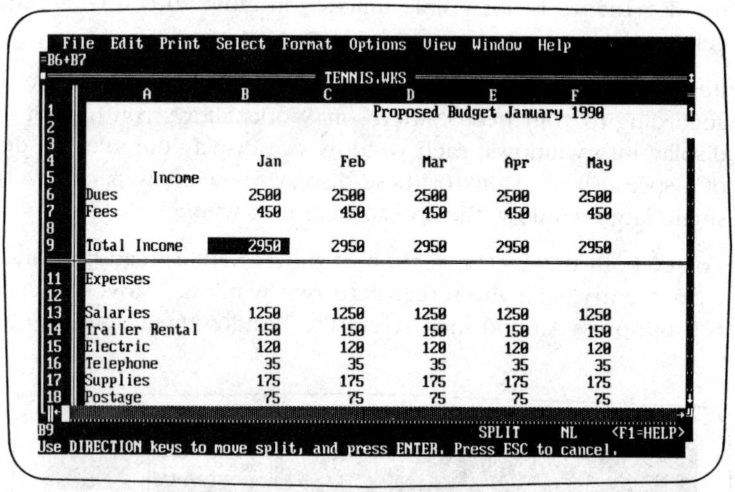

Fig. 6.12.
The horizontal line indicating the new window.

Moving between Windows

You move from one window to another by pressing the F6 key. Press F6 to move to the bottom window. Now, scroll the screen up by pressing the down-arrow key so that the Total Expenses and Net Income lines are the only rows displayed (see fig. 6.13).

Press F6 again to move the cell selector to the top window. By having the screen split, you can easily see the results of any change made in the income figures.

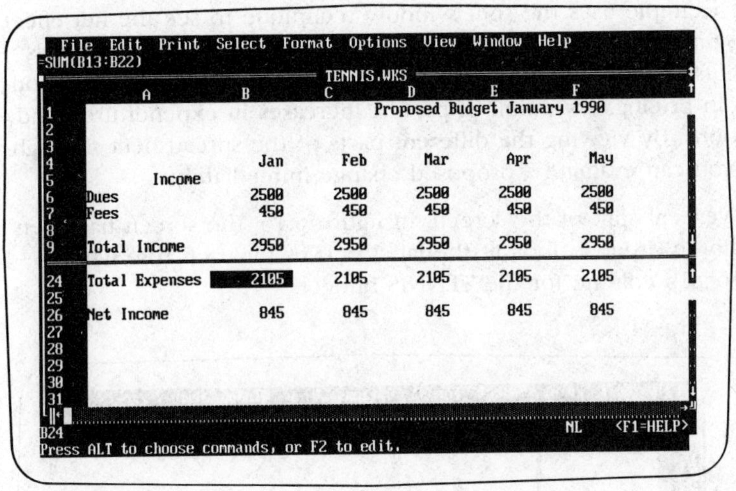

Fig. 6.13.
Total expense and net income displayed.

For example, what effect will a change in the Dues income entered in the month of January have on Net Income? The current January dues income is $2,500 producing a net income of $845 dollars per month. What happens if dues drop off to a total of $1,500 per month? Enter *1500* for Dues in Jan in cell B6.

As you might expect, the picture changes dramatically for the club. Net Income becomes a negative number, −155 (see fig. 6.14).

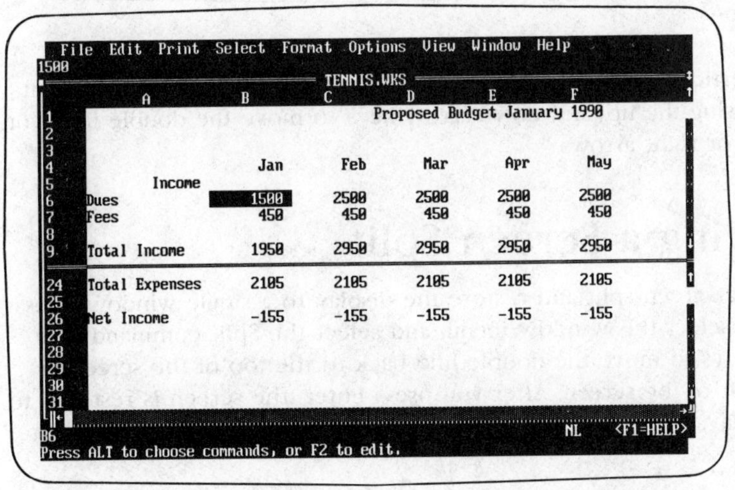

Fig. 6.14.
The new net income.

This simple example uses the split window technique to see the net effect of a change on the income side of the club. In a more complex business situation, the split window allows for simultaneous viewing of information on changes in pricing, allocation of profits, increases in expenditures, and other variations. By viewing the different parts of the spreadsheet through a window, you can evaluate a proposed change immediately.

Consider a vertical split of the screen. In figure 6.15, the screen has been split vertically in order to look at the label entries for each row while creating a `Totals` column for the TENNIS budget.

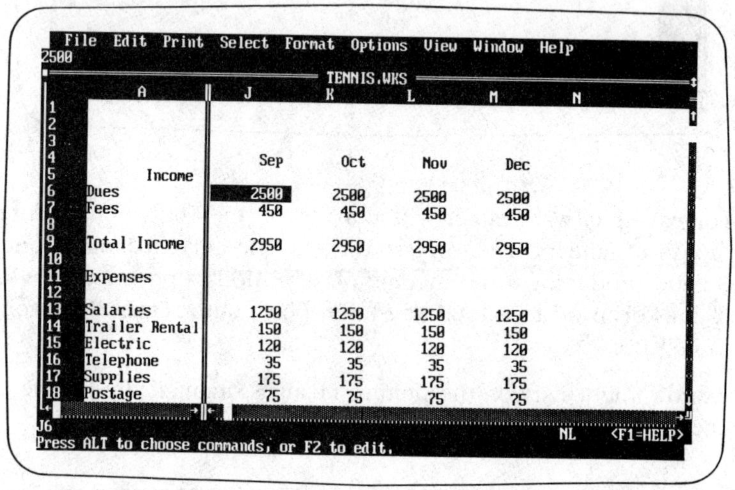

Fig. 6.15.
The vertical screen split.

Making a vertical split is identical to making a horizontal split except that instead of using the up- and down-arrow keys to move the double line, you use the left or right arrows.

Removing a Screen Split

To remove a screen split and restore the display to a single window, press the Alt key, select the Window menu, and select the Split command. Use the arrow keys to move the double line back to the top of the screen or to the far left of the screen. After you press Enter, the screen is restored to normal display.

Using the F5 (GoTo) Function Key

Many times as you are working in a spreadsheet, you need to go back and forth between different cells. If you make a note of which cells you need to travel to, you can speed the journey by using the GoTo key, the F5 function key.

In addition, you can use the Go To function (press Alt, S, and G) to move the cell selector to named ranges of cells. Figure 6.16 shows the Go To dialog box.

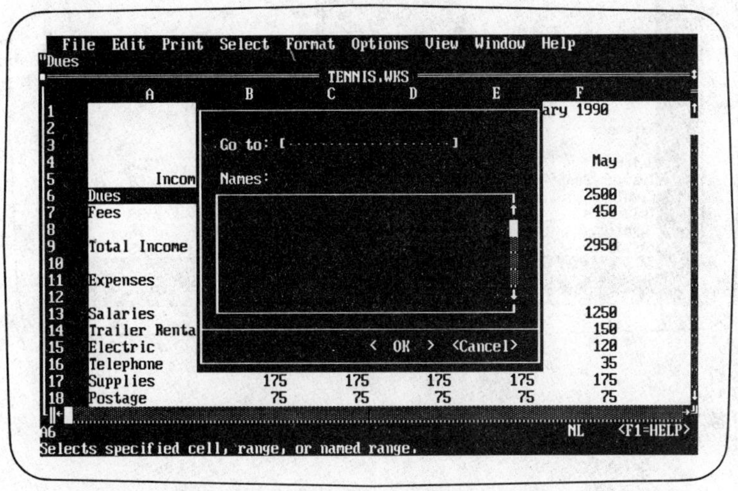

Fig. 6.16.

The Go To dialog box.

To move to another location in your spreadsheet, type the cell address, range, or range name of your destination. Under Names is a box that lists names of ranges already created. Many times you need only to find a specific cell to jump to. Enter the cell address as you enter cell addresses in a formula: A1, B2, and so on. Then press Enter or use the mouse to click OK at the bottom of the dialog box. Immediately, Works closes the window and moves the cell selector to the designated cell address. You can also use the mouse to click and drag the small black box on the right side of the list of names to select the range.

Formatting Cells

To this point in building the TENNIS spreadsheet, no numbers have been formatted to reflect the kinds of values they represent. Microsoft Works displays numbers in a default format called General, plain with no symbols of any kind. Other formats are available on the Format menu (see fig. 6.17). To access this menu, press Alt for the menu bar and T for Format.

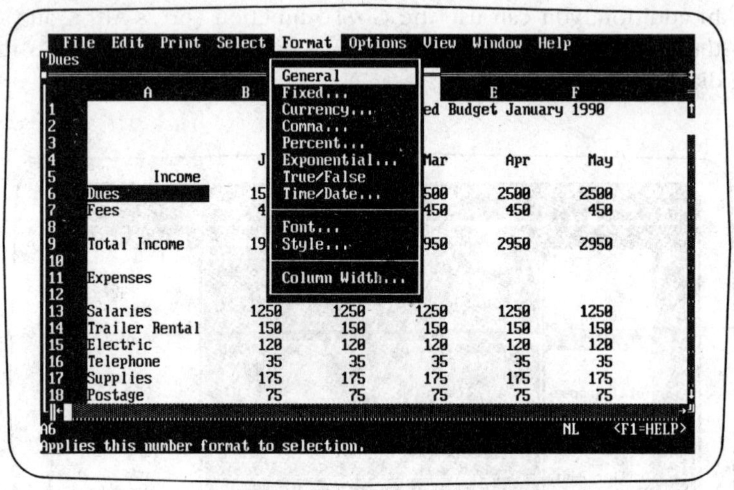

Fig. 6.17.

The Format menu.

The following is a list of the formats and the resulting display:

Format	*Effect*
General	Formats numbers as precisely as possible: 466 or 4.66 or 4.66E+6.
Fixed	Formats numbers to the number of decimal places you specify. If you specify 3 places, a number like 456.7896 becomes 456.790. Any negative numbers are displayed with a leading minus (−) sign.
Currency	Formats numbers to include a leading dollar sign and a comma every three places to the left of the decimal point.
Comma	Formats numbers by separating every three places with a comma. Negative numbers are displayed in parentheses.

Percent	Formats numbers so that they are displayed with a trailing percent sign and the decimal place moved two positions to the right. A number such as .0567 becomes 5.67%.
Exponential	Displays numbers in scientific notation. 9999999 displays as 9.99E+06. An exponent has a range of ±300. Negative numbers are displayed with a leading minus (−) sign.
True/False	Formats cells to display either TRUE or FALSE. All numbers are displayed as TRUE. Cells with zero entries are displayed as FALSE.
Time/Date	Formats cells to display entries as time or date in the format you specify.

Figure 6.18 illustrates the different effects of Format.

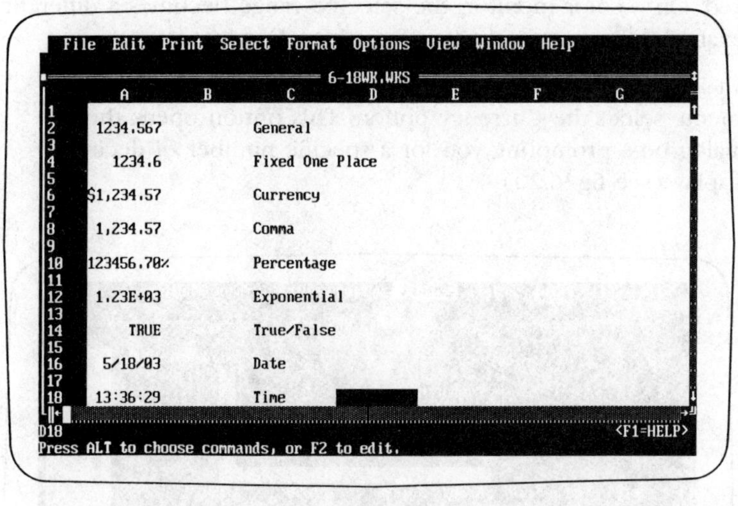

Fig. 6.18.

Effects of formats.

In the TENNIS spreadsheet, the numbers are all formatted as General. A better way to display them is as Currency. To change the format, select the cells that are to be reformatted.

Microsoft Works has a command that selects every cell in the spreadsheet. To select all the cells, press the Alt key and open the Select menu by pressing S. Figure 6.19 shows the Select menu.

From the Select menu, choose the All option. Selecting that command changes the screen display indicating that the entire screen display has

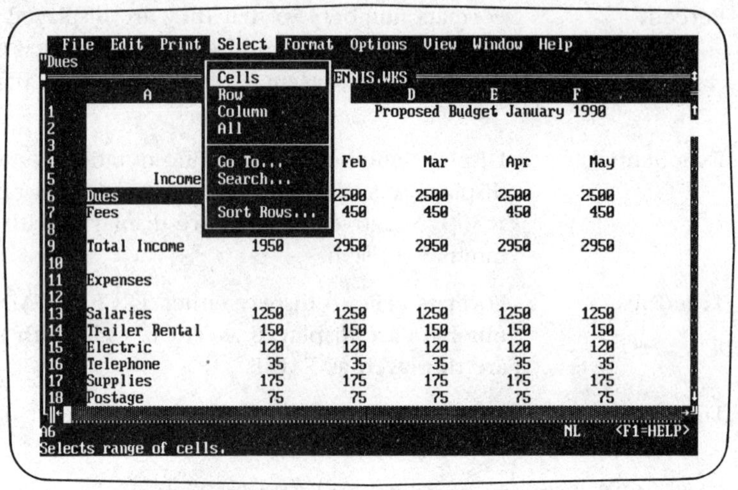

Fig. 6.19.

The Select menu.

been selected. On a color monitor, the selected range becomes a different color; for example, the screen changes from blue to white.

Press the Alt key to activate the menu bar and select the Format menu. From this menu, select the Currency option. This option opens the Currency dialog box, prompting you for a specific number of decimal places to display (see fig. 6.20).

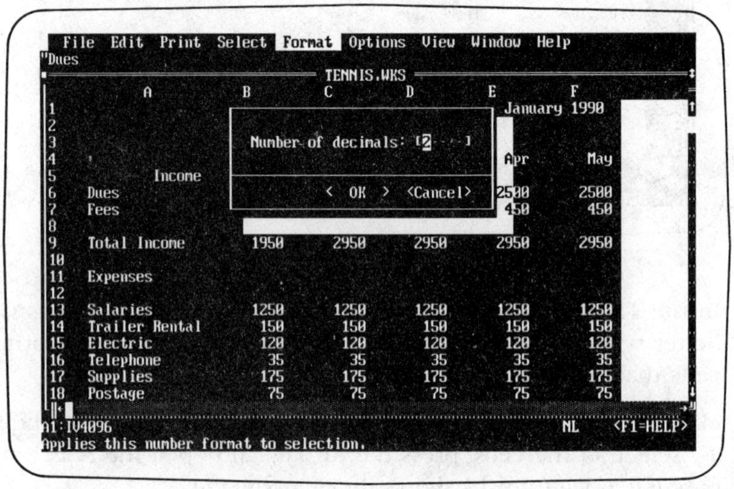

Fig. 6.20.

The Currency dialog box.

In most financial reports, the decimals are not necessary for the sake of precision. Therefore, enter 0 as the number of decimal places and press Enter. The spreadsheet now looks like the one shown in figure 6.21.

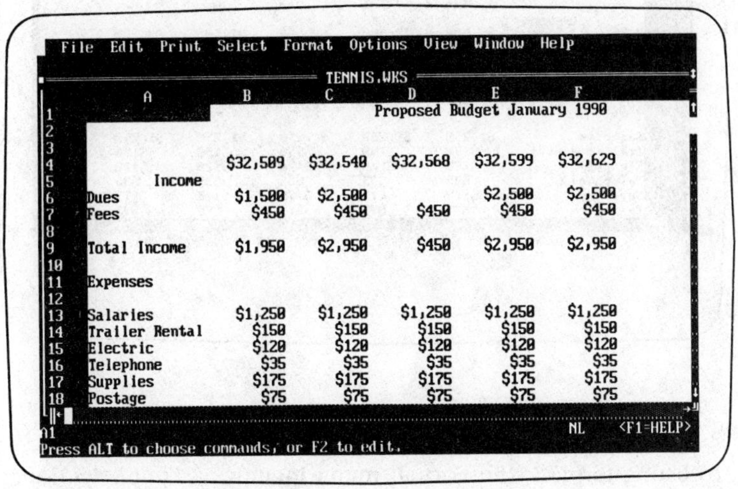

Fig. 6.21.

The TENNIS worksheet formatted for Currency.

A formatting feature that financial spreadsheets often have is a line to separate the income section from the expense section. To add a line, follow these steps:

1. Move the cell selector to cell B10 and type

   "----------

   (a leading quotation mark, followed by 10 hyphens). Press Enter and the B10 cell is filled with a line. (The reason for typing 10 hyphens is that the cell is 10 characters wide.)

2. With the cell selector in cell B10, press and hold the Shift key and press the right-arrow key until cells B10 through M10 are highlighted.

3. Press the Alt key to activate the menu bar, select the Edit menu, and then select the Fill Right command. Press Enter. The line fills cells B10 through M10 (see fig. 6.22).

Another formatting attribute that financial people add to spreadsheets is the double line to indicate the "bottom line" of a spreadsheet. Adding a double underline requires that you enter a series of equal signs in a cell as a label and then fill the cells in which you want a double line, just as you enter the single line.

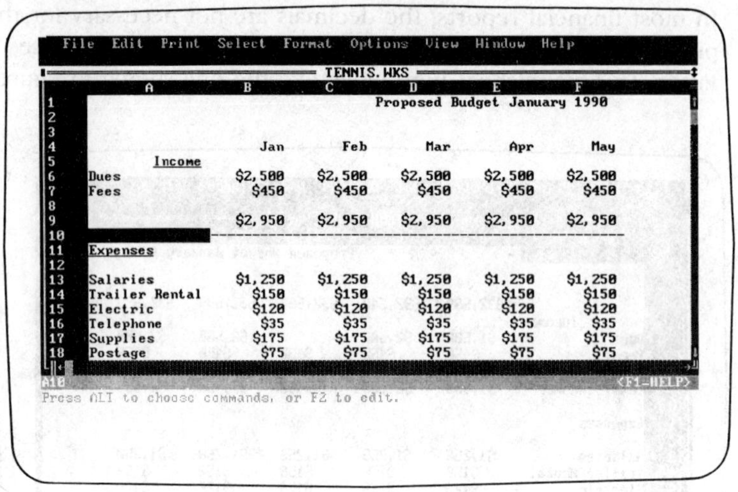

Fig. 6.22.

The income section underlined.

Before going to the next example, save your TENNIS spreadsheet.

In addition to listing formats, the Format menu includes a Font selection. Fonts are type styles that Microsoft Works can send to your printer. Whether your printer can actually print the font is a separate issue. Microsoft Works checks with the type of printer you have installed and displays the types of fonts your printer is capable of printing.

A selected font applies to the entire spreadsheet file. Every character in the spreadsheet is printed with the same font; you cannot print a selected cell or range of cells in a font different from the remainder of the spreadsheet.

Using Range Names

Use range names to simplify spreadsheet work by identifying groups of cells that normally are considered a single unit for use in formulas, copying, or searching. In figure 6.23, you see a spreadsheet that calculates payments for varying mortgage rates. Enter this spreadsheet to work with range names.

To open a new spreadsheet, select the File menu option Create New File. In cell A2, enter the title

HOME LOAN

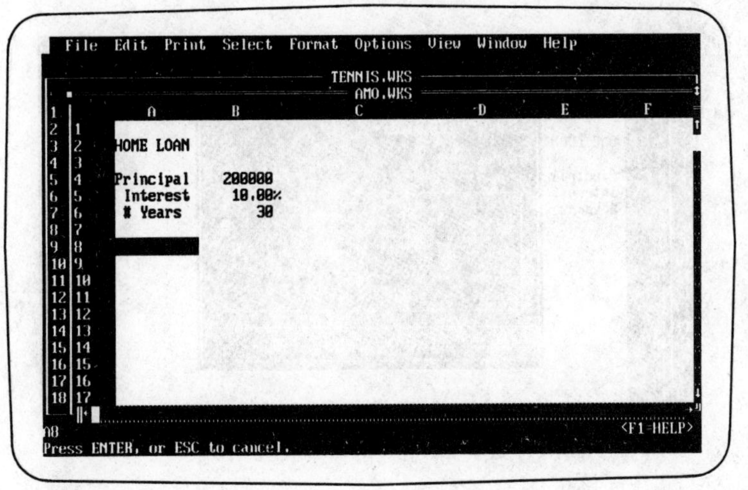

Fig. 6.23. *Sample spreadsheet with named ranges.*

In cell A4, enter the label

Principal

In cell A5, enter the label

Interest

In cell A6, enter the label

\# Years

Across from the labels, enter the values *200000* for `Principal`, *10%* for `Interest`, and *30* for `# Years`. Because Works understands the percent sign following the number 10, the program formats the cell as a percentage.

The next step is to connect the labels with the corresponding values:

1. Move the cell selector to B4.
2. Press the Alt key to activate the menu bar, select the Edit menu, and choose the Range Name command. The Range Name dialog box opens (see fig. 6.24).

Microsoft Works assumes that the range B4 is the range to use. The label `Principal` is the default range name. Press Enter to select (or use the mouse to click) `Create`. Cell B4 is now a named range called `Principal`.

When you use the Range Name command, Microsoft Works assumes that you want to name the range with the text in the cell the cursor is on, the text in the cell directly to the left of the cursor location (as in this case), or the text directly above the cell location. The assumed range name is

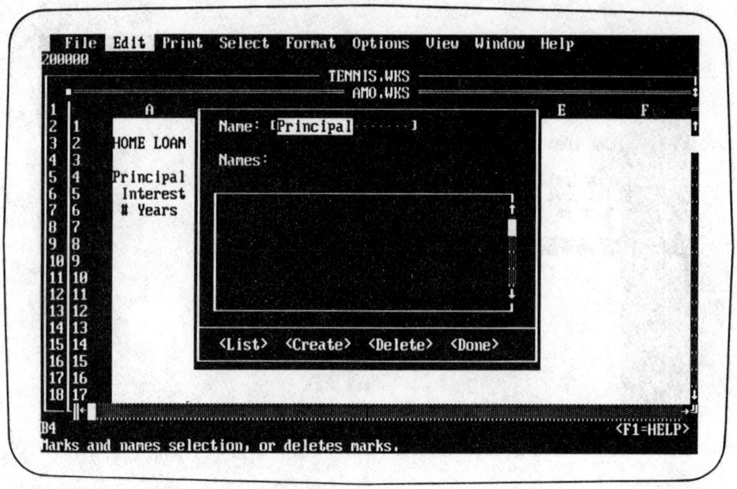

Fig. 6.24.

The Range Name dialog box.

displayed in the Name field of the Range Name dialog box. Pressing Enter or Alt-C finishes the task.

Repeat the procedure with Interest and # Years so that cell B5 is named Interest and cell B6 is named # Years.

With the ranges named, you can use them in a formula. Move the cell selector to cell A8 and begin the formula with the equal sign followed by the function PMT for payment and the opening parenthesis, as follows:

=PMT(

Instead of entering the cell addresses, use the range names to finish the formula:

=PMT(Principal,Interest/12,# Years*12)

Do not leave any spaces between the arguments of the formula and use only commas as separators. The interest is calculated on a monthly basis, thus the division by 12, and the number of years is also figured monthly (30*12=360). If everything is entered correctly, your spreadsheet should resemble figure 6.25.

Any cell, or contiguous group of cells, can be a named range. Later in this chapter, you will treat the entire spreadsheet as a named range in order to simplify printing. The length of any range name cannot exceed 15 characters.

After you have created many range names, a list of those range names may be useful for reference. To list all range names, move the cell selector to

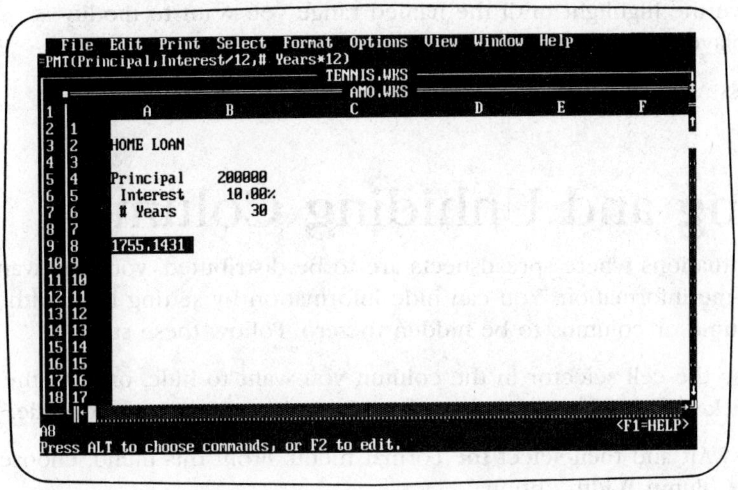

Fig. 6.25.

The loan payment with range names.

any area of the spreadsheet where you want the upper left corner of the list to begin.

Press Alt, select the Edit menu, and then choose the Range Name command. In the dialog box, use the Tab key or the mouse to select the `List` option. Press Enter or click.

The range names are displayed, two cells for each name: one for the name and the second for the cell reference.

To change the name of a range, do the following:

1. Open the Range Name dialog box and press the down-arrow key twice. The first range name listed will appear at the top of the dialog box in the `Name` field.
2. Move the cursor to highlight the range name you want to change.
3. Delete the current range name by pressing Alt-T.
4. Return to the worksheet and repeat the steps to create a range name by moving the cursor either to the left of the text, directly below the text, or in the same cell. Then press Alt, select Edit, and select Range Name.

If you want to change the cell reference for a named range, follow these steps:

1. Select the new range.
2. Press Alt, open the Edit menu, and select Range Name.

3. Move the highlight until the named range you want to modify is displayed in the Name field.

4. Press Alt-C to create the new range.

Hiding and Unhiding Columns

In some situations where spreadsheets are to be distributed, you may want to hide some information. You can hide information by setting the width of the column or columns to be hidden to zero. Follow these steps:

1. Place the cell selector in the column you want to hide, or with the Shift key and the arrow keys, select the columns you want to hide.

2. Press Alt and then select the Format menu. From this menu, choose the Column Width option.

3. In the Width dialog box, type *0* and press Enter.

The columns are now hidden. To redisplay the column, first use the GoTo key, F5, to access the hidden column. When the column address is displayed in the lower left corner of the screen, press Alt and select the Format menu. Then choose the Column Width option and change the width to a normal setting.

Protecting Cell Contents

After working diligently on a spreadsheet, you do not want inadvertently to alter a critical formula and destroy all your work.

You should take two steps to prevent this alteration. First, make a copy of the spreadsheet and save it on a separate disk. Second, lock the critical cells so that neither you nor anyone else can mistakenly ruin the labor.

In the loan amortization example, you should lock the cells with the labels to avoid accidentally erasing the range names. Microsoft Works initially locks all cells of the spreadsheet, but the protection is not activated until you select it from the Options menu.

To lock all the cells in the loan amortization spreadsheet, press the Alt key to activate the menu bar and select Options.

Press P to select the Protect Data command. This command is a toggle; selecting it again turns off the protection. An asterisk precedes the command when it is activated.

All cells in the spreadsheet are now protected. Move the cursor to the label `Principal` and press F2 to attempt to make an edit. Erase a few characters and press Enter. Microsoft Works displays a dialog box, which lets you know that you cannot change locked cells.

Unlocking Cells

Unlocking cells requires that you reverse the process of locking. If you have activated the Protect Data command, all cells in the spreadsheet are locked.

To unlock specific cells in a spreadsheet, do the following:

1. Press the Alt key to activate the menu bar and open the Options menu.

2. Select the Protect Data command. If an asterisk is next to the Protect Data command, select the command again to turn off the locking.

3. In the spreadsheet, select the cell or cells that you want to remain unlocked after you once again turn on the Protect Data command.

4. With the cell or cells selected, press Alt and open the Format menu.

5. From the Format menu, select the Style command. The Style dialog box appears (see fig. 6.26).

6. Press Alt-K to erase the mark in front of the `Locked` option. Press Enter or use the mouse to click `OK`.

7. Press the Alt key and open the Options menu. Select the Protect Data command.

The cells you have selected are unlocked. The remaining cells are again locked.

Tip: Use the `Locked` option to protect the contents of cells vital to correct spreadsheet results.

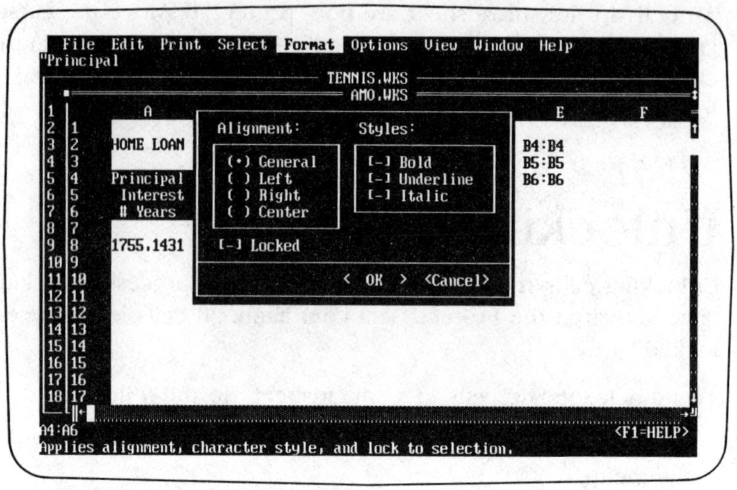

Fig. 6.26.

The Style dialog box.

Entering Date and Time

You have several ways to use date and time entries. They can be used for calculating, time-stamping a spreadsheet, or separating data entered into the spreadsheet by time.

Works accepts time and date in specific formats as described in table 6.1.

Table 6.1
Works Date and Time Formats

Display long format	*Type this*
Month,Day,Year	July 17, 1990
Month,Year	July, 1990
Month,Day	July 17
Month	July
Display short format	*Type this*
Month,Day,Year	07/14/90
Month,Year	07/90
Month,Day	07/14
Time display 24 hour	*Type this*
Hour,Minute,Second	10:15:00
Hour,Minute	10:15
Time display 12 hour	*Type this*
Hour,Minute,Second	3:30:00PM
Hour,Minute	3:30PM
Hour	3PM

If the format you choose is too large for the cell width, Works displays # signs across the cell until you change the width.

The current date and time can be entered with a shortcut. It requires some finger dexterity because you press three or four keys at once. For the current date, press Ctrl-+-; (Ctrl, plus, and semicolon). For the current time, press Ctrl-+-: (Ctrl, plus, and colon).

The time or date is entered based on the computer's internal clock or based on the date and time you entered when starting your computer at the date and time DOS prompts. Unfortunately, these quick entries are not updated when Works performs a recalculation.

To have a continuously updating time or date, you need to enter a formula. One of the functions included with Works is the NOW function.

In the cell where you want a current time or date, type

=NOW()

Works inserts the time or date, depending on how you have formatted the cell with the Format Style Time/Date option. The cell entry is updated to the current time or date as you recalculate the spreadsheet.

Showing the Spreadsheet Formulas

As you build more complex spreadsheets, auditing your formula trails is a good idea. A small error in inserting a formula can lead to gross errors later, as one formula result builds on another. Unfortunately, many spreadsheet users have the tendency to believe whatever the spreadsheet produces. Remember to make every spreadsheet pass the common-sense test. After finishing your work, use the Microsoft Works calculator to test a few crucial numbers.

One method of auditing is to change the spreadsheet display to show only the formulas instead of the results of the calculations. The Show Formulas option on the Options menu reveals the formulas.

Figure 6.27 is the TENNIS spreadsheet with the formulas shown.

The formulas are shown instead of the actual numbers the formulas produce. Of particular interest are the entries in cells B4 and C4. Those cells contain the names of the months, but Works displays values because the month names are serial dates. Works displays the serial value as

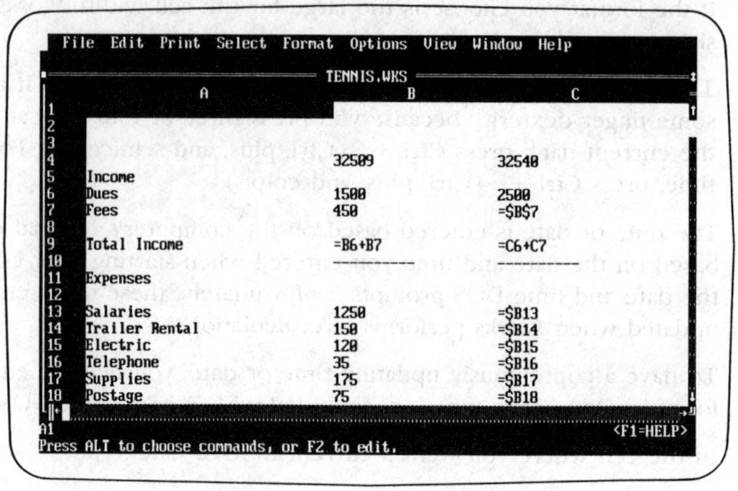

Fig. 6.27.

The TENNIS spreadsheet formulas shown.

opposed to a text entry. Remember, when the names of the months were inserted, the Fill Series command was used to complete the row. If the name of the month had been entered with a specific year included, such as *January 1980*, the entry would have remained a text entry.

Manual versus Automatic Recalculation

Works has the capacity to recalculate automatically whenever a change is made in the spreadsheet. Automatic recalculation can be turned off, however, so that the recalculation is performed as you specify.

To turn off the automatic recalculation, press Alt to activate the menu bar; select the Options menu and choose the Manual Calculation option.

Turning off recalculation can be helpful if your spreadsheet gets so large that a recalculation takes a long time or if you want to make several changes before the recalculation takes place. When in this mode, the CALC message is displayed on the status line.

To recalculate when the automatic recalculation is off, press the F9 function key.

The automatic recalculation is a toggle switch; to turn automatic recalculation back on, repeat the steps used to turn it off.

Sorting the Spreadsheet

In some spreadsheet applications, sorting the entries alphabetically or by numeric value may be useful. The sort function works on selected rows and columns. The sort is performed in ascending order (1, 2, 3... or A, B, C...) or in descending order (9, 8, 7... or Z, Y, X...), as you designate. In ascending order, if the column contains numbers and text, the text comes before the numbers. In descending order, text follows the numbers.

Tip: When sorting, Works adjusts the relative references but not those that are absolute. Use caution whenever formulas are included in the sorted material.

Figure 6.28 shows a spreadsheet used for performing payroll calculations. The first column of the spreadsheet is used to give a unique number to each record. If you forget to make a copy of the spreadsheet before you sort the contents, this column provides a measure of protection and allows you to re-sort the list of names based on the numbers in column A.

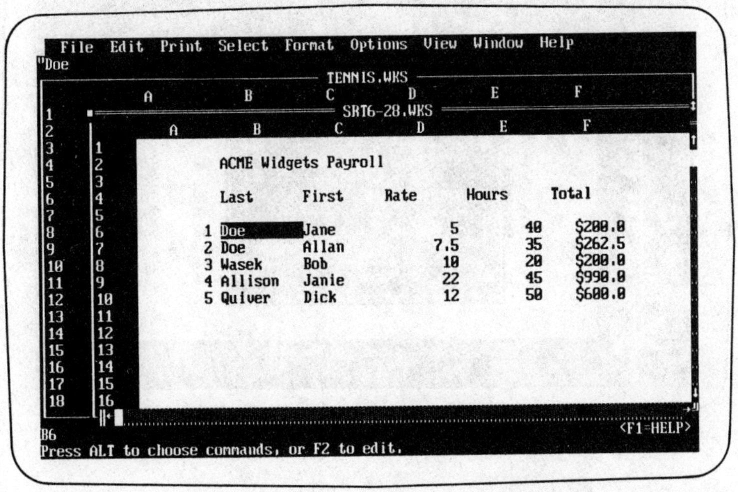

Fig. 6.28. *A payroll spreadsheet.*

You may make a copy of this spreadsheet to follow the examples. The only formula is in column F; the formula is Rate times Hours (D6*E6) copied down.

Tip: Before performing a sort on any spreadsheet, first make a copy of the spreadsheet under a unique name. If you perform a sort and are not happy with the results, you still have a copy that reflects the spreadsheet before the sort.

Because the rates of pay and the number of hours worked vary, even a small payroll can be difficult to sort. The first sort is alphabetical, performed on the last name of the employees.

To perform a sort, do the following:

1. Highlight the `Last` name column with the cell selector.
2. With the Shift and down-arrow keys, highlight the range B6:B10.
3. Press the Alt key to activate the menu bar and open the Select menu. From this menu, choose Sort Rows. The Sort dialog box appears (see fig. 6.29).

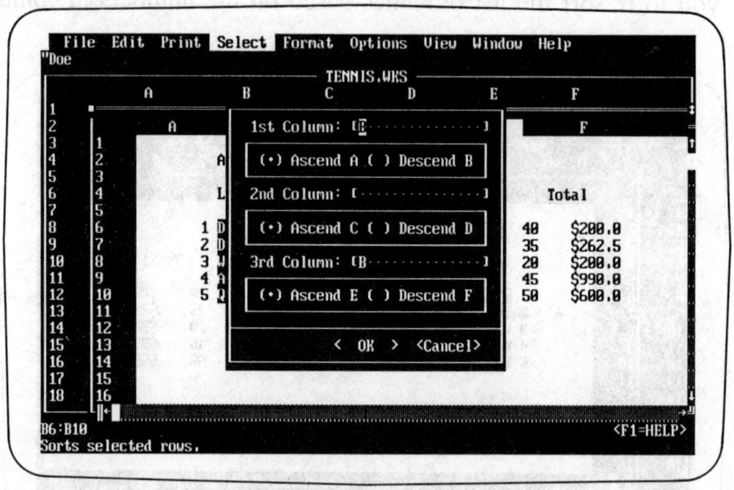

Fig. 6.29.

The Sort dialog box.

The Works sort function allows you to sort on three columns. In the example used here, you have highlighted only a single column of cells—column B as listed in the dialog box. Therefore, the default setting, sorting the first column in ascending order, is adequate for this sort.

Press Enter or click the mouse pointer on the `OK` option. The names are sorted as shown in figure 6.30.

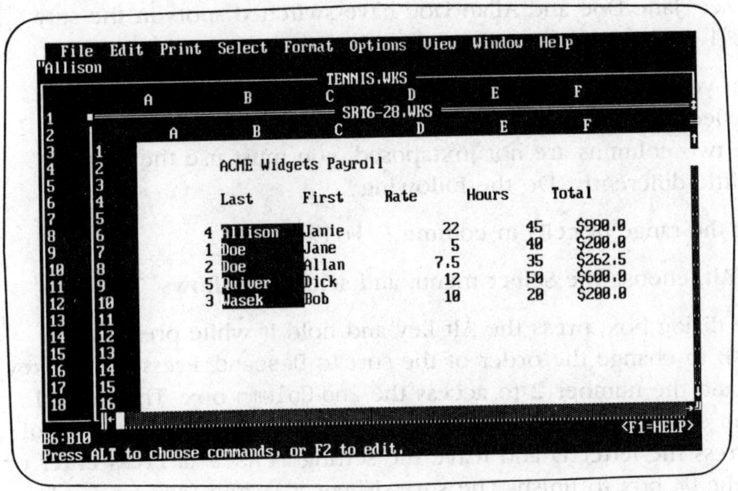

Fig. 6.30.
The payroll sorted by last name.

Add another sort column that requires Works to break a tie. Because records for Jane and Allan Doe have the same last name, you want to sort the `First` name column. Do the following:

1. Select cells B6:C10.
2. Press Alt, choose Select, and then select Sort Rows.
3. The first column to be sorted is column B, as Works shows in the dialog box. Press the Tab key to move the cursor to the `2nd Column` entry. Type the letter *C* as the second column to sort. Press Enter or click the `OK` box (see fig. 6.31).

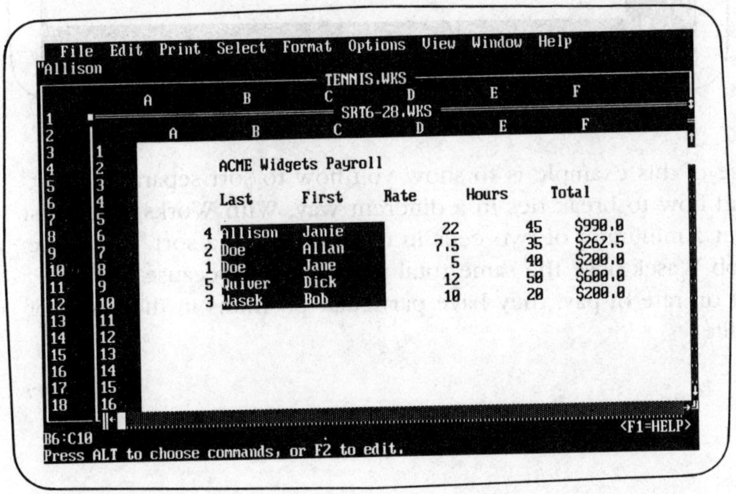

Fig. 6.31.
Two-column sort.

As you can see, Jane Doe and Allan Doe have switched spots in the sort because the *A* in *Allan* comes before the *J* in *Jane*.

Suppose that you want to sort on a descending scale the total dollars earned as reflected in column F and the rate of pay as in column D. Because the two columns are not juxtaposed, you must use the Sort function a little differently. Do the following:

1. Select the range of cells in column F, F6:F10.
2. Press Alt, choose the Select menu, and select Sort Rows.
3. In the dialog box, press the Alt key and hold it while pressing the letter B to change the order of the sort to `Descend`. Press the Alt key again and the number 2 to access the `2nd Column` box. The second column on which to sort is the D column because it has the rate of pay. Press the letter D and leave the setting as `Ascend`. Press Enter or click the `OK` box to finish. The spreadsheet is sorted (see fig. 6.32).

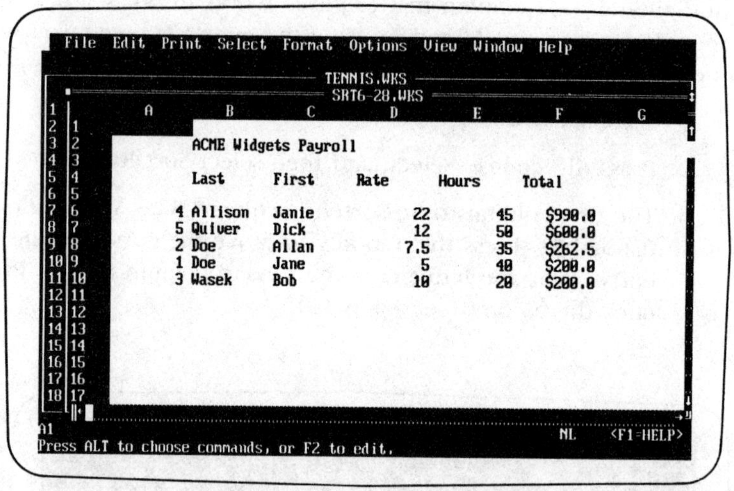

Fig. 6.32.
The `Total` *and* `Rate` *columns sorted.*

The purpose of this example is to show you how to sort separated columns and how to break ties in a different way. With Works, you must always select a minimum of two cells in order to begin a sort. Both Jane Doe and Bob Wasek have the same total earnings, but because of the second sort on rate of pay, they have particular positions in the order of the sorted file.

Searching Cells

In the preceding exercise, you saw how a sort can rearrange your lists of entries into more usable forms.

Suppose that you have several hundred employees or have a formula that is repeated many times in a large spreadsheet. To find a certain employee or a specific formula, use the search technique.

Although the employee database (it is a type of database) is rather small, the search function can be illustrated. If you need to find an employee with the first name of Jane or Janie but don't remember the name exactly, you can use a wild-card search to help.

Press Alt, open the Select menu, and choose the Search option. The dialog box opens (see fig. 6.33).

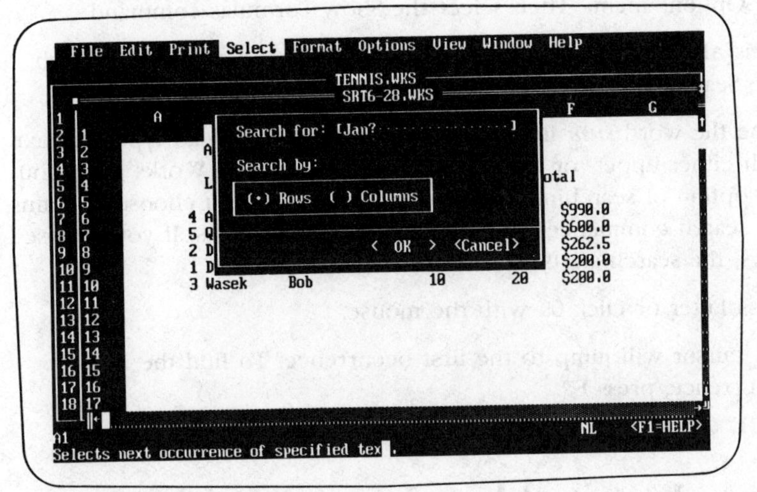

Fig. 6.33.
The Search dialog box.

The entry in the `Search for` blank is

`Jan?`

The question mark acts as the wild card and asks Works to find any entry that begins with the specific letters *Jan* and ends with any other letter.

If you want, you can direct Works to search row by row or column by column, if you believe either would be faster.

Press Enter or click the `OK` box to begin the search. Works stops on the first entry that makes a match, `Jane Doe`. Press the F7 function key, and the cell selector jumps to the next match, `Janie Allison`. If you press F7 again, the cell selector jumps back to the `Jane Doe` entry because Works searches the entire spreadsheet for matches.

The question mark stands for a single character. You can use asterisks to perform a broader search. If you want to find all entries that start with the letter Q, type *Q**.

The search function works just as well for finding formulas. You cannot use operators, such as > or <, but you can use wild cards, such as 5?5 or 6*.

In the TENNIS spreadsheet, many numbers are calculated with the SUM function. Suppose that you want to find all the cells containing this function. Because the SUM function name is contained in formulas, you must format the spreadsheet to show formulas. Do the following:

1. With the TENNIS spreadsheet as the active file, press Alt and choose the Options menu. Then select the Show Formulas command.
2. Press Alt, open the Select menu, and choose the command Search. The Search dialog box opens.
3. Type the word *sum* in the `Search for` field. (You can type the text with either upper- or lowercase letters.) Microsoft Works gives you the option of searching by rows or columns. If you choose columns, the search commences in column A and goes across. If you choose rows, the search starts in row 1 and goes down.
4. Press Enter or click `OK` with the mouse.
5. The cursor will jump to the first occurrence. To find the next occurrence, press F7.

More about Absolute and Relative Entries

In figure 6.34, the TENNIS spreadsheet is displayed with only the entries in columns A and B. You decide that you want to see what each expense is as a percentage of the total expenses. The formula is the individual expense divided by the total. The C column has been formatted to display as percentages with no decimals.

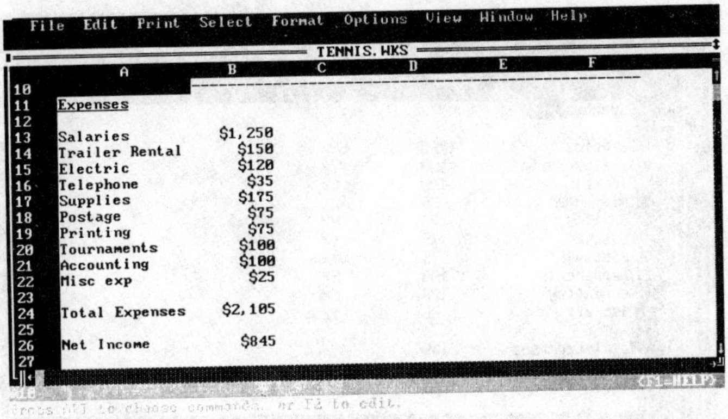

Fig. 6.34.

Column C formatted as percent with zero decimals.

In cell C13. make the following entry:

=B13/B24

Next, copy the formula into the range C14:C22 with the Edit menu's Fill Down command.

Because the formula adjusts relative to its position, and Works cannot divide by blank cells, Works responds with the ERR message, except in cell C15, which displays a value that is wrong because it is dividing by the Net Income number in cell B26.

To fix this problem, adjust the formula to have a divisor that is absolute. Move the cell selector back to C13 and press the F2 (Edit) key. Move the cursor to letter B after the / and type a dollar sign ($). Move the cursor to the 2 and again type a dollar sign. The formula should read

=B13/B24

Press Enter and recopy the formula with the Fill Down command. The correct results are shown in figure 6.35.

Printing a Spreadsheet

Printing the spreadsheet allows you to share your completed spreadsheet with your colleagues. Figure 6.36 shows the Works Print menu. Consider each option before actually printing the spreadsheet.

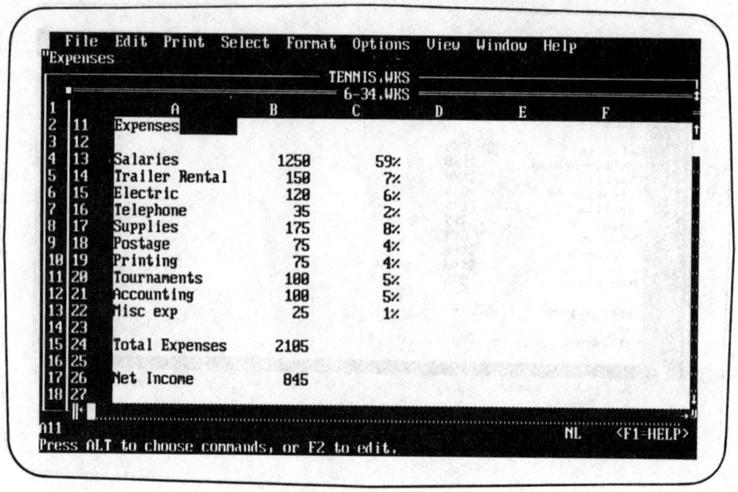

Fig. 6.35.

The percentage expenses.

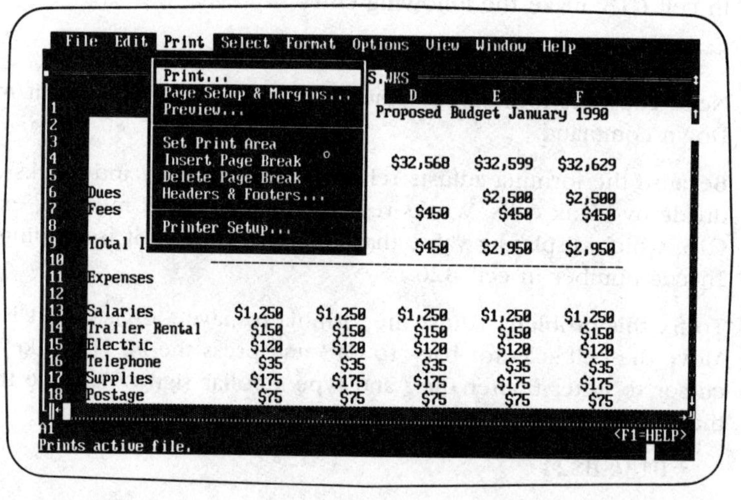

Fig. 6.36.

The Print menu.

The first option is simply to print the active file. If your spreadsheet file is small or needs no formatting, this method is the simplest way to print your file. However, you must consider that your spreadsheet is probably going to be wider than your printer can manage (usually 80 or 132 characters). Therefore, when Works prints the spreadsheet, part of it goes on the first page and the rest is printed on a second page.

When you select the Print option, the Print dialog box opens (see fig. 6.37).

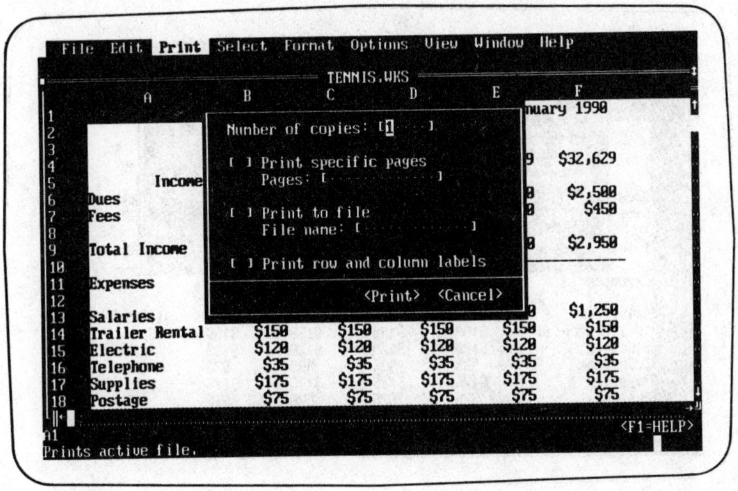

Fig. 6.37.

The Print dialog box.

Works is flexible in its printing capabilities. It allows for multiple copies, prints entire spreadsheets or only specific pages, or prints to a disk file in order to use the file with other applications.

To print only specific pages, enter the page numbers. For example, if your spreadsheet is 10 pages long and you need to print only pages 3, 6, and 8 through 10, you make this entry: 3,6,8:10.

When you separate page numbers with commas, Microsoft Works prints individual pages. When you separate page numbers with colons, Microsoft Works prints pages in sequence; for example, if you enter *8:10*, the program prints pages 8, 9, and 10.

Printing to a file creates a DOS file that can be printed with the DOS print command. Other applications, such as some word processors, can read this file.

With the Print menu's Page Setup & Margins option, you can determine the size of the paper output for Works (see fig. 6.38).

The default Print settings are set for standard 8 1/2-by-11-inch paper. As you add headers or footers, you may want to adjust these settings. For most applications, the defaults work well.

Using Set Print Area, Works prints only the cells you select. Use this option when you need to have hard copy of a small area of the spreadsheet.

After printing a spreadsheet, you may find that it looks better on paper with a page break or with breaks different from the breaks Works has

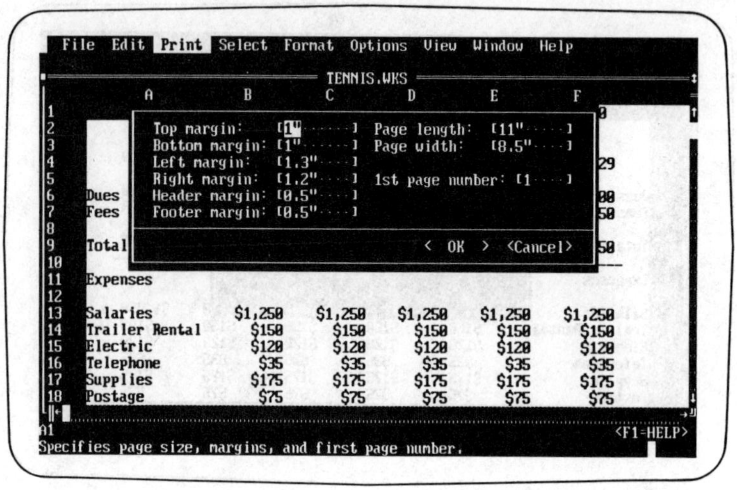

Fig. 6.38.

The Page Setup & Margins dialog box.

selected. Selecting Insert Page Break displays a dialog box that allows you to pick a new page break at a specific row.

The Delete Page Break option deletes any page break you choose.

The Headers & Footers option takes you to the dialog box shown in figure 6.39.

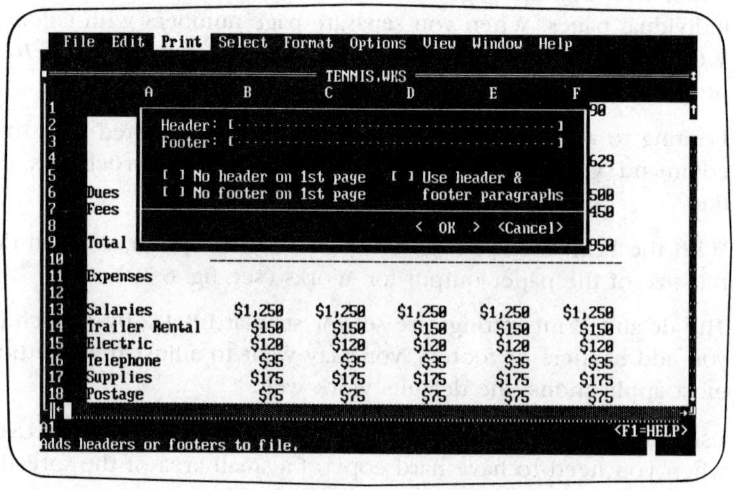

Fig. 6.39.

The Headers & Footers dialog box.

With the Headers & Footers dialog box, you can enter any header or footer you need and also choose whether headers or footers are printed on the first page. You can also use special formatting commands by combining the ampersand with a letter as follows:

Special Formatting	*Command*
Left or right align	&l or &r
Center	&c
Print page number	&p
Print file name	&f
Print the date	&d
Print the time	&t
Print an ampersand	&&

Printer Setup is an important option. Check this dialog box before you begin printing (see fig. 6.40).

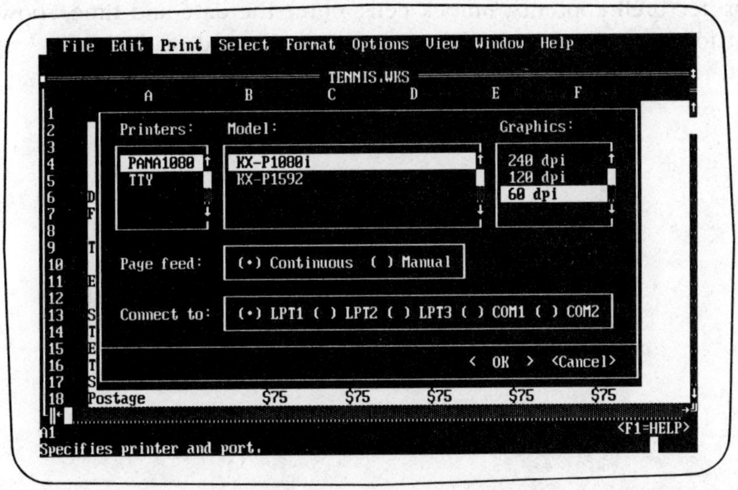

Fig. 6.40. *The Printer Setup dialog box.*

The information in the Printer Setup dialog box depends on what you told Works about your printer when you installed Works. If you described your printer correctly when installing Works, you should have no trouble printing. If you have more than one printer attached to your computer, you can select the second printer from this dialog box.

Because it is difficult to judge where everything will come out on a printed spreadsheet before you actually print your spreadsheet, Works prints on-screen a preview of the pages. This preview gives you the opportunity to add or delete formatting as appropriate.

To see the print preview, press Alt to open the Print menu and select the Preview command. Microsoft Works displays the pages, one at a time, as they will print. If you are using a color monitor, note that the preview pages are displayed in black and white.

Chapter Summary

In this chapter, you examined how to create a fully interactive spreadsheet. Copying cell contents, changing the width of columns, and splitting the screen were examined. You learned how to use the GoTo feature to move to any cell instantly. And you learned about the formatting features, which allow you to display cell contents as you want—in percentage, currency, and other formats. In addition, you examined how you can name cell ranges so that the names can be used in formulas.

You also learned other techniques, such as how to hide and unhide columns, protect cell contents, unlock cells, enter the date and time, show spreadsheet formulas, sort a spreadsheet, search cells, and print a spreadsheet.

7

Using Functions

Microsoft Works contains built-in functions that can be used with the Microsoft Works spreadsheet or database. These functions are abbreviations of longer formulas that would be difficult to use in a spreadsheet or database if they were not already a part of Microsoft Works.

Using Microsoft Works functions in spreadsheet formulas requires that you use the correct format. This is not difficult, but the format is exacting; you will find that if you take care to enter the functions and arguments correctly, you will save yourself from much frustration.

The format of a function is called the *syntax*. The syntax for each function is the same in that the name of the function comes first, followed by a left parenthesis, then one or more arguments separated by commas, and then a right parenthesis. For example, a spreadsheet formula using a function is

=DATE(*Year,Month,Day*)

In the preceding function, the equal sign indicates to Works that a formula is to follow. Next, the name of the function, DATE, appears. Following the name of the function is the left parenthesis and then three arguments: *Year*, *Month*, and *Day*. Then you close the function with the right parenthesis. There are no spaces between the function name, the parentheses, and the arguments.

Each function is reviewed in this chapter. The functions are in alphabetical order by name. Several categories of functions exist:

- ❑ Date and time functions
- ❑ Financial functions
- ❑ Information functions
- ❑ Logical functions

- Lookup functions
- Mathematical functions
- Statistical functions
- Text functions
- Trigonometric functions

Microsoft Works' Built-In Functions

This section examines each function contained in Microsoft Works. An example usage of the function follows the syntax and the usage description. In the explanations of the functions, the word "Returns" denotes the result of using the function.

ABS

Syntax: ABS(*x*)

Usage: Returns the absolute value of *x*.

Example: =ABS(−8) returns 8

ACOS

Syntax: ACOS(*x*)

Usage: Returns the arccosine of *x*, which is the angle whose cosine is *x*. The value of ACOS is returned in radians. *X* must be in the range from −1 through 1. The angle can be between 0 radians (0 degrees) and pi radians (180 degrees).

Example: =ACOS(−.05) returns 2.094 (2pi/3 radians)

ASIN

Syntax: ASIN(*x*)

Usage: Returns the arcsine of *x*, which is the angle whose sine is *x*. The value of ASIN is returned in radians. *X* must range from −1 through 1. The angle ranges from −pi/2 radians (−90 degrees) through pi/2 radians (90 degrees).

Example: =ASIN(−0.5)*180/pi returns −30 (degrees)

ATAN

Syntax: ATAN(*x*)

Usage: Returns the arctangent of *x*, which is the angle whose tangent is *x*. The value of ATAN is returned in radians. The angle ranges from −pi/2 radians (−90 degrees) to pi/2 radians (90 degrees).

Example: =ATAN(1) returns 0.785 (pi/4 radians)

ATAN2

Syntax: ATAN2(*X coordinate,Y coordinate*)

Usage: Returns the arctangent of an angle defined by the X and Y coordinates. The arctangent is the angle, in radians, determined by the point described by the coordinates. The angle ranges from −pi radians (180 degrees) to, but excluding, pi radians (180 degrees). Table 7.1 shows the ATAN2 results with the X and Y coordinates as shown.

Table 7.1
ATAN2 Results with X and Y Coordinates

If X coordinate is	*And Y coordinate is*	*ATAN2 gives angle*
positive	positive	between 0 and pi/2
negative	positive	between pi/2 and pi
negative	negative	between −pi and −pi/2
positive	negative	between −pi/2 and 0

When both X and Y coordinates are 0, ATAN2 returns the error value ERR.

Example: =ATAN2(−1,−1) returns −2.356 (−3pi/4 radians)

AVG

Syntax: AVG(*RangeReference0,RangeReference1,...*)

Usage: Returns the average of the values specified in *RangeReference*. *RangeReference* may be numbers, cell references, or formulas. When using cell references, blank cells are considered 0. When using range references, blank cells are ignored. Text is treated as 0 in all references.

Example: =AVG(B2:F2) returns 88 (values are 97,83,78,85 and 97)

CHOOSE

Syntax: CHOOSE(*Choice,Option0,Option1,...*)

Usage: The CHOOSE function uses *Choice* to select an *Option* from the list. If *Choice* is 0, CHOOSE selects *Option0*; if *Choice* is 1, CHOOSE selects *Option1*, and so on.

If *Choice* is either 0 or greater than the number of options available in the list, CHOOSE returns the error value ERR.

Example: =CHOOSE(A1 – 1,10,20,30) returns 20 (when cell A1 holds the number 2)

COLS

Syntax: COLS(*RangeReference*)

Usage: Returns the number of columns in *RangeReference*.

Example: If the range B2:D5 is named Sales, then

=COLS(Sales) returns 3

COS

Syntax: COS(*x*)

Usage: Returns the cosine of *x*, which is an angle measured in radians.

Example: =COS(1.047) returns 0.5

COUNT

Syntax: COUNT(*RangeReference0,RangeReference1*,...)

Usage: Returns the number of cells contained in *RangeReference*. COUNT adds 1 for every cell that holds a number, formula, text, ERR, and N/A. *RangeReference* can be numbers, cell references, range references, or formulas. When using range references, blank cells are ignored. With cell references, blank cells add 1 to the count.

Example: =COUNT(B2:F2) returns 5

CTERM

Syntax: CTERM(*Rate,FutureValue,PresentValue*)

Usage: Returns the number of compounding periods needed for an investment earning a fixed rate per compounding period to grow from a present value to a future value. *Rate* is the interest rate for a single compounding period.

Example: You have $1,000 in a savings account with an annual rate of 8 3/4 percent. Interest is compounded monthly. How long will it take to double your investment?

=CTERM(8.75%/12,2000,1000) returns 95.41 months (nearly 8 years)

DATE

Syntax: DATE(*Year,Month,Day*)

Usage: Returns a date number for the date specified by *Year*, *Month*, and *Day*. The date number is an integer ranging from 1 to 65534. The integer represents the dates from January 1, 1990, to June 3, 2079.

The value for *Year* must be a number ranging from 0 (1900) to 179 (2079). *Month* ranges from 1 to 12. *Day* ranges from 1 to 31. If you enter a value outside of these ranges, DATE adjusts the value to the correct date. If *Year*, *Month*, and *Day* are not a valid date in the Works range of dates, ERR is returned.

You can use DATE to enter a constant date in a cell by using a formula.

Example: =DATE(60,11,30)

Generally, typing the date directly as 11/30/60 is easier. Use DATE within a larger formula to calculate the number of days between two other dates. It is easier to type the formula ="3/20/89" - "10/20/60".

Example: If cell B5 holds the number of the current quarter (1, 2, 3, or 4) of 1989, then

=DATE(89,B5*3+1,1) returns the date number of the first day of the next quarter

DAY, MONTH, YEAR

Syntax: DAY(*DateNumber*)
MONTH(*DateNumber*)
YEAR(*DateNumber*)

Usage: Returns the day, month, or year of the date specified by *DateNumber*. DAY returns a number from 1 through 31. MONTH returns a number from 1 through 12. YEAR returns a number from 0 through 179.

Date numbers use the integers 1 through 65534 to represent the dates January 1, 1900, through June 3, 2079, with January 1, 1900, being date number 1. June 3, 2079, is date number 65534.

Example: =YEAR('4/15/89') returns YEAR(31882) returns 89

DDB

Syntax: DDB(*Cost,Salvage,Life,Period*)

Usage: Uses a double-declining balance method to find the amount of depreciation in the period specified. *Cost* refers to the amount paid for the asset. *Salvage* is the value of the asset at the end of its working life. *Life* refers to the number of time periods you expect to use the asset. *Life* is usually entered as years. *Period* is the period of time for which you want to find the depreciation.

The formula for computing depreciation for a given period is

$$\frac{\text{Value*2}}{\text{Life}}$$

Example: You buy machinery for $50,000. The life expectancy of the machinery is 10 years. The salvage value is $8,000. The depreciation expense for the seventh year, using the double-declining balance method, is

=DDB(50000,8000,10,7) returns $2,621.44

ERR

Syntax: ERR()

Usage: Returns the error value ERR. Use it to force a cell to display ERR whenever a specified condition exists. Use ERR to find cells whose formulas depend on the erroneous cell.

Example: If B2 contains the number 0, then

=(IF(B2=0,ERR(),B2)) returns ERR

EXP

Syntax: EXP(*x*)

Usage: Returns e to the power of *x*, where e equals 2.71828...., the base number of natural logarithms. Use the exponentiation operator (^) to compute the powers of other bases. EXP is the inverse of LN.

Example: =EXP(1) returns 2.718... (the value of e)

FALSE

Syntax: FALSE()

Usage: Returns the logical value 0 (FALSE). Use FALSE rather than 0 to create more readable logical formulas.

Example: If B2 contains the number 5, then

=IF(B2>10,TRUE(),FALSE()) returns =IF(B2>10,1,0) returns 0

FV

Syntax: FV(*Payment,Rate,Term*)

Usage: Returns the future value of an ordinary annuity of equal payments, earning a fixed interest rate per term, compounded over several terms. Microsoft Works makes the assumption that the first payment occurs at the end of the first period. Works uses the formula that follows to calculate the future value of an ordinary annuity:

$$\frac{\text{Payment}*((1+\text{Rate})\ \text{Term}-1)}{\text{Rate}}$$

Example: You deposit $1,500 into your savings every year for 8 years. The interest rate is 8.75 percent, compounded annually. At the end of 8 years, how much money will be in the account?

=FV(1500,8.75%,8) returns $16,393.61

HLOOKUP, VLOOKUP

Syntax: HLOOKUP(*LookupValue,RangeReference,RowNumber*)
VLOOKUP(*LookupValue,RangeReference,ColumnNumber*)

Usage: These two functions find an entry in a table. HLOOKUP searches the top row of the specified *RangeReference* until it finds the number that matches *LookupValue*. It then goes down the column the number of rows specified in *RowNumber* to find the entry.

Arrange the numbers in the top row in ascending order. Works searches the top row for the largest number that is less than or equal to the *LookupValue*.

VLOOKUP searches the leftmost column in *RangeReference* until it finds the number that matches *LookupValue*. VLOOKUP then goes to the right the number of columns in *ColumnNumber* to get the entry. Arrange the numbers in the left column in ascending order. Works searches the left column for the largest number that is less than or equal to *LookupValue*.

You will get an error value ERR if *ColumnNumber* or *RowNumber* is negative, or is greater than or equal to the number of rows or columns in a *RangeReference*.

Example: =HLOOKUP(1986.5,C5:G8,0) returns 1986 (cell D5)

HOUR, MINUTE, SECOND

Syntax: HOUR(*TimeNumber*)
MINUTE(*TimeNumber*)
SECOND(*TimeNumber*)

Usage: Returns the number for the hour, minute, or second, respectively, of the time represented by *TimeNumber*. HOUR returns an integer from 0 through 23. MINUTE and SECOND return integers ranging from 0 through 59. *TimeNumber* ranges from 0 through 0.999 to represent the times 12:00 a.m. through 11:59:59 p.m.

Example: =MINUTE('16:48:30') returns MINUTE(0.70035) returns 48

IF

Syntax: IF(*Condition,ValueIfTrue,ValueIfFalse*)

Usage: Determines whether *Condition* is true or false and then returns either *ValueIfTrue* or *ValueIfFalse*.

Example: If A1 holds the number 20, then

=IF(A1>10,B1,C1) returns the value in B1

INDEX

Syntax: INDEX(*RangeReference,Column,Row*)

Usage: Returns the value in a cell in *RangeReference* at the intersection of the specified *Column* and *Row*.

If either *Column* or *Row* is negative, or is greater than or equal to the number of rows or columns in *RangeReference*, Works returns the error value ERR.

INT

Syntax: INT(*x*)

Usage: Returns the integer part of *x*. INT deletes the digits to the right of the decimal point with no rounding. (Use ROUND to round *x* to the nearest integer.)

Example: =INT(7.9) returns 7

IRR

Syntax: IRR(*Guess,RangeReference*)

Usage: Returns the internal rate of return for the cash flow series in *RangeReference*. The internal rate of return is the interest rate that gives the cash flow series a net present value of 0.

This function uses an iterative technique that can have more than one solution. IRR gives the error value ERR if the computations do not converge to within 0.0000001 after 20 iterations.

Enter a *Guess* to tell IRR where to begin. Enter a different *Guess* if Works is unable to determine the IRR. Normally a starting value between 0 and 1 yields a meaningful result.

Example: You have an investment represented by cash flow numbers: (7,000), 2,000, 2,000, 2,000, (3,000), 2,000, 6,000. It should yield about 10 percent. What is the internal rate of return?

=IRR(10%,A1:G1) returns 12.32%

ISERR

Syntax: ISERR(*x*)

Usage: Returns the logical value 1 (TRUE) if *x* is the error value ERR; otherwise, it returns the logical value 0 (FALSE). Use ISERR to test for errors in a spreadsheet. You can use ISERR to prevent errors from flowing to other related cells.

Example: If A1 contains the error value ERR,

=IF(ISERR(A1),2,1) returns 2

ISNA

Syntax: ISNA(*x*)

Usage: Returns the logical value 1 (TRUE) if *x* is the value N/A. If *x* is not the value N/A, then the logical value 0 (FALSE) is returned. Use ISNA to test for N/A values in the spreadsheet. Like ISERR, you can use ISNA to prevent N/A values from flowing to other cells.

Example: If A1 contains the value N/A, then

=ISNA(A1) returns 1

LN

Syntax: LN(*x*)

Usage: Returns the natural logarithm of *x*, which uses the mathematical constant e, 2.71828..., as a base. The value for *x* must be a positive integer.

Example: =LN(2.7182818) returns LN(EXP(1)) returns 1

LOG

Syntax: LOG(*x*)

Usage: Returns the base 10 logarithm of *x*, which must be a positive integer. The inverse of LOG is exponentiation.

Example: =LOG(10) returns 1

MAX

Syntax: MAX(*RangeReference0,RangeReference1,...*)

Usage: Returns the largest number contained in *RangeReference*. The *RangeReference* may be numbers, cell references, range references, or formulas. In cell references, blank cells are treated as 0. In range references, blank cells are ignored. In each type of reference, text is treated as 0.

Example: With values of 97, 95, 83, 70, and 97 in cells B2 through F2,

=MAX(B2:F2) returns 97

MIN

Syntax: MIN(*RangeReference0*,*RangeReference1*,...)

Usage: Returns the smallest number contained in *RangeReference*. The *RangeReference* may be numbers, cell references, range references, or formulas. In cell references, blank cells are treated as 0. In range references, blank cells are ignored. In each type of reference, text is treated as 0.

Example: With values of 97, 95, 83, 70, and 97 in cells B2 through F2, and 1000 in cell G2,

=MIN(B2:F2,G2,70) returns 70

MINUTE

Syntax: MINUTE(*TimeNumber*)

Usage: Returns the number for the minute represented by *TimeNumber*, an integer ranging from 0 through 59. *TimeNumber* ranges from 0 through 0.999 to represent the times 12:00 a.m. through 11:59:59 p.m.

Example: =MINUTE('16:48:30') returns MINUTE(0.70035) returns 48

MOD

Syntax: MOD(*Numerator*,*Denominator*)

Usage: Returns the remainder (modulus) of

$$\frac{\text{Numerator}}{\text{Denominator}}$$

The remainder or modulus has the same sign as *Numerator*. MOD returns an ERR value if *Denominator* is equal to 0.

Example: =MOD(−3,−2) returns −1

MONTH

Syntax: MONTH(*DateNumber*)

Usage: Returns the number, in the range of 1-12, for the month represented by *DateNumber*.

DateNumber uses the integers 1 through 65534 to represent the dates January 1, 1900, through June 3, 2079, with January 1, 1900, being date number 1. June 3, 2079, is date number 65534.

Example: =MONTH(31882) returns 4. 31882 is the *DateNumber* for April 15, 1989.

NA

Syntax: NA()

Usage: Returns the numeric value of N/A. Use NA() to indicate that information is not available.

Example: If A1 holds the number 0, then

=IF(A1=0,NA(),A1) returns N/A

NOW

Syntax: NOW()

Usage: Returns the date and time number for the current date and time. At every recalculation, this value is updated. The integer portion of NOW() is the date number, and the decimal fraction is the time number. The decimal portion is not displayed unless the cell format is changed from general to fixed, two decimal places.

Use the Format menu's Time/Date command to display the actual date or time.

Example: If the current date and time is 4:48:00 p.m. on April 15, 1989, then

=NOW() returns 32613

NPV

Syntax: NPV(*Rate,RangeReference*)

Usage: Returns the net present value of a series of cash flow payments, represented by numbers in *RangeReference*, discounted at a fixed *Rate* per period.

For *Rate*, insert the interest rate you want to use to discount each period. If you have a 12 percent annual interest rate but want to discount on a monthly basis, divide the annual interest rate by 12 to find the monthly rate; for a 12 percent annual interest rate, the monthly rate would be 1 percent.

RangeReference is the reference of a single cell or part of a single row or column. It cannot be a range that holds more than one row or column.

Works assumes that payments occur at the end of periods of equal length. To find the net present value of a cash flow series whose first payment occurs at the beginning of the periods, you must add the amount of the first payment to the net present value of the payments that follow. Works uses the following formula to calculate net present value:

$$NPV = \sum_{i=1}^{N} \frac{Payment[i]}{(1+Rate)i}$$

Example: You are looking into a rental contract that promises a 10 percent yield with monthly payments at the end of the month for the subsequent five months. Cells B2:F2 contain the expected monthly payments ($500, $1,500, $3,000, $4,000, and $5,000). The value for the investment is entered in B1 as $8,000. Calculate how much you should pay for the investment:

=NPV(10%,B2:F2)−B1 returns $2,763,30

PI

Syntax: PI()

Usage: Returns the number 3.14159..., which is an approximation of the mathematical constant pi.

Example: =COS(60*PI()/180) returns 0.5 (cosine of 60 degrees)

PMT

Syntax: PMT(*Principal,Rate,Term*)

Usage: Returns the periodic payment for a loan or an investment of *Principal* based on a fixed interest *Rate* for each compounding period over a given *Term*. Works assumes that payments occur at the end of equal periods.

Specify the interest rate in *Rate* for the compounding period. Works uses this formula to calculate the periodic payment:

$$\frac{Present\ Value*Rate}{(1-(1+Rate)-Term)}$$

Example: You decide to buy a car requiring a loan for $12,000, at 9 percent interest per year. What would your payments be if you decided to pay the loan with 24 monthly installments?

=PMT(12000,9%/12,24) returns $548.22

PV

Syntax: PV(*Payment,Rate,Term*)

Usage: Returns the present value of an ordinary annuity of equal *Payments*, earning a fixed interest *Rate* per period, over the *Term* of several periods.

Works assumes that the first payment is paid at the end of the first period. The following formula is used for calculating the present value of an ordinary annuity:

$$\text{PV} = \frac{\text{Payment}*(1-(1+\text{Rate})-\text{Term})}{\text{Rate}}$$

Example: You learn that you are to inherit some money from your uncle. You will be paid $1,500 at the end of each year for the next 10 years. You estimate the annual inflation rate over the next 10 years will be 9 percent. The value of this inheritance in today's dollars is

=PV(1500,9%,10) returns $9,626.49

RAND

Syntax: RAND()

Usage: Returns a random number from 0 up to but not including 1. A random number is generated every time the spreadsheet is recalculated.

Example: =RAND()*10+1 returns a random number between 1 and 11, but not including 11

RATE

Syntax: RATE(*FutureValue,PresentValue,Term*)

Usage: Returns the fixed interest rate per compounding period needed for an investment of *PresentValue* to grow to a *FutureValue* over several compounding periods or *Terms*. Use the following formula to calculate the rate:

$$\text{RATE} = \frac{\text{FutureValue 1/Term}}{\text{PresentValue}} - 1$$

Example: You are operating a limited partnership that intends to purchase an apartment building for $750,000. You intend to sell it for $1,500,000 after 6 years. The annual rate of return for this investment is

=RATE(1500000,750000,6) returns 12.25%

ROUND

Syntax: ROUND(*x*,*NumberOfPlaces*)

Usage: Rounds *x* to the specified number of places either to the left or right of the decimal point. Insert a positive *NumberOfPlaces*, and the number is rounded that many places to the right of the decimal point. Inserting 0 in *NumberOfPlaces* forces *x* to be rounded to the nearest integer. A negative *NumberOfPlaces* rounds *x* the number of places to the left of the decimal point. *NumberOfPlaces* can range from −14 to 14.

Example: =ROUND(2.149,1) returns 2.1

ROWS

Syntax: ROWS(*RangeReference*)

Usage: Returns the number of rows in *RangeReference.*

Example: If the range B3:D6 is named Table, then

=ROWS(Table) returns 4

SECOND

Syntax: SECOND(*TimeNumber*)

Usage: Returns the number for the second represented by *TimeNumber*, an integer ranging from 0 through 59. *TimeNumber* ranges from 0 through 0.999 to represent the times 12:00 a.m. through 11:59:59 p.m.

Example: =SECOND('16:48:30') returns SECOND(0.70035) returns 48

SIN

Syntax: SIN(*x*)

Usage: Returns the sine of *x*, which is an angle measured in radians.

Example: =SIN(1.047) returns 0.866

SLN

Syntax: SLN(*Cost*,*Salvage*,*Life*)

Usage: Finds the amount of depreciation in one period using the straight-line depreciation method. Insert the amount you paid for the asset in *Cost.* Insert the amount you expect to obtain when you sell the asset at the end of its life span for *Salvage.* Insert the number of periods you expect to use the asset (usually measured in years) for *Life.* SLN uses this formula to compute depreciation for the specified period:

$$\text{SLN} = \frac{\text{Cost} - \text{Salvage}}{\text{Life}}$$

Example: You buy machinery for $50,000. The machinery should last 10 years, after which you think you can get $8,000 for it. The depreciation expense per year using the straight-line method is

=SLN(50000,8000,10) returns $4200

SQRT

Syntax: SQRT(*x*)

Usage: Returns the square root of *x*. Works returns the error value ERR if *x* is negative.

Example: =SQRT(25) returns 5

STD

Syntax: STD(*RangeReference0,RangeReference1,...*)

Usage: Returns the population standard deviation of *RangeReference*. The values in *RangeReference* may be numbers, cell references, or formulas. Blank cells are ignored in range references. Blank cells are treated as 0 in cell references. Text is treated as 0 in any of the references.

The standard deviation of a sample of the population is given by the following formula:

STD(*RangeReferences*)*SQRT(COUNT(*RangeReferences*)/(COUNT (*RangeReferences*) − 1))

Example: =STD(B2:F2) returns 8.43

SUM

Syntax: SUM(*RangeReference0,RangeReference1,...*)

Usage: Returns the total of all values in *RangeReference*. The values in *RangeReference* may be numbers, cell references, or formulas. Blank cells are ignored in range references. Blank cells are treated as 0 in cell references.

Example: =SUM(B2:F2) returns 355

SYD

Syntax: SYD(*Cost,Salvage,Life,Period*)

Usage: Finds the amount of depreciation for a specific period, using the sum-of-the-years-digits method. The amount you paid for the asset is the *Cost*. The amount you expect to get when you sell the asset at the end of its life is *Salvage*. The number of periods, usually measured in years, you expect to use the asset is the *Life*. The period for which you want to find the depreciation is the *Period*.

The formula that follows shows the computation of SYD for a specified period:

$$\text{SYD} = \frac{(\text{Cost} - \text{Salvage})*(\text{Life} - \text{Period} + 1)}{\text{Life}*(\text{Life} + 1)/2}$$

Example: You buy machinery for $50,000. The machinery should last 10 years, after which you will sell it for $8,000. The depreciation expense for the seventh year using SYD is

=SYD(50000,8000,10,7) returns $3,054.55

TAN

Syntax: TAN(*x*)

Usage: Returns the tangent of *x*, which is an angle measured in radians.

Example: =TAN(0,785) returns 1

TERM

Syntax: TERM(*Payment,Rate,FutureValue*)

Usage: Returns the number of compounding periods necessary for a series of equal *Payments*, earning a fixed interest *Rate* per period, which should grow to a *FutureValue*. Use the following formula to calculate the future value of an ordinary annuity:

$$\text{TERM} = \frac{\text{FutureValue*Rate LN}(1 + (\text{Payment}))}{\text{LN}(1 + \text{Rate})]}$$

(when *Rate* is not equal to 0)

$$\text{TERM} = \frac{\text{FutureValue}}{\text{Payment}}$$

(when *Rate* is equal to 0)

Example: Each month you add $200 to a savings account with an 8 3/4 percent interest rate, compounded monthly. How long will it take before you have $5,000?

=TERM(200,8.75%/12,5000) returns 23.05 months

TIME

Syntax: TIME(*Hour,Minute,Second*)

Usage: Returns a time number for the time specified by *Hour*, *Minute*, and *Second*. The time number is a fraction ranging from 0.0 through 0.999, which represents time from 0:00:00 or 12:00:00 p.m. through 23:59:59 or 11:59:59 p.m.

Hour is a number ranging from 0 through 23. *Minute* and *Second* are numbers ranging from 0 through 59. If either *Minute* or *Second* is outside the specified range of 0 through 59, TIME adjusts the number to the correct time.

Example: =TIME(16,48,0) returns 0.7 (time number of 4:48:00 p.m.)

TRUE

Syntax: TRUE()

Usage: Returns the logical value 1 (TRUE). Use TRUE() rather than 1 to create more readable logical formulas.

Example: If A1 holds the number 20, then

=IF(A1>10,TRUE(),FALSE()) returns =IF(A1>10,1,0) returns 1

VAR

Syntax: VAR(*RangeReference0*,*RangeReference1*,...)

Usage: Calculates the variance in the numbers in *RangeReference*. *RangeReference* may be numbers, range references, cell references, or formulas. Blank cells are ignored in range references. Blank cells are treated as 0 in cell references. Text is always treated as 0. Use the following formula to calculate the variance of the population:

VAR(*RangeReferences*)*COUNT(*RangeReferences*)/(COUNT(*RangeReferences*) − 1)

Example: =VAR(B2:F2) returns 71.18

YEAR

Syntax: YEAR(*DateNumber*)

Usage: Number of the year represented by *DateNumber*, a number from 0 through 179.

DateNumber uses the integers 1 through 65534 to represent the dates January 1, 1900, through June 3, 2079, with January 1, 1900, being date number 1. June 3, 2079, is date number 65534.

Example: =YEAR('4/15/89') returns YEAR(31882) returns 89

Chapter Summary

In this chapter, you examined the built-in functions of Works. These functions make constructing complex formulas easy. The key to using functions is to use the correct syntax; without the correct order, Works cannot calculate an answer.

In the next chapter, the charting tool of Works is examined. If you have a well-constructed chart, even the most arcane numbers can be deciphered easily.

8

Creating Charts

You can do a terrific job of manipulating and analyzing numeric information when you use a spreadsheet. A spreadsheet's flexibility makes it easy for you to compare hundreds of variables for a particular situation. But many people have trouble correlating black-and-white numbers on a piece of paper with their implications for a real-life situation. For this reason, the idea of charting information was developed. With a chart, relationships are more easily grasped because numbers are represented by forms rather than abstract figures.

Works has the capacity to create many kinds of charts to illustrate the information contained in your spreadsheets. You have probably seen many of the types of charts Works can create: line, bar, stacked bar, combination, hi-lo-close, and pie.

This chapter presents the information you need to create series charts and pie charts from the data in your spreadsheets. You will learn how to define a chart and how to specify the data to be used in that chart. The many enhancements that can be added to a chart, such as horizontal and vertical lines, chart titles, and legends, also are explained. You will learn how to print and plot charts; how to save chart definitions with the spreadsheet; and how to duplicate, modify, or erase chart definitions. An error-finding section is also included.

Learning the Basic Chart Types

Before you learn how to create and work with charts, take a look at the many types of charts available with Works.

Bar Chart

A *bar chart* shows differences between categories of data. Such a chart is useful for comparing values at particular points in time. Figure 8.1 shows the seasonal sales variation of two products.

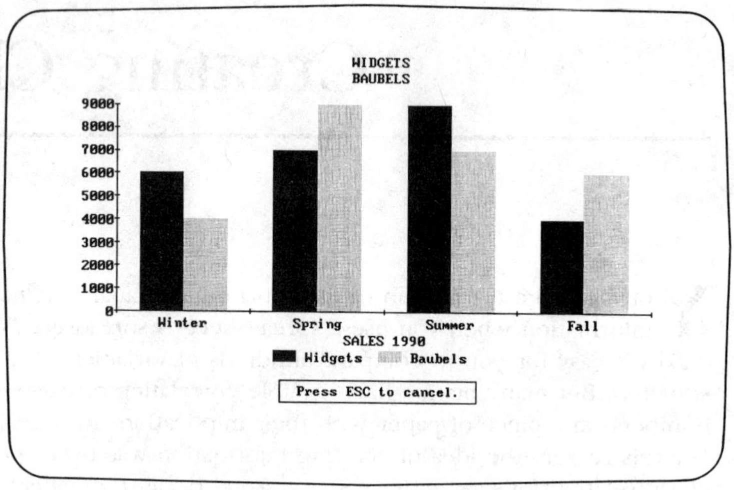

Fig. 8.1.

A bar chart.

Stacked Bar Chart

A *stacked bar chart* shows the relative value of a series of numbers as they contribute to a whole. In figure 8.2, the sales of three products are stacked to show their relative contributions to the total sales.

100% Bar Chart

Displaying data as a portion of a 100% bar is another means of displaying separate contributions to a whole. In figure 8.3, the same sales numbers used in figure 8.2 are used in this type of chart.

Line Chart

The most common chart used in business is the *line chart*. This chart does an excellent job of reflecting trends over time. Figure 8.4 depicts a series of sales figures over time.

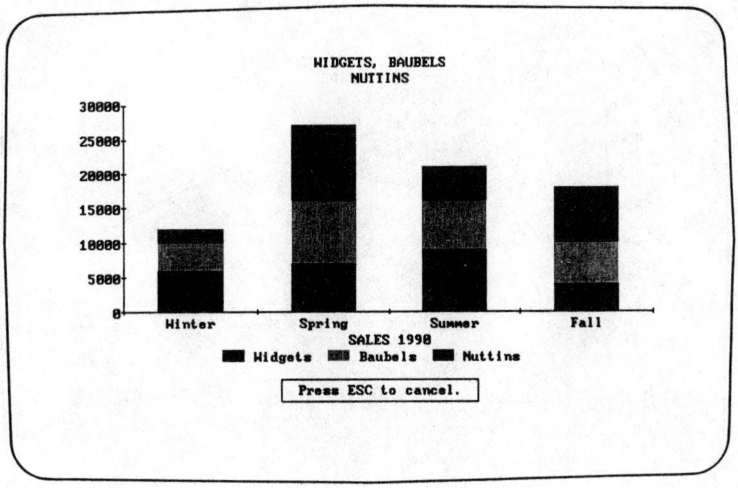

Fig. 8.2.

A stacked bar chart.

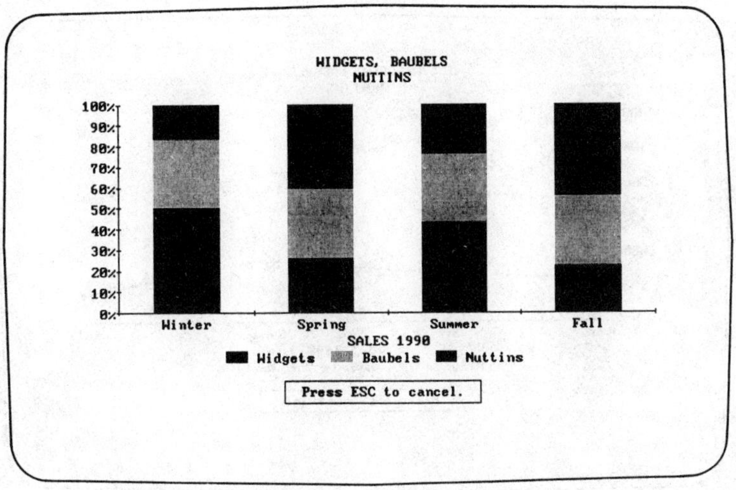

Fig. 8.3.

A 100% bar chart.

Area Line Chart

An *area line chart* stacks the values chosen as a total of the lines plotted, similar to a stacked bar chart. In figure 8.5, the contributions of three products to sales are charted.

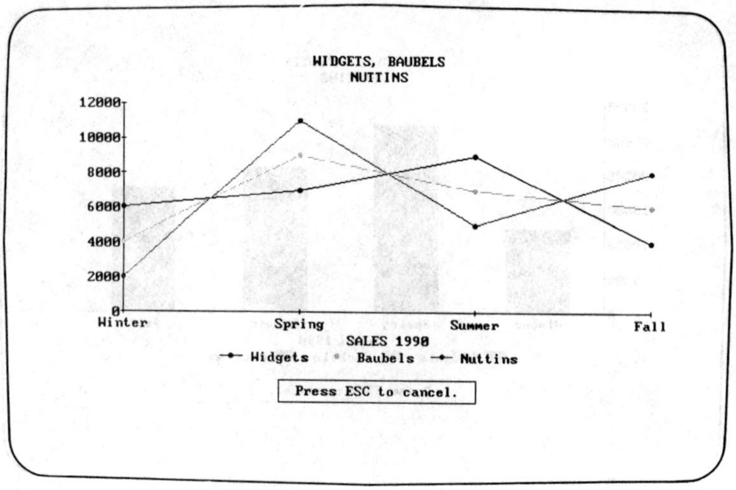

Fig. 8.4.

A line chart.

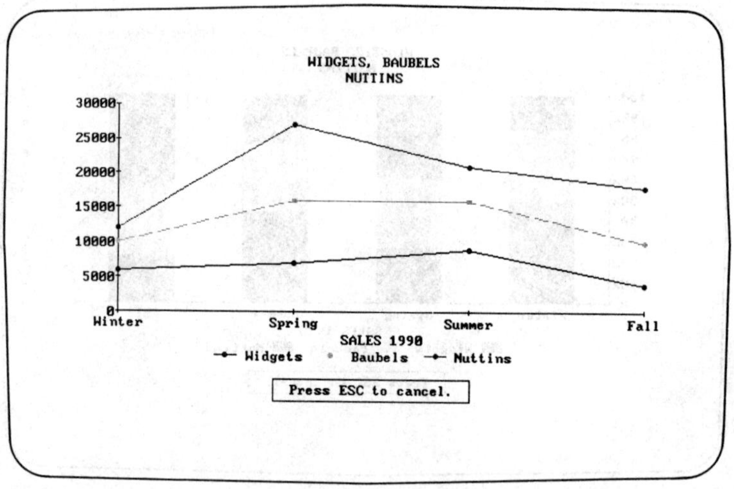

Fig. 8.5.

An area line chart.

Hi-Lo-Close Chart

The *hi-lo-close chart* is used primarily in tracking the price movements of stocks. In figure 8.6, a mythical company's stock price movements are charted.

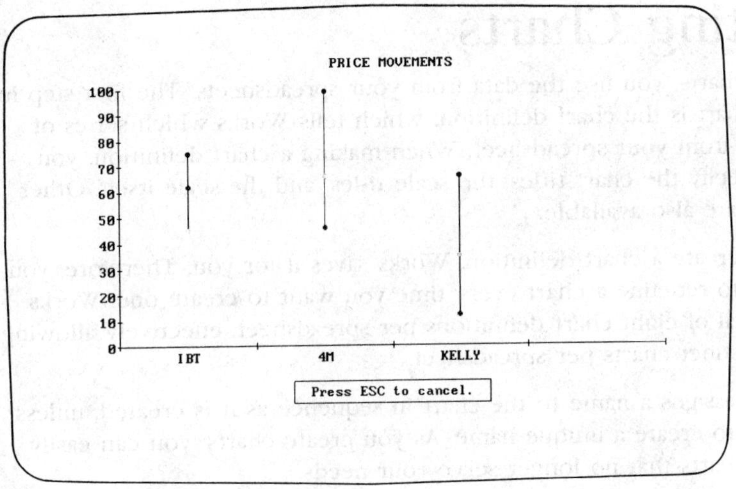

Fig. 8.6.
A hi-lo-close chart.

Pie Chart

A *pie chart* shows the relationship of numeric components to a whole. In figure 8.7, the sales of a product in different geographic areas is charted. Assuming that every component is included in a pie chart, the pie itself will equal 100 percent of the numbers being charted.

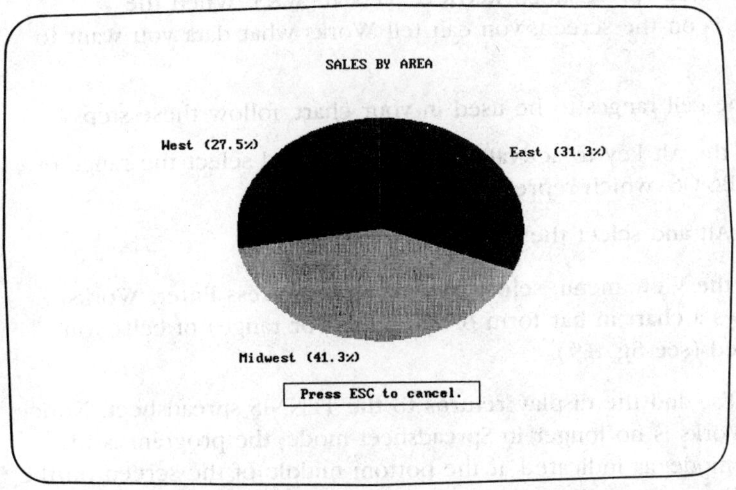

Fig. 8.7.
A pie chart.

Creating Charts

To create charts, you use the data from your spreadsheets. The first step in making a chart is the chart definition, which tells Works which series of data to use from your spreadsheet. When making a chart definition, you also can specify the chart titles, the scale titles, and the scale itself. Other style types are also available.

When you create a chart definition, Works saves it for you. Therefore, you don't have to redefine a chart every time you want to create one. Works allows a total of eight chart definitions per spreadsheet, effectively allowing for eight distinct charts per spreadsheet.

Works also assigns a name to the chart in sequence as it is created, unless you decide to create a unique name. As you create charts, you can easily delete old charts that no longer serve your needs.

Displaying the charts is called *plotting* in Works. You can plot as well as print the charts you create.

Creating a Bar Chart

In order to create a chart, you must first have the spreadsheet file displayed on your computer screen. For this example, the first six months of the TENNIS.WKS spreadsheet will be used. You are already familiar with retrieving a saved spreadsheet. Retrieve TENNIS.WKS. When the spreadsheet is on the screen, you can tell Works what data you want to chart.

To select the cell ranges to be used in your chart, follow these steps:

1. Press the Alt key to activate the menu bar and select the range of cells B6:G6, which represents January to June.
2. Press Alt and select the View menu (see fig. 8.8).
3. From the View menu, select New Chart and press Enter. Works displays a chart in bar form of the series (or range) of cells you selected (see fig. 8.9).
4. Press Esc and the display returns to the TENNIS spreadsheet. Notice that Works is no longer in Spreadsheet mode; the program is in Chart mode, as indicated at the bottom middle of the screen on the same line as the cell address indicator.

You have created a simple series bar chart. Admittedly, this is not a very interesting chart, just a single series of data with no variation in that data.

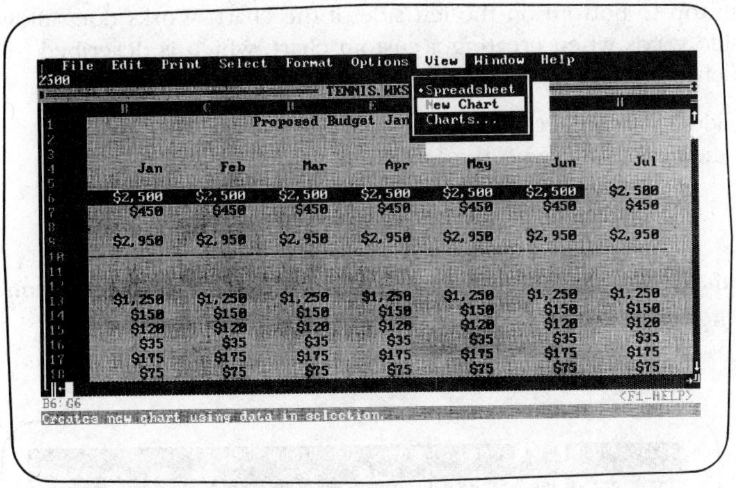

Fig. 8.8.

The View menu.

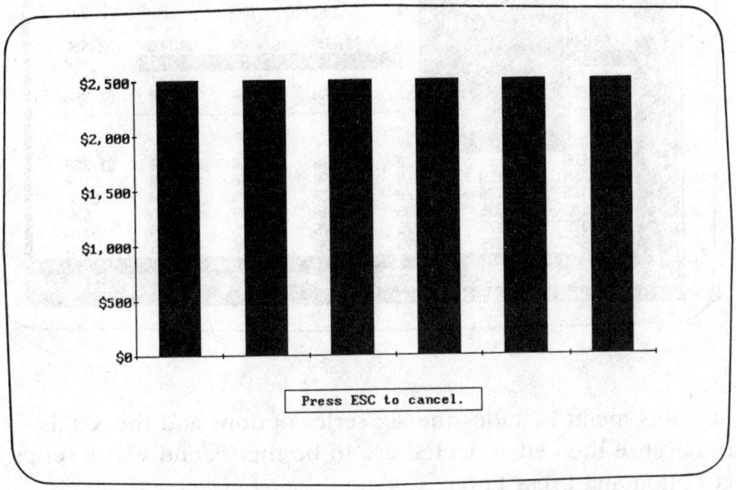

Fig. 8.9.

The dues income charted on a bar chart.

This example simply shows how easily you can create a chart. The bar chart style is the default setting.

All the series charts have a consistent structure. The horizontal line on the chart is the x-axis, and the vertical line is the y-axis. When adding data to a chart, the series are added as the first, second, third, and so on, with a total of six series allowed. Hence, the y-axis series are charted across from left to right, and the x-axis series, which can only be a single series, is charted from top to bottom on the left side of the chart. Works does allow for a right-side y-axis when creating a custom chart, which is described later in this chapter.

In order to add a second series of values to your chart, follow the same steps as for the first series, with the following changes:

1. Use the Shift and End keys to select the cells B7:G7, the Fees row entry.

2. Press the Alt key to activate the menu bar and select the Data menu (see fig. 8.10).

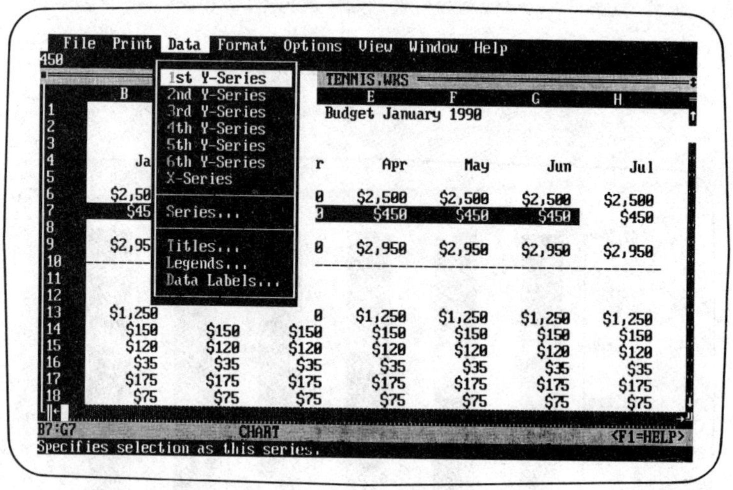

Fig. 8.10.

The Data menu.

As you can see, this menu includes the six series options and the x-axis series option. Because the cells selected are to be the second y-axis series, highlight that option and press Enter.

To view the chart with the new series added, press Alt and select the View menu. Choose the Chart1 option. When you create a chart, Works automatically adds the third option, Charts, to the View menu; and if you add more charts to the spreadsheet, Works will list them sequentially beneath the Charts heading.

Creating a Stacked Bar Chart

With two data ranges in your chart, you can change the type of chart to a stacked bar chart, which—in the case of the `Income` section of this spreadsheet—will reflect the total income for every month. To create this chart, follow these steps:

1. If you are still looking at the chart, press Esc to return to the spreadsheet in Chart mode. Press the Alt key to activate the menu bar and select the Format menu. Select the Stacked Bar option.

2. Press Enter and then press Alt. Then select the View menu. Choose Chart1 again. The chart is displayed as in figure 8.11.

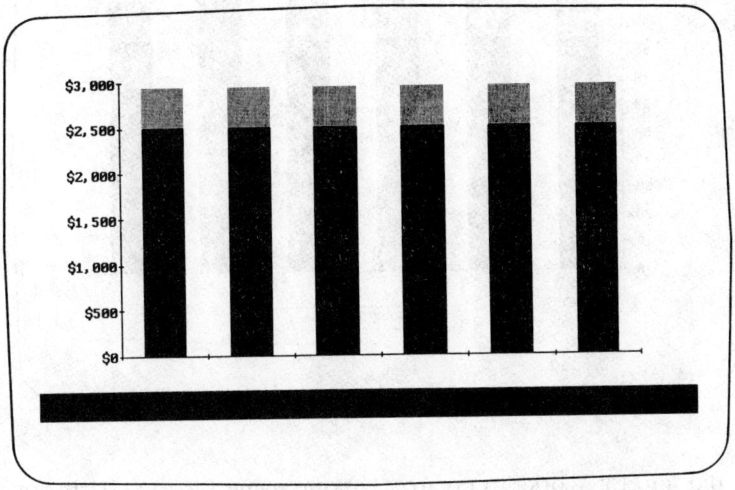

Fig. 8.11.

The stacked bar Income chart.

The stacked bar chart plots the two series of numbers that you highlighted: the `Dues` income in cells B6:G6 and the `Fees` income in cells B9:G9.

As you can see, you can easily change the type of chart displayed. Simply select the Format menu; then highlight the option desired or press the letter that is displayed in reverse video or in a different color in the word. Works will use the same data series as was used in your previous chart.

Creating a 100% Bar Chart

The 100% bar chart is used for looking at data from the perspective of a baseline amount. By setting all data to be charted as a percentage of the whole chart, you can more easily identify the most crucial components. The 100% bar chart is a close relative of the pie chart, because the total pie, by definition, must be 100 percent.

To create a 100% bar chart, do the following:

1. Using the same data as before, go to the Format menu and highlight the 100% option. Press Enter.
2. Press the Alt key, select the View menu, and then select the Chart1 option. The chart will be displayed (see fig. 8.12).

Fig. 8.12.

The 100% bar chart.

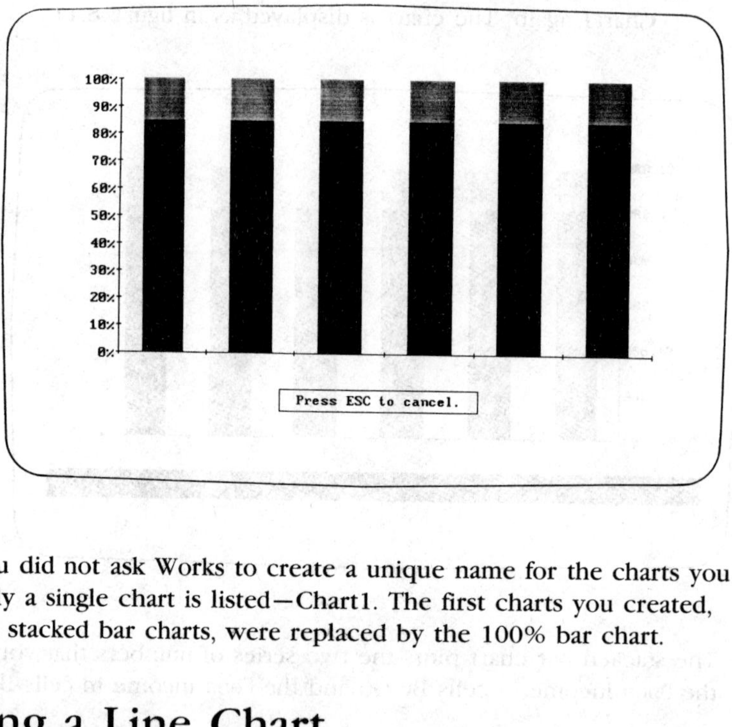

Because you did not ask Works to create a unique name for the charts you created, only a single chart is listed—Chart1. The first charts you created, the bar and stacked bar charts, were replaced by the 100% bar chart.

Creating a Line Chart

For an illustration of the interactive capability of the spreadsheet and the chart or charts you create from it, modify the data you have selected for charting:

1. Press the Alt key and select the View menu.
2. Change the view mode from Chart to Spreadsheet.

The menu bar has new menu choices, alerting you that you can now modify the spreadsheet entries. Do the following:

1. In cell C6, type *3000*.
2. In cell D6, type *500*.
3. In cell E6, type *4500*.
4. In cell F6, type *4200*.
5. In cell G6, type *1000*.

To create the line chart, follow these steps:

1. Press Alt and select the View menu; then choose Chart1. After viewing the new chart with varying bars, press Esc.
2. Use the Format menu to change the format of the chart to line.
3. Press Alt and select the View menu. From the View menu, choose Chart1. The chart will be displayed as shown in figure 8.13.

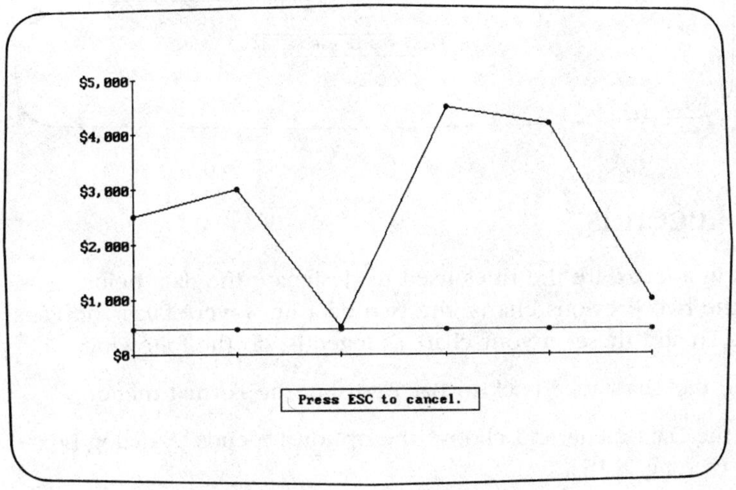

Fig. 8.13.

The line chart.

Creating an Area Line Chart

Using the same data as in the previous example, you can change Chart1 to an area line chart. This type of chart reflects the totals of the line charts as they are added together, in much the same way as the stacked bar chart. The first line is drawn, and then the next line is added to the first series, creating the stacked effect.

To create the area line chart, follow these steps:

1. Press the Alt key and select the Format menu.
2. Choose Area Line and press Enter.
3. Press Alt and select the View menu. Choose the Chart1 option and then press Enter to display the chart (see fig. 8.14).

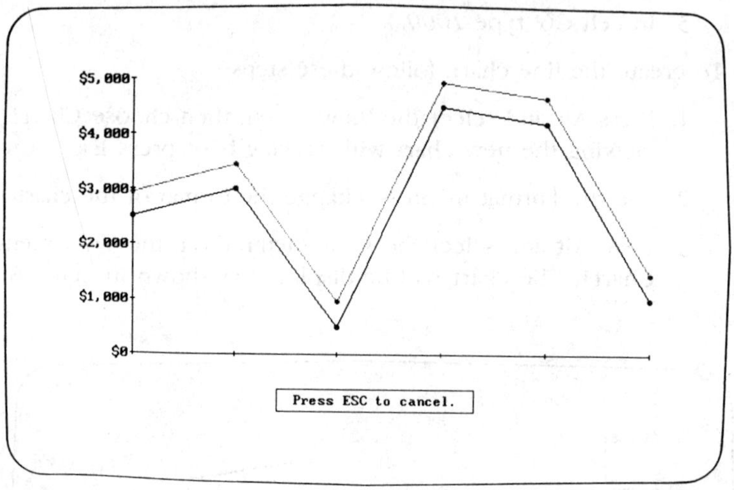

Fig. 8.14.

The area line chart.

Adding Legends

The legends in a chart are the titles used to designate the data being charted. In the two previous charts, the two data lines were Dues and Fees, respectively. To add these to your chart as legends, do the following:

1. Change the chart type back to Bar by using the Format menu.
2. Open the Data menu and choose the option Legends. A dialog box opens (see fig. 8.15).
3. Press Alt-L (press and hold down the Alt key while you press L). You can type in the first legend for the first y-axis series, *Dues*, and then press Enter. Highlight the option 2nd Y and then press Alt-L. Type in the legend for the second y-axis series, *Fees*.
4. Press Alt-C to create the legends and finish by pressing Alt-D to tell Works you are done.

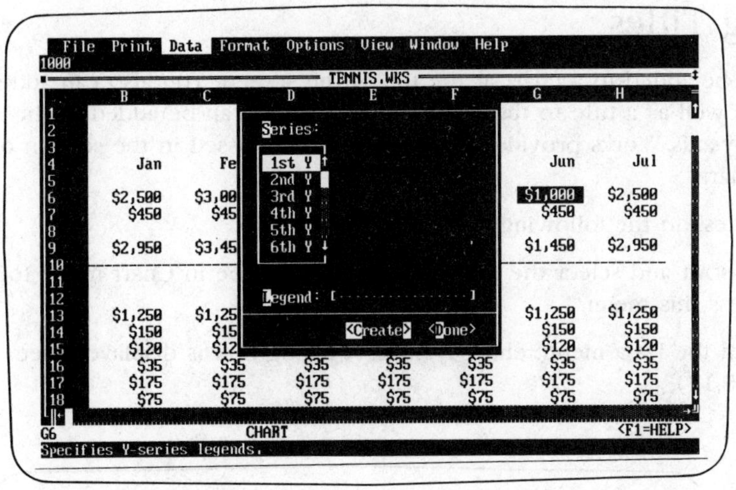

Fig. 8.15.

The Data Legends dialog box.

To see the legends added, use the View menu and choose the option Chart1. The legends will be added (see fig. 8.16).

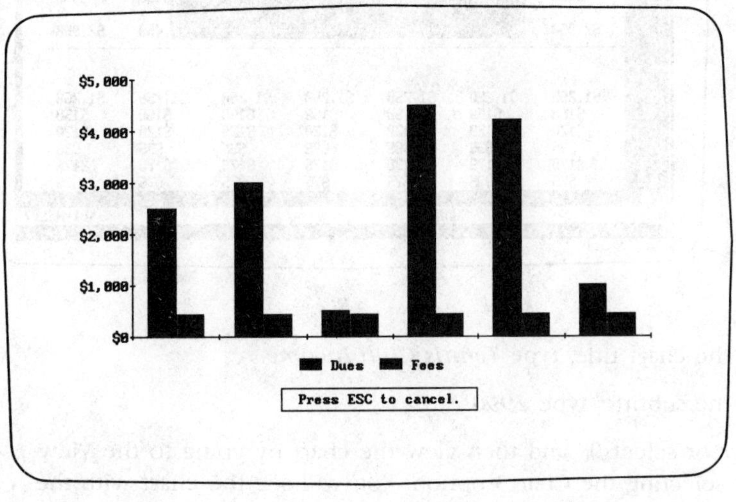

Fig. 8.16.

The legends added to the bar chart.

If you plan to change the legends or just want more flexibility, you can type in a cell address instead of an actual legend name. In the preceding example, the cell address A6 can substitute for *Dues*, and A7 for *Fees*. Then, if you change the entries in those cells, the legends on your chart also will change.

Adding Titles

Titles can be added to a chart at the top of the screen. You also can add a subtitle as well as a title to the x- and y-axis. A title can be added to the right-side y-axis Works provides. This feature is discussed in the section on custom charts.

To add titles, do the following:

1. Press Alt and select the Data menu. You must be in Chart mode to access this menu.

2. From the Data menu, choose Titles. A dialog box is displayed (see fig. 8.17).

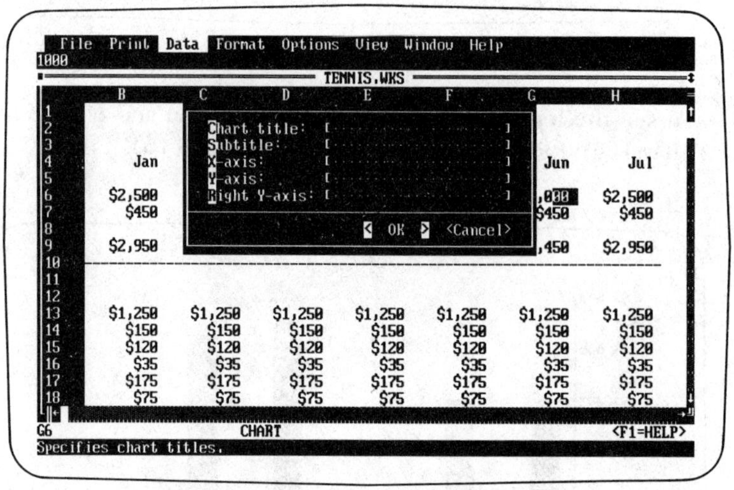

Fig. 8.17.

The Data Titles dialog box.

3. For the chart title, type *Tennis Club Income.*

4. For the subtitle, type *1990.*

Press Enter or select OK and then view the chart by going to the View menu and selecting the Chart3 option. You will see the chart with the titles displayed (see fig. 8.18).

To enhance this chart even more, you can add the names of the months across the bottom of the x-axis. To do so, follow these steps:

1. Select the range of cells B4 to G4, which contain the names of the months.

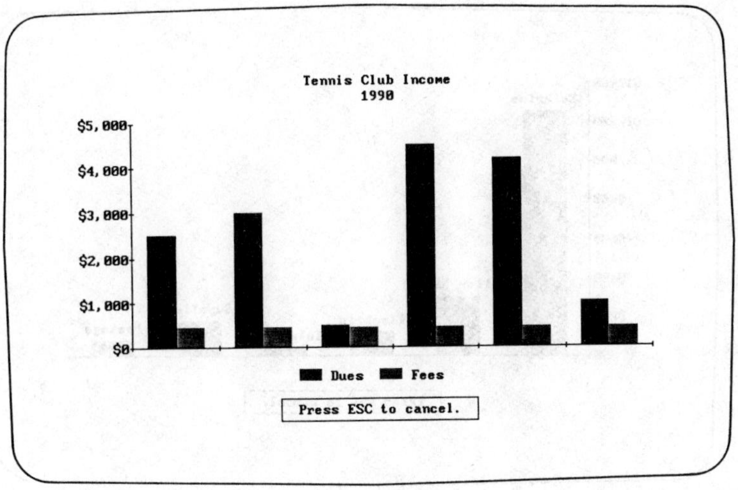

Fig. 8.18.
Titles added to the bar chart.

2. Press Alt, select the Data menu, and then choose the option X-Series.

Go to the View menu to see the chart, which now looks like figure 8.19.

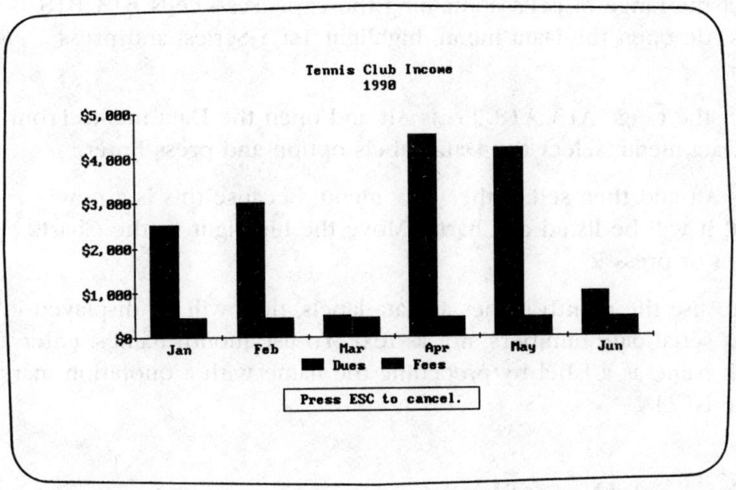

Fig. 8.19.
The completed Tennis Club Income chart.

Adding Data Labels

In some charts, you may find that adding data labels is necessary. These labels are inserted into the chart at the top of a bar or along the points plotted in the chart. Figure 8.20 shows a chart with data labels inserted.

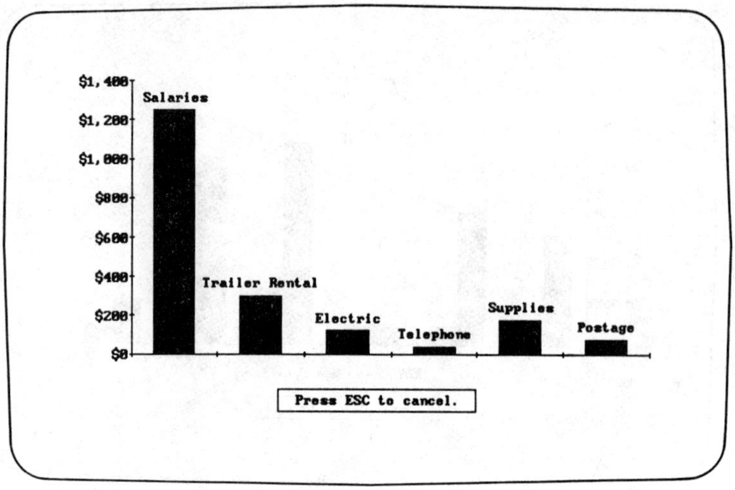

Fig. 8.20.

A chart with data labels added.

To create this chart from the Tennis spreadsheet, do the following:

1. Change from the Spreadsheet view to the Chart view by pressing Alt, pressing V, and then selecting the New Chart option.
2. Select the range of cells containing the expenses—cells B13..B18. Press Alt, open the Data menu, highlight 1st Y-Series, and press Enter.
3. Select the range A13..A18. Press Alt and open the Data menu. From the Data menu, select the Data Labels option and press Enter.
4. Press Alt and then select the View menu. Because this is a new chart, it will be listed as Chart2. Move the highlight to the Chart2 option or press 2.

If you try to use the month names as data labels, they will be displayed in the chart as serial date numbers, not as text. To use month names, enter each month name as a label by preceding the name with a quotation mark. An example is *"JAN*.

Creating a Pie Chart

A pie chart represents a set of numbers that together create the whole pie. In this example, you will create a pie chart to show the Expense section numbers as pieces of a pie. To create the pie chart, follow these steps:

1. Move the cell selector to cell B13 and select the cells in the range B13 to B22.
2. Press Alt and open the Format menu. Choose the Pie option.
3. Open the View menu, make this a new chart, and press Enter. The pie chart will look like the example shown in figure 8.21.

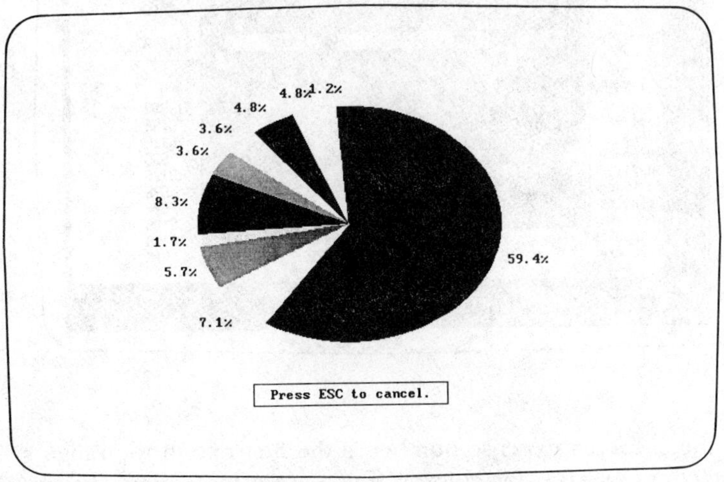

Fig. 8.21.

The Expense pie chart.

The labels for each slice on a pie chart are the the most important pieces of information you can add. The way to add these labels is to select the cells A13 to A22 and then make them the x-axis series from the Data menu. However, if you select all those entries as labels, you will find that the screen appears cluttered. By leaving off the last entry in cell A22 and using the range A13 to A21, the labels appear much better.

As with any other chart, you can add titles or change the series depicted in a pie chart. Remember that only one series can be displayed at a time on this kind of chart.

After creating a pie chart, you may want to emphasize one of the pieces of the pie. The traditional means to do so is to explode, or pull away from the other pieces of the pie, the one piece that represents the desired number.

Using the pie chart from the previous example, explode the Salaries piece and also make it a specific color. If you have only a monochrome monitor, you can change the pattern of the piece rather than the color. To make these modifications, follow these steps:

1. Access the Format menu and choose the option Data Format. The Data Format dialog box appears (see fig. 8.22).

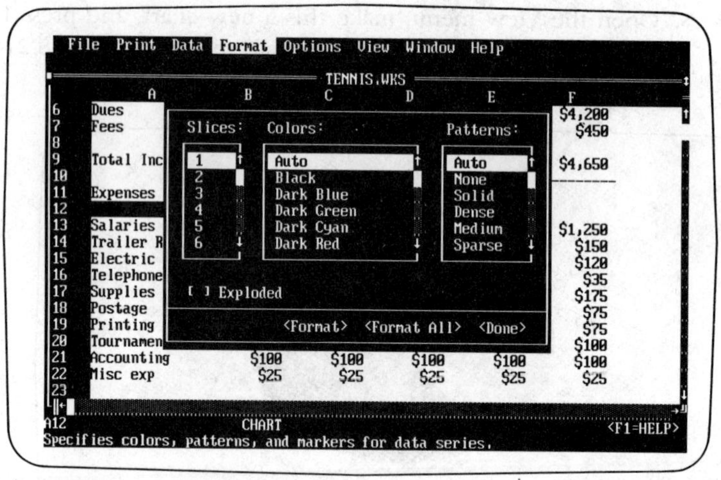

Fig. 8.22.

The Data Format dialog box.

2. Because the `Salaries` expense number is the first one in the range you selected, press Alt-C for colors. (If you are using a monochrome monitor, press Alt-P for patterns.)

3. Select the `Black` option as the color. Then press Alt-E to put an X in front of the word `Exploded`. Pie slice 1 is now exploded and black. (On a monochrome system, select the pattern style you want.)

4. To finish, press Alt-F to reformat the slice. Then press Alt-D when you're done.

View the pie chart by going to the View menu and choosing Chart4. The chart appears as in figure 8.23.

Changing Fonts

You can change the font type for the titles or the other fonts displayed in your charts. Select the chart you want to modify. Access the Format menu and select the Title Font option. The Title Font dialog box appears (see fig. 8.24).

Works provides a dazzling array of fonts and type sizes for you to experiment with. To see the fonts on-screen, you must select the Options

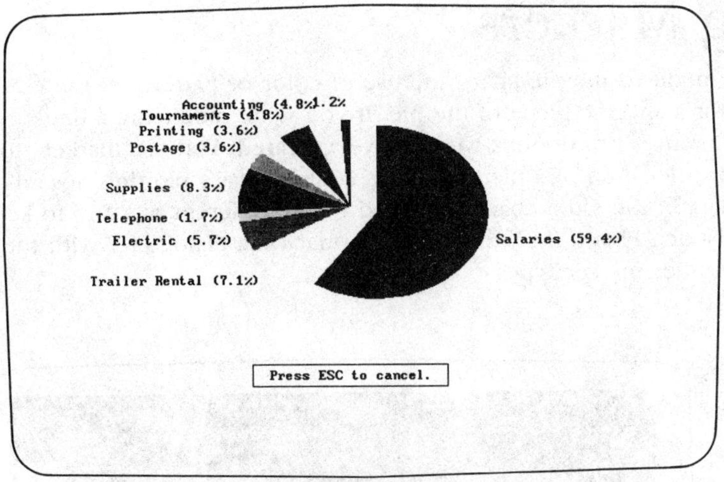

Fig. 8.23.

The exploded Salaries pie slice.

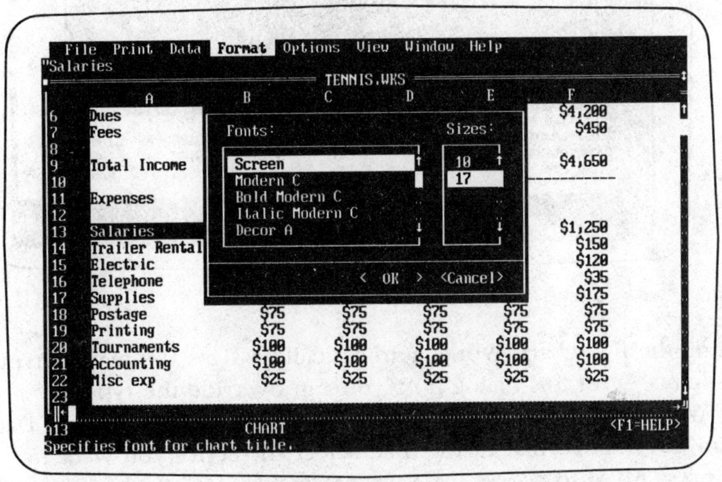

Fig. 8.24.

The Title Font dialog box.

menu and then choose Show Printer Fonts. This option requires a good deal of processing power and, depending on the kind of computer you have, can significantly slow your screen display. If you leave this option set to off, the fonts will print as directed, but you will not be able to see them on-screen. The best way to become familiar with this capability is to try a variety of sizes and fonts to see what you like best.

Using Markers

When you modified the pie chart, the use of color or pattern was examined for a specific piece of the pie. If you were modifying a line chart, a different set of options would have appeared. You use markers to plot the exact location of a piece of data. When you are plotting several pieces of data in the same chart, you need to use different markers to keep the lines distinct. Figure 8.25 shows the Format Data dialog box with the options for other marker types.

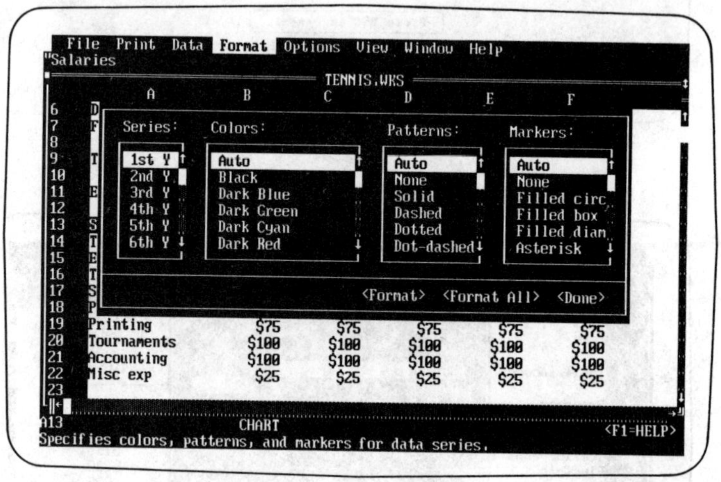

Fig. 8.25.

The Format Data dialog box.

When creating the line chart, Works automatically assigns the marker types to the data points. With this dialog box, you can override the types assigned by Works. To do so, access the the Format menu and choose Data Format. From the Data Format dialog box, select the series you want to modify and press Alt-M to access the `Markers` section. Make your selection and be sure to press Alt-F for `Format` before pressing Alt-D for `Done`. The change you have made will appear in the chart. If you want to have the format change apply to all the data plotted, select the `Format All` option before pressing Alt-D.

Creating Customized Charts

You may get the idea that you have been creating customized charts throughout this chapter. Actually, you have enhanced standard charts. Four types of charts are not standard:

- ❑ Charts with a right y-axis
- ❑ A mixed line and bar chart
- ❑ A hi-lo-close chart
- ❑ An XY chart

This section examines how to create these charts.

Adding a Right Y-Axis

Figure 8.26 shows a typical line chart. To add a right y-axis, first make sure that you're in Chart mode; then go to the Options menu and select the Two Y-Axis option. The Two Y-Axis dialog box opens (see fig. 8.27).

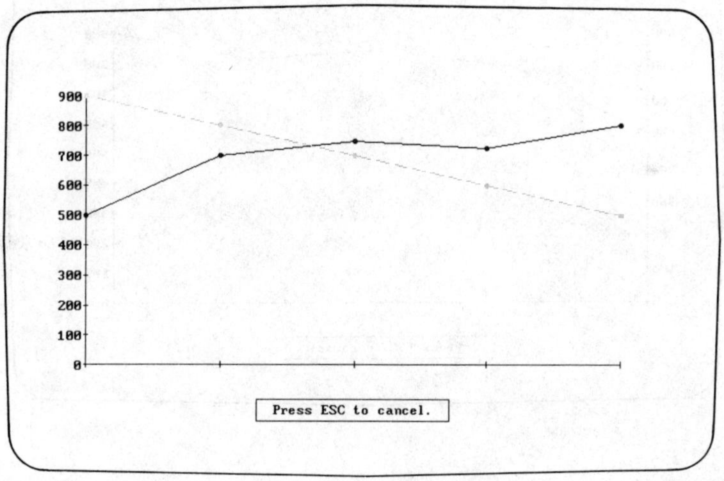

Fig. 8.26.
A line chart.

The first y-axis series remains assigned to the left y-axis. You want to assign the second y-axis series to the right axis. You can assign any series to either a left or right axis. This feature may seem complex, but with a little practice, you will feel comfortable using this feature. Figure 8.28 shows the resulting chart with the right y-axis.

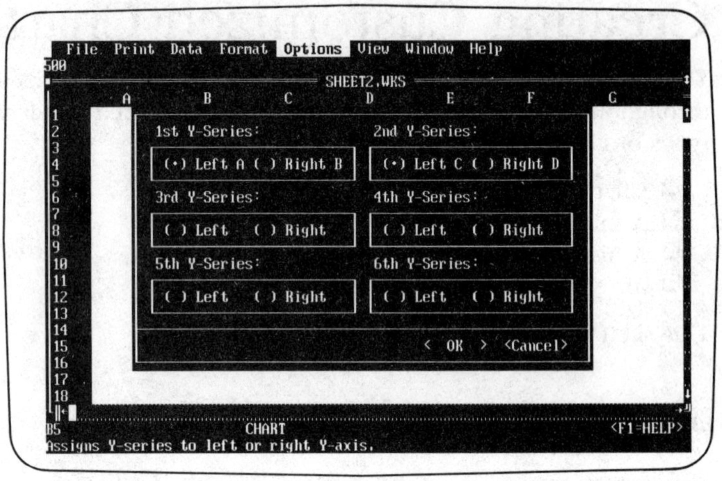

Fig. 8.27.

The Two Y-Axis dialog box.

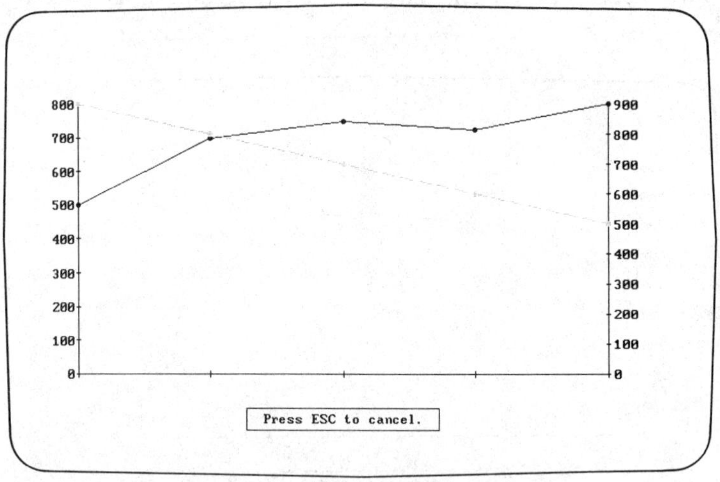

Fig. 8.28.

The two y-axes chart.

In addition to having two y-axes, you have the ability with Works to scale the y-axis and the x-axis. *Scaling* simply means that you determine the frequency of the numbers that will be used to enumerate the y-axis. These options are found on the Options menu. In figure 8.29, the y-axis Scaling dialog box is shown.

The settings for the scale are automatically made by Works based on the range of data you select to be plotted. However, you can override the settings in this dialog box. Again, you can learn best about the options by

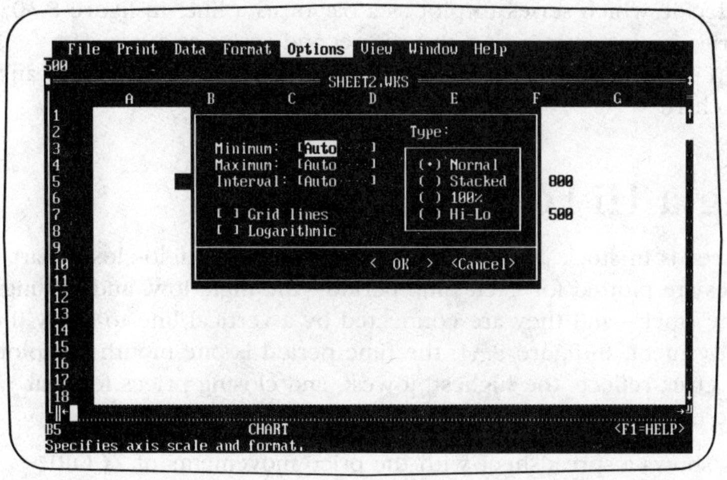

Fig. 8.29.

The y-axis Scaling dialog box.

trying many variations. For example, adding grid lines enhances the readability of some charts but adds too much clutter to others.

Mixing Lines and Bars

Another choice on the Options menu is the Mixed Line and Bar option. Choosing this option opens the dialog box shown in figure 8.30.

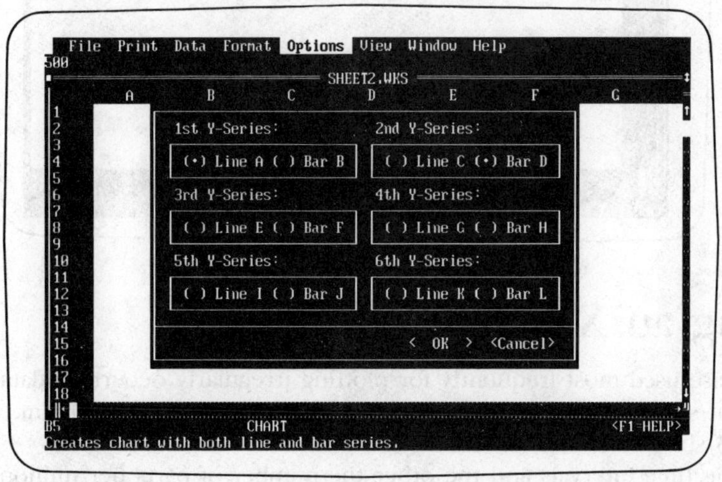

Fig. 8.30.

The Mixed Line and Bar dialog box.

You must decide which series to plot as a bar or as a line. In figure 8.30, the first series is plotted as a line and the second series as a bar. The combination of having the y-axis on the left and the grid lines creates an interesting chart.

Making a Hi-Lo-Close Chart

Following trends in stock prices is made easier with the hi-lo-close chart. Three values are plotted for each time period—the high, low, and closing prices of the stock—and they are connected by a vertical line to show the range of movement. In figure 8.31, the time period is one month per plot. Hence, the chart reflects the highest, lowest, and closing prices for that stock in the entire month.

Figure 8.31 shows a spreadsheet with the price movements of ZCORP. Figure 8.32 shows a chart reflecting the spreadsheet prices. Each month is a single y-axis series with three values. The Hi-Lo-Close option from the Format menu was chosen to plot the numbers.

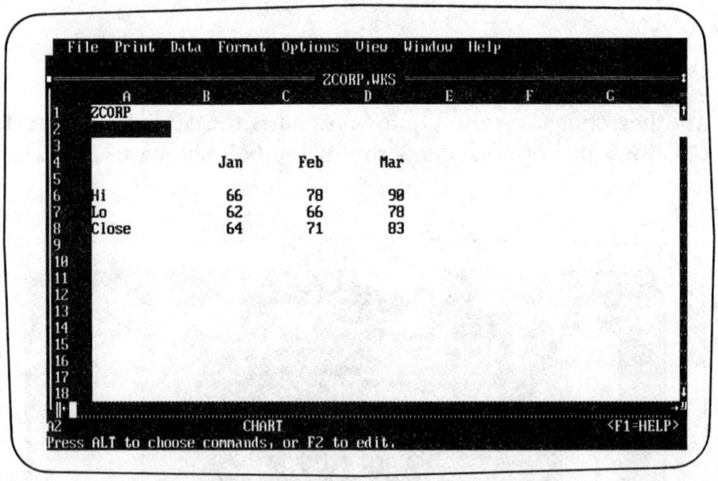

Fig. 8.31.

The Stock Price spreadsheet.

Making an XY Chart

XY charts are used most frequently for plotting irregularly occurring data, such as that supplied by the absorption of a drug into the blood stream. Figure 8.33 shows a spreadsheet with two columns of numbers—one representing time intervals and the other the number of parts per million detected in the patient's bloodstream.

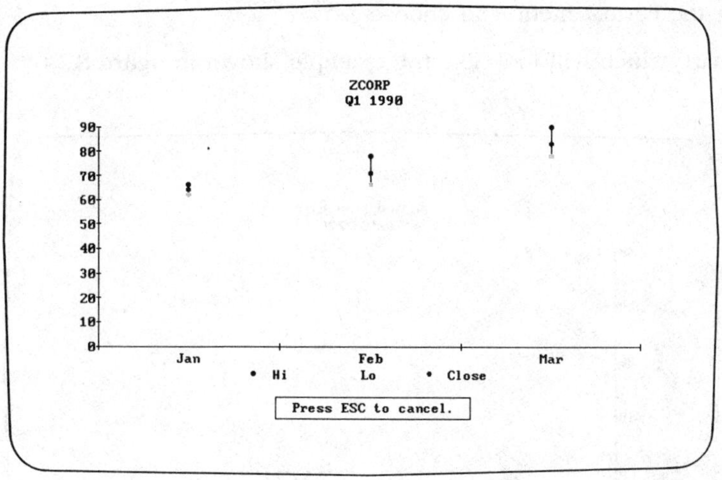

Fig. 8.32.

The ZCORP stock prices, plotted.

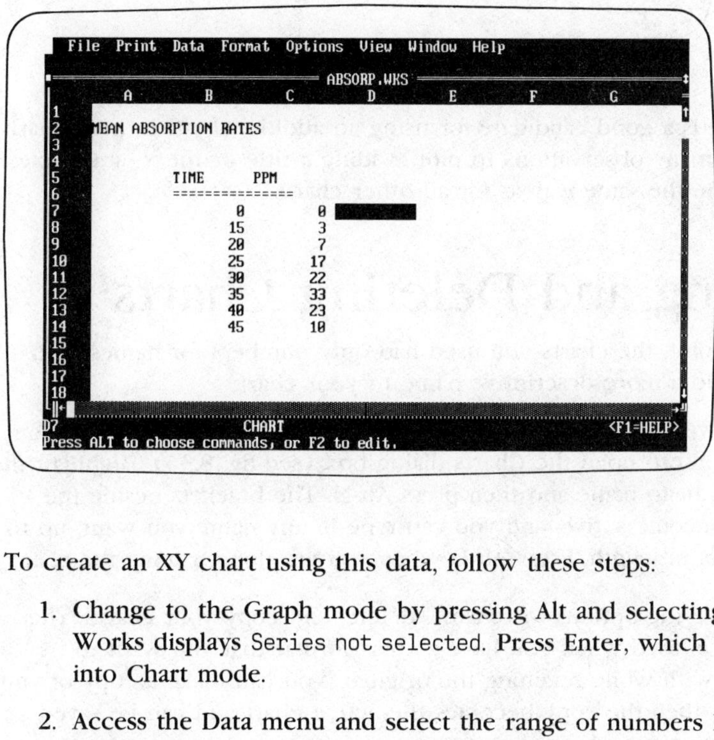

Fig. 8.33.

The Absorption spreadsheet.

To create an XY chart using this data, follow these steps:

1. Change to the Graph mode by pressing Alt and selecting New Chart. Works displays `Series not selected`. Press Enter, which will take you into Chart mode.

2. Access the Data menu and select the range of numbers B7:B14 as the x-axis series.

3. Select the range of numbers C7:C14 as the first y-axis series.

4. Select the Format menu and choose X-Y.

View the chart, which will look like the example shown in figure 8.34.

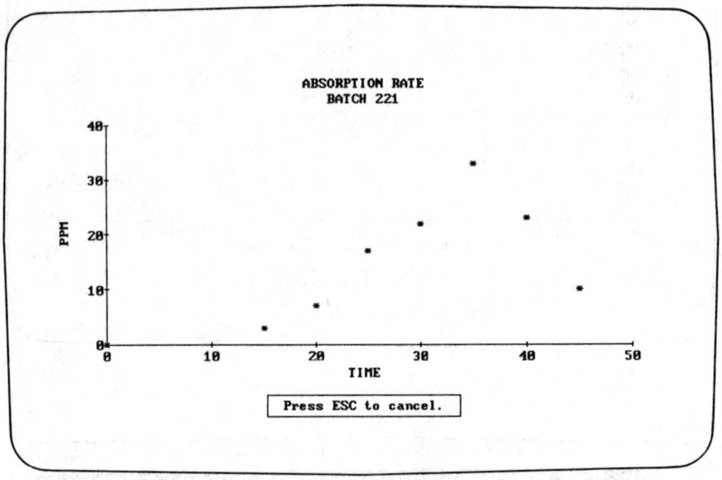

Fig. 8.34.

The XY plot.

An XY chart is a good candidate for using an additional y-axis, particularly if you have many observations to plot. Adding a title or the x- and y-axes labels is done the same way as for all other charts.

Naming and Deleting Charts

Up to this point, the charts you used had only numbers for names. You easily can add a more descriptive name to your chart.

After you have created a chart to your liking, use the Charts option from the View menu to open the Charts dialog box (see fig. 8.35). Highlight the chart you want to name and then press Alt-N. The brackets beside the word Name become active, and you can type in any name you want, up to 16 characters in length. Press Alt-D when you are done naming the chart.

You also have the options to rename, delete, and copy your charts. The Copy option is used when you have a chart format that you want to experiment with while retaining the original. You can make a copy of your original, and then the copy becomes the active chart and can be saved with a unique name.

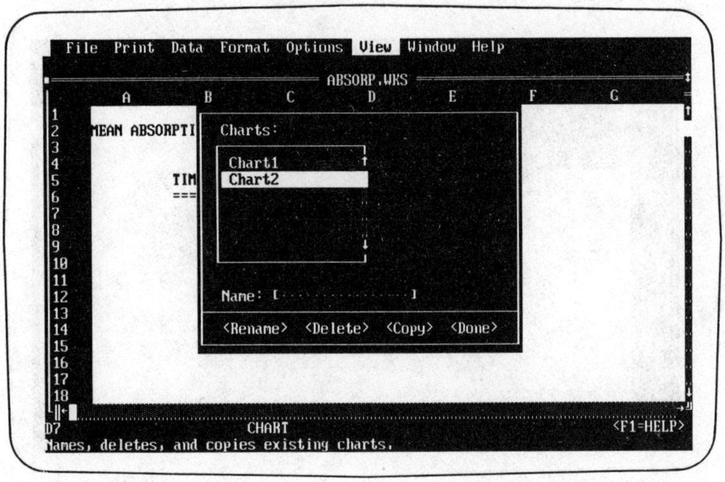

Fig. 8.35.
The Charts dialog box.

Using a Color or Black-and-White Display

If you are using a system with a color monitor, you may want to see how the chart will look in black and white before printing. Doing so gives you the opportunity to modify the markers or the cross-hatching required for printing in black and white.

To see a chart displayed in black and white, do the following:

1. Press Alt and select the Options menu.
2. From the Options menu, choose Format for B&W.

View your chart now, and it will appear just as it will print.

Printing Charts

Printing charts is straightforward if you have installed your printer correctly. The Print menu is shown in figure 8.36.

Choosing this option opens a dialog box that asks for input on the number of copies desired or asks whether you want to print the chart to a file. You can use the File option to save the chart for transfer to other programs or over a modem. If none of these choices is necessary, simply press Enter again to print the chart on your printer. Printing charts takes a long time,

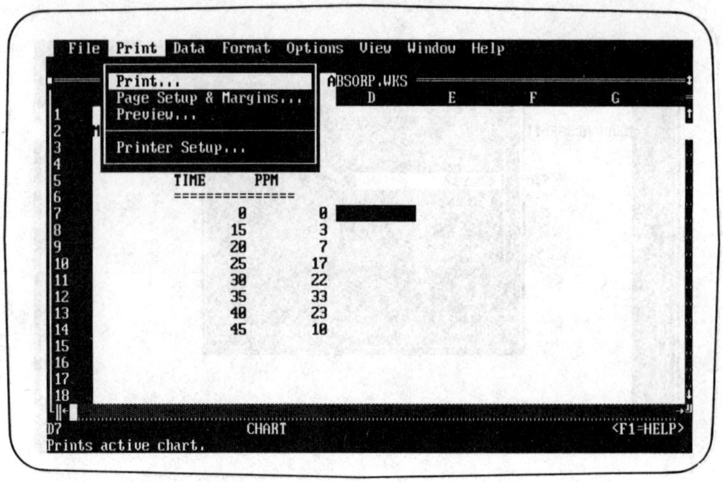

Fig. 8.36.

The Print menu.

especially if you are using a dot-matrix printer. Use this time to take a break.

Working with Page Setup and Margins

If you want to modify the size of a chart in relation to the page or change the size of the paper you are using for printing, you can use the Print dialog box (see fig. 8.37).

Works has inserted the default settings, assuming that you want to print the chart on standard-size paper. You also have the option of printing the chart either in Landscape or Portrait mode. All the charts printed in the text have been in Portrait mode.

Two other useful printing features follow:

- ❑ Before your chart is printed, you can use the Preview feature to look at your chart on-screen as it will appear on paper. In view of the time it takes to print a chart, this feature alone will save you hours. Figure 8.38 shows a chart in Landscape mode as it will appear on paper.

- ❑ Although Works installs the printer driver that you specified when you first started using the software, you can modify some of the

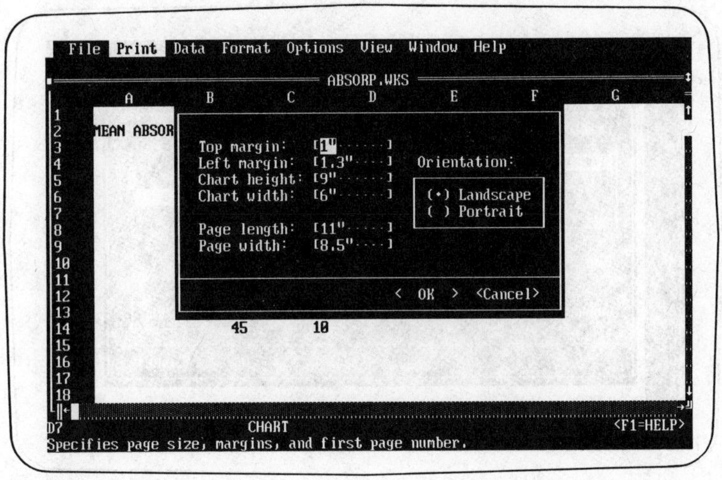

Fig. 8.37.

The Print dialog box.

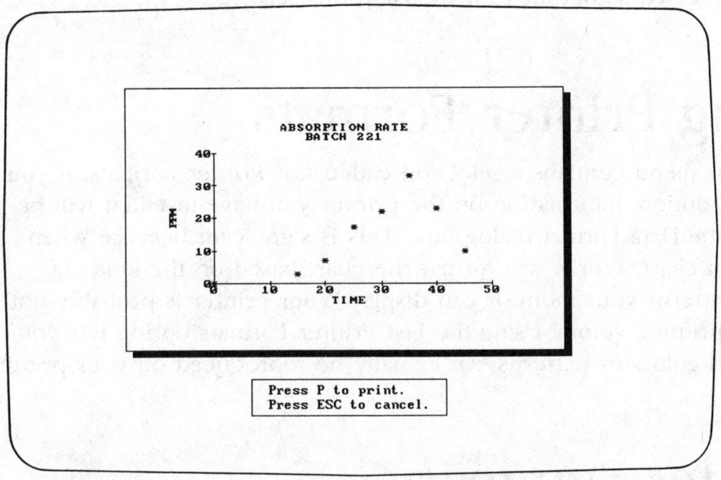

Fig. 8.38.

The Chart Preview feature.

settings; or, if you have two printers, you can switch from one printer to another. Figure 8.39 shows the Printer Setup dialog box. In the example, two printers are listed, indicating that two were set up when Works was installed. Depending on the printer, you can print heavier or lighter graphics, as indicated by DPI (dots per inch).

In some instances, you may want your printer to print one page at a time instead of printing continuously, which is the way a dot-matrix printer normally works. This setting also can be switched in the Printer Setup dialog box. If you acquire a new printer, you need to install it. But you

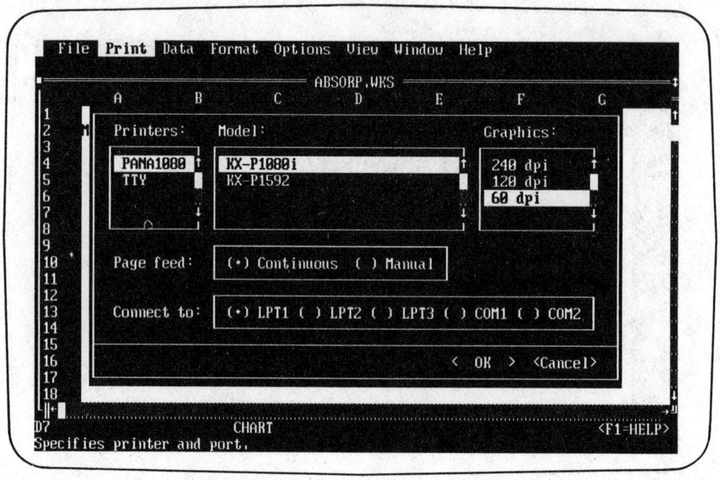

Fig. 8.39.

The Printer Setup dialog box.

can connect an additional printer, provided that you have the printer port, and direct the Works output to it by using this screen.

Listing Printer Formats

The Options menu contains a selection called List Printer Formats. If you choose this option, information on the printer you have installed will be printed to the Data Format dialog box. This is significant because when you create a chart, Works will format the chart based on the kinds of colors or patterns your monitor can display. Your printer is probably not capable of printing colors. Using the List Printer Formats option lets you know which colors or patterns can actually be reproduced on your printer.

Chapter Summary

Charts illuminate relationships that are difficult to perceive when represented by numbers on a spreadsheet alone. The key to using charts is to pick the appropriate chart format to illustrate your data. This chapter explored the many aspects of creating charts and examined the ease of switching among different chart formats.

In Chapter 9, the Microsoft Works database is examined. A database makes it easy for you to store and recall large amounts of information, such as names, invoices, and part numbers.

Part IV

Databases

Includes

Quick Start 3

Creating a Database and Database Report

This quick-start lesson will briefly examine the Works database feature. Simple steps are given for creating, naming, entering, and editing fields and data. Change from the Form view to the List view. Then move fields, change their sizes, alter their styles, and sort the data. Save the newly created database to keep a magnetic copy of the information.

Creating a New Database

When you start Works, the File menu appears on your screen. With the cursor on Create New File, press Enter. Move the highlighting down to New Database (or press D). Press Enter and a new database file is opened. You are using a new database file in the Form view.

Name your database by typing the name across the top of the screen. Press Enter to insert the label into the cell.

If you're using a mouse, point to Create New File and click. Point to New Database and click.

Naming Database Fields

Decide where you want the first field and move the cursor to that location. Type the name of the first field and end it with a colon. If the field name is Last Name, for example, the entry will look like this:

Last Name:

Press Enter to insert the field title into the database cell. The Field Size dialog box appears. The default width is 20 characters, and the default height is 1 line. Accept the default values by pressing Enter (change them by typing in different values and then pressing Enter).

Continue to enter fields until all the information you need can be recorded in the database record. Figure QS3.1 shows the screen with several fields entered.

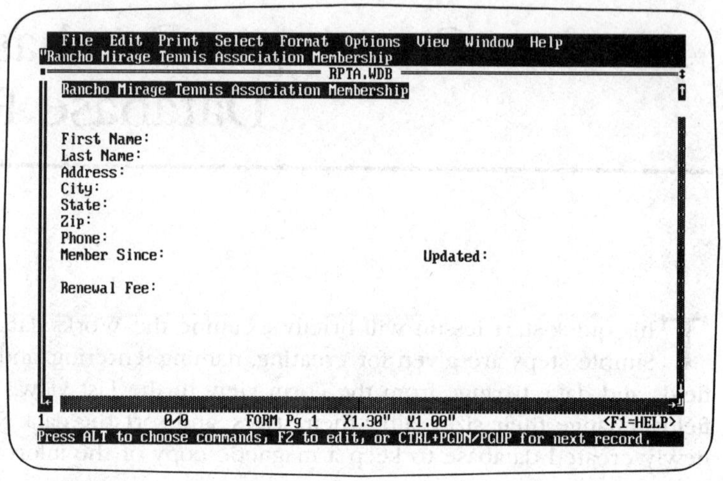

QS3.1.

The database screen with fields entered.

Editing a Field

Change the contents of a field name cell by moving the cursor to that cell. Press F2. EDIT appears on the status line. Edit the cell by moving the cursor, using the cursor-movement keys, deleting incorrect text, and replacing the incorrect text with correct text.

If you want to change the entire field name (not just edit it), simply type a new entry in the cell and press Enter. The new text will replace the old text.

Entering Data

Each field name is followed by a dotted line indicating the space for the data to be entered for each field. Move the cursor highlighting to the data cell and type the data you want to enter for that field. Press Enter. Figure QS3.2 shows the data filled in for this record.

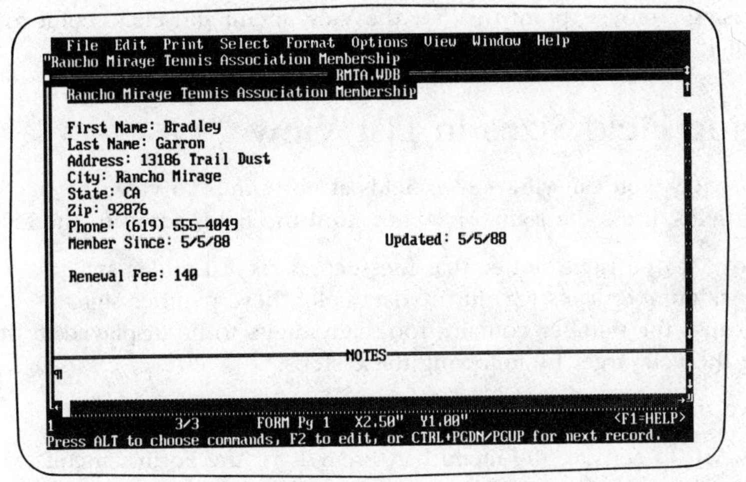

QS3.2.
Data filled in for fields in a record.

Enter data in the next record, too. To get to the next record, press Ctrl-PgDn. You will scroll to the second record in the new database. Move the cursor to the data cell and enter the data for the second record.

Changing to List View

Once the database is created in Form view, list the records by switching to List view. Press Alt to activate the menu bar. Press V for the View menu. Press L for the List option of the View menu. The data is now listed as shown in figure QS3.3.

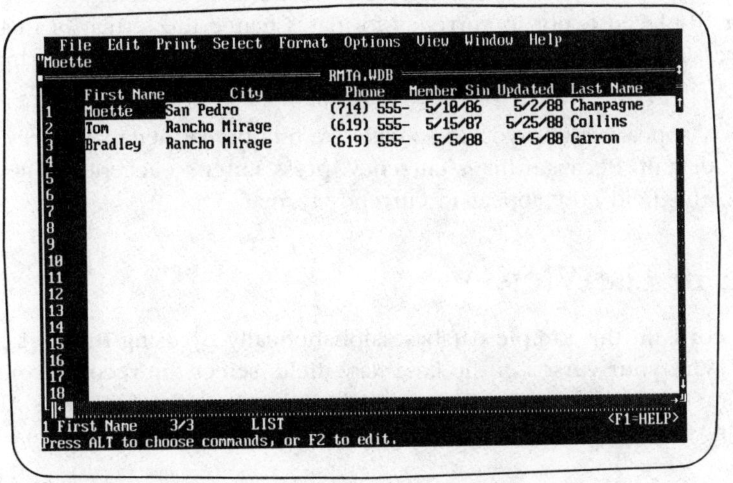

QS3.3.
The database in List view.

If you're using a mouse, point to V for the View menu and click. Point to List and click.

Changing Field Sizes in List View

In this List view, you can view seven fields at one time. To view the remaining fields, press the right-arrow key until the fields scroll to the left.

As you move to the right, notice that the second record under `Amt of Purchase` has number signs (#) in the data cell. These number signs appear because the number contains too many digits to be displayed in the cell. Make the cell larger by following these steps:

1. Move the cursor to the `Amt of Purchase` field.
2. Press Alt to activate the menu bar. Press T for the Format menu. Press W for the Field Width option. The Field Width dialog box appears, containing the original width of 10 characters.
3. Type *13* and press Enter. The field is widened to 13 characters, allowing plenty of room for $10,899.00.

Choosing Field Styles and Alignment

Move to the last field in the records on the screen (the field named `Balance Due`). The two previous fields are entered in currency format. The `Balance Due` field contains a calculation subtracting the amount paid from the amount of purchase. (The formula is =Amount of Purchase−Amount Paid.)

Even though the formula is a calculation of two fields in currency format, the answer displayed is not in currency format. Change the format of this field by pressing Alt to activate the menu bar. Then press T for the Format menu and U for the Currency option.

A dialog box appears asking you to specify the number of decimal places. Two is the default. Because this is currency, press Enter to accept 2. The numbers in this field now appear in currency format.

Sorting in List View

Sort the records in this sample database alphabetically by using the `Last Name` field. With your cursor in the `Last Name` field, select the records you want to sort. Because you want to sort all the records in the file, press Alt for the menu bar, S for the Select menu, and A for the Select All option.

With the entire screen highlighted, press Alt to activate the menu bar. Press S for the Select menu. Press O to sort records.

The Sort Records dialog box appears. Because your cursor was in `Last Name` when you started, `Last Name` appears in the dialog box as the field by which you want to sort. With the indicator on ascending order, press Enter.

The records in this database are sorted alphabetically in ascending order as shown in figure QS3.4.

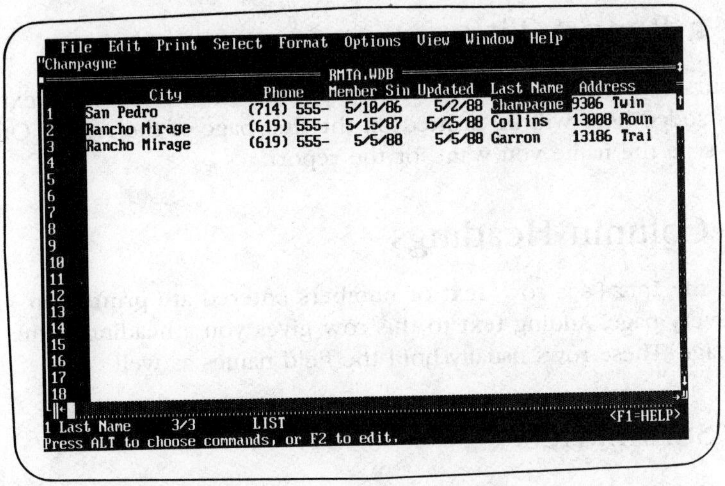

QS3.4. The database sorted in List view.

Saving the Database

Save the database you have created to disk by pressing Alt to activate the menu bar. Press S for the Save option. The file will be saved as DATA1.WDB. If you do not want that name, type in another name and press Enter.

Creating a Database Report

Creating a database report in Microsoft Works is as easy as choosing another view while you are in your database. You can see database records in the Form view, the List view, and when you are ready to prepare a report, the Report view.

JULY.WDB is the database used in the examples in this quick start. If you prefer, use a database you have already prepared.

Moving to the Report View

With your cursor in the List view, press Alt to activate the menu bar, V for the View menu, and N to create a new report of the data. The data is listed in report format on your screen. In the example file, JULY.WDB, two fields appear on the first screen. Follow the instructions given on the status bar to move through the report.

Press Esc to get to the Report Definition screen. This is where you will control the results of the printed report.

Adding a Report Title

Move the cursor to a position across from the row title `Intr Report`. Text or numbers added here will be printed on the first page of the report. On this report, type the name you want for the report.

Adding Column Headings

Across from the `Intr Page` row, text or numbers entered are printed on the top of every page. Adding text to this row gives you a heading at the top of the page. These rows usually hold the field names as well.

Adding Summaries

The `Summ Report` rows are at the bottom of the Report Definition page. Enter text or functions in these rows to summarize the report data. If you want to know the total number of records for a particular field, enter this function in a `Summ Report` row:

=COUNT(Country)

Works will count the number of records in the `Country` field.

Sorting Reports

Do simple report sorts by pressing Alt to activate the menu bar, S for the Select menu, and O for the Sort Records option. The Sort dialog box appears. As you can see in figure QS3.5, in this dialog box, you can sort and create breaks for specific groups.

Complete the following steps for each field by which you want to sort (you may sort by as many as three fields). Enter the name of the field.

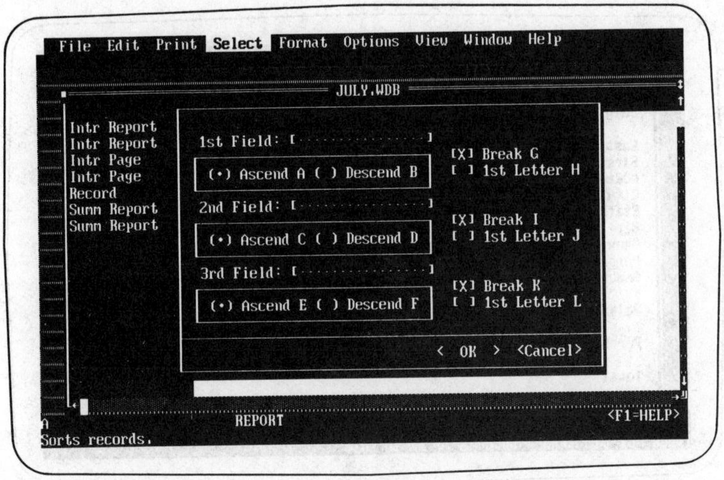

QS3.5.

The Sort dialog box.

Indicate if you want the sort done in descending or ascending order and then select to break by group or by first letter.

If you sort by `Country` in ascending order (*ascending* means it will be alphabetical), you will probably choose to break by the specified group. That way all the records in one country will be listed in one group.

After a sort, go to the Report view (press Alt, V, and then R) and view the list of records. The records in that database now are listed according to your sort choices.

Preparing a Query

Sort the data in a report according to more than one criteria by using a query. Press Alt to activate the menu bar, press V for the View menu, and Q for the Query option. A screen that looks like the Form view appears. No data is in the field data cells.

Search for the specific information you want by placing that information in the field data cells. If you want to get a report of only those records that are from Brazil, with purchases over $50, type *Brazil* in the `Country` field data cell and *>$50* in the `Purchase Amt` field data cell. Your query form will look like the one in figure QS3.6.

When the query criteria have been entered in the data cells, press Alt to activate the menu bar, V for the View menu, and L for the List view. Only the records that match your query criteria are displayed in List view.

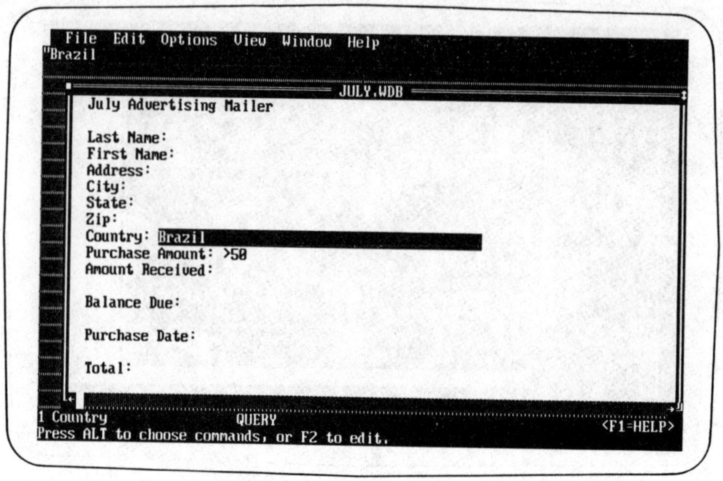

QS3.6.

The query form.

With your cursor in this specified list of records, press Alt to activate the menu bar, V for the View menu, and then N to create a new report. The result of your query will become a new report with a new title.

Naming the Report

Because you want the report title to be more specific than Report2, press Alt, then V, and then R. Move the highlighting to Report2. Press Alt and then N. Move the cursor to the Name box. Type a new name for the report, such as *Brazil.* Press Alt and then R. Press Alt-D when you are done changing report names.

Printing the Report

With your cursor in the report you want to print, press Alt to activate the menu bar and press P for the Print menu. Specify the options you want, including multiple copies. Press Enter and your report will print.

Saving Reports

Saving your reports is easy. Press Alt to activate the menu bar and then F for the File menu. Press S and Works will save your reports as a component of the database in which you are working. This includes any variations on reports that you have made.

9

Creating and Using Databases

In the Introduction, you read about what a database is and what it can do. The database helps you store and organize information. Your life is full of databases—from the people listed in your address book to your list of suppliers.

The Microsoft Works database helps you organize lists of data, select items that are most important, and report on certain aspects of the information you have stored. Because all of this is done electronically, you can get reports, lists, and forms printed within minutes.

Inserting database information into word-processed documents is easy. You can send database information across telephone lines or to another computer in a network. The integration features of Microsoft Works make using a database simple.

In this chapter, look for the basics of creating a database. You will learn how to enter field names, enter data into a record, and edit cell contents, as well as enter dates and move fields and records.

As you become more familiar with database basics, you will learn about searching a database for specific records, selecting records, and sorting records. When you know how to find the records you want, you can start copying, deleting, and clearing data. You will read about formulas, formatting data and numbers, and adding functions to database tasks. As with word processing and spreadsheets, you can add character styles and various alignments to a database.

At the end of this chapter, you will learn how to protect a database to keep it confidential. You also will read about hiding field names, fields, and records. Chapter 10 will contain the information you need to create database reports.

Creating a Database

At the opening Works screen (see fig. 9.1), press N to create a new file. On the new menu that appears, you can choose whether you want to open a new word processing file, a new spreadsheet file, a new database file, or a new communications file (see fig. 9.2). Use the down-arrow key to highlight New Database. Press Enter.

The database screen appears. The file is named DATA1.WDB as a reference. The work space is clear, and you are ready to create a database. Before you plunge into the task of creating a database, take a moment to learn about its various components:

Database Record. This holds all the information about one person, one company, or one event on your list, and consists of database fields. All the records in one database file will hold the same information about each person, company, or event.

Database Field. In a database of companies, each piece of information about the company is a *field.* The name, address, and phone number of the company, the type of company, and the main contact person are all fields in the record for that specific company.

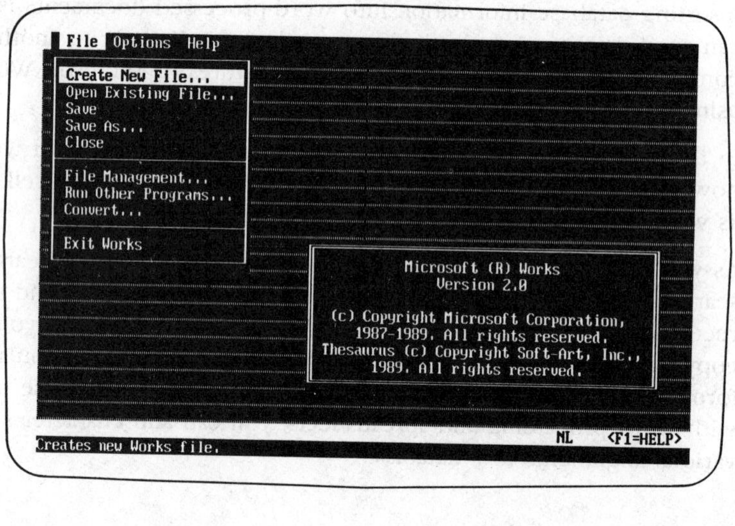

Fig. 9.1.

The opening Works screen.

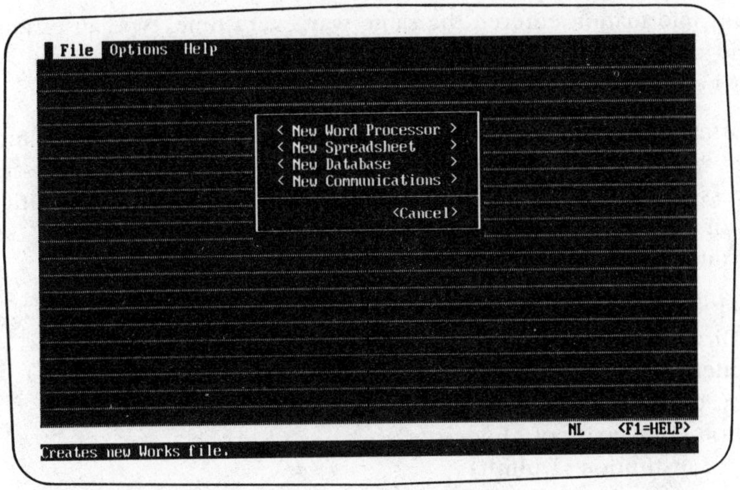

Fig. 9.2.
The Works screen to choose which type of file you want to open.

Label. A title or note is considered to be a *label*, which means that you will not be adding field information to it. The name at the top of the database is an example of one.

Cell. When you list or report information that is in a database, the information is presented in rows and columns. A *cell* is the point where a row and column intersect.

Deciding What You Want To Accomplish with Your Database Information

Now you need to get a clear idea about what you want your database to do. Decide what information is going to be crucial to have, what you would like to add, and what order or format you prefer to use. For example, the database you create for your personal name and address file is going to be different than the one you create for your suppliers.

Create a format that is easy to read and easy to use. Consider those persons who will have access to the database. If you use an abbreviation, will everyone who uses the database know what it stands for?

Field names should be meaningful and unique so that others can understand them. Use your own secret code only when you are the sole person who will have access to the database.

If you want information entered the same way every time, type an example in the field name, such as *Date (MM/DD/YY)*. Date format is especially important because you often will retrieve information by date.

What information do you want on mailing labels? Do you want first names, last names, or professional titles? You may need to add plenty of space for long addresses, plus a field for the company name. When you work with academic or government institutions, you may have to include all the following information:

Name (Joe Brown, Ph.D., D.D.S.)
Title (Director)
Department (Public Heath Dentistry)
School (School of Public Health)
Institution (University of Minnesota)
Branch of Institution (Duluth)

With some entries, you may want to include credentials as a separate field. In a database of expert consultants, you may want to record the professional credentials of those listed, such as M.D., M.S.W., M.B.A., or Ph.D.

Enter the information in a logical order. If you rearrange the sequence (name, company name, address, city, state, and ZIP code), another person entering data into the database may be confused or inconsistent.

You may want to add a number for each field. Purchase orders and invoices often have numbers assigned to them. Add to the record a field that holds a field number.

Entering Field Names

You will create a simple database for the Rancho Mirage Tennis Association. Suppose that it is April 1990, and the Association wants to send a letter to its members who need to renew their membership in May. Therefore, the database contains the members' names, addresses, phone numbers, date of membership, date of most recent membership payments, and amount of money the members' need to pay each year.

Limit the information in the database to the fields just named, although much more could be added for each member. You could list a member's playing level, tournament standings, doubles partner, and locker number, and you could list the last time the member had his or her racquet restrung.

Note: This is the database used for creating form letters and mailing labels in Chapter 4.

To create your databse, do the following:

1. With your cursor in the upper left corner of the database screen, type *Rancho Mirage Tennis Association Membership*. The text is highlighted on the screen and appears both below the menu and above the line with the file name. This area is called the *formula bar* (see fig. 9.3).

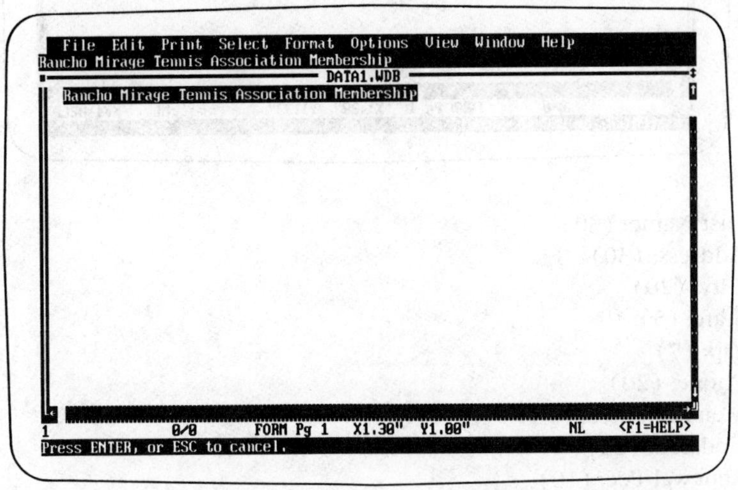

Fig. 9.3.
The title of the database.

2. Press Enter. Move the cursor down two lines using the down-arrow key. Type *First Name:*, and the words appear both in the work space and on the line below the menu. The colon tells Works that you are now entering a field into the database.

3. Press Enter and a dialog box appears. You are to select the width and height of the field. The default values are 20 and 1, respectively (see fig. 9.4). If you know you have many long first names, change the value to more than 20. With `OK` highlighted, press Enter.

4. Repeat steps 2 and 3, entering the following fields with the space allotted (shown in parentheses):

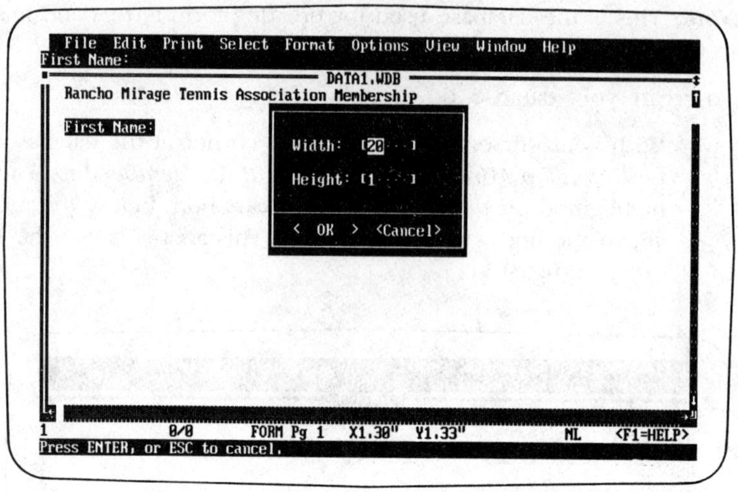

Fig. 9.4.

The Width/Height dialog box.

Last Name: (30)
Address: (30)
City: (20)
State: (5)
Zip: (7)
Phone: (20)
Member Since: (20)
Updated: (20)
Renewal Fee: (10)

Your screen should look like the one shown in figure 9.5.

Entering Data into a Record

You have the basic format for the information you want in your database, and you are ready to add data to each field of information:

1. Move the cursor with the up-arrow key so `First Name` is highlighted. Press the right-arrow key one time, and the highlighting moves to the right of the field name as shown in figure 9.6. The highlighting covers 20 spaces, as specified when you entered the field previously.

2. Type *Bradley*. Continue to move the cursor down to fill in each field until the following data is entered:

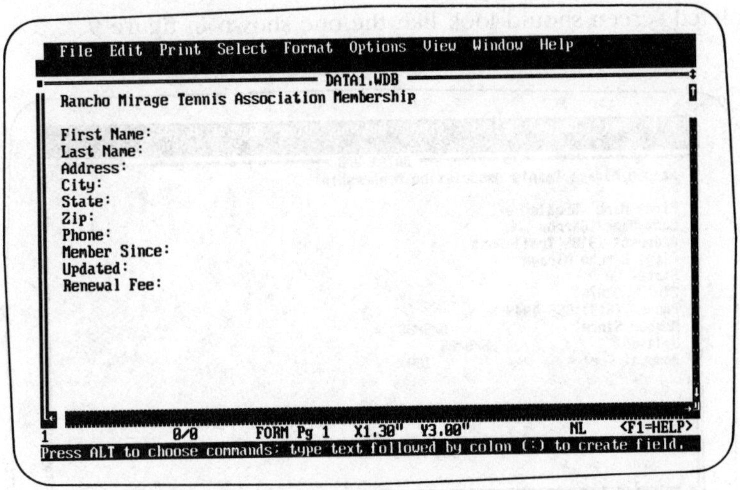

Fig. 9.5.

The database fields entered in DATA1.WDB.

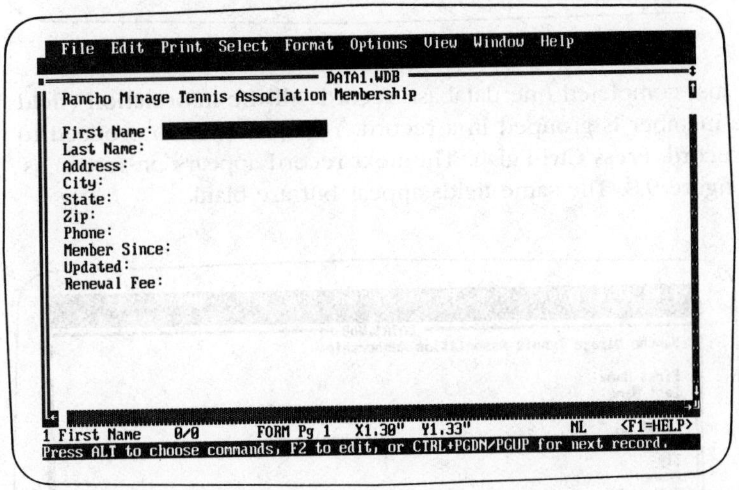

Fig. 9.6.

Space for the First Name *field highlighted.*

Garron
13186 Trail Dust
Rancho Mirage
CA
92876
(619) 555-4049
5/5/88
5/5/88
180

The completed screen should look like the one shown in figure 9.7.

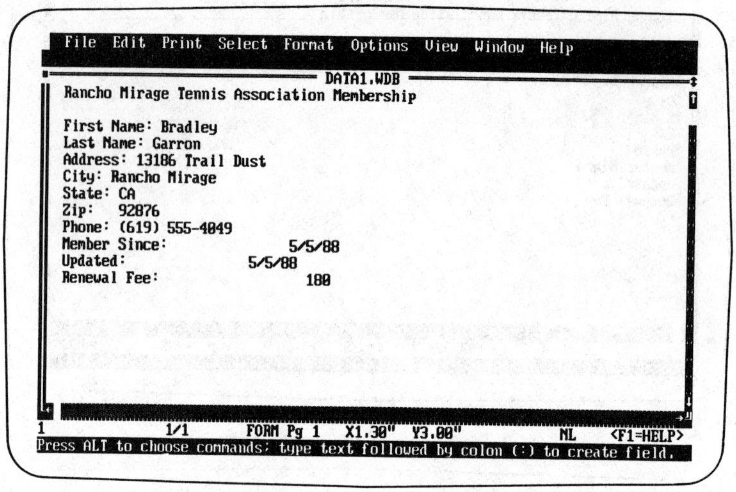

Fig. 9.7.

The completed record.

You have just completed one database record. All the information (fields) about one member is grouped in a record. You are ready to proceed to the next record. Press Ctrl-PgDn. The next record appears on-screen as shown in figure 9.8. The same fields appear but are blank.

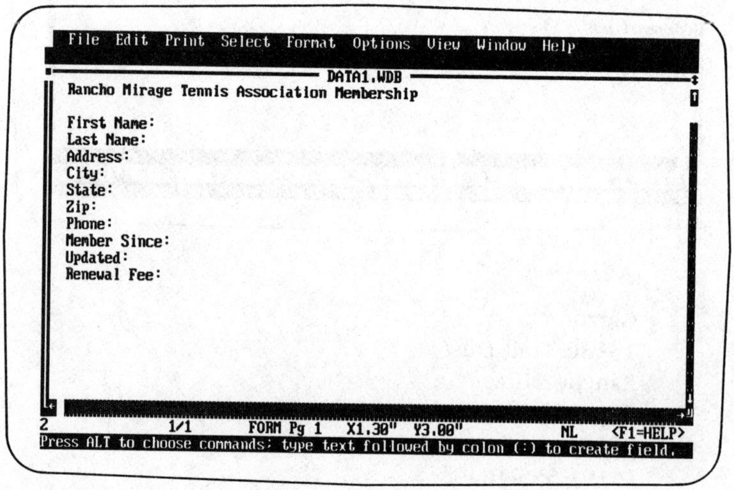

Fig. 9.8.

The second record in the database.

Tip: Notice the 2 that appears on the far left side of the status line. This number tells you that you are in the second record that you entered into your database.

Fill in this record and the third record with the field information presented here:

Record 2:

Moette
Champagne
9306 Twin Trail
San Pedro
CA
92929
(714) 555-3838
5/10/86
5/2/88
140

Record 3:

Tom
Collins
13008 Round Up Ave.
Rancho Mirage
CA
92928
(619) 555-4989
5/15/87
5/25/88
140

Examining the Form View Database Screen

With Record 3 on-screen (see fig. 9.9), notice that the database screen displays a great deal of information. This information helps you keep track of where you are and what you are doing.

Across the top of the screen is the Works menu. Access these menu selections by pressing Alt and then the highlighted letter for each menu.

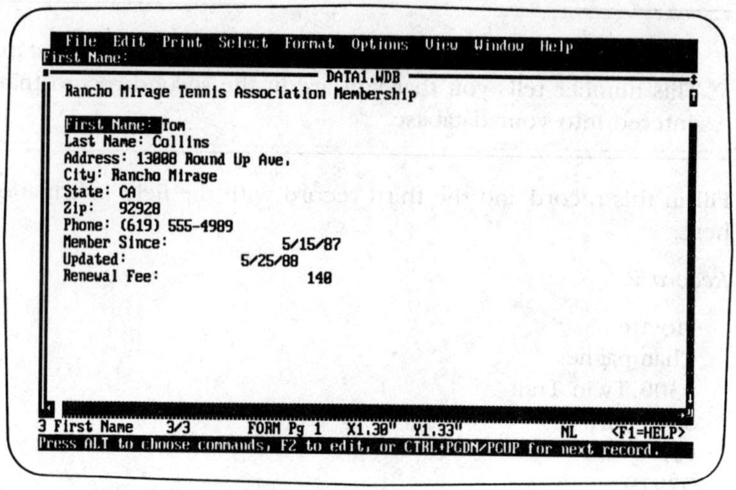

Fig. 9.9.

Record 3 on-screen.

The second line from the top, the formula bar, holds the contents of the active cell. In this example, you see that the cursor is on the `First Name` field. Move the cursor by pressing the right-arrow key one time and `"Tom` appears on this line. The quotation mark that appears before `Tom` indicates that this is data entered into a field, or a label, as in the name of the database. Move the cursor to make ***Rancho Mirage Tennis Association Membership*** the active cell, and `"Rancho Mirage Tennis Association Membership` appears on the formula bar.

Tip: Whenever you enter field names, text, numbers, or field formulas, they are displayed in the formula bar and in the active cell. Press Enter to insert them in the active cell. Works gives you the chance to correct and edit them before they are placed in the database. You can, of course, edit them after entries are made in the active cell by pressing F2 to edit.

The name of the file in which you are working appears on the third line from the top of the database screen.

The work space takes up the majority of the Works database screen, showing the name of the database and listing the fields and their contents.

The shaded line directly below the work space is where mouse activity occurs. Use the arrows to resize windows and use the blocks to move quickly around the database.

The *status line* holds a great deal of information. In essence, as its name implies, it informs you of your status in the database. The 3 that appears on the far left side indicates that the third database record is being displayed.

First Name appears next, giving you the name of the field in which you are working. On this screen, First Name appears on both the formula bar and the status line. If, however, you move the cursor to Tom, "Tom will appear on the formula bar, and First Name will remain on the status line.

As you move right, you see 3/3. All three records are being displayed. With a larger database, it may appear as 28/40, which tells you that 28 of the 40 possible records in that database are being displayed.

Next, you see the word FORM, telling you the type of screen you are looking at. The options are Form, List, and Query screens. Press Alt and then V for the View menu, and the three screen types are listed. A diamond appears next to the Form option, again indicating that you are looking at a Form display. Move the cursor to the List option and press Enter. LIST now appears in place of FORM on the status line. The three records in your database also appear in List mode on the screen. Return to the Form mode by pressing Alt, then V, and then F.

Pg 1 appears next on the status line, denoting a record that has only one page. As you develop a database, you may have records with more than one page. You know where to look to find which page of the record the cursor is in.

More specific information is displayed about your location in the record or database. X1.30" and Y1.33" are displayed next. Imagine a row of Xs across the top of your screen and a row of Ys going down the left side. Like the spreadsheet, the database is divided into cells. The X and Y notations tell you in which cell you are. As you move the cursor across the page to the right, the numbers go in the sequence shown here:

X1.00, X1.10, X1.20, X1.30, X1.40, X1.50, X1.60, X1.70, X1.80, X1.90, X2.00, X2.10, . . .

As you move down the screen, following the y-axis, the sequence is as follows:

Y1.00, Y1.17, Y1.33, Y1.50, Y1.67, Y1.83, Y2.00, Y2.17, Y2.33, Y2.50, Y2.67, Y2.83, Y3.00, . . .

Using the cell indicators, you can find specific locations in a small or large database.

In the short, blank space that follows, you will see the name of command modes you are presently using. Press Alt and then E for the Edit menu.

Press M to move text, and MOVE will appear in this location on the status line. The same is true for Copy or Extend modes. Press F2 and you are in the database Edit mode as indicated in this same location.

The NL you see on-screen tells you that your keyboard is in the Num Lock position. If you press the Caps Lock key, CL appears on the status line. Most of you will have an indicator light on your keyboard for these options, in addition to the on-screen indication.

The last item on the status line is the ever-present reminder to press F1 if you need help with any Works task. Works reads which command you have just selected so that it is able to help you when you indicate that you need assistance.

The bottom line of the Works screen is the *message bar*. While you're in the database, this bar may display the message Press ALT to choose commands, F2 to edit, or CTRL+PGDN/PGUP for next record. Another standard message in the database is Press ALT to choose commands; type text followed by colon (:) to create field. The message bar offers a one-line help message for any task you might perform.

Press Alt and the message bar displays the message Press letter on menu title, or use direction keys and press Enter. So you press E for the Edit menu, and the message bar reads Must select field or label. You are constantly receiving a cue with each key you press.

Now that you are aware of the information available on-screen, practice one of the suggestions on the message bar. Press F2 to edit a field.

Editing a Field

You decide that many other tennis association members will be adding data to this database. Therefore, you choose to take the advice offered earlier in this chapter. You are going to edit the Member Since and Updated fields by adding the format in which you want the date to appear.

Unlike the procedure you use with word processors, the database requires you to enter information into its cells. Move your cursor to the Member Since cell. If you start typing, the new text overwrites the old within that cell. Because you are going to add text to the field, you first need to make the field larger.

Tip: Earlier, when you decided a cell should be 20 or 40 characters wide, that included the field name. When adding text to a field, you have to expand the size of the field in order to have all the text visible on-screen.

Changing the Size of a Field

With the cursor on the underlined section of text next to `Member Since`, press Alt, then T, and then Z to choose the Field Size option. When the dialog box appears, type *40* instead of the 20 chosen earlier to represent the size of this field. Leave the height at 1 line. Press Enter.

Because the size of the field is expanded, you can now go back and enter the date format to the field.

Changing Data in a Field

If you find that you have entered the wrong data into the cell following the field, you can correct it by using the edit key (F2) or by simply typing in new data. When you don't have much information in a cell, you may want to type in the new data. For example, a date is in the cell following the `Member Since` field. If the date is wrong, you have to change the data. To do so, move the highlighting to that cell and simply type in the correct date. Press Enter and the new data is inserted into the cell.

Use the edit key (F2) when you have a long entry in the field or when you are editing something that is difficult to spell. With the highlighting on the cell you want to correct, press F2 and `EDIT` appears on the status line. Using the cursor-movement keys, move your cursor to the incorrect text and then edit just as you would in the word processor. Backspace over the incorrect text and then insert the correct information at the cursor location.

Selecting Fields and Records in Form View

When you prepare to edit, move, and copy records or fields, you must first select them. You have already seen how a Form view cell is selected by simply moving the highlighting to it. In Form view, you are able to select only one record or field at a time. Go to the section on List view to learn how to select more than one record or field.

Select a record by placing your cursor in it. The entire record will not be highlighted, as you would expect with fields. With your cursor in a record, you can move, copy, or delete that record.

Use the keyboard to select a field or data cell by pressing the cursor-movement keys until you get to the cell you want.

Use a mouse to select a field or data cell by pointing to the cell you want and highlighting it.

Moving a Field

Looking at your database, you decide it is not in the order you want. Instead of having the `Updated` field below `Member Since`, you decide you want to move it to the right. This way the dates are on one line and can be easily spotted. Start by selecting the field you want to move.

With Works you can move the field around on the Form view to make the job of reading and finding data easier. You can also move a record from the end of the list to the beginning or insert it anywhere in the list of records. All subsequent records will be renumbered automatically if you choose to move records around.

With the highlighting on the field name you want to move, press Alt, E, and then M to select the Move option. When you press M, the field name and data are highlighted. Figure 9.10 depicts the screen as it will look when you prepare to move a field. Notice the `MOVE` indicator on the status line.

Press the cursor-movement keys to move the highlighting to the new location. In this case, press the right-arrow key to move the highlighting to the right, past the end of the field above. Press the up-arrow key, moving the highlighting up one line.

To use the mouse, move the highlighting by pointing to the right side of the highlighted bar. Click and move the arrow to the right. Click again and the right side of the highlighting will be moved to the location of the mouse arrow. Click on the highlighting again and move the arrow up one line. Click and the highlighting is in the new location.

Figure 9.11 shows the highlighting in the new location. At this point, the field is still in the original location. Press Enter and the field moves to the highlighting (see fig. 9.12).

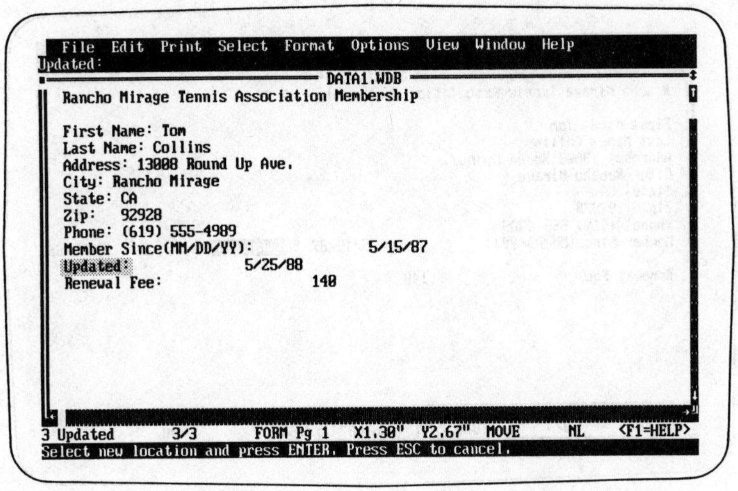

Fig. 9.10.

Prepared to move a field.

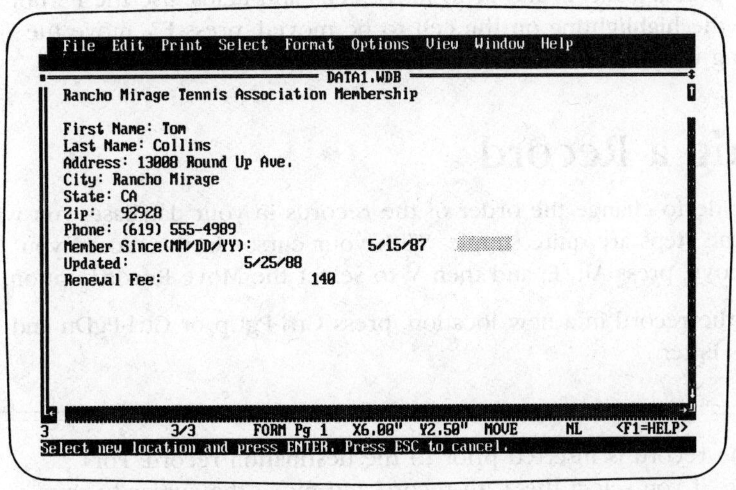

Fig. 9.11.

The highlighting in the new location.

Glance through the two remaining records in this database (press Ctrl-PgUp or Ctrl-PgDn), and you will notice that the change you made in one record appears in every record. This convenient feature means that you don't have to repeat the move procedure in every record.

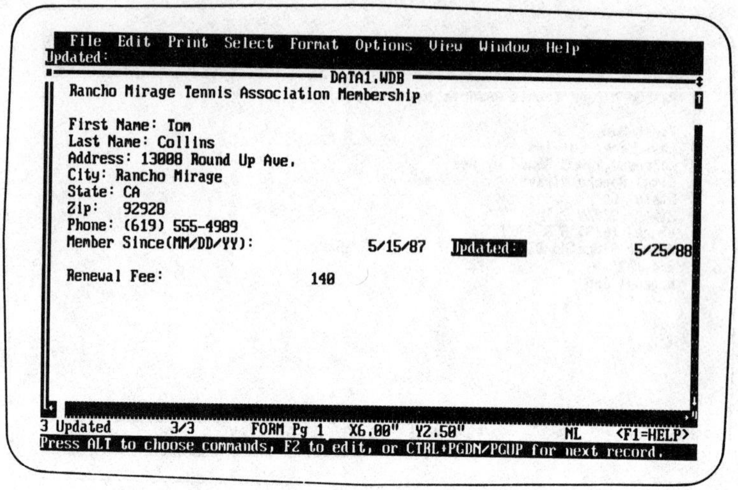

Fig. 9.12.

The field in the new location.

Using the Move Hot Key

Instead of pressing Alt, E, and M to move cells and fields, use the F3 hot key. With the highlighting on the cell to be moved, press F3, move the highlighting to the new location, and press Enter.

Moving a Record

If you decide to change the order of the records in your database, you will find that the steps are quite simple. With your cursor in the record you want to move, press Alt, E, and then V to select the Move Record option.

To insert the record in a new location, press Ctrl-PgUp or Ctrl-PgDn and then press Enter.

Tip: The record is inserted prior to the destination record. For example, if you select the 12th record and move the cursor to the 10th, you insert the record, and then the moved record becomes record number 9.

Copying Labels

You cannot copy field cell data or field names from one record to another using Works. Actually, there is no need to do so because once you establish a database form, every field appears in every record.

You may choose to copy a label from one database to another. As in the previous sections, highlight the label you want to copy by moving your cursor to the label. Press Alt and then E for the Edit menu. From the Edit menu, select the Copy option. `COPY` appears on the status line, informing you that you are in the Copy mode.

Move the cursor to a new location for the label you want to copy. This new location may be in another record or database. Press Enter and the label is inserted in the new location.

The hot key for copying is Shift-F3. Instead of pressing Alt, E, and then C to copy, select the label you want to copy and press Shift-F3. Move the highlighting to the new location and press Enter. The label remains in the original location and is inserted in the new location.

A hot key is also available for you to continue copying the same data. Continue copying the same label by moving the cursor to a new location and pressing Shift-F7. The same label will be copied to the new locations.

Copying and Replacing

Use the Copy Record command to copy an entire record to a new location and replace an existing record. With your cursor in the record you want to copy, press Alt, E, and then P to select the Copy Record option. Press Ctrl-PgUp or Ctrl-PgDn to move to the record you want to replace and then press Enter. The record is copied, but nothing is replaced.

If you do not want to replace an old record, move the cursor to a blank record and press Enter. The record is copied, but no other record is replaced.

Deleting and Clearing Data

Deleting and clearing data are two distinct tasks. Deleting data removes records or fields you no longer need, along with their formatting. Clearing data removes the contents of a cell but leaves its formatting commands so that new information typed in will have the same format as the replaced information. Clear a cell when you want to erase what you have and replace it.

In the RMTA database, highlight `Renewal Fee.` Press Alt and then E to open the Edit menu. Figure 9.13 shows the screen at this point.

Note: The Edit menu will display different menu options, depending on what you have highlighted. In this case, Delete Field is listed; however, the menu would list Delete Label if a label were selected or Delete Line if a blank line were selected.

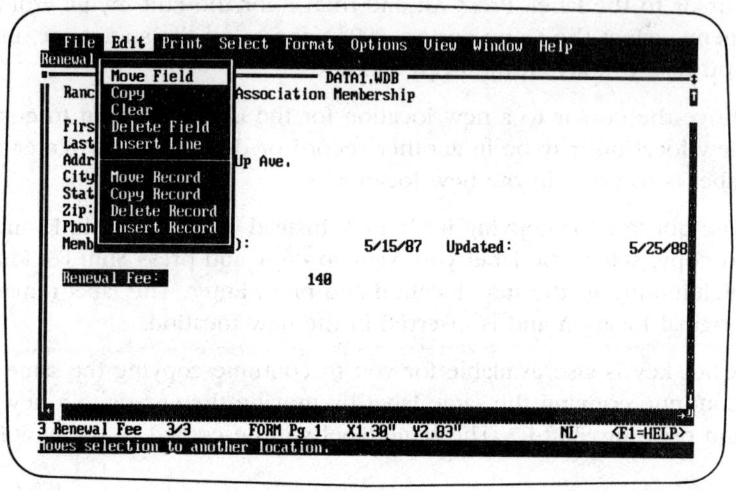

Fig. 9.13.

The screen prior to deleting a field.

Press D for Delete Field. When you do, a warning box will appear, asking whether to delete the data in this field. If you want to delete the field, press Enter after selecting the `OK` option. If you don't want to delete the field, highlight `Cancel` and press Enter. You also can press Esc to remove yourself from this situation at any time.

Clear cell contents by selecting either the label or data you want to remove. Press Alt, E, and then E again to select the Clear option. By choosing this option, you can reenter data into these cells with the same formatting you previously employed.

Examining the List Screen and Functions

Until now you have been working with the Form database screen and with its functions. With the Form screen, you see one record at a time while viewing the fields in that record. When you want to see more than one record at a time to compare field data, use the List database screen. To get a more realistic view of a List screen, move to a database with more entries in it.

For the examples that follow, a database has been created with 25 entries. The 25 entries are names and addresses to whom an advertising mailing was sent in July 1989. All the addresses are outside the United States. In this database, the user is going to track the response to the advertising, noting which persons purchased products as a result of the mailer and the length of time it took for the order to arrive (purchase date).

As with most databases, you could keep track of much more information than this. Perhaps you want to know the date the order was received, when it was shipped, its transit time, whether it was returned, or what the recipient's fax number is. By keeping track of this information, you would know how cost-effective it is to advertise outside the United States.

With the cursor in this database, press Alt and then V to see the View menu (see fig. 9.14). A diamond appears next to the Form option. Move the highlighting to the List option and press Enter. You see what looks like a cluttered list of items found in the database (see fig. 9.15).

On this screen you still have the menu bar, followed by the formula bar. Pay close attention to the formula bar in the List view. Although you may not be able to see an entire entry on the work space, you can see it in the formula bar. As you move the cursor across the top of the screen, you may see `General De` in the work space. On the formula bar, you see `General Delivery`, which is the entire entry (see fig. 9.16).

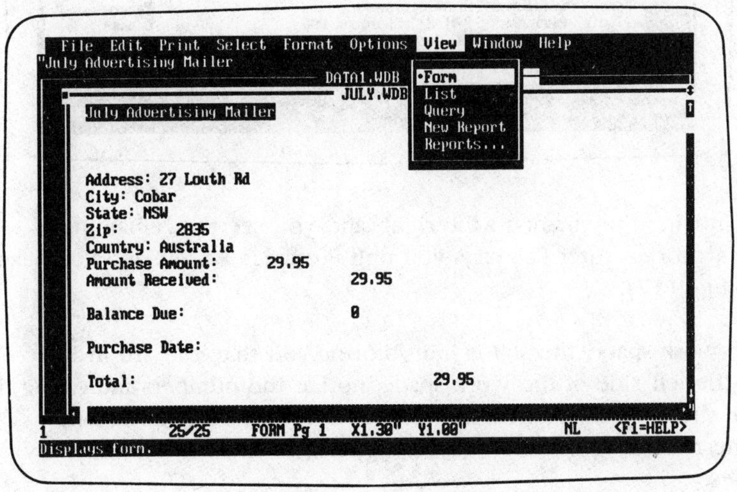

Fig. 9.14.

The View menu.

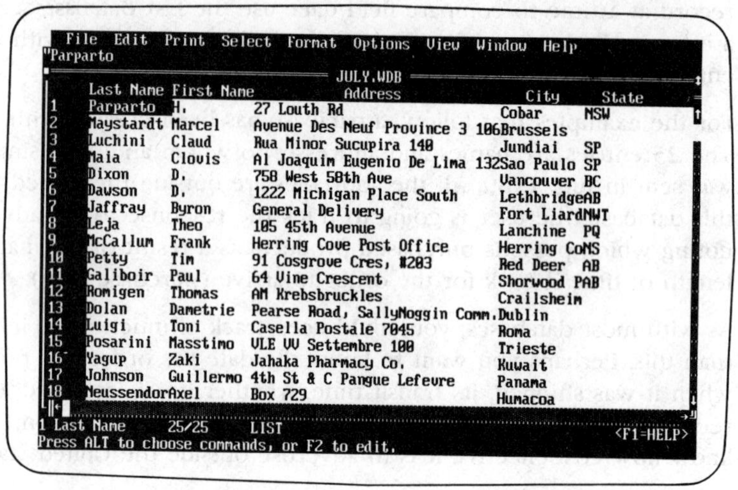

Fig. 9.15.

The database in List view.

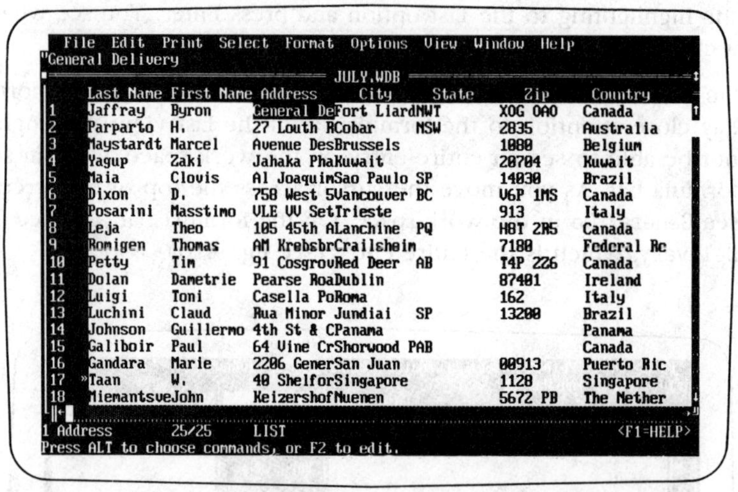

Fig. 9.16.

`"General Delivery` *on the formula bar.*

Continue moving the cursor to the right, and you see the remaining database categories. After `Country`, you find `Purchase Amount` and `Purchase Date` (see fig. 9.17).

Below the work space, the status line informs you that you are in List view. On the left side of the work space, notice the numbers indicating the number of the database record. The numbers 1 to 17 appear on one screen. The remaining List view screen appears much as the Form view screen does.

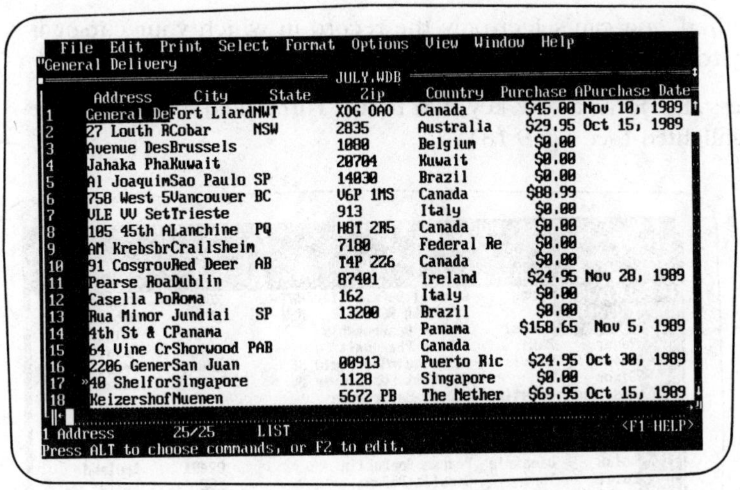

Fig. 9.17.
The right side of List view.

In the work space, notice that the fields are listed from left to right in the same order that you entered them in Form view. As you get to the numeric entries, you also will see various alignments. Because the Canadian postal codes start with letters, they are aligned on the left; postal codes from other countries, made up of numbers, are aligned on the right. The same is true in the `State` column. The `Purchase Amount` column came out neatly because the values were entered in dollars

Selecting Data in the List View

In the Form view, you can select only one field, data cell, or record at a time. In the List view, you can select five records and hide them, you can select an entire field and move it, and you can select any portion of the data and copy it.

Select one cell as you would in the Form view. Move the cursor highlighting to that cell, or point to the cell and click to turn on the highlighting.

Select 3 records out of a 25-record database by moving the cursor to the left side of the screen and following these steps:

1. Move the cursor to the left-most field of the records you want to select.
2. Press F8. (You also can use the menu method by pressing Alt, S, and R to select the Record option. However, if you use the menu

method, you can select only the record in which your cursor is located.) EXT appears on the status line.

3. Press the down-arrow key two times. Three field entries will be highlighted (see fig. 9.18).

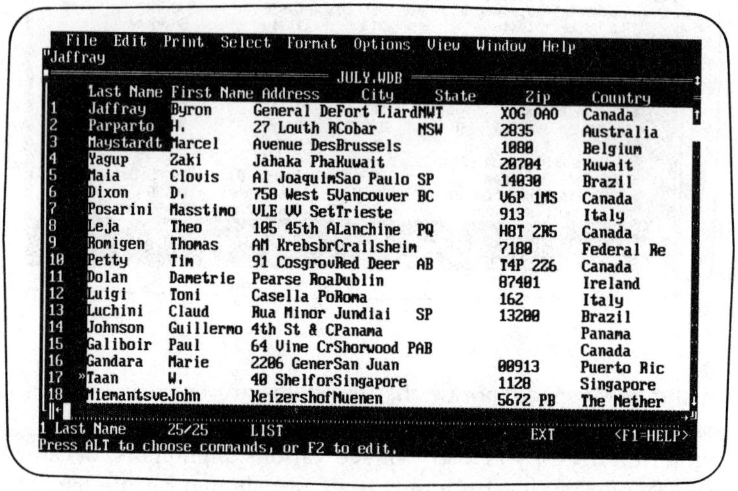

Fig. 9.18.

Three fields selected.

4. Press the right-arrow key until every field in the three records is highlighted (see fig. 9.19). Or press the End key to move to the end of the record.

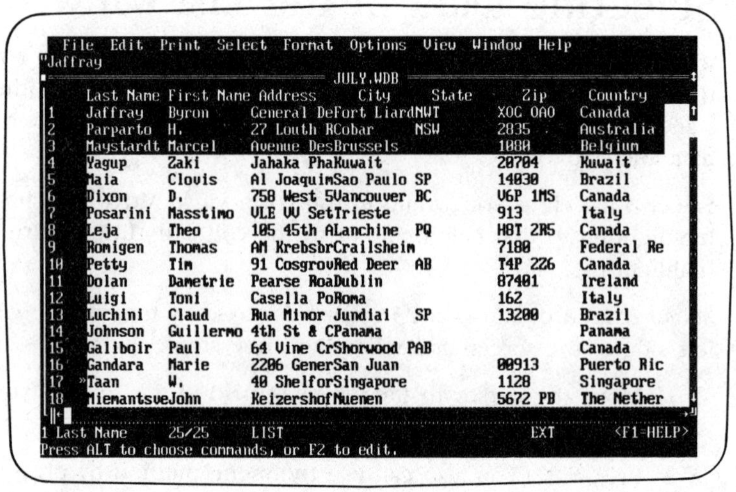

Fig. 9.19.

Three records selected.

Three records are highlighted. Now you are ready to perform tasks such as moving, copying, and deleting records.

Tip: Turn the highlighting off by pressing F8 again. `EXT` is removed from the status line. Now press any cursor-movement key to turn off the highlighting.

Select any field by placing the cursor at the top of the field, pressing F8, and then using the cursor-movement keys to move the highlighting until the entire field is selected.

If you want to format, move, hide, copy, or delete the entire database, save yourself some keystrokes by using the Select All command. With your cursor in the database you want to select, press Alt, S, and then A to select the All option, and the entire database is highlighted.

Tip: Press any cursor-movement key to turn off all the highlighting when `EXT` is no longer on the status line.

In larger databases, you can save yourself the chore of paging back and forth to find the field or record you want to select. Use the Go To command to select a specific record or field:

1. Press Alt, S, and then G to select the Go To option.
2. The Go To dialog box appears. All the fields in your database are listed. Move the highlighting to the field or record number you want to select. In this example, `Purchase Amount` was selected (see fig. 9.20).
3. Press Enter. Your cursor is jettisoned to the first record in the `Purchase Amount` field. Although this column is not highlighted, it is selected.

Editing a Field

The process for editing a field in the List view is basically the same as for the Form view. You move the highlighting to the field and either type in a new entry or edit the old entry. When you start typing, the new text replaces the old in that field. Edit the field by pressing F2. The cursor moves to the entry on the formula bar. From there, move the cursor, delete, and reenter text as needed.

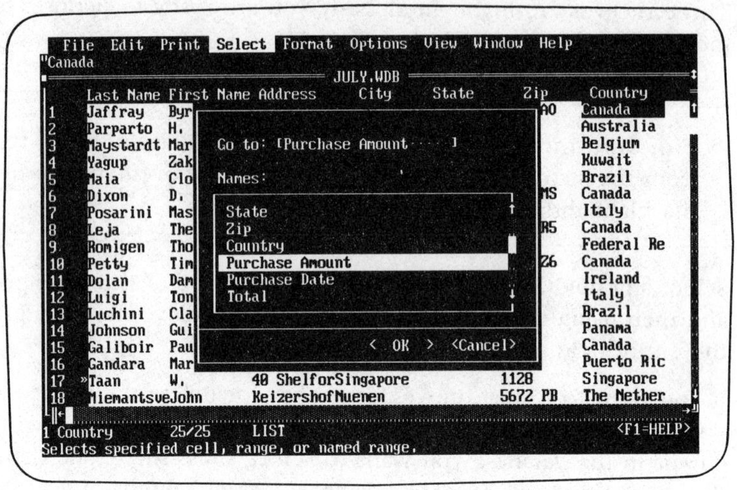

Fig. 9.20.

Purchase Amount *highlighted in the Go To dialog box.*

Changing the Size of a Field

Suppose, while perusing the List view of your database, that you need to see an entire column, even though it doesn't all appear on-screen. You want to make the field larger so that you can view it.

To do so, move the cursor to the column you want to expand. Press Alt and then T for the Format menu and select the Field Width option by pressing W. A dialog box appears, showing the current width, which is 10. Type *40* (see fig. 9.21) and press Enter.

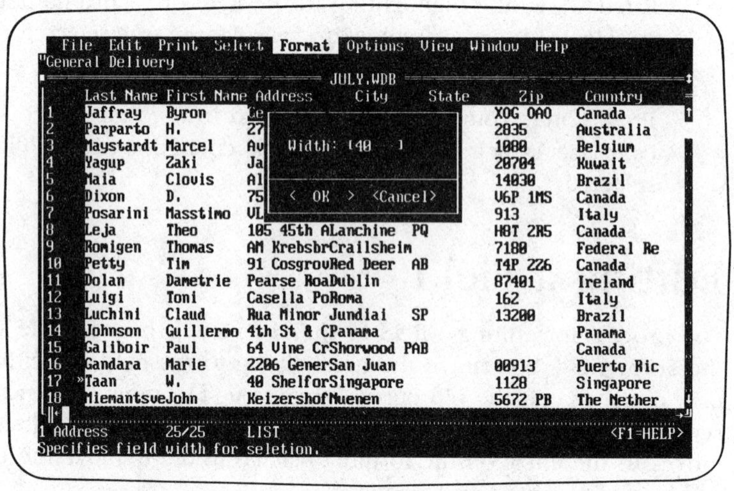

Fig. 9.21.

The Column Width dialog box.

The width of the `Address` column expands to 40 characters wide. As you move the cursor down the page, you can view the entire address for every record in this database. Notice how the database is neater now that there is some space between the columns. To make the List view even easier to read, continue increasing the size of other columns so that no overlap occurs.

Moving a Field

Eventually, this database will be sorted alphabetically, according to last name. To make the List view easier to read, move the `Last Name` field to the left margin and the `First Name` field to the right of it. First, add a blank field between the `Last Name` and `Address` fields. You create a blank field first because when you move a field to a new location, it replaces the data in the field to which you move it. In other words, if you move the `First Name` field to the `Address` field's location, the latter will be replaced.

Tip: Before you start moving columns, fields, or cells, save the file so that you have a backup file on disk.

As you see in figure 9.22, the highlighting is on `General Delivery` beneath the `Address` field. You are going to insert the blank field to the left of the `Address` column. Press Alt, E, and then I to select the Insert Record/Field option. Press Enter and the dialog box shown in figure 9.23 appears.

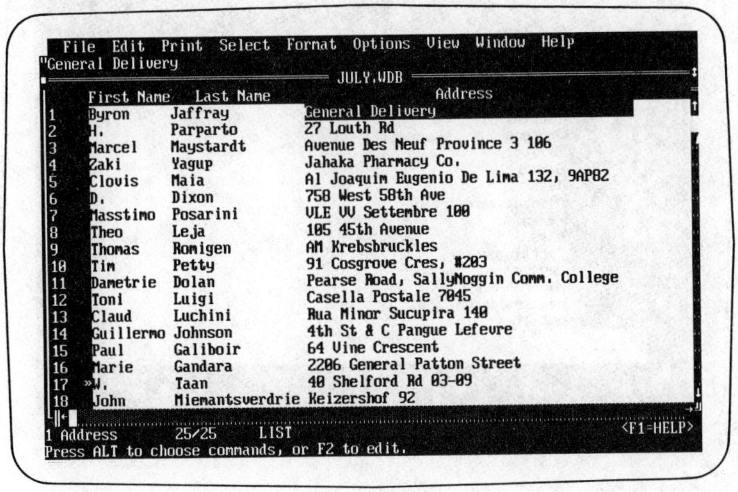

Fig. 9.22.

Highlighting in preparation for inserting a field.

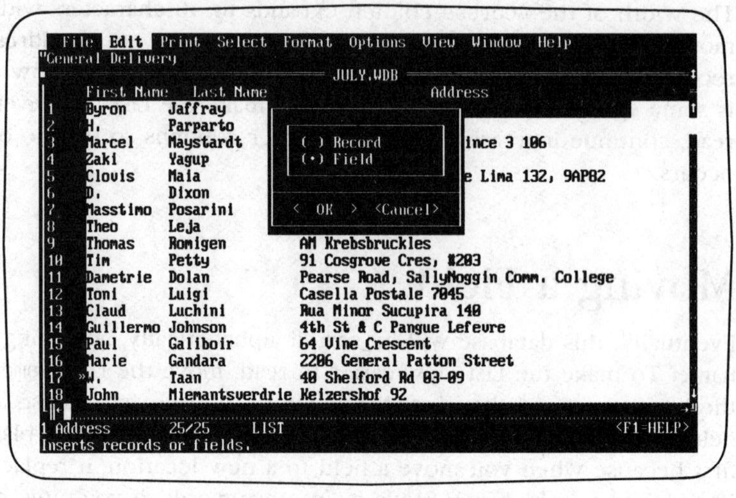

Fig. 9.23.

The Insert Record/Field dialog box.

In the Record/Field dialog box, you can select either Record or Field. You are in the List view, so you want to insert a blank field to the left of the cursor. Move the indicator to Field and press Enter. A blank field is inserted to the left of the Address column. Now you are ready to move the First Name column to its new location.

With the cursor on the first data entry under the First Name field, press F8 so EXT appears on the status line. Move the cursor with the down-arrow key until all the entries in that field are highlighted (see fig. 9.24).

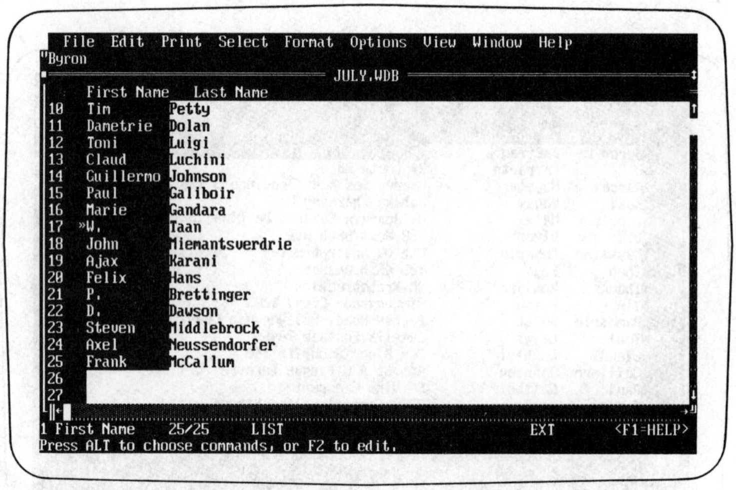

Fig. 9.24.

The First Name *field column selected.*

With the field you want to move selected, press Alt, E, and then M. If you prefer, press F3, the Move hot key. On the status line, you are told to select the new location. Do so by moving the cursor to the blank field you just created. Press Enter. The `First Name` field is blank. The previously blank `Field3` now holds the first names. Figure 9.25 shows the screen after the completed move.

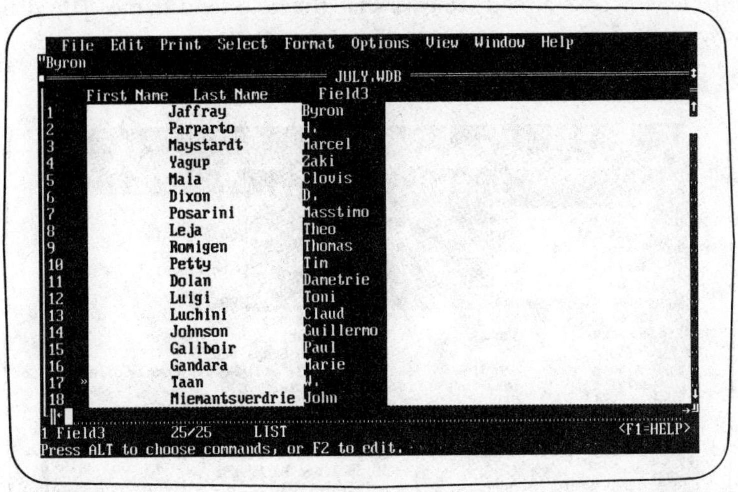

Fig. 9.25.

The `First Name` *field data moved to* `Field3`.

To move the `Last Name` column to the left margin, first select it. With the cursor at the top of the column, press F8 and then press the down-arrow key until the entire column is highlighted. Press F3. Move the cursor to the top of the far left column and press Enter.

This rearranged List view needs to be cleaned up somewhat. First expand the column that holds the last names. Press Alt, T, and then W to select the Field Width option. Type *16* in the dialog box that appears and press Enter. Move the first names in `Field3` to the last name category following the move steps already given and then delete `Field3`.

Delete a field by moving the cursor to the top row in that field. Press Alt, E, and then D to select the Delete Record/File option. Choose `Field` in the dialog box that appears and press Enter.

Editing the Field Name

The last names are on the left, and the first names are listed beside them. However, the field names at the top of the columns are incorrect. Change the field names by following the steps listed here:

1. Move the cursor to any cell in the `First Name` column, which is holding the last names.

2. Press Alt, E, and N to select the Field Name option. A dialog box appears.

3. Type the new field name for this column. In this example, that is *Lst Name*. Press Enter. Do not include the colon here as you did in the Form view. Works already knows that this is a field name. The dialog box with the new name is shown in figure 9.26.

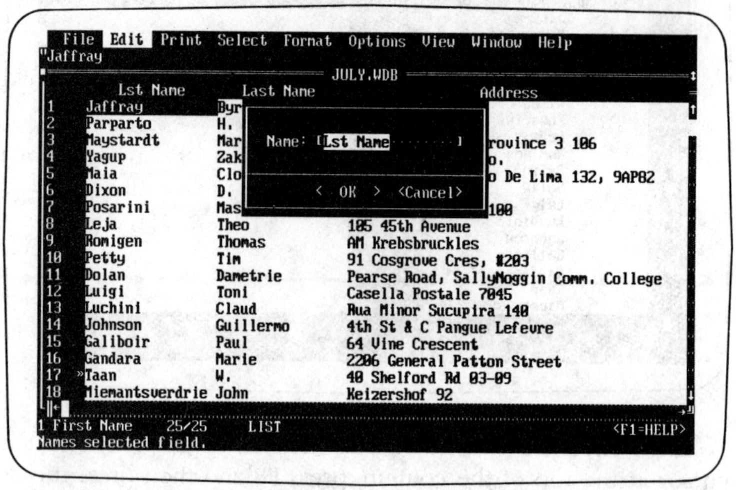

Fig. 9.26.

The Field Name dialog box.

Tip: The name of the column was changed slightly because Works will not allow you to give two fields the same name.

Next, you can change the name of the `Last Name` field to *First Name*. Beyond that, you can change the field name `Lst Name` to *Last Name* because *Last Name* is no longer used elsewhere in the database. After all this maneuvering, the List view database looks like the one shown in figure 9.27.

Note: There is a 15-character limit on field names.

Moving a Record

In the List view, the records appear horizontally across the screen. You follow the same procedure already described, but you select the row the

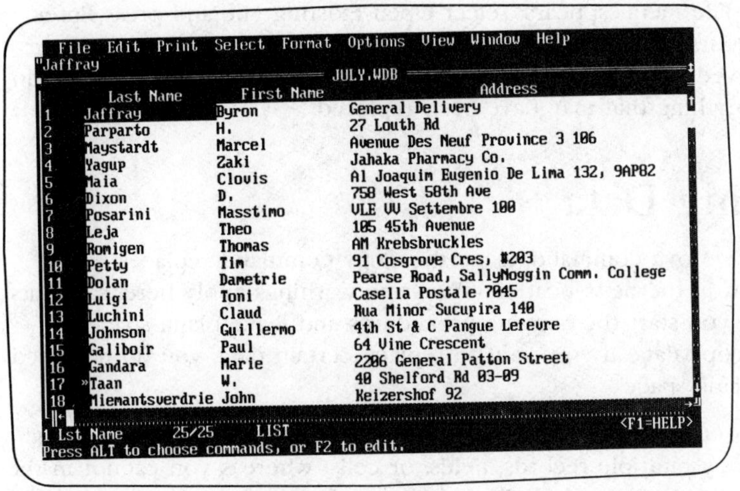

Fig. 9.27.

Fields moved and names changed.

record is in instead of the column going down the screen. For practice, move the first record to the end of the list:

1. Move the cursor to the upper left cell of the record or range of records you want to move. In this example, the highlighting should be on the first record and the first column.
2. Press the End key.
3. Press F3 to place you in the Move mode.
4. Move the cursor to the new location. In this case, choose line 30. Press Enter. The first record is placed on line 30. You can see that row 1 is now blank.

Tip: To protect your data, save your file before you start moving records and fields. If you had moved a record to record number 10, it would have been replaced and would no longer exist. If you want to move a record or field to a new location among other records or fields, create blank space in which to insert the data before you start the move process so that you will not replace data. If you do replace something by accident, you can always return to the saved database to retrieve it.

If you replace data on a saved database, press Alt, F, and then C to select the Close option. When you do, a dialog box appears, asking whether you want to save the changes to the file in which you are working. Move the highlighting to No and press Enter. Works will not save the changes.

When the File menu appears, select Open Existing File and press Enter. Move the cursor to the saved version of the file you closed. Press Enter and the saved version will appear. You retrieve your original data and do not lose anything that may have been replaced.

Copying Data

As with the Move command, using the Copy command replaces information in the new location. The same warnings apply here: save the file before you start the copying procedures and leave blank space in which to copy data. If you want to replace certain data, you do not need to leave blank space.

Select the records, fields, or cells you want to copy. When in the List view, you can copy multiple records, fields, or cells, whereas you cannot in the Form view. With your cursor in the upper left corner of the data you want to copy, press F8. The Extend mode is now on. Press the cursor-movement keys until all the data you want to copy is highlighted.

In this example, highlight the `Purchase Amount` column and press Shift-F3. Move the cursor to the new location and press Enter. The `Purchase Amount` column remains in the original location and is copied to the new location.

Repeat copy commands by pressing Shift-F7. This means that you can copy this same data several times in different files or different parts of a file, while having selected the data only once.

Deleting and Clearing Data

Delete and Clear data in the List view by first selecting the text. Select data to be cleared when you want to keep any formatting but want to remove the cell contents. Delete data when you want to erase it. Deleting will not keep the formatting in the cells.

Select the text you want to delete or clear; then press Alt, E, and then E again to select the Clear option. Or press Alt, E, and D for the Delete Record/Field option.

Because you are using the List view, you can delete several records, fields, or cells at a time. By selecting three inactive records, you can delete or clear them and enter three new names. Carrying out these types of functions in the List view saves you several steps compared with the procedure for deleting three records, one at a time, used in the Form view.

Now that you're familiar with functions you can perform in the List view, you will learn how to use the Works search function. To use the search function, stay in the List view.

Searching a Database

When in the List view, you can search the entire database, selected fields, or certain records. While in the Form view, you can search the entire database only.

The search function helps you designate groups of records to print, to include in a report, or to add to a word-processed document. Find the data you need quickly and easily with a database search. In the database JULY.WDB, you are particularly interested in the native country of the potential customer.

Search the database for records with a German origin. With the cursor at the top of the database, follow these steps:

1. Press Alt, S, and then S again for the Search option.
2. When the Search For dialog box appears, type the data for which you are searching. In this case, type *Germany*.
3. Select either `Next record` or `All records` from the dialog box. The `Next record` option allows you to find only the next occurrence of the data you entered. No records are hidden when you select the `Next record` option. Choose `All records`, and Works will display the records that match the data for which you are searching. The records that do not match are hidden from view. For this example, choose `All records`. Press Enter when the dialog box looks like the one shown in figure 9.28.

Three records are displayed in the search for addresses from Germany. Figure 9.29 shows how only the records that hold the searched-for data are revealed. All others are hidden.

Tip: If you select `Next record` in the Search For dialog box, find one record, and are ready to find the next record with the same data, press F7 to repeat the search.

Now that the three searched-for records are displayed, you want to get back to the List view where all the records are displayed. To see the

Fig. 9.28.

The Search For dialog box.

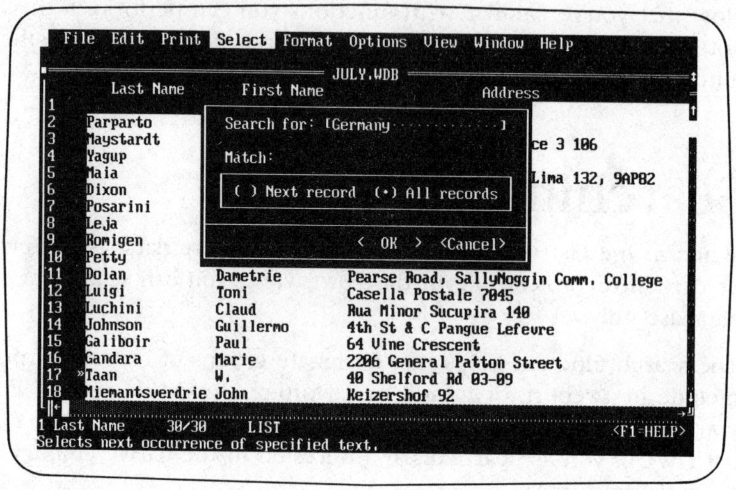

Fig. 9.29.

Three records from Germany.

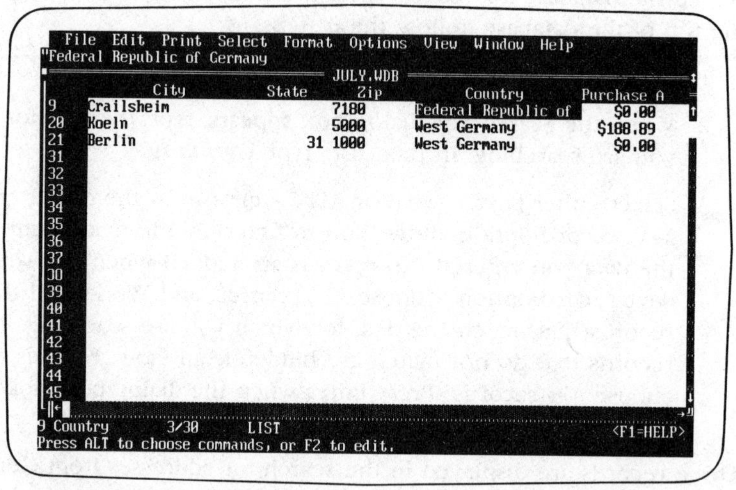

whole picture once again, press Alt and then S for the Select menu (see fig. 9.30). Press L for the Show All Records option. The entire database is again on-screen.

You can search for any character or string of characters in a database. If you cannot remember the exact spelling or sequence of a string of characters, use the Works wild cards. A question mark (?) represents any single character, and an asterisk (*) represents any string of characters.

Search for *Christens?n*, and Works will find *Christensen* and *Christenson*. Search for *a*y*, and Works will find *anatomy, allegory,* and *androgyny,* as

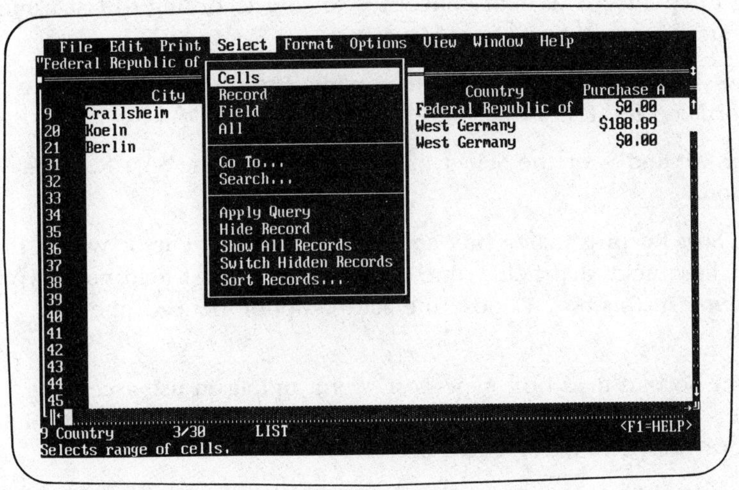

Fig. 9.30.

The Select menu.

well as any other words that begin with A and end with Y. Works finds all upper- and lowercase references to the words you're searching for.

If you are interested in going beyond searches and want to search for ranges of data, you need to create a query. A query is useful when you want to find ZIP codes higher than 90000, for example, or last names that begin with the letters L through S. Review the Query view information in Chapter 10 for complete instructions on creating queries.

You noticed that when you searched for the preceding data, three records were displayed while the rest were hidden. At the end of this chapter, you will read more about hiding fields and records in a database.

Sorting Records

Placing the database records in a specific order can save you time. You can put the records in ZIP code order so that when you print the labels for a bulk mailing, they will be printed in the proper order. You can have the records arranged in ascending order by invoice number. Or you can list the `Last Name` field in the database according to alphabetical order.

Works allows you to specify up to 3 sort fields at one time. Put the most important field first, with the remaining 2 fields in descending order. An ascending sort is done from the beginning to the end, as in A to Z or 0 to 100. Descending order is the opposite, as in Z to A or 100 to 0.

Because the main concern of the user of this database is the country of origin shown in records, the sorting task at hand is to sort, alphabetically, according to country. The next concern is to sort according to last name in alphabetical order. Here is how it works:

1. Press Alt and then S for the Select menu. Press A to select all the records on the List view.

2. Press Alt and S for the Select menu. Press O for the Sort Records option.

3. The Sort Records dialog box appears. Because the cursor was in the `Last Name` field, that field name is placed in the first field box. Type *Country* in this box. Choose the `Ascend` option beneath the first field.

4. In the second field box, type *Last Name* and again use ascending order. The dialog box should look like the one shown in figure 9.31 before you press Enter. Press Enter.

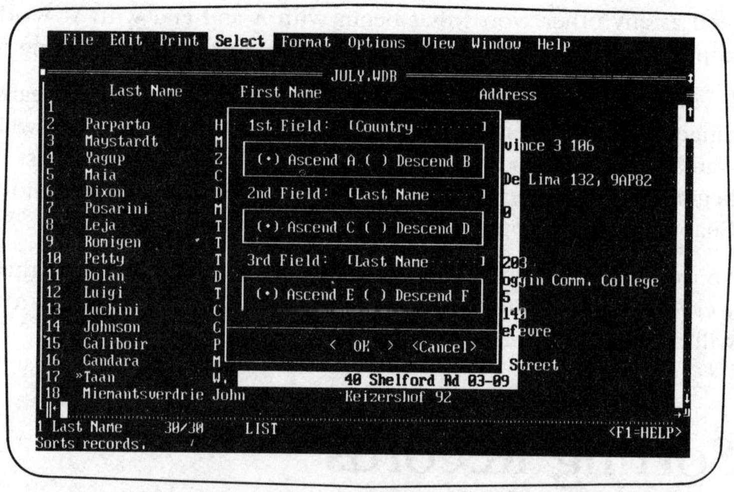

Fig. 9.31.
The Sort Records dialog box with entries.

The records in the database are listed alphabetically by country. Within each country, the individuals are listed alphabetically by last name.

Tip: You can sort by more than three sort fields. Do one sort with the least important fields listed. Do a second sort with the more important fields listed on the Sort Records dialog box.

Using Formulas in a Database

Formulas can be used in database cells as they were in spreadsheet cells. Use formulas either to create a proposed response in a field where one condition is likely to be true or to use the values in two fields calculated together.

Formulas must be preceded by an equal sign (=). You are setting up the formula to equal the value that appears in that cell. Only one formula is allowed per database field. A formula entered into a field in one record is automatically entered in every other record in that database.

When you are calculating a value based on the values in other fields, you use the name of the other fields in the formula. In an invoice record, you may have the amount of purchase, the amount paid, and the balance due. Put that in a formula in which the Balance Due field would contain this formula:

=Purchase Amount−Amount Paid

You could take the last example a step farther and create an incrementing value. For example, you want a balance due for each invoice, but you also want the total amount due for this time period. Use a Total Balance Due field to add the balance due from the previous record or records to the balance due in the current record. The Total Balance Due formula would be

=Balance Due+Total Balance Due

Works will then get the total balance due from the field in the previous record and add it to the balance due from this record, giving you a running total.

The formula also can be used with text. The Rancho Mirage Tennis Association has 95 percent of its members living in Rancho Mirage. Instead of entering Rancho Mirage in the `City` field of 500 records, simply type the following in the `City` field:

="Rancho Mirage

The equal sign (=) tells Works that this is a formula to be inserted into every record. The quotation mark (") tells Works that this is text. For the few members who live in another city, enter their city name as you normally would. That label will replace the universal label you typed with the formula.

Database formulas can contain operators such as +, −, *, /, constant values, field names, and functions. The Works operators are listed in table 9.1.

Table 9.1
Works Operators

Operator	*Meaning*
^	Exponential
−	Negative or subtraction
+	Positive or addition
*	Multiplication
/	Division
=	Equal to
<>	Not equal to
<	Less than
>	Greater than
<=	Less than or equal to
>=	Greater than or equal to
~	Not
|	Or
&	And

The same functions that work in the spreadsheet also work in the database. You will find the functions and their descriptions in Chapter 7. Insert these built-in mathematical equations in formulas to reduce the time it takes to enter complex formulas.

Here is an example of using a formula in the JULY.WDB database. You are going to get a running total of purchases made outside the United States.

Add a new field in the Form view. To return to the Form view, press Alt and then V for the View menu. Select Form and press Enter.

Move the cursor to the bottom of the first record. Type *Total:* and press Enter. Type *40* for the field size. With your cursor in the highlighting for the data, type this formula:

=Purchase Amount+Total

Press Enter and a value appears in the data cell. The formula you entered appears on the formula bar. This formula gives you a running total. It adds the purchase amount to the total for the previous record. As you move through the records, the total becomes larger. Figure 9.32 shows the total value for a later record. Notice the formula on the formula bar.

Making each form more like an invoice, fields for amount received and balance due have been added. For each record, the data was entered for the amount received. In the `Balance Due` data cell, type the following formula:

=Purchase Amount−Amount Received

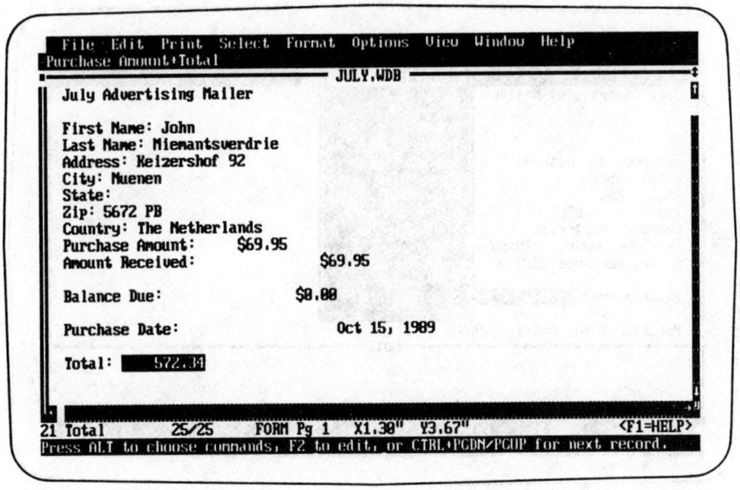

Fig. 9.32.

Record 21 with running total.

Press Enter. For the first record, a balance due of zero is shown. Moving to a record where a balance due value is present, see how Works has done your calculating for you. The formula you used to get the balance due is displayed on the formula bar.

Formatting Data

Numbers in the database can be in formulas or data in a field. The formats that affect numbers are found on the Format menu shown in figure 9.33. The top portion of the menu shows the formats from General to Time/Date.

Format numbers differently when they are dates, when they appear in a balance sheet, or when you are rounding data. Here is a description of the various number formats:

General. This is the default number format; if you do not specify a format, Works uses the General format. Integers are used in a precise form. For example, you will find 548.989 in this format. Numbers that take up more than the allotted space in a cell are written in exponential notation, such as 5.48E+06. Negative numbers are preceded by a minus (−) sign.

Fixed. You specify the number of decimal places you want displayed using this format. Specify three decimal places, and .05898 will appear as .059. Negative numbers are precedd by a minus (−) sign.

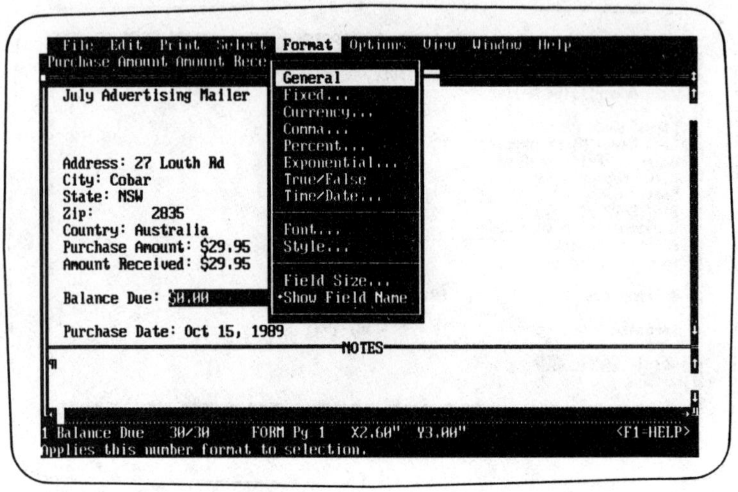

Fig. 9.33.

The Format menu.

Currency. In this format, a currency sign, commas every three spaces, and a decimal point to two locations are displayed (the number of decimals can be changed). When you enter data with a currency symbol, Works recognizes the symbol and formats the number as currency. Negative numbers are placed in parentheses.

Comma. This format inserts commas at every three places, and negative numbers are placed in parentheses.

Percent. This format displays numbers as percentages with the specified decimal places. For example, .67 becomes 67% with zero decimal places specified. Negative numbers are preceded by a minus (−) sign. As with the Currency format, type a percent symbol (%) after a number and Works recognizes the Percent format.

Exponential. Values are shown in scientific notation in this format. For example, 158600000 becomes 1.59E+08 if you specify two decimal places. Negative numbers are preceded by a minus (−) sign.

True/False. Logical values are displayed in this format. Cells with a value of zero display FALSE, and cells with a nonzero value display TRUE.

Time/Date. Go to the next section for details concerning this format.

Tip: When you want to format a number that begins with a zero, type a quotation mark and then type the number. This makes the number text rather than a numeral. In JULY.WDB you enter the ZIP code for San Juan, Puerto Rico, by typing *"00913*. Without the quotation mark, the leading zeros would be eliminated, leaving you with an incorrect ZIP code of 913.

Now that you have been introduced to the formatting options, add one to the JULY.WDB database. The balance due is a calculated value. It is displayed to two decimal places only if there are two decimal places with a numerical value. Change the format to Currency so that two decimal places are present. In figure 9.34 the highlighting is on the data cell for the `Balance Due` field. No decimal places appear for the value.

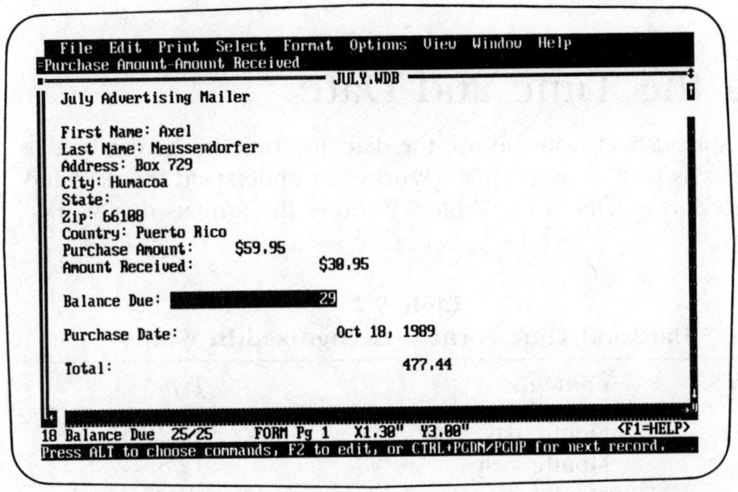

Fig. 9.34. *The highlighted cell to be formatted.*

Press Alt, T, and then U to select the Currency option. You are asked to specify the number of decimals. Press Enter with the default value of 2 on-screen. The value of the `Balance Due` field is reformatted with a dollar sign and two decimal places (see fig. 9.35).

Note: When you format the cell in one record, all the records in that file have the same format.

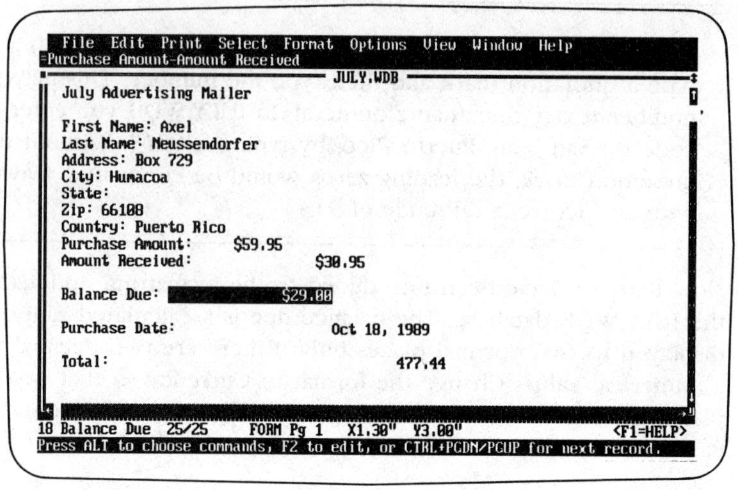

Fig. 9.35.

Balance due formatted in Currency format.

Using the Time and Date

As in the spreadsheet, you can use the date and time in the database as data in cells as well as in formulas. Works can understand the date and time entered in specific ways. Table 9.2 shows the formats that Works recognizes.

Table 9.2
Date and Time Formats Recognized in Works

Format	*Contents*	*Type*
Short	Month, day, year	12/28/55
	Month, year	12/55
	Month, day	12/28
Long	Month, day, year	Dec 28, 1955
	Month, year	Dec, 1955
	Month, day	Dec 28
	Month only	Dec
12-hour	Hour, minute, second	7:36:00 PM
	Hour, minute	7:36 PM
	Hour only	7 PM
24-hour	Hour, minute, second	21:18:00
	Hour, minute	21:18

Type the date or time, using the formats shown in table 9.2, in any field cell in the database. As long as they are in the correct format, Works will recognize and accept them.

Works automatically formats dates and times according to those listed in table 9.2. If several people are entering data into the database, format the date cell and all the entries will be the same. Do the following:

1. In any record, in the data cell of the `Purchase Date` field, press Alt, T, and then T again to select the Time/Date option.
2. The Time/Date dialog box appears. Select the format for the date in the `Purchase Date` field. In this example, choose `Month, day, year` as the format for entering dates.
3. Press Enter. The field data cell is formatted. Type a month, day, and year in any format, and it will appear in a standard format every time. Type *10/15/89* and `Oct 15, 1989` appears in the data cell.

In addition, you can enter the current date and time in any database cell. With your cursor in a field attribute location in the Form view or a cell in the List view, press Ctrl-; (press and hold down the Ctrl key while you type a semicolon). When you do, the current date is inserted within the cell. Press Ctrl-Shift-; to insert the current time in a cell. Figure 9.36 shows the date and time entered in two separate cells.

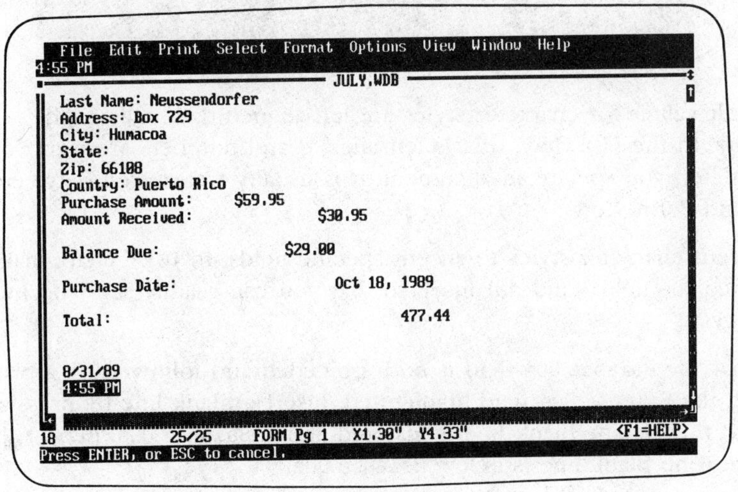

Fig. 9.36.

The current date and time inserted.

Using Different Character Styles and Alignment

Works gives you many choices in character styles and alignments. You can choose boldface, underline, and italic character styles. Data can be left aligned, right aligned, centered, or justified. Works also has a slide-to-left feature so that you can keep blank spaces from being printed. These options are on the Style dialog box, which you access by pressing Alt, T, and then S for the Style option. Figure 9.37 shows this dialog box.

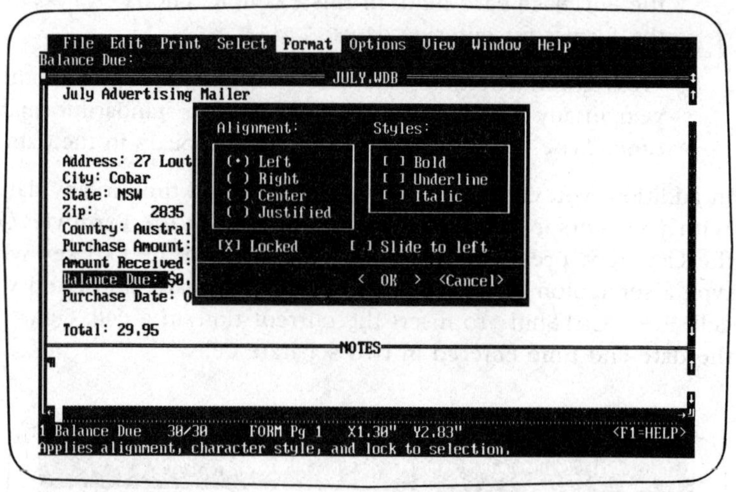

Fig. 9.37.

The Style dialog box.

The default values for character styles are left-aligned data cells in the Form view. In the List view, text is left aligned and numbers are right aligned. When you specify an alignment, it is usually transferred between the List and Form view.

Use different character styles to accent specific fields. In JULY.WDB, make the `Balance Due` field stand out more so that you can readily see who owes you money.

Notice that the `Balance Due` field is both preceded and followed by a blank line. With the `Balance Due` field highlighted, insert a blank line by pressing Alt, E, and then I. The blank line is inserted above `Balance Due`. Repeat this procedure if no blank line is below `Balance Due`.

Move the highlighting to `Balance Due` and press Alt, T, and S for the Style option. With the Style dialog box on-screen, select the `Bold` option. An `X` appears next to `Bold`, indicating that the option is turned on. Move the cursor to `OK` and press Enter.

Balance Due is in boldface on-screen. As you peruse the Form view, you can easily spot one of the most important fields on the page.

Adjust a column alignment in the List view. Press Alt, V, and then L for the List menu. Move the cursor to the right until you are in the Zip field. Figure 9.38 shows how the postal codes that begin with letters are left aligned and the postal codes that are numbers are right aligned. Make the entire column left aligned by following the steps listed here:

1. Press Alt, T, and then S for the Style option.
2. While in the Style dialog box, press L for left-aligned text. Press Enter.

The postal codes in the Zip field column are all left aligned as they would be if they were text. Look at figure 9.39 to compare the left-aligned Zip field with the same column in the previous figure.

When you print forms and you want the text to slide to the left so that less blank space is printed, use the Slide to left check box on the Style dialog box.

Note: The Slide to left option is available only on the Form view of a database.

First, select the text you want to slide to the left. Press Alt, T, and then S for the Style option. Press S to turn on the Slide to left option. When you print this form, no leading spaces will be printed before the selected field or label.

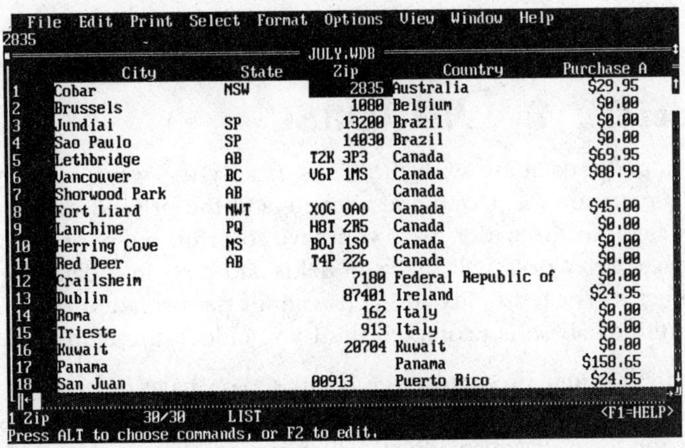

Fig. 9.38.

Left- and right-aligned postal codes.

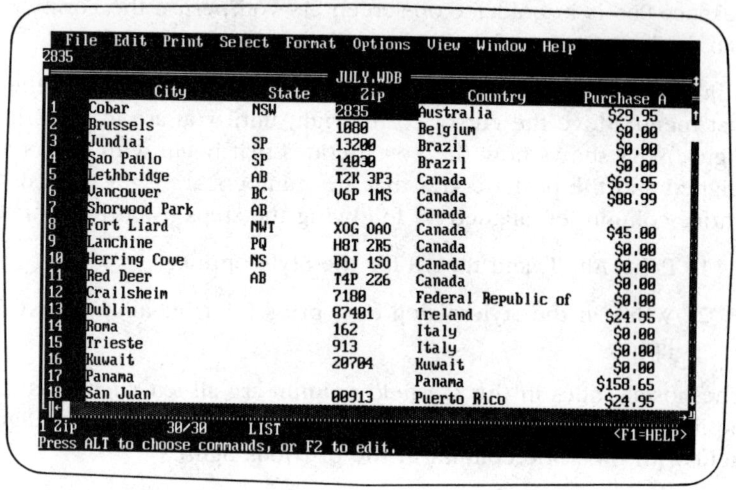

Fig. 9.39.
Left-aligned postal codes.

Using Different Fonts

Changing fonts is another effective way to set off certain text in your database. Your ability to change fonts will depend on the capabilities of the printer you are using. Select the text you want to appear in another font and press Alt, T, and then F to select the Font option. The Font dialog box appears, listing the fonts available with the printer you indicated in the Works setup program.

Move the cursor to the font of your choice and press Enter. The selected text will be printed in that font. Text can be affected by only one font at a time, unlike character styles.

Protecting a Database

You have developed a database with the fields exactly the way you want them. The characters are formatted and aligned, and the printed version of the Form view fits into the paper form you have to print. It's perfect! Now protect your database. Works will lock the fields and cells in a database when you protect it. Locked fields and cells cannot be formatted or changed when the database is protected until you unlock the field or cell.

You will want to consider protecting the database you have created, especially when other people will be entering data into it. Works allows you to protect the form design while still allowing you to enter and edit data. Protect the form design, and other employees can enter and edit data but cannot change the field names, labels, format, or size.

Protect the JULY.WDB database form design by pressing Alt, O, and then F for the Protect Form option (Form view only). When the Protect Form option is on, the indicator symbol is placed next to it on the menu (see fig. 9.40).

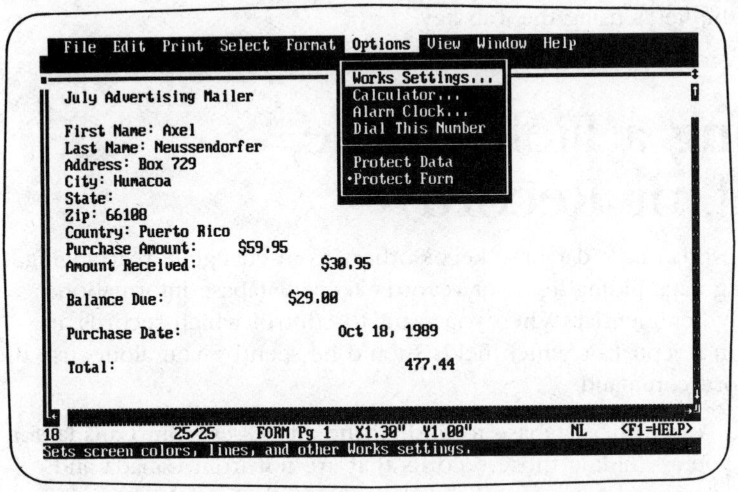

Fig. 9.40. *The Protect Form indicator turned on.*

When you enter data in a field, it is entered in the locked form. Press Alt, T, and then S for the Style option. The Style dialog box appears. Below the list of types of alignment, the locked box has an X beside it. The Locked option is turned on by default. In other words, it is always on until you turn it off.

With the data entered in the Locked mode, you can still continue to enter and edit data. When you are ready to lock the entire database, and not just the form, press Alt, O, and then P for the Protect Data option. The indicator appears next to this option now, showing that it is on.

With the Protect Data option on, locked fields and data cells cannot be edited or entered. A student can access his or her grade report but cannot change the final grade. An employee can look at his or her work schedule but cannot add a few extra hours of overtime.

You have the option to keep some of the fields unlocked. Then, when the Protect Data option is on, those fields are not affected. That is, they remain unlocked and can have either new data entered or old data edited.

Unlock a field by pressing Alt, T, and S to reach the Style dialog box. Press K to turn off the Locked option. This option is a toggle. Press K again and the option is turned on. When the X no longer appears next to the option, move the cursor to OK and press Enter. The field or cell in which you are working is unlocked.

With all your fields locked and the Protect Data option on, put your cursor at the top of the Form screen and press Tab. Nothing happens because Tab selects only unprotected fields. If none exist, the Tab key does not move you to the next field. Turn off the Protect Data option, and you can again move to the fields using the Tab key.

Hiding a Field Name, Field, or Record

Whereas protecting a database keeps others from changing, rearranging, and editing data, hiding fields or records keeps database information completely confidential. When you want to control which records are included in a report or which fields should be seen by you alone, use the Hide Record command.

When you search the database to find all the addresses from Canada, for example, you are hiding those records that are not from Canada and displaying the ones that are. Beyond that, the Hide Record command allows you to choose which records you want to hide, regardless of searches.

A hidden record is not listed in List view and does not appear in the Form view. A hidden record cannot be included in a report or be printed with other records. The status line displays the number of displayed records compared to the total number of records. If 22/25 appears on the status line, 22 of the total 25 records are displayed; three records remain hidden.

With your cursor in the record you want to hide (Form view), press Alt, S, and then H for the Hide Record option. The record disappears from the screen. On the status line, you see that one less record is displayed.

In List view, you can select several records and hide them all with one series of keystrokes. In JULY.WDB, hide all the records from West Germany. To do so, first select the two records from West Germany. Now press Alt, S, and H for the Hide Record option. Figure 9.41 shows the screen before the records are hidden.

Return to the List view screen, and 23 of 25 records are displayed.

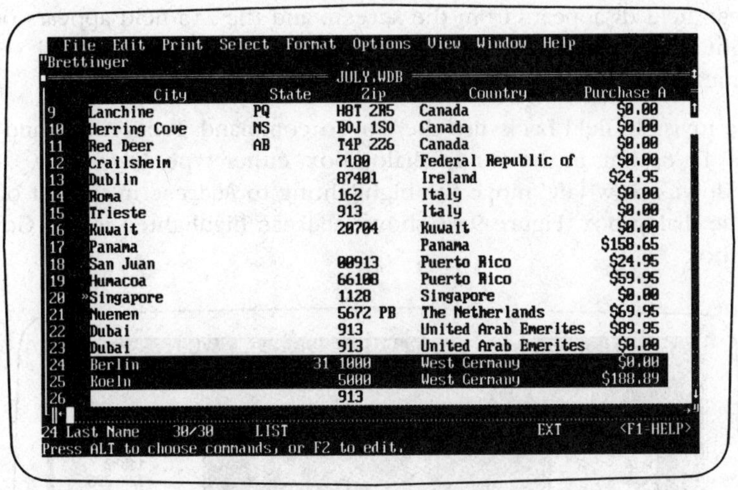

Fig. 9.41.

Two records selected for hiding.

When you hide a field, you get a slightly different result than when you hide a record. Hide a field in the List view, and the field is still displayed in the Form view. You usually will want to hide a field when you are in the List view. If you hide a field, the other fields will be more visible.

Suppose that you are working in JULY.WDB and are only interested in the last name of the person on the mailing list and his or her postal code. Hide the `Address` field, and you will be able to see the last name and the postal code on the screen at the same time.

With your cursor highlighting in the `Address` column, press Alt, T, and then W for the Field Width option. In the dialog box, press 0 (see fig. 9.42). Press Enter.

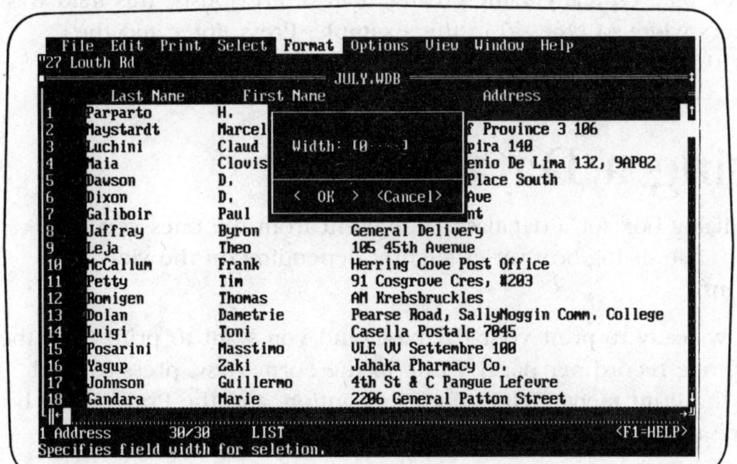

Fig. 9.42.

The Field Width dialog box.

The `Address` field disappears from the screen, and the `Zip` field appears on the far right side. Don't worry, because the address information is still there, in memory, although it is not visible on-screen.

To get the invisible field back, use the Go To command. Press Alt, S, and G for the Go To option. In the Go To dialog box, either type *Address* or, using the down-arrow key, move the highlighting to `Address` in the list of fields in the dialog box. Figure 9.43 shows `Address` highlighted in the Go To dialog box.

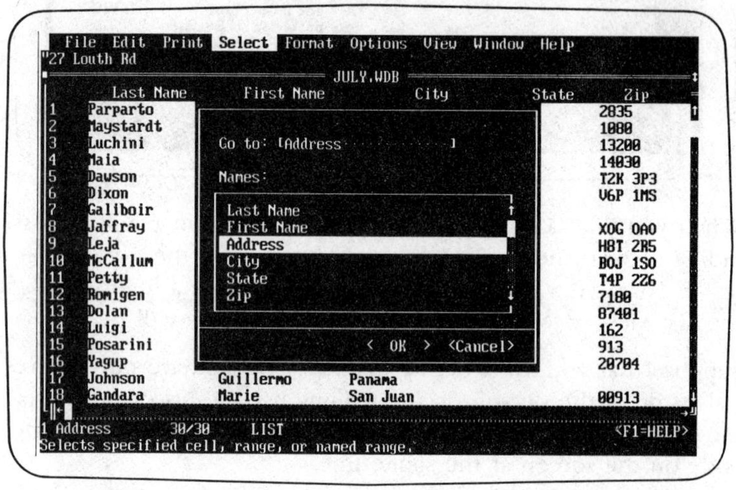

Fig. 9.43. `Address` *highlighted in the Go To dialog box.*

Press Enter and you select the hidden field, even though it is not displayed. Now press Alt, T, and W for the Field Width option. In the Field Width dialog box, type any value greater than 0. Previously, this field was 40 characters wide, so type *40* in this example. Press Enter and the `Address` field reappears in its original location.

Printing a Database

The Print dialog box for a database is different from the ones you have seen before. The dialog box varies slightly depending on the view you want to print.

You are now ready to print your database, and you want to print from the Form view, one record per page. While in the Form view, press Alt and then P for the Print menu. Select the Print option, and the Print dialog box appears (see fig. 9.44).

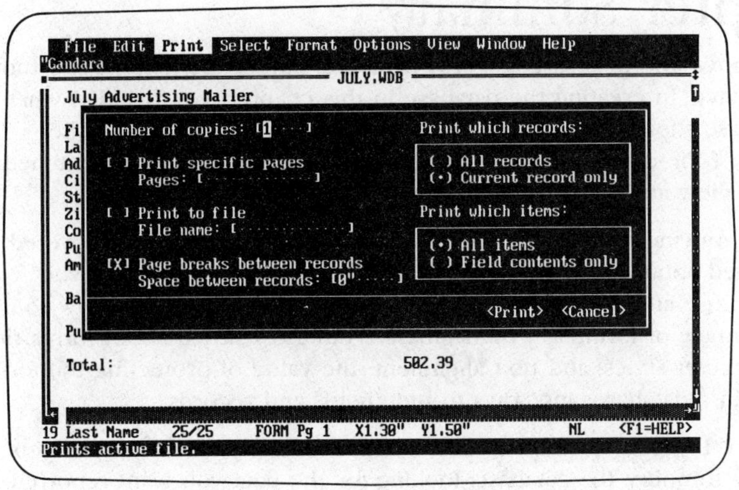

Fig. 9.44.

The Print dialog box.

As usual, you can print any number of copies you choose. The `Page breaks between records` option is turned on, which means that you will get one record per page. On the right side of the dialog box, you can choose to print all records or the current record only. Press Alt-A to print all records. Press Alt-M to print forms only. Finally, you can choose between printing field names and contents or printing data only. When you have made all these decisions, press Alt-P to print the Form view of the database.

Note: The dialog box options that are dimmed are not available in the view from which you are printing. Monochrome monitors have options without reverse-video letters.

Print from the List view by pressing Alt, P, and then P again for the Print option. In the List view, you can choose the number of copies and whether you want to print labels. Press Enter and the list of records will print.

In the List view, you can control page breaks by inserting a page-break marker into the list of records. If you want 20 records per page, move the cursor to record number 20 in the List view. Press Alt, P, and then I for the Insert Page Break option. You will be asked to select `Record` or `Field`. Choose `Record` and press Enter. The page-break symbol (») is inserted beside record 20.

Chapter Summary

You are now able to create a Works database, one of the most useful tools you can have. In creating the database in this chapter, you decided what the database should do for you. Once you were able to compose the elements of the database, you entered fields and data. And you examined the Form view and List view modes of the database.

Selecting, moving, copying, and deleting text in each view were covered. You learned about searching and sorting data; you chose the data you wanted to use and put it into a more useful order. You learned how to take advantage of formulas in a database. You also learned about formatting cells, character styles, and text alignment; the value of protecting the form and data in a database; and ways to hide fields and records.

In Chapter 10, look for ways to create reports from your data. After you learn how to query the database, looking for the data you want reported, you will learn the finer skills, such as duplicating, deleting, sorting, viewing, and customizing reports. After you have created the report, you will need to know how to format it with headers, footers, fonts, and titles. The printing options available for reports also will be discussed.

10

Creating and Using Database Reports

You have made a plethora of database entries. Make that data more useful to you. Create paper copies you can show your friends, your boss, or the board of directors. You have already done some simple sorting of data. Now you are ready to prepare queries and print the data by creating practical reports.

Creating a Database Report

Place a report on your screen and look at the components in this method of displaying your data. With your cursor in a database you have created, place your first report on the screen. (In the example here, you are using JULY.WDB, a database with 25 records of recipients of a July advertising mailing. In the database, you are tracking their response and purchase amount.)

Press Alt to activate the menu bar. Press V for the View menu (see fig. 10.1). Press N for the New Report option. You have created a report by pressing N.

On the first screen that appears (see fig. 10.2), you see the `Last Name` and `First Name` fields, followed by the data for those fields.

Press Enter again and more fields appear on the screen. Continue to press Enter. You will see all the fields listed and the record data listed. You then will come to the screen shown in figure 10.3.

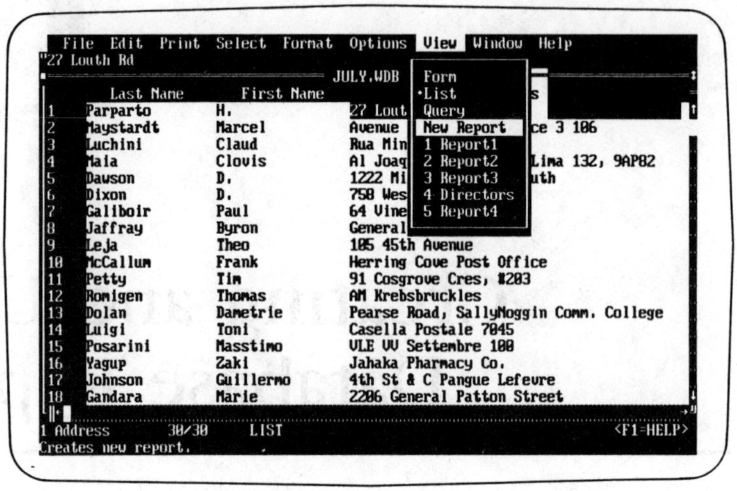

Fig. 10.1.

The View menu.

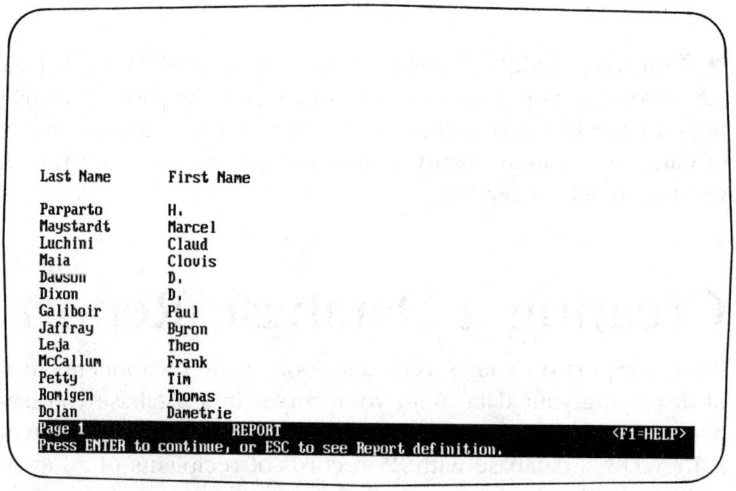

Fig. 10.2.

The `Last Name` *and* `First Name` *fields in the report.*

This is the Report Definition screen. On this screen, you can enter report titles, column labels, and summary formulas. Across the top of the screen are the alphabetical column headings. Down the left side of the screen are the row names. A description of each of the rows follows:

- `Intr Report`. Two `Intr Report` rows are printed at the beginning of each report. Insert text for report titles in these rows.
- `Intr Page`. These two rows start each page. Usually they hold the field name. However, you can add to or change the text in the `Intr Page`

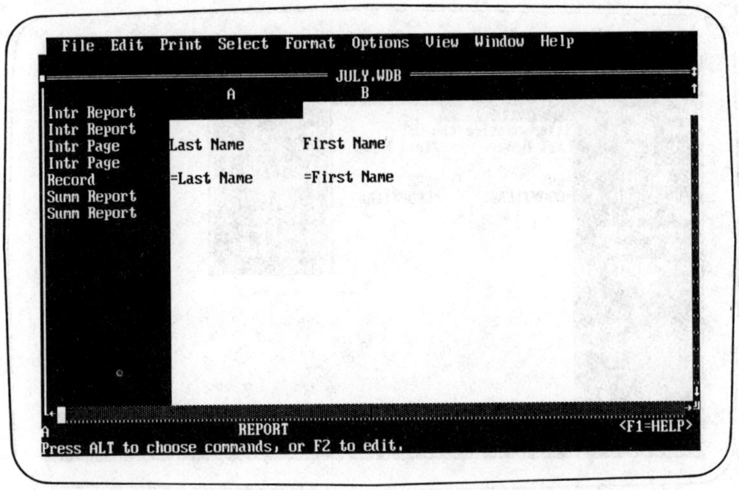

Fig. 10.3.
The Report Definition screen.

rows. The text you have in these rows is printed at the top of every page.

- ❑ `Record`. The `Record` row holds the record data for each database. One entry for each record is listed.
- ❑ `Summ Report`. The `Summ Report` rows appear at the end of a report. You can place statistical data or text summaries of each report in these rows. You also have the option of leaving these rows blank to create groupings.

These are the basic row definitions you will find in this first report. As you customize your report, some new rows will be added. You will look at the new rows and row definitions as they occur.

Returning to a List or Form View

While in a report, press Alt to activate the menu bar, V for the View menu, and either L or F for the List or Form view of your database. When the View menu appears, you will see that the report you just created is now listed on the menu. Report1 is indicated on the menu as the active view (see fig. 10.4).

Tip: Return quickly to the view you were in before the Report view by pressing F10. With one quick keystroke, you can be back in the List or Form view. You must be in the Report Definition screen to use the F10 key.

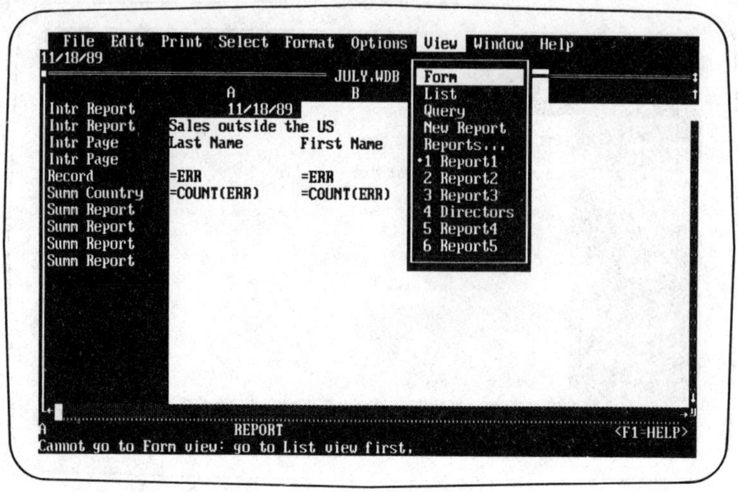

Fig. 10.4.

Report1 added to the View menu.

Sorting a Report

In Chapter 9, JULY.WDB was sorted alphabetically by country. When JULY.WDB is listed in the Report view, it maintains the same order in which it was previously sorted. This same sort can be accomplished in the Report view as well. You also can be much more specific in a Report view, creating breaks and summaries where you need them.

When you choose to sort records in the Report view, you will notice that the Sort dialog box is a little different from the Sort dialog box in List view. In addition to listing the fields by which you can sort, the dialog box offers the option of creating breaks after each group created by the sort.

Go to the Sort dialog box (see fig. 10.5). First make sure that you're in the Report Definition screen; then press Alt to activate the menu bar, S for the Select menu, and then O for the Sort Records option.

You can sort by three fields at a time. The first field is at the top. When you sort, you name the field by which you want to sort. Also indicate whether you want to sort in ascending or descending order. Choose ascending order, and Works sorts the data from A to Z or from 1 to 100. Choose descending order, and Works sorts from Z to A or from 100 to 1. So far, the sort is the same as in the List view.

To the right of the field-sorting selection, you can choose to break the sorted data into groups. With Break turned on (indicated by an X next to the option), Works creates a grouping by inserting a blank summary row in the report when the contents of the field change.

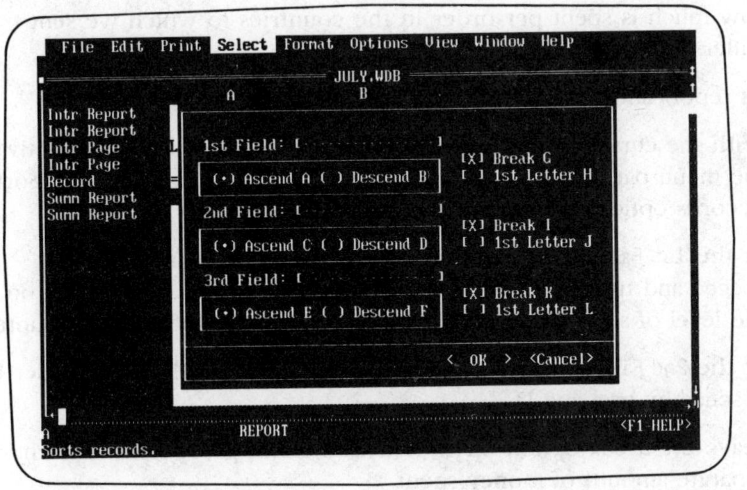

Fig. 10.5.
The Sort dialog box.

Choose the `1st Letter` option, and Works creates a grouping in the report when the first letter of the sort changes.

The break by letter, the default break, is used most often. The length of the database determines which type of break you want to use. In JULY.WDB, there are only 25 records. If you put a break after every change in first letter, you will have a break after almost every record.

With a database of 1,000 entries, you may have 60 records with a last name that starts with S. Choose a break after the first letter change for the field `Last Name`, and you will have a group of data in a workable size.

Tip: When you make report sorting and grouping decisions, consider your original goals when you created your database. Do you want to end up with every record grouped according to the first letter in the last name, or do you want to know the total of the orders by country? If you are clear about your original intent, sorting and grouping decisions will be easier to make.

The purpose in developing the JULY.WDB database is to learn which advertising recipients order the most products. If you sort by country, you can learn where to spend your advertising dollars most effectively. The report will try to answer these kinds of questions:

- ❑ If we advertise in Italy, are we just wasting our money?
- ❑ In which country do we get the most return for our advertising dollar?

- ❑ How much is spent per order in the countries to which we sent mailers?

Sort this report and set up breaks by following these steps:

1. With the cursor in the Report Definition screen, press Alt to activate the menu bar. Press S for the Select menu and press O for the Sort Records option. The Sort dialog box appears.

2. At the `1st Field` prompt, type *Country*. Leave the indicator on `Ascend` and turn on `Break` by pressing Alt-G, I, or K, depending on the level of sort. Works will break the record list after each country.

3. At the `2nd Field` prompt, type *Purchase Amount*. Move the order to `Descend` by pressing D.

4. Leave the `Break` option off so that data is not grouped after each separate amount of money spent.

5. Figure 10.6 shows the dialog box with these entries. Move the cursor to `OK` and press Enter.

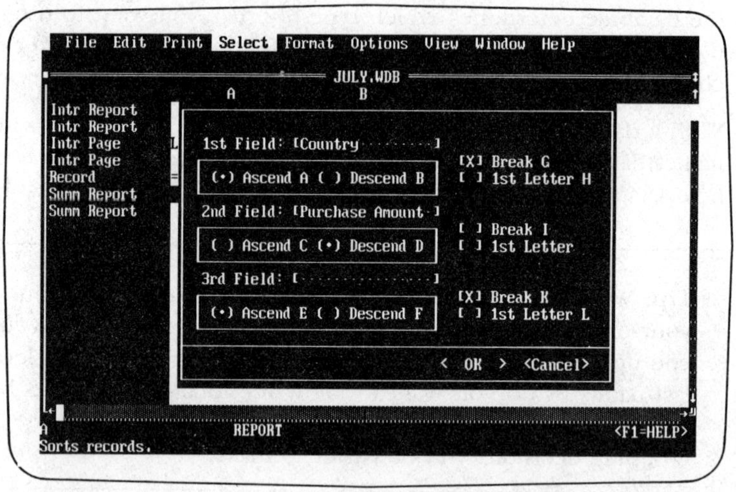

Fig. 10.6.

The Sort dialog box with entries.

You are returned to the Report Definition screen. Below the `Record` entries, the row `Summ Country` is inserted. For every field, you will find the following equation in the `Summ Country` row:

=COUNT(*Field Name*)

When you view or print this report, the total number of records per group will appear in this cell. As you move the cursor to the right to reveal the Purchase Amount field, you see the equation

=SUM(Purchase Amount)

This equation can be seen in figure 10.7 on the formula bar. At the end of the list of purchases, you will get a total of the amount purchased per country.

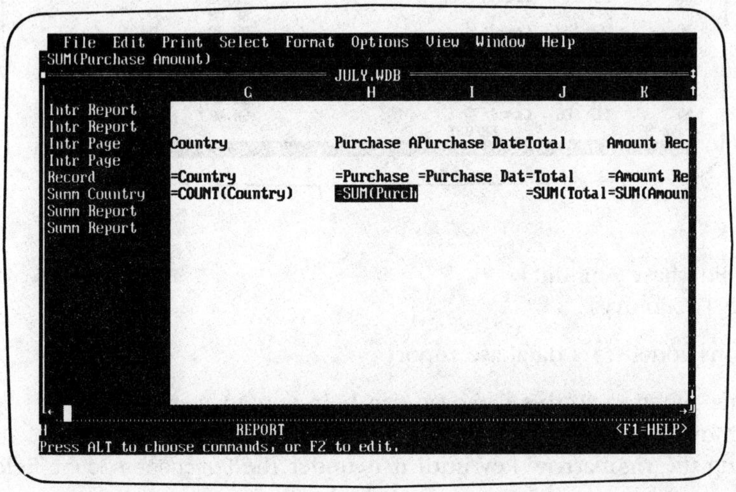

Fig. 10.7.

The =SUM(Purchase Amount) equation.

Now view the results of your sort. Press Alt to activate the menu bar, V for the View menu, and 1 to see Report1 after the sort. On the first page are the First Name and Last Name fields. Press Enter until you see the Country field listed.

Figure 10.8 shows the Country field. The countries are in alphabetical order. To the right are the purchase amounts listed in descending order by country. The purchase amounts for Canada are $88.99, $69.95, and $45, respectively. Press Enter and you see the remaining countries and purchase amounts.

Using Functions in a Database Report

In Chapter 9, you learned that functions could be used in a database much like they are in a spreadsheet. The preceding example shows a function in a database report. The phrases

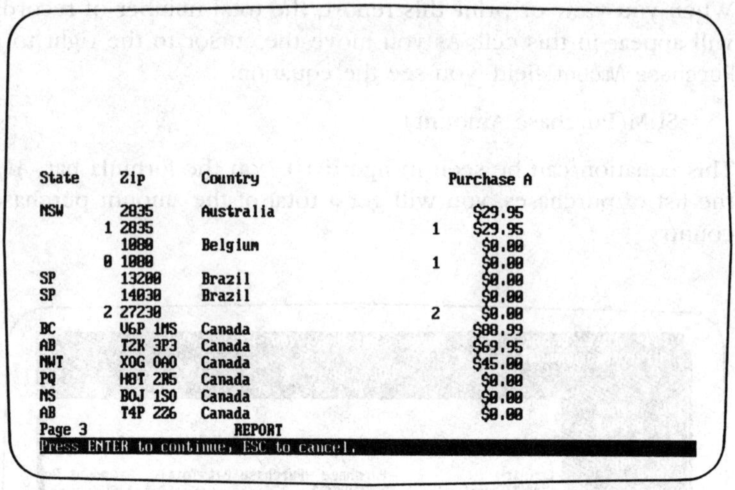

State	Zip	Country		Purchase A
NSW	2835	Australia		$29.95
	1 2835		1	$29.95
	1080	Belgium		$0.00
	0 1080		1	$0.00
SP	13200	Brazil		$0.00
SP	14030	Brazil		$0.00
	2 27230		2	$0.00
BC	V6P 1MS	Canada		$88.99
AB	T2K 3P3	Canada		$69.95
NWT	XOG 0A0	Canada		$45.00
PQ	H8T 2R5	Canada		$0.00
NS	B0J 1S0	Canada		$0.00
AB	T4P 2Z6	Canada		$0.00

Page 3 REPORT

Press ENTER to continue, ESC to cancel.

Fig. 10.8.

The Country *field.*

=SUM(Purchase Amount)
=COUNT(Country)

are functions added to a database report.

Add another function so this database can help you answer another question. Move the cursor to one of the Summ Report rows. Move the cursor using the right-arrow key until it is under the Purchase Amount field. Type

=AVG(Purchase Amount)

and press Enter.

You have just asked Works to figure the average amount of a purchase of product according to the records in this database. Works will automatically add all the purchase amounts together and divide by the total number of purchase amounts. For more information about functions, see Chapter 7.

Press Alt to activate the menu bar, V for the View menu, and 1 for Report1. As the report appears on-screen, press Enter until you see the end of the Country and Purchase Amount page. The average purchase amount is displayed below the list of purchase amounts. The value is 35.465833. In other words, the average purchase amount is approximately $35.47.

Functions can make complex mathematical equations as easy as typing a single line in a cell.

Using Formulas in a Database Report

Formulas in a database report can be treated almost the same as formulas in a database. Enter the formula of your choice in one of the `Summ Report` rows. Always start the formula with an equal sign (=). Use operators such as an asterisk (*) for multiplication, a slash (/) for division, a plus sign (+) for addition, and a minus sign (−) for subtraction.

Developing a Query for a Database Report

Use a database query to look for certain records in your database that meet *two or more criteria*. If you are going to find records that meet just one criterion, using a search is easier. When you want to find records that have *Canada* in the `Country` field, for example, use a search. When you want to find records that have *Canada* in the `Country` field, a purchase amount over $50, and also a balance due, use a query.

The result of your query can be a report. You may want to create a report that lists the names of your friends in New York City with more than 2 children with whom you have corresponded in the last 12 months. You can create a report that lists the number of employees with degrees in electrical engineering, have more than 10 years experience with your company, and who are also interested in traveling to a new position in Brazil. All the data in the fields in the records can be used in queries.

When you apply a query, you establish criteria for each field in the database. Works searches the hidden and displayed records to find the records that match your criteria.

With your cursor in the List view, press Alt to activate the menu bar. Press V for the View menu and press Q for the Query option. In JULY.WDB you see what looks like a Form view of a record but with no data in the fields. Type the criteria for your query in these spaces.

Using Query Formulas

Set up a query formula to find an exact match to two or more criteria. You can build very complex queries using the equation for queries:

=(formula stating search conditions)/combining operator/(formula stating search conditions)

In either formula stating search conditions, use comparison operators. The comparison operators are listed in table 10.1. The table shows the operator, the formula, and what the query will find.

Table 10.1
Comparison Operators

Operator	*Field*	*Formula Used*	*Finds These Records*
Equal to (=)	Country:	="Canada"	Country is Canada
Not equal to (<>)	Country:	<>"Canada"	Country is not Canada
Less than (<)	Balance Due:	<50	Balance due is less than $50
Greater than (>)	Balance Due:	>50	Balance due is more than $50
Greater than or (>=)	Purchase Amt:	>=50	Purchase amount is equal to $50 or more
Less than or (<=)	Purchase Amt:	<=50	Purchase amount is equal to $50 or less

The comparison operators find ranges of data. The logical operators find records that meet more than one set of conditions. For example, you can look for

Balance Due: >50 AND <1000

The logical operator AND indicates that you will find amounts above $50 and below $1,000 in your query. The logical operators and their symbols are

AND &
OR |
NOT ~

Entering a Query

In JULY.WDB, find the records with orders from Canada and purchase amounts greater than $10:

1. If you are not already in the Query view, make sure that you're in the List view and press Alt to activate the menu bar. Then press V for the View menu and press Q for the Query option.

2. Move the highlight down until you are in the data cell for the field `Country`. Type *Canada*. Press Enter to insert the data into the cell.

3. Move the cursor to the `Purchase Amount` field. In the data cell, type *>10* (see fig. 10.9). Press Enter.

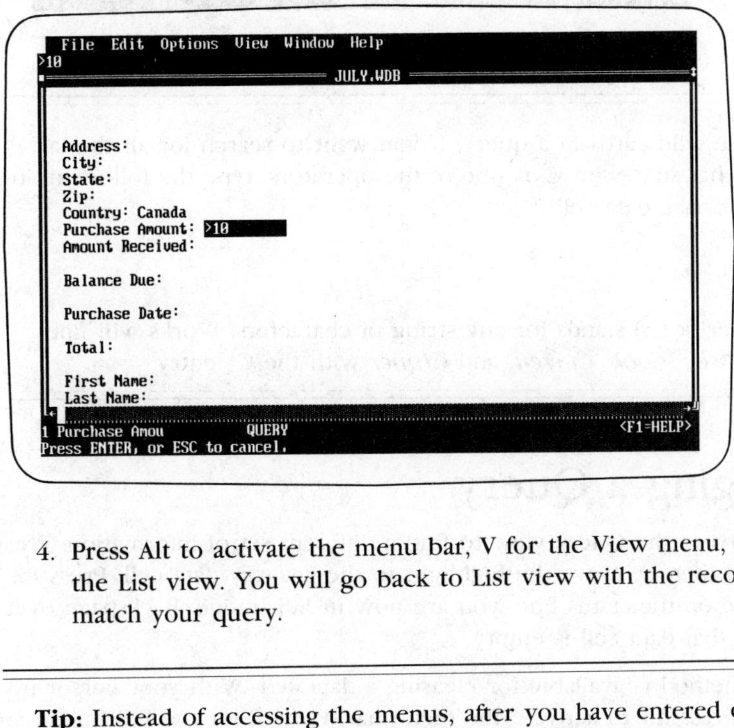

Fig. 10.9.
The Query screen with data entered.

4. Press Alt to activate the menu bar, V for the View menu, and L for the List view. You will go back to List view with the records that match your query.

Tip: Instead of accessing the menus, after you have entered query information, press F10. You will be back in List view with the records that match your query.

In this case, three records show orders from Canada with purchase amounts over $10. Figure 10.10 is a screen shot of the `Country` and `Purchase Amount` fields in the List view following the query.

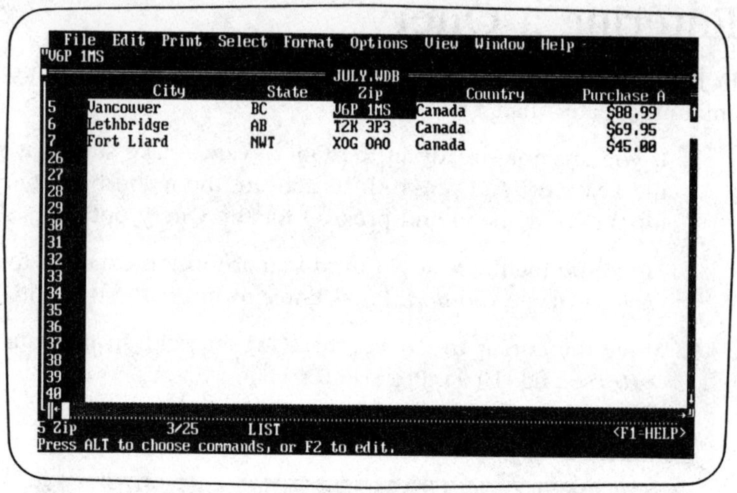

Fig. 10.10.

The Country *and* Purchase Amount *fields after query.*

Tip: Use wild cards in a query. If you want to search for all the last names that start with C as one of the operators, type the following in the Last Name data cell:

C*

The asterisk (*) stands for any string of characters. Works will find *Christensen*, *Cook*, *Curren*, and *Climer* with the C* entry.

Changing a Query

Now return to the Query view to find a different set of information. Press Alt, V, and then Q. Move the highlight to the Country data cell. Press F2. As you see on the status line, you are now in Edit mode. Backspace over Canada so that data cell is empty.

Another method is available for clearing a data cell. With your cursor in that cell, press Alt to activate the menu bar. Press E for the Edit menu and then press E for the Clear option. The cell in which your cursor is placed is cleared of data. Any formatting or style conditions for that cell remain. Use this menu method of clearing data when you have an entry in the data cell that is too long to backspace over.

Clear the Purchase Amount field as well. Move the cursor to the Balance Due data cell. Place a formula in the cell that will cause Works to find all records showing a balance due greater than 0 and less than 100. The formula should look like this:

>0&<100

Press F10 to return to the List view. In this example, 7 records are displayed with the balance due exceeding 0 but less than $100. Figure 10.11 shows the Balance Due field resulting from this query.

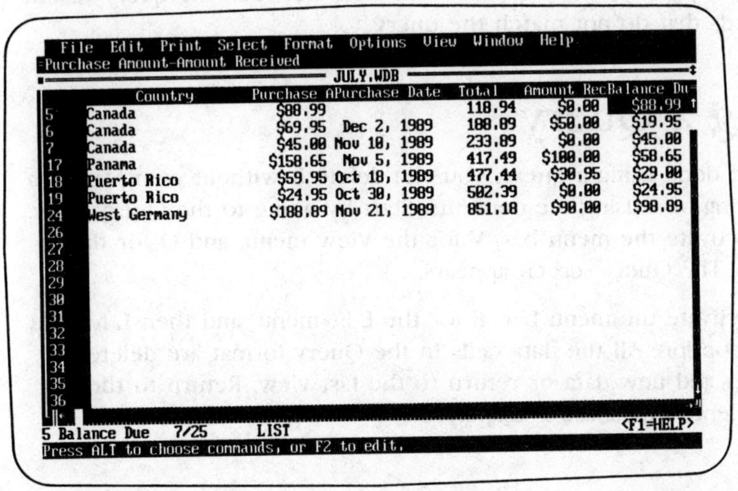

Fig. 10.11.

The Balance Due *field resulting from the query.*

Returning to Your Complete Database

While in the list of records that resulted from your query, press Alt to activate the menu bar and press S for the Select menu. Press L for the Show All Records option. Every record in this database is displayed.

Tip: When you use the Show All Records option, you do not delete the active query. It is still available to you. Press Alt to activate the menu bar, S for the Select menu, and Q for the Apply Query option. The screen displays the result of your last query.

Tip: After you have designed a query, you can go back, add, change, or delete records, and then apply the active query again. Press Alt to activate the menu bar, S for the Select menu, and Q for the Apply Query option. The screen displays the query again with the new data.

Viewing the Records That Do Not Match the Query

You have a list of selected records as a result of your query. To view all the records that do not match this query, press Alt to activate the menu bar, S for the Select menu, and W for the Switch Hidden Records option. Using this menu path, you can go back and forth between the query results and the records that do not match the query.

Deleting a Query

When you are done using a query, you can delete it without going to each cell and clearing or erasing the contents. Start by going to the Query view. Press Alt to activate the menu bar, V for the View menu, and Q for the Query option. The Query screen appears.

Press Alt to activate the menu bar, E for the Edit menu, and then L for the Delete Query option. All the data cells in the Query format are deleted. You can either add new data or return to the List view. Return to the List view, and the entire database is displayed.

Copying Data in a Database Report

Copy rows or columns in a database report by first selecting the rows or columns and then moving them to the desired location. You must be in the Report Definition screen of the Report view in order to copy. In this example, copy the `Last Name` and `First Name` fields to the end of the report:

1. With the cursor on the `Last Name` field in the Report Definition screen, press F8. `EXT` appears on the status line. You also can press Alt, E for the Edit menu, and C for the Copy option if you prefer the menu method.

2. Move the cursor down until the `Record` row is highlighted.

3. Move the cursor to the right, using the right-arrow key, until the `First Name` column is highlighted. Figure 10.12 shows the highlighting.

4. Press Shift-F3. On the status line, you see `Select new location and press ENTER. Press ESC to cancel.`

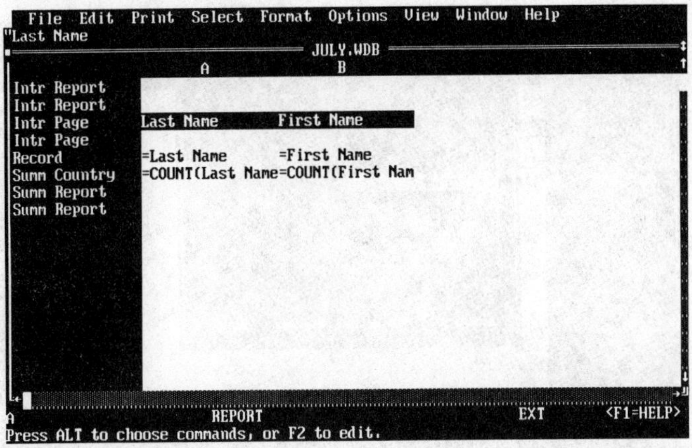

Fig. 10.12.

Columns A and B highlighted.

5. With the arrow keys, move the highlighting to column N and press Enter. The `Last Name` and `First Name` fields remain in the original location and are copied to the end.

Deleting Reports

You have several reports that are similar. You find that you need to work with and print only one of the reports. Delete the reports you don't need. In another database, you find that you have created eight reports and you need one more. You must delete an old database report before you can create another one, because the limit is eight.

While in the Report Definition screen, press Alt to activate the menu bar, V for the View menu, and R for the Reports option.

The Reports dialog box appears. In it are listed the reports you have created for this database. Report3 is no longer needed. Move the highlight to `Report3` (see fig. 10.13).

Press Alt-T. A prompt asks whether deleting this report is OK. Press Enter to delete it. Press Esc during the process or choose `Cancel` if you change your mind and do not want to delete the report.

When you delete the report, you are returned to the dialog box where you can delete more reports, rename reports, or copy entire reports.

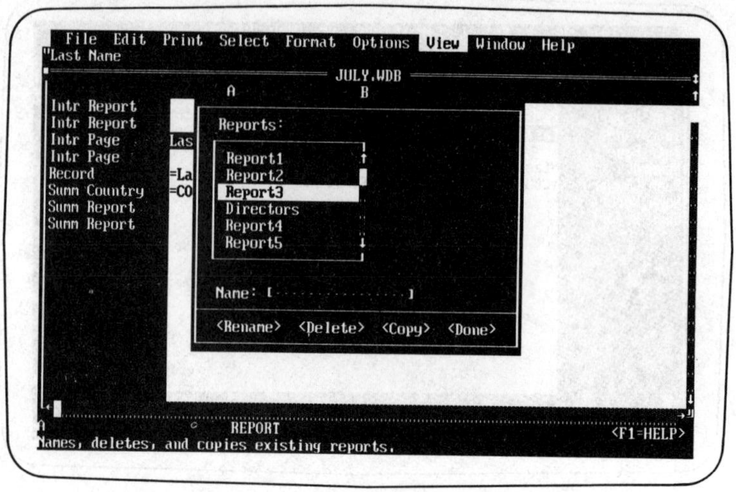

Fig. 10.13.

Report3 highlighted in the Reports dialog box.

Renaming a Database Report

While in the Reports dialog box, move the highlight to `Report1`. That is the report in which most of the work has been done. The records in that report are grouped by country with totals for each country. Instead of leaving the name as Report1, which is not descriptive, change the name of the report to Country:

1. With `Report1` highlighted, press Alt-N to move the cursor to the `Name` box.
2. Type the new name. You can add a title of up to 15 characters (see fig. 10.14).

Press Alt-R to have the new name inserted in the `Report1` position. Follow these same steps to rename other reports. When you are done working in the Reports dialog box, press Alt-D.

Duplicating Database Reports

You have prepared a report for the board of directors. Now you want to create a similar report from the same database for your management staff and another report for your own records. Create variations on a report by duplicating the report or using the `Copy` option on the Reports dialog box.

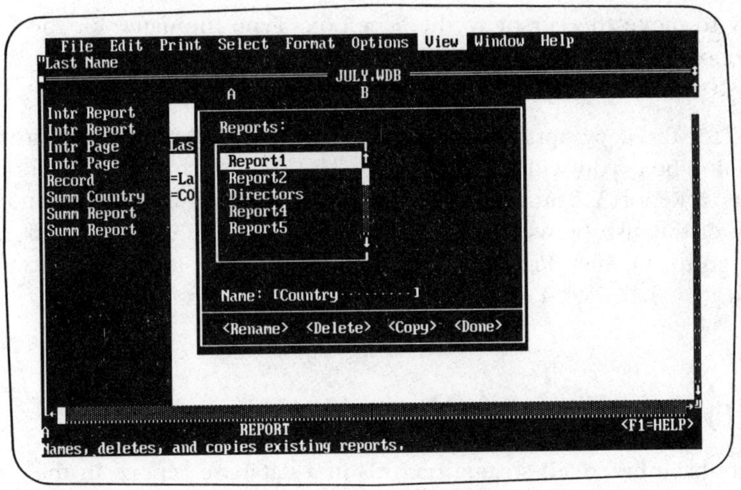

Fig. 10.14.

The Reports dialog box with Country *in the* Name *box.*

You then can make changes to the copied report without changing the original report.

The Reports dialog box lists the reports already created. Remember, the limit is eight reports per database, so if you already have eight, you have to delete one before you can duplicate a report.

While in the Report Definition screen, press Alt to activate the menu bar, V for the View menu, and R for the Reports option. Move the highlighting to the report you want to copy. In figure 10.15, the highlight is on Report5.

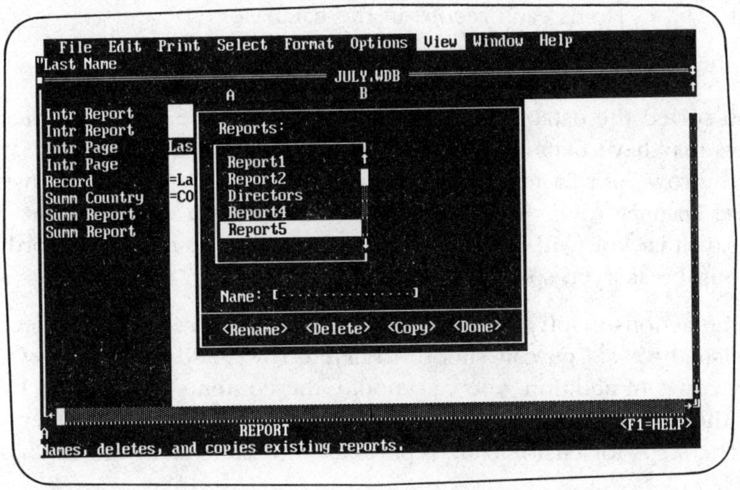

Fig. 10.15.

Report5 *highlighted in the Reports dialog box.*

Press Alt-N to move the cursor to the Name box. Type the name for the copy of Report3. In this example, make this the copy for the board of directors, so name the report Directors.

Press Alt-C for the Copy option in the dialog box. Just below Report3 in the Reports dialog box, you will see Directors. The report named Directors is a duplicate of Report3. You can view the duplicate, make alterations, and then easily distinguish between the reports that go to the directors and those that go to the staff. Press Alt-D when you are done in the Reports dialog box.

Customizing a Report

You already have practiced sorting records in a database report. In the example earlier in this chapter, you grouped the data by country and then had the purchase amount listed in descending order. When you customize a report, you are again working with the rows of a report definition. The rows are named down the left side of the screen. The columns, labeled A, B, C, and so on, appear across the top of the screen and usually contain field names and records.

The rows in a database report are listed in a predetermined order as follows:

Row	*Contains*
Intr Report	Holds a report title (first page only)
Intr Page	Label or field name for the column (every page)
Record	Holds each record in the database
Summ Report	Text or value at the end of the report

When you sorted the database JULY.WDB or the database of your choice, other rows may have been added. Because JULY.WDB was sorted by country, the row Summ Country was inserted before the Summ Report rows. In the Summ Country row, you find a formula that holds a function. The function says that you will get a count of the number of records according to the group breaks you specified.

Many of the actions involved in customizing a database report also affect the established rows. You can choose to delete rows, add or insert rows, or modify rows. In addition, you can modify the contents of the rows by changing the formatting of cells, including character styles and number formats. The steps for customizing reports are the same as in the database.

Note: The actions taken to customize a report must occur in the Report Definition screen. You cannot access the menus while viewing the report unless you are in the Report Definition screen.

Deleting a Row or Column

In JULY.WDB, Report1, the `Total` field is not really necessary and only takes up space. In the Report Definition screen, move the cursor to the `Total` column, or column J, and press F8 to turn on the EXT mode (see fig. 10.16).

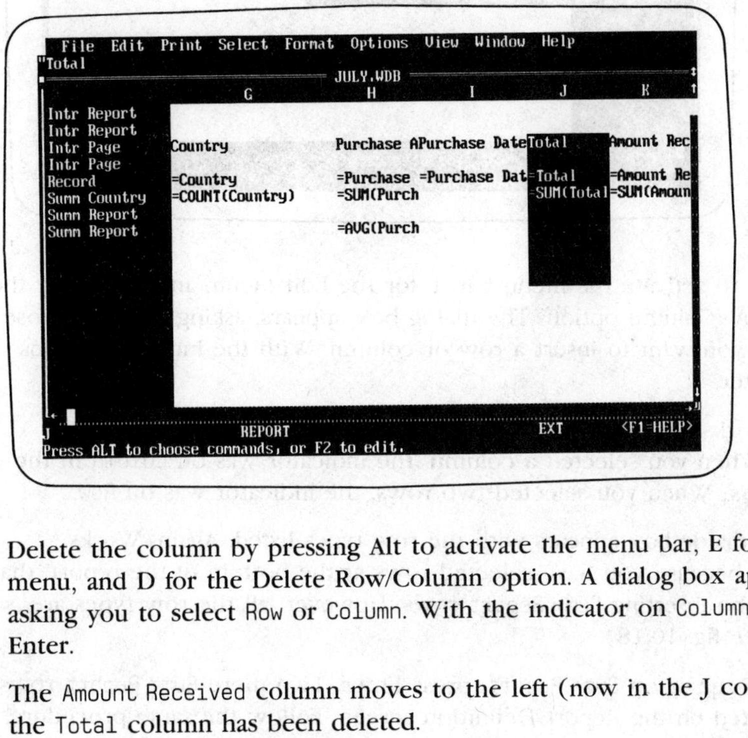

Fig. 10.16.
The `Total` *column highlighted.*

Delete the column by pressing Alt to activate the menu bar, E for the Edit menu, and D for the Delete Row/Column option. A dialog box appears, asking you to select `Row` or `Column`. With the indicator on `Column`, press Enter.

The `Amount Received` column moves to the left (now in the J column), and the `Total` column has been deleted.

Follow these same procedures to delete a row. First select the row; press Alt, E, and then D. Then choose `Row` from the dialog box.

Inserting a Row or Column

Insert two rows to do more calculations at the end of the report. With the cursor below the bottom `Summ Report` row, press F8 to turn on the EXT mode. Press the right-arrow key until all the active columns are highlighted across. Then press the down-arrow key to select two rows. Figure 10.17 shows the highlighted rows.

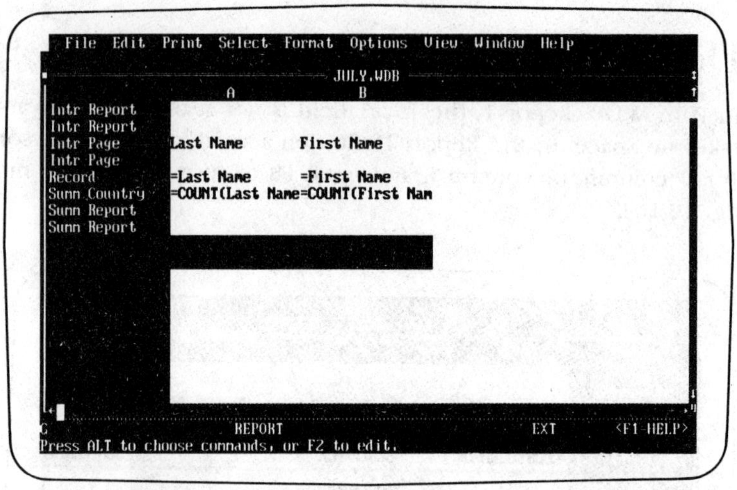

Fig. 10.17.

The blank highlighted rows.

Press Alt to activate the menu bar, E for the Edit menu, and then I for the Insert Row/Column option. The dialog box appears, asking you to choose whether you want to insert a row or column. With the indicator on `Row`, press Enter.

Note: Works makes an assumption on what you are going to insert or delete. When you selected a column, the indicator was on `Column` in the dialog box. When you selected two rows, the indicator was on `Row`.

Another dialog box appears with the row types listed. Again, Works assumes, because you have selected rows at the bottom of the report, that you will be inserting `Summ Report` rows. However, all the row types are listed (see fig. 10.18).

With the cursor on `Summ Report`, press Enter. Two more `Summ Report` rows are inserted on the Report Definition screen. Follow the same procedures to insert a column.

Entering Information in a Database Report Cell

In the Report Definition screen, you can add data, labels, formulas, or functions in the cells. At the top of the screen are two `Intr Report` rows.

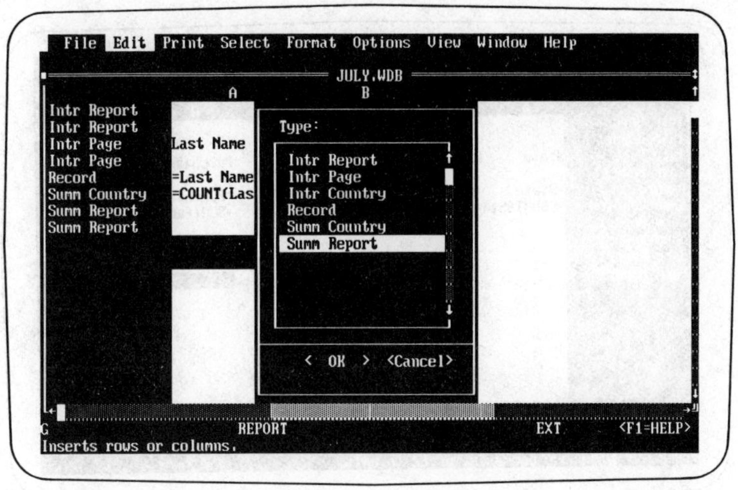

Fig. 10.18.

The Row Type dialog box.

In the top row, add the date; in the second `Intr Report` row, insert a title for the report. The contents of the `Intr Report` rows appear on the first page of the report.

With the cursor in column A in the first `Intr Report` row, type *11/18/89*. Press Enter. In the next row, type *Sales Outside the US*. Press Enter.

Tip: Remember to press F2 to edit the formula bar.

Notice that the text entered was preceded by a quotation mark ("). The text is considered to be a label, which is indicated by the quotation mark.

With these two additions, the date and title of the report will appear on the first page when the report is printed.

Add additional formulas in the `Summ Report` rows you entered at the bottom of the Report Definition screen. Move the cursor to the bottom `Summ Report` row. Using the right-arrow key, move the highlight to the `Purchase Amount` field column. The cursor location is shown in figure 10.19. You already have added the average function to this column. In addition, add the standard deviation. This is a statistical calculation described more fully in Chapter 7.

Press Alt to activate the menu bar, E for the Edit menu, and then S for the Insert Field Summary option. The Summary dialog box appears. On the left side of the box are the fields in this database. On the right side of the box are statistical calculations available on a report.

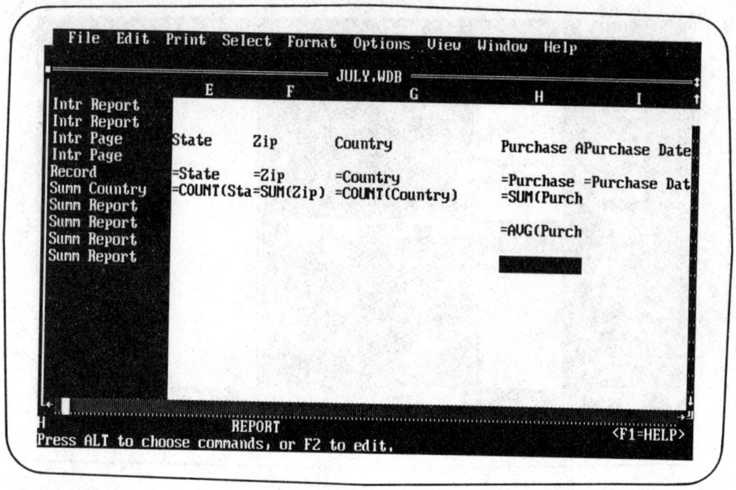

Fig. 10.19.

The cursor location for adding a function.

Press the down-arrow key until `Purchase Amount` is highlighted. Press the right-arrow key to move to the right side of the dialog box. Move the indicator to `STD` so the dialog box looks like the one shown in figure 10.20. Press Enter.

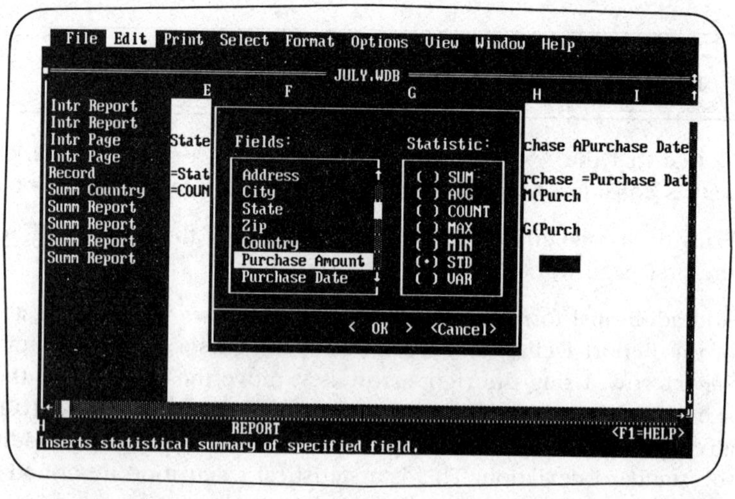

Fig. 10.20.

The Summary dialog box completed.

Other statistical calculations are listed on the Summary dialog box. Table 10.2 lists the calculations available with a brief description.

Table 10.2
Statistical Calculations on the Summary Dialog Box

Function	*Description*
SUM	Total of the group
AVG	Average of the group
COUNT	Number of items in the group
MAX	Largest number in the group
MIN	Smallest number in the group
STD	Standard deviation of the group
VAR	Variance of the group

Inserting Field Names and Field Contents

Insert the field names and contents in any cell by placing your cursor in the appropriate cell. Press Alt to activate the menu bar and then press E for the Edit menu. On the Edit menu, you see two options: Insert Field Name and Insert Field Contents. Press N for the Insert Field Name option.

The available fields with this database are listed. With this list, you can insert any field name as a label at the cursor location.

Look at the Insert Field Contents list by pressing Alt to activate the menu bar and E for the Edit menu. Then press O for the Insert Field Contents option (see fig. 10.21). This should be used only on the `Record` row, where it is most useful. Select any option on this list and Works inserts =*fieldname* in the cell. The actual contents of the cell can be seen when you view the report.

Changing Character Style

In JULY.WDB, the title has been entered in column A in the second `Intr Report` row. Change the style of this title by placing the highlighted cursor in this cell. Press Alt to activate the menu bar, T for the Format menu, and then S for the Style option. The Style dialog box appears.

The style options are `Bold`, `Underline`, and `Italic`. You can select one or more of the options. Set off the title of the report by making it both bold and underlined. Press B and U. Then press Enter.

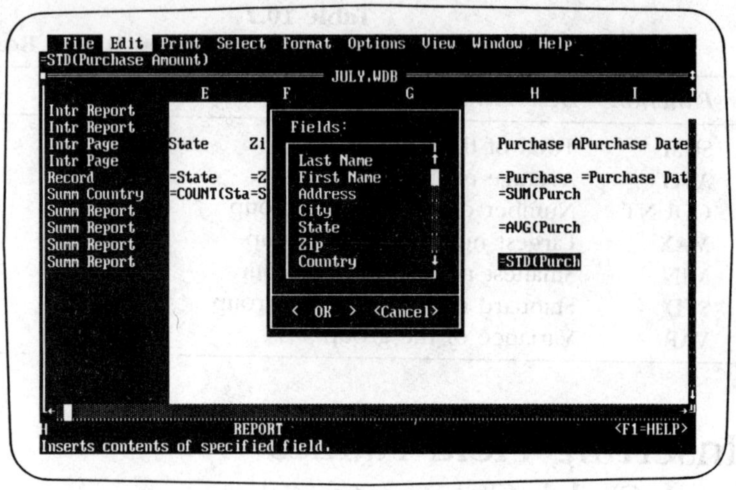

Fig. 10.21.

The field contents list.

Figure 10.22 shows the title of the report formatted in bold and underlined style.

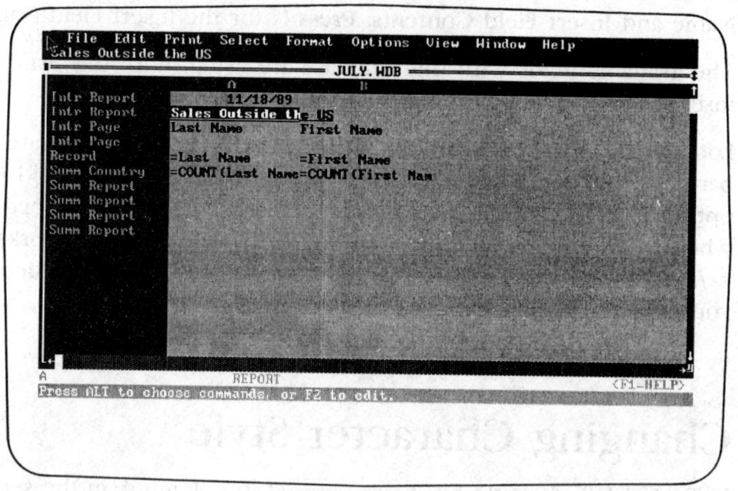

Fig. 10.22.

The bold and underlined title.

Use any of the cell alignment and character styles to format cells in a report. The steps are the same as the ones listed previously. Change the choices, and you change the character style or alignment. For more details on how to change styles and formats, see Chapter 9.

Formatting a Report

Before printing a report, add some final touches to the document. These final touches will give your document a more finished, professional look.

Changing Fonts

Alter the fonts in your report based on the fonts available with your equipment. The fonts available with your printer are displayed when you press Alt to activate the menu bar, T for the Format menu, and F for the Font option. Figure 10.23 displays the font selection for one hardware setup. Your screen will likely be different, depending on your printer. The list of fonts available will be a result of the printer you selected in the setup program.

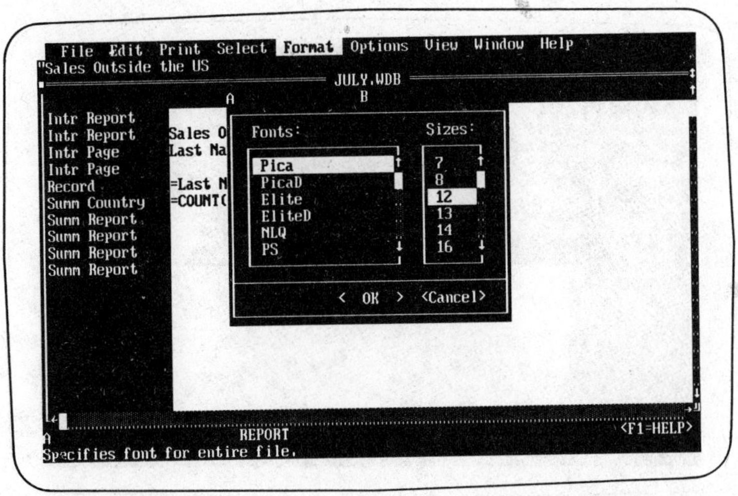

Fig. 10.23.

The list of fonts available.

Next to the list of fonts is the list of sizes in which the fonts are available. The sizes are listed in points. One point is approximately 1/72 inch.

Change the font by pressing Alt to activate the menu bar, T for the Format menu, and F for the list of fonts. Move the highlight to the font and size you want. Press Enter. The font and size you choose will not appear on the screen but will be printed.

Adding Headers and Footers

In the word processing chapters, the two types of headers and footers were discussed. The *paragraph* headers and footers are used in word processing documents. *Standard* headers and footers are used in spreadsheet and database documents.

Add the headers and footers you want by pressing Alt to activate the menu bar and pressing P for the Print menu. Then press H for the Headers & Footers option. The Headers & Footers dialog box appears. Notice how the paragraph header and footer option is dimmed, which means you cannot use this option in a database report.

Press Alt-F to move the cursor to the `Footer` option. Type *Board of Directors*. The dialog box should look like the one shown in figure 10.24. Move the cursor to `OK` and press Enter.

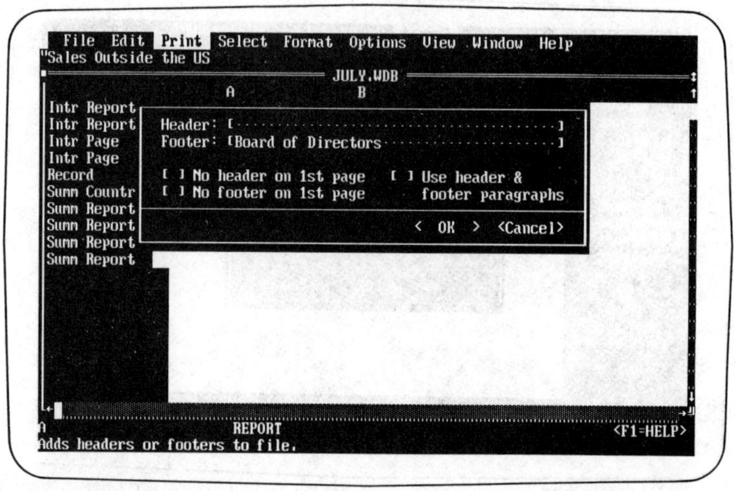

Fig. 10.24.

The Headers & Footers dialog box.

The footer you have added to the document does not appear on the Report Definition screen. You can view the footer by pressing Alt to activate the menu bar, V for the View menu, and 1 for Report1. Figure 10.25 shows how the footer looks at the end of the first page of the report.

Printing Database Reports

When you print a report, you can choose to print the entire document or specified rows from the document. Select the report you want to print by placing your cursor on that report on the Report Definition screen.

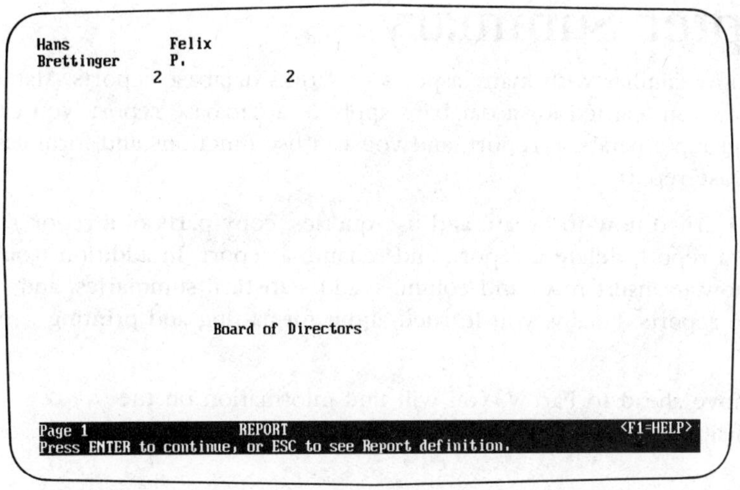

Fig. 10.25. *The footer on-screen.*

Press Alt to activate the menu bar, P for the Print menu, and then P or Enter for the Print dialog box (see fig. 10.26).

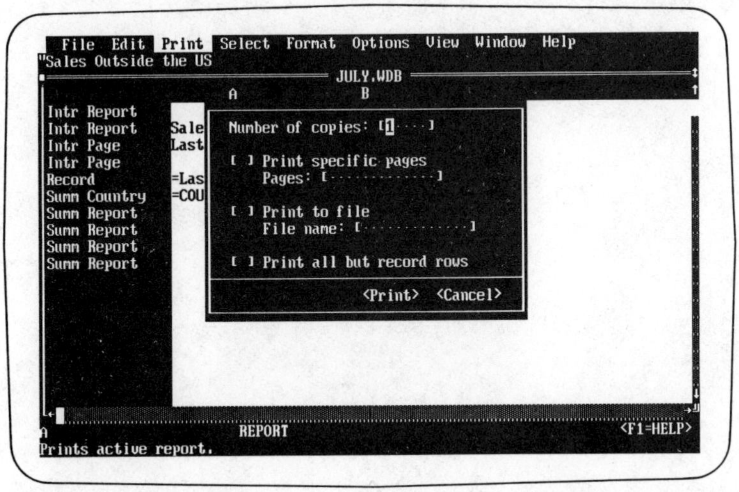

Fig. 10.26. *The Print dialog box.*

When printing a report, you can choose to print multiple copies of the report, or you can choose the option `Print all but record rows`. The two remaining options are dimmed and are not available when you're printing a report. Choose the options you want. If you want just one copy of the report, press Enter.

Chapter Summary

You are now familiar with many aspects of Works database reports. Many of the tasks you learned for a database apply to a database report; you can sort and group a database report, and you can use functions and formulas in a database report.

You also learned how to create and use queries, copy parts of a report, duplicate a report, delete a report, and rename a report. In addition, you learned how to insert rows and columns, add statistical summaries, and customize reports. Finally, you learned about formatting and printing reports.

As you move ahead to Part V, you will find information on the communications component of Works and on macros.

Part V

Communications and Macros

Includes

11

Communicating with Works

If your hardware system includes a modem, you have at your fingertips the tools necessary to communicate with other computers, FAX machines, MCI mail boxes, and on-line information services. The modem connects you to these sources of information via an ordinary telephone line. Microsoft Works sets up your computer so that it can communicate with those other communications devices.

With Microsoft Works and your modem, you can send information to other computers and receive it. You can send information from a file or directly from the keyboard. You also can receive information into the computer buffer or directly into a file.

The Microsoft Works communications tool supports a wide variety of communication protocols, or systems, that enable your computer to communicate with a wide variety of computers. These other computers do not have to be IBMs or compatibles; they can be Apples, Macintoshes, or mainframe computers.

The use of the Microsoft Works communications tool is limited only by your imagination. You can use this tool in a business environment to send electronic mail, spreadsheets, or customer lists via a database file.

Examining Communication Terms

Before you begin to use the communications tool, take a few minutes to examine the following list of definitions:

Off-line	This is the state your computer is in when you are in the Works communications tool but not yet connected to another computer. In Works, `OFFLINE` will be displayed in the lower left corner of the screen when you are in the communications tool but not connected to another computer.
On-line	This is the state your computer is in when you are connected to another computer. In Works, `ONLINE` will be displayed on the status line.
Logging on	This is the process of connecting to another computer. The process includes phone dialing, entering a user identification, and perhaps entering a password.
Logging off	This is the process of disconnecting your computer from another computer.
Modem	This is the device that converts computer information into a signal that can be transmitted over telephone lines.
Host	This is the name of the computer service to which your computer becomes connected. CompuServe, The Source, and The Official Airline Guide are examples of host systems.
BBS	This is an electronic bulletin board usually set up by an individual to share free software, information on products, or information on particular computers (the Amiga Users Forum, for example). These bulletin boards are popular among the hacker crowd, and you can gain a great deal of information on computing and other things. Normally, there is no charge for on-line time. Your total cost is just the phone line usage.

Getting Started

In order to use the communications feature, you must have a modem connected to your computer. Modems come in a variety of packages. Some are internal on a computer board that you plug into an open slot on the computer motherboard. Some are external and sit outside your computer. The internal modems are usually less expensive than external modems. If you don't have open slots in your computer, you may have to purchase an external modem. The kind you have makes no difference from a performance standpoint.

Assuming that you do have a modem and it is connected to a phone line, to use the Works communications tool you must first open a communications file. As with all the other modes of Works, use the Create New File option from the opening Works menu.

From the dialog box that appears, select the option New Communications. A new screen appears (see fig. 11.1).

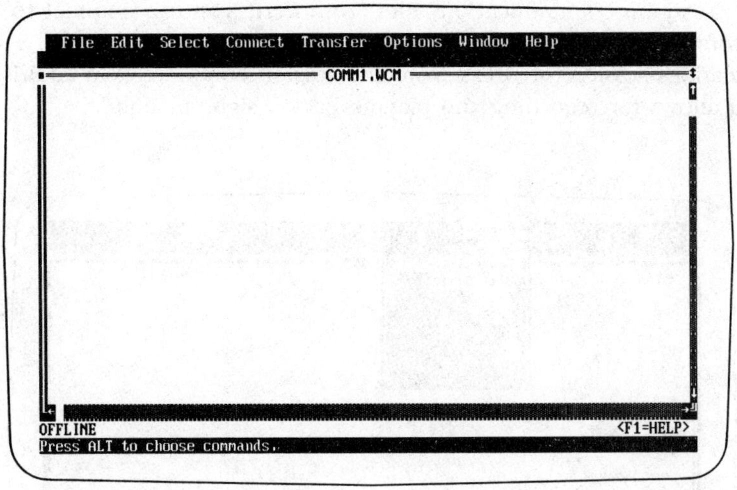

Fig. 11.1.

The New Communications screen.

For a moment, explore the menus available with the communications tool. Press the Alt key to activate the menu bar. Begin by pressing F to open the File menu. Or you can use the mouse to move the pointer to the word File and click. Consistent with every tool in Works (the word processor, spreadsheet, and database) the communications tool's File menu contains the same familiar options.

Edit

Press the right-arrow key once to open the Edit menu. It is different from the Edit menus in other modes. You will find only a single option, Copy, which allows for the copying of selected text.

Select

Press the right-arrow key again and open the Select menu. Here you can select text that is on the screen or, with the All option, capture all text that has been transmitted to your computer from another computer and is residing in the communications buffer.

Connect

Press the right-arrow key to open the next menu, the Connect menu (see fig. 11.2). The Connect menu contains all the options you will use once you have created a communications file. From here, you can connect to another computer, ask Works to redial a busy number, pause the communications session, or break from the session completely. In addition, this menu allows for recording and playing back a sign-on sequence.

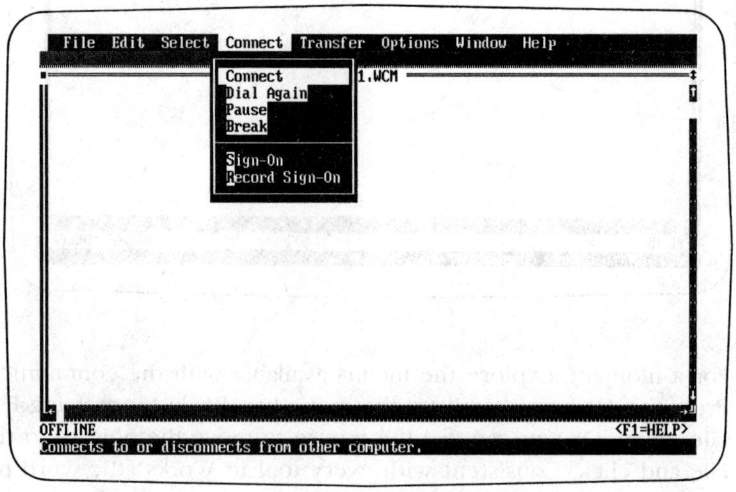

Fig. 11.2.

The Connect menu.

Transfer

The Transfer menu contains the options you use to capture text being sent to your computer. The text is captured in a specific file. The Transfer menu also allows you to send a designated file. You must first instruct Works to receive a file or send a file, as the situation requires.

Options

This Options menu contains the same elements of the Options menu in the other modes, but some specific communications options are available: Terminal, Communication, and Phone. This menu is the first used when you're beginning the communications session. This menu and its options are examined in detail later in this chapter.

Window

The Window menu options are the same as in other modes. The windows can be moved, sized, rearranged, or split.

Help

Help in this mode is identical to the help you receive in other modes of Works.

Creating a Communications File

When you begin communicating with other computers, you enter a world with its own jargon and nuances. Because there is no accepted standard for intercomputing communications, a number of settings must first be established. Works includes the default settings that are effective 99 percent of the time. These settings are examined in this section.

To open the dialog box containing the communications settings, press the Alt key for the menu bar and press O for the Options menu. Then press M for the Communications options (see fig. 11.3).

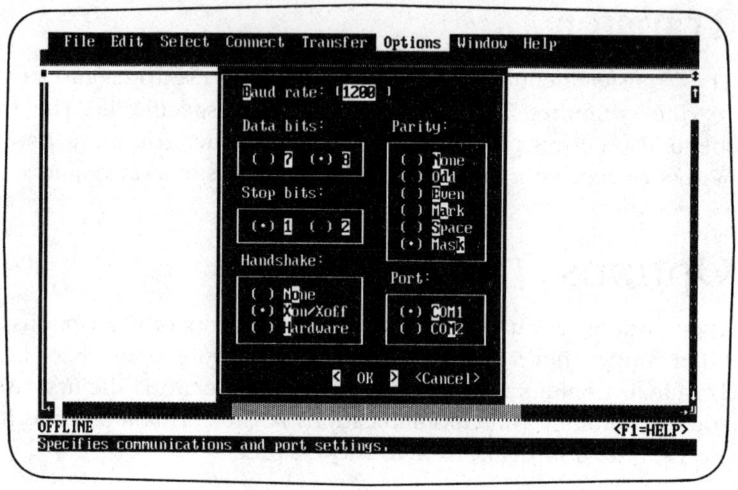

Fig. 11.3.

The dialog box that appears after choosing Communications from the Options menu.

Baud Rate

The first setting at the top of the dialog box is `Baud rate`. The rates can vary from 300 to 2400, and the default rate is 1200. If yours is a 1200-baud modem, you're in business. If your modem is not 1200 baud, change to the rate that supports your modem. If you are connecting to another computer directly with only a cable and without a modem, the rate will probably be 9600.

Data Bits

Each character transmitted is represented in computer code by either 7 or 8 bits. The normal setting is 8 bits.

Stop Bits

For the beginning and ending of each character to be interpreted correctly, a *stop bit* is included. The normal setting is 1 stop bit.

Parity

The `Parity` setting allows an internal auditing process to check whether enough bits are being sent in the correct amount. An asterisk is displayed in place of the character wherever an error occurs. To avoid confusion,

Works has a `Mask` setting, which enables the program to work with any other computer's settings.

Handshake

As the name implies, computers do have an electronic handshake when they get together. If you are using a modem, the best setting is `Xon/Xoff`. If a direct cable connection is made, the `Hardware` setting is appropriate. Select `None` only if you know that the other computer to which you will be communicating does not have a handshake method.

Port

If your computer is outfitted with two ports for serial communications, you must specify which port is being used for the modem. `COM1` is the normal setting.

The Terminal Dialog Box

The other possible settings you may have to modify are on the Terminal dialog box (which you access from the Options menu). Figure 11.4 shows the Terminal dialog box.

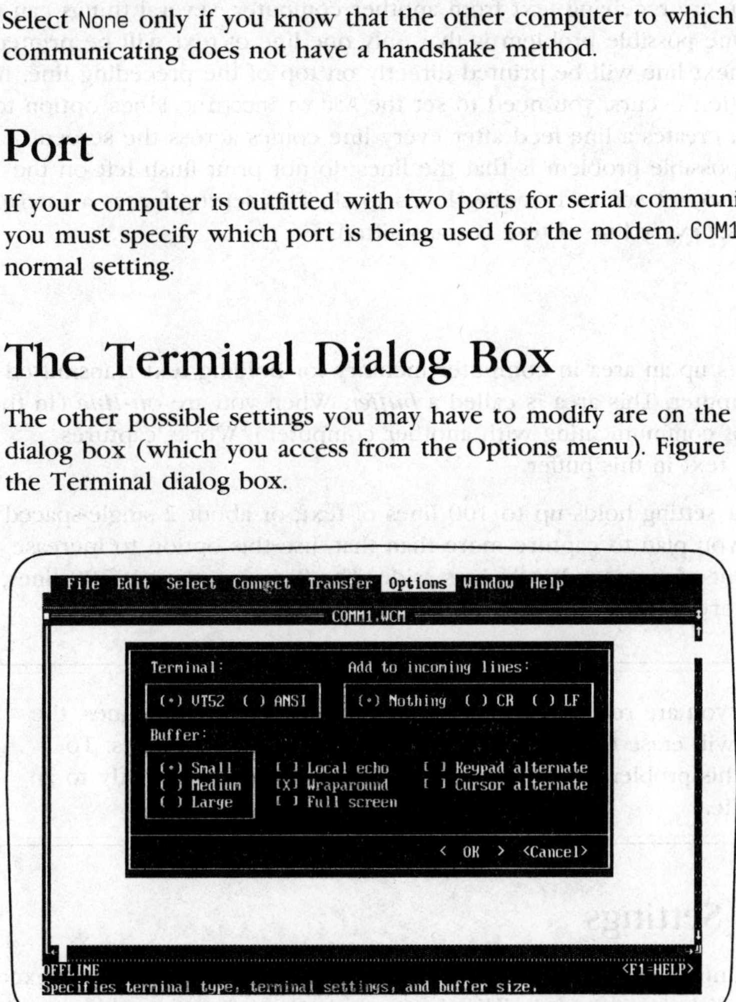

Fig. 11.4.

The Terminal dialog box.

Terminal

The Terminal option is included so that when you are using the communications tool, the computer actually functions as a terminal. Two basic types are available, but the VT52 option is most common.

Add to Incoming Lines

When you are receiving text from another computer, several things can go wrong. One possible problem is that only one line of text will be printed, and the next line will be printed directly on top of the preceding line. If this situation occurs, you need to set the Add to incoming lines option to LF, which creates a line feed after every line comes across the screen. Another possible problem is that the lines do not print flush left on the screen. If so, set Add to incoming lines to CR. This setting forces a carriage return after every line of text is transmitted.

Buffer

Works sets up an area in computer memory for holding text transmitted to your computer. This area is called a *buffer*. When you are *on-line* (in the process of communicating with another computer), Works captures incoming text in this buffer.

The Small setting holds up to 100 lines of text, or about 2 single-spaced pages. If you plan to capture more than that, use this option to increase the amount of memory Works sets aside. The Medium setting is 300 lines, and the Large setting is 750 lines.

Tip: If you are receiving a text file that is larger than 750 lines, the buffer will erase the beginning lines to receive the new lines. To avoid this problem, transfer the incoming information directly to an open file.

Other Settings

The remaining settings in this dialog box should not come into play except under special circumstances. The Wraparound setting wraps to the next line on the screen any text longer than 80 characters. The Local echo setting is used when you are communicating with another computer and a user is at the other keyboard. One of the fun things you can do when connected to another person's computer is type messages back and forth. As you type, the characters are printed on your screen and on the screen of the computer to which you are connected. Sometimes the letters you type will not be seen on your screen, so you must turn on the `Local echo` option.

You can remove the Works communications display entirely and see only the computer display in full-screen mode. You may want to do this in order to avoid screen clutter.

The `Keypad alternate` and `Cursor alternate` settings are for use in ANSI-terminal emulation. With `Keypad alternate` chosen, the numbered keypad keys will send escape sequences when the Num Lock key is turned on. The cursor-movement keys also will send an escape sequence, but the Num Lock key must be turned off.

Connecting to an Information Service

One of the many information services available, CompuServe, has a wide variety of offerings. Of course, its services are not free. At a minimum, you will have to pay for the connect time to the service plus the phone time. When you connect to CompuServe, your computer is communicating with a mainframe computer. The mainframe has the capacity to communicate with thousands of users simultaneously.

A description of the physical process of connecting to another computer is as follows: The modem in your computer dials the connecting number just as a phone does. The computer on the other end, the host computer, answers the phone and then sends a high-pitched tone over the line to your computer. At that point, Works recognizes that the connection has been established, and the host computer sends a question to your computer. The question is displayed on-screen. At that point, you begin the sign-on protocol, such as a user identification and password. Once this information is accepted by the host computer, you are presented with a menu particular to the host system.

Once you reach this point, the navigation within CompuServe is controlled by your selection of menu options.

Setting Up Works To Initialize a Connection

Regardless of which service you decide to connect to, Works must be set up to start the process. Follow these steps:

1. Assuming that you are already in the COMM1.WCM file, press Alt and then select Options. From the Options menu, select Phone. The dialog box shown in figure 11.5 appears.

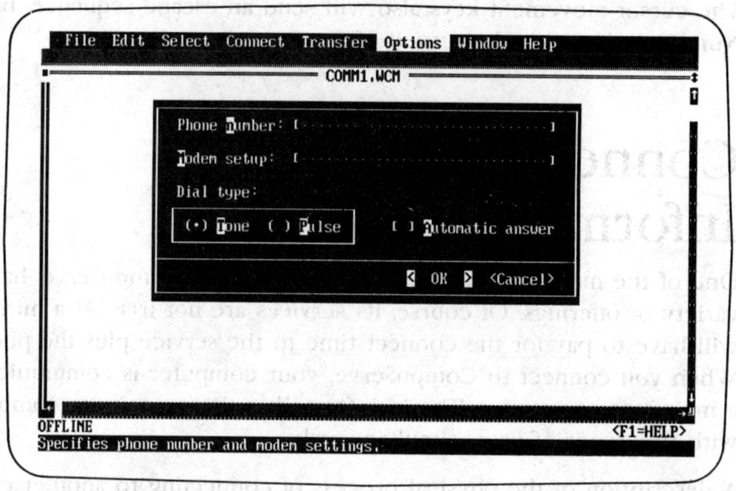

Fig. 11.5.
The Phone dialog box.

If you are connecting to CompuServe, a local number or an 800 number is available that you can type at the field labeled `Phone number`. To get started with CompuServe, you must first contact the company to obtain a user ID and a password. The phone numbers for several information vendors are included in Appendix A.

If your local number is an 800 toll-free line, do not forget to have the modem dial the 1 for long distance. Or, if you work in an office with the need to catch an outside line, dial 9, then a comma, and then the outside number. The comma creates a pause in the dialing sequence. If you fail to reach an outside line, another comma can be used. (Works includes another setting here; if you are using a rotary dial phone, you can set `Dial type` to `Pulse`.)

2. Select `OK` to close the dialog box. Then press Alt for the menu bar and choose the Connect menu. Select the Connect option from the menu. Works will dial the phone, and you will hear the tone over

your computer speaker. When the connection is made, the high-pitched tone is the host computer. Works will change the status line in the lower left corner from `OFFLINE` to a clock showing elapsed time. This clock keeps you aware of the cost of being on-line.

3. Pressing Enter a couple of times may be necessary to get the host computer's attention. When the computer does respond, it will ask, in the case of CompuServe, for the host system (which is CompuServe), the user ID, and the password. The password is not displayed on your screen so that unauthorized people will not be able to see it.

4. After you finish your communications session, you stop by logging off within the service. To stop the session within Works, you must press Alt, select the Connect menu, and then select the Connect option.

If, during the course of your session, you decide to have Works capture text, the text is stored in the buffer. To save the information in the buffer, press Alt, choose File, and then choose Save.

Works records the sign-on procedure you used to connect to the service so that when you decide to call that service (or other computer services) again, the process is automated.

Calling a Service the Second Time

All the information you entered to reach and connect with a service (or other computer) is stored in the communications file. By default, the first file is given the name COMM1.WCM, unless you changed it when you saved the file. At that point, the communications file can be given a more descriptive file name, such as CPSERVE.WCM for CompuServe.

Whatever the file name is, use the Open Existing File option and then select the file from the list presented in the Works file manager. After the file is open, select the Connect menu and then choose the Sign-On option.

Sometimes, when you attempt to connect with a service, the line will be busy. Press Alt, select the Connect menu, and choose the Dial Again option from the Connect menu in order to try again.

Sending a File

Works includes the XMODEM protocol, which will enable the transfer to take place.

First, you must be connected to another computer or a service. If you are connected to another computer (a friend's computer in another office, for example), your configurations must match as to the baud rate, parity, and so on. If the configurations do match, to send a file you will use the XMODEM modem setting. Let the other computer know you are ready to send the file. With a service, such as CompuServe, a menu offering will be available for it to become aware of your intention.

To send the file, do the following:

1. Press Alt and select the Transfer menu.
2. From the Transfer menu, select the Send File option. A dialog box appears.
3. From this dialog box, select the file you want to transmit.
4. Select `Binary` or `Text` file. In most transfers, you will want to use the `Binary` option. It will preserve the file as you constructed it (the formatting will remain intact, for example).

   If you are sending a text file, you may need to select the `CR` or `LF` option in order for it to transmit correctly.
5. Choose `OK` and the file will begin transferring. The status line will alternate between `SEND` and `WAITING`. Don't be surprised if transferring the file takes awhile.

When Works finishes sending, press `OK` to resume your session. At any point in the transfer, you may stop the process by pressing Esc. Works responds with a dialog box asking whether you want to quit.

Receiving a File

The opposite of sending a file is receiving a file. With an information service, the first step is to establish the connection and find the file you want to receive. With CompuServe, a menu choice is listed that will begin sending you the file. You will want to use the XMODEM transfer protocol.

After you have asked the host computer to send the file, press Alt, select the Transfer menu, and select the Receive option. The File dialog box opens, and you can select the drive and file name in which you want to store the file with the Save As option from the File menu.

Select the type of file, binary or text, and then select OK. The Works status bar alternates between RECEIVE and WAITING as the file transfers. The process will likely take longer than you expect. At any time during the transfer, you may stop the process by pressing Esc.

Copying Information from Communications to Another Tool

At some point, you may want to transfer files containing spreadsheets or databases from the communications buffer. An example would be when you have two offices working on a budget, each with separate and discrete parts. To receive a spreadsheet file and copy it into the Works spreadsheet tool, do the following:

1. Connect to the other computer and open a new spreadsheet file in the spreadsheet tool.
2. Go through the process of receiving the file. Up to 750 lines can be held in the communications buffer. The DOS file is necessary after the file gets too large.
3. Press Alt, choose the Connect menu, and then choose the Pause option. This option allows you to put the communications session on hold. Choose the Edit and Copy commands.
4. Press Alt again and open the Window menu. The spreadsheet file you opened will be listed as an open window. Select the spreadsheet file with the highlight. It will be displayed on the screen. Because you are in a spreadsheet, move the cell selector to the cell where you want the information to be inserted. Press Enter and select the appropriate option as requested by Works.
5. Select OK. After the insertion, return to the Communication window by pressing Alt, selecting the Window menu, and choosing the name of the communication file. It will be displayed in place of the spreadsheet.
6. Return to the session by reselecting the Pause option from the Connect menu.

As an alternative to transferring information from the communications buffer to another tool, you can have the file sent directly to a file on your computer. Follow these steps:

1. After connecting to the other computer, press Alt and select the Transfer menu. From there, use the Capture Text option to open the File dialog box.

2. In the `Save file as` entry field, type a file name for the incoming text. You can choose any extension you want and save the file to any drive or directory.

3. To append the new text to an old file, press Alt-A. To overwrite the old file, press Alt-R.

Using the Automatic Answer Feature

In order to save money and use the computer when normal business hours are over, you can set the Works communications tool to wait for another computer to call it and then receive information.

If, for example, the company you work for has an office on the East Coast and an office on the West Coast, you can send messages via the modem. Assuming that you are in the East Coast office, you can set your computer to receive a file from the West Coast office after your normal working day. Leave the computer turned on and ready to receive the file as follows:

1. Select the Options menu and choose Phone.

2. Choose the `Automatic answer` option on the Phone dialog box (see fig. 11.5).

3. Choose `OK`.

4. Select the Connect menu and choose the Connect option.

Works will wait patiently for the incoming call. When the call comes, Works will answer and receive any information into the buffer. When you return to work the following day, the information will be waiting for you. You receive two benefits with this feature. One benefit is that you are able to extend your work day with computer automation. The second benefit is that telephone rates are much cheaper after normal work hours.

Examining Common Communication Problems

Even though major improvements have occurred in the communications industry, there is still little standardization. Each phone company and phone equipment supplier has a slightly different way of doing things, making for annoying inconsistencies. The following sections examine some common problems that may occur in the course of using the communications tool.

Call Waiting

If the phone line to which the modem is connected has call waiting, a problem can occur that has nothing to do with Works. When you are on-line and a call comes into your line, the call will garble the transmission.

You have two options. One is to disable the call-waiting feature before going on-line. Usually, you can disable call waiting by dialing a special code to the telephone company computer before going on-line. The second choice is to install a separate line without the call-waiting feature.

If you can disable call waiting from your own phone, you can add the Disable command to your communications files. Then, every time you attempt to access another computer, the disable procedure proceeds the dial out.

In some telephone service areas, to ussue the Disable command, you press the asterisk (*) and then dial the number 70. Your script at the Options Phone screen would read

*70, 123-4567

Call waiting will resume automatically when you end the communications session. You don't need to reestablish call waiting after you are finished.

Extension Phones

Another hazard for home computer users is the ubiquitous extension phone. Not knowing that you are communicating, another person can pick up an extension phone. The line interference will garble the transmission. Many modern phones, however, do have a light that turns on when the line is active.

PBX Problems

Working in an office setting usually means that you will be dialing through some type of PBX system. The best solution is to obtain a dedicated line specifically for the modem communications. This solution may not be feasible, depending on the amount of traffic and the business justification for its use.

In hooking into a PBX, the jack you need is called an RJ-11. PBX systems normally do not have such an adapter. The company that installed the telephone system should be able to assist you in getting hooked up correctly.

Finally, PBX systems are speed oriented. If you are forced to dial through one, keep your use of commas to a minimum in order to avoid having the PBX assume that there is no activity on the line and release your station. The PBX can be adjusted for wait times, too, by the installation company.

Modem Problems

If you are properly set to dial and nothing happens when you instruct Works to dial, check the following:

- ❑ Is the modem plugged in at all the necessary places? Make sure that an internal modem is firmly seated in the slot (particularly if you installed it yourself).
- ❑ Is the port you selected (or default to) correct? Works will check to see whether a modem is in the port indicated. If Works cannot find the modem, it will not work.
- ❑ If you are using an external modem, check the connections again. Sometimes you may have to turn the modem off and on again to reset its internal software.
- ❑ Is the modem truly Hayes compatible? Hayes set the standard for use with personal computers, and it is imperative that your modem is compatible.

No Dial Tone

When you ask Works to dial and you hear no noise from your speaker that sounds like a dial tone, check to see whether the telephone lines are connected correctly. On a home setup, most of the internal modems allow for the incoming line to the modem and an outgoing line to the user's telephone set. This setup makes it easy to use both the phone and the modem without having to plug in the telephone line every time. However, you could have the two lines in the wrong jacks.

If this check fails, plug the phone into the jack to be certain it works.

The Called Computer Fails To Respond

Check the phone number dialed. If it is correct, try calling the service to see whether a problem exists with the system. Perhaps the hours of access are restricted. If you are trying to access a BBS, the line may be tied up frequently. The line may even have disappeared because BBSs are often operated by private individuals.

Screen Garbage and Unintended Disconnection

Check with the settings on the other computer to make certain that everything matches. To avoid frustration, jot down the settings for each service you use.

If the computer you are connected to is an Apple or DEC, expect that the connection will not be perfect.

If the communication works great for a time and then deteriorates, suspect the telephone company or a bad electrical storm. Computers and telephones hooked together are sensitive to electrical interference.

You Cannot Log On

CompuServe is accessed through shared telephone networks called Tymnet or Telenet. These networks are front-end computers, and although they may be working, the host itself may be down for repairs. Incorrectly entering your identification or password also can cause trouble, particularly if the entry must be in all uppercase or all lowercase letters.

XMODEM

You tried to transfer a file and had no luck. Unfortunately, not all XMODEM protocols are exactly compatible. Again, a lack of standardization exists. Try sending your file in Text mode as opposed to Binary.

Chapter Summary

In this chapter, you learned how to use the Works communications tool, with a modem, to access the many outside information services available. In the world of electronic communications, a computer and a modem have become a potent tool. With the increasing number of information services, home offices, and bulletin boards, the use of electronic communications is growing. With Works and a subscription to an information service, you can have at your fingertips an unlimited source of information on every conceivable subject—all from your keyboard.

In the next chapter, you will learn how to use macros to automate tasks that you use repeatedly in Works.

12

Creating and Using Macros

A macro is a short computer program that automates a routine set of keystrokes. Macros simplify the steps required to run database reports, total spreadsheets, and create graphs or form letters. This chapter will cover how to construct, test, and modify macros.

Creating a Macro

The Works macro function acts as a recorder of the keystrokes you enter to make a certain thing happen in Works. In fact, that is all the macro does. The macro plays back the keystrokes you pressed in Works.

The macro is stored under a specific name, and you can replay it by pressing specific keys together. For example, you may use the Ctrl and T keys to name a macro that will add a total of numbers in a spreadsheet.

To reach the Macro dialog box, press Alt-/ (press and hold down the Alt key while you press the slash key). These two keys must be pressed together. If you have a separate numeric keypad, the slash (/) key on the keypad will not work. Figure 12.1 shows the Macro dialog box.

Using the Macro Dialog Box

In this section, you will examine the options available on the Macro dialog box.

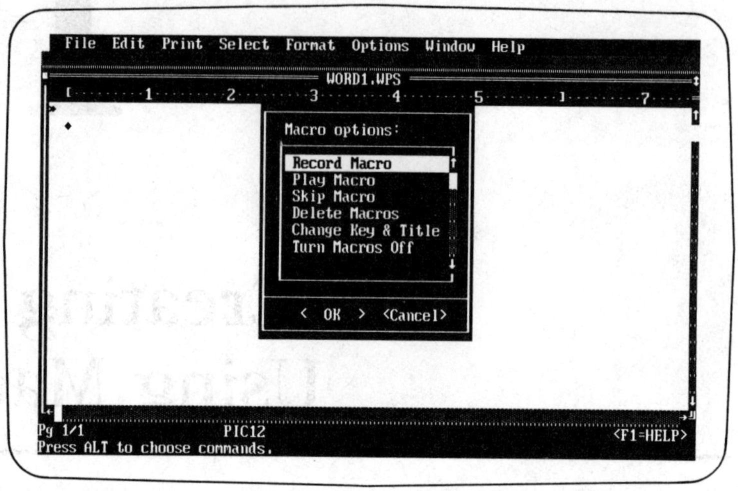

Fig. 12.1.
The Macro dialog box.

Record Macro

The Works Record Macro feature is like a tape recorder; the difference is that a tape recorder captures sound, and the macro recorder captures input from the keyboard. If you select the Record Macro option, the dialog box exits the screen, and from that point on, every keyboard input is recorded. RECORD is displayed on the status line in the lower right corner of the screen. This is your indicator that the Record Macro option is functioning.

The RECORD indicator will remain until you reopen the Macro dialog box and select the End Recording option.

Play Macro

This option opens a dialog box that lists all the macros you have created. Because you can open the Macro dialog box at any time, any of the macros listed can be replayed. If you create a macro to save a file, for example, it can be replayed in the spreadsheet, word processor, and database. To replay a listed macro, move the highlight to the macro name and press Alt-P.

Skip Macro

If you created a macro and assigned its playback as a key that is also used by Works (the F1 Help key is an example), you can stop the macro from running at the wrong time and still have the macro stored where you desire.

One method is to select the `Skip Macro` option. When the dialog box closes, press the keystroke that would normally play back the macro. Works ignores the macro playback once. If you reinvoke the macro key a second time, it will play the macro.

The second method for shutting off the macro key is to type an accent grave (`). The key to use is usually located in the upper left corner of the keyboard. The accent grave symbol shares the key with the tilde symbol (~). Press the Accent Grave key and then the macro key. This procedure shuts off the macro key for one use and then returns to the macro playback function. As a general rule, do not use function keys by themselves as macro keys. Add a second key preceding the function key.

Delete Macros

The `Delete Macros` option erases the keystrokes recorded to a particular key. This option frees the assigned key so it will no longer be assigned to a macro. You then can use the key again for another macro.

Change Key & Title

The `Change Key & Title` option provides you flexibility in designating the particular key for a macro and changing the macro title if necessary. Choosing this option opens the Macro List dialog box so that you can select the macro to be modified.

Turn Macros Off

At some point, you may want to turn off all the macros you have recorded. The `Turn Macros Off` option is a toggle. Selecting the option once turns the macros off. Select the Macro dialog box again, and the option will be displayed as `Turn Macros On`.

Creating a Word Processing Macro

Macros in word processing are useful. If you write often, you can record addresses, favorite phrases, or entire letters in a macro. Many people use macros to record words that they frequently use or words that they often misspell. Commonly used words may include the names of companies or jargon.

Open a word processing document with the New Word Processor command. You are going to create a macro that will insert your name and address into a letter. The macro can perform this operation whenever you want. You will not be required to type the information each time. To create the macro, do the following:

1. Open the Macro dialog box by pressing Alt-/.
2. Select the `Record Macro` option.
3. The Playback & Title dialog box appears (see fig. 12.2).

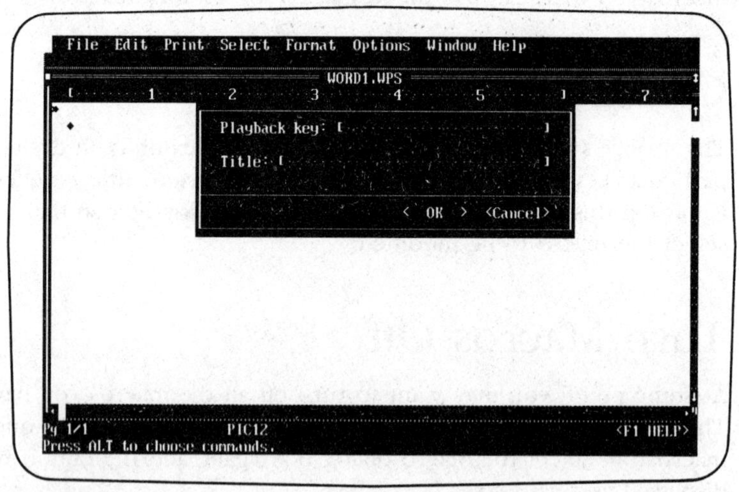

Fig. 12.2.
The Playback & Title dialog box.

At the `Playback key` field, you can assign the key you want to hold this recording. For this macro, you do not want to use a key that you use for other purposes on a regular basis (such as a letter key). A good alternative to using single keys for storing macros is to use two-key combinations. Remember that Works uses the Alt key to activate the menu bar, so you don't want to use Alt as part of the two-key combination. You may want to use the Ctrl key with another key for this example.

4. For this macro, press Ctrl-N. The N will stand for *Name*.
5. Press the Tab key to move the highlight to the `Title` field. Type *Name and Address.*
6. Press Enter (or click `OK`) and Works is now ready to record the keystrokes.
7. Type your name and address on the word processing screen. You may make any changes you want because Works is recording every keystroke. Only the finished entry will be displayed. Figure 12.3 shows a sample name and address.

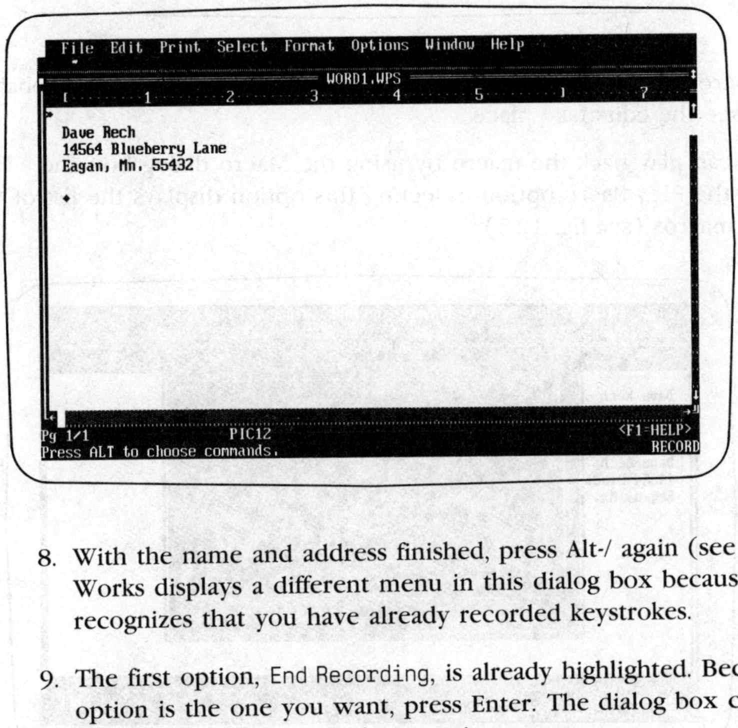

Fig. 12.3.
A sample name and address.

8. With the name and address finished, press Alt-/ again (see fig. 12.4). Works displays a different menu in this dialog box because it recognizes that you have already recorded keystrokes.
9. The first option, `End Recording`, is already highlighted. Because this option is the one you want, press Enter. The dialog box closes, and you are back at the word processing screen.
10. To run the macro, move the cursor several lines below the address you typed and then press Ctrl-N.

Almost instantly, the name and address you typed are displayed. If you made any edits when you originally typed the name and address, the

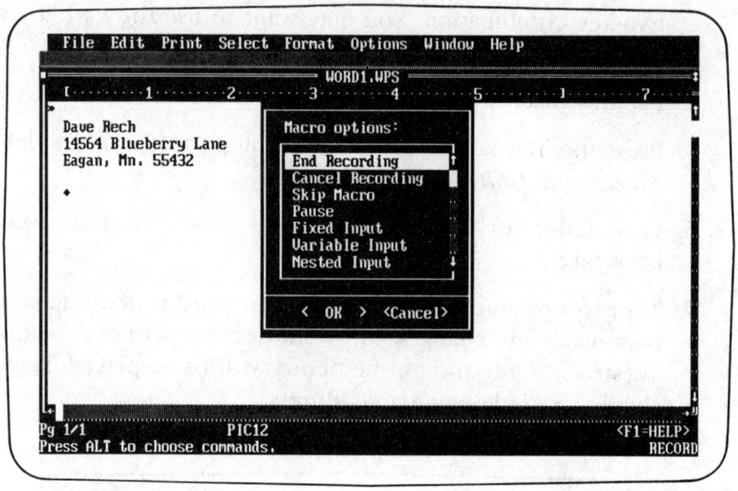

Fig. 12.4.

The End Macro Options dialog box.

mistakes are played back. Because everything happens so fast, you probably will not see the edits take place.

You also can play back the macro by using the Macro dialog box and selecting the `Play Macro` option. Selecting this option displays the list of available macros (see fig. 12.5).

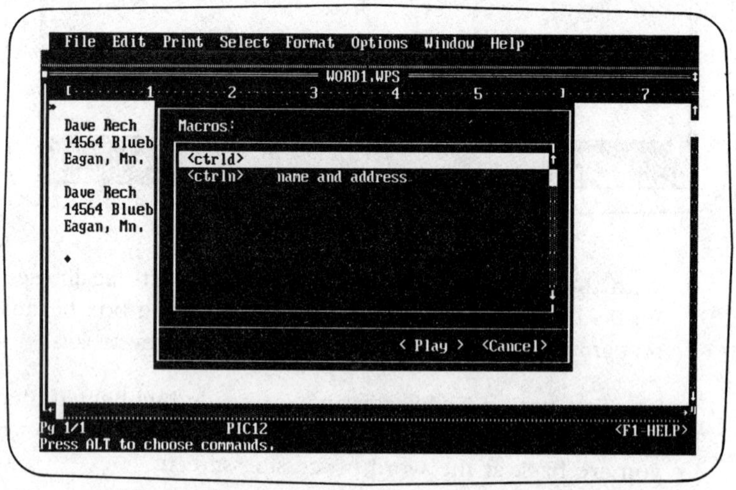

Fig. 12.5.

The Macro List dialog box.

In figure 12.5, two macros are listed. To play one of the macros, move the highlight to it and press Enter. The macro will run as usual. Notice that the first macro listed has no title. This omission demonstrates the clear advantage of adding a title to every macro you create. If every macro has a title, even if you don't use a macro for several months, you can come back to it and remember what it does. Using macro titles is particularly important because macros can be written to do anything that can be done in Works.

Suppose that you create a macro to select all the text in a word processing file and then to delete it. If you fail to name the macro and then accidentally ask Works to play it back, you may delete a valuable file. Add a title to all your macros.

Creating a Spreadsheet Macro

In the spreadsheet, a macro can accomplish a routine chore for you instantly. The macro can even be used for automating the spreadsheet for printing and copying. A sample macro for inserting the current date and time follows:

1. Open a spreadsheet file.
2. Press Alt-/ to begin recording a macro.
3. Use the combination Ctrl-D as the playback keys. For a title, type *Inserting the Date and Time.*
4. The dialog box closes. With the cell selector in cell A3, type the following formula:

   =NOW()

5. Press Enter.
6. Now format the cell. Press Alt for the menu bar, select the Format menu, and select the Time/Date option. When the Time/Date dialog box opens, select the `Month, Day, Year` option and then press Enter or click `OK`.
7. Press the down-arrow key to make A4 the active cell. Then type the following formula:

   =NOW()

8. Format the cell for the time. Press Alt and then select Format; then select the `Hour,Minute` option from the Time/Date dialog box.
9. Press Alt-/ to open the Macro dialog box and select `End Recording`.

Now you can run the macro by pressing Ctrl-D. The menus will flash by on the screen, and the time and date will be inserted wherever the cell selector was located.

Creating a Database Macro

Databases are frequently used for doing repetitive tasks. For an example, consider that investors holding various mutual funds need to be informed periodically of the status of their holdings. Not every investor has the same mutual funds, so a sort task is required for sending updates to only those clients holding a particular fund. If you have to sort the investor database by hand every time you intend to update the investors on their accounts, you will never get the job done.

You can create a macro that will begin the sort and then pause for you to input the name of a particular fund. This fund can then be used as a selection criterion.

To create this macro, you will use the sample database from Chapter 9:

1. Open the file RMTA.

2. Press Alt-/ to begin the macro recording.

3. You will perform a query based on the renewal date. When the Query screen appears, however, don't proceed with a date-based query. Instead, press Alt-/. The dialog box shown in figure 12.6 appears.

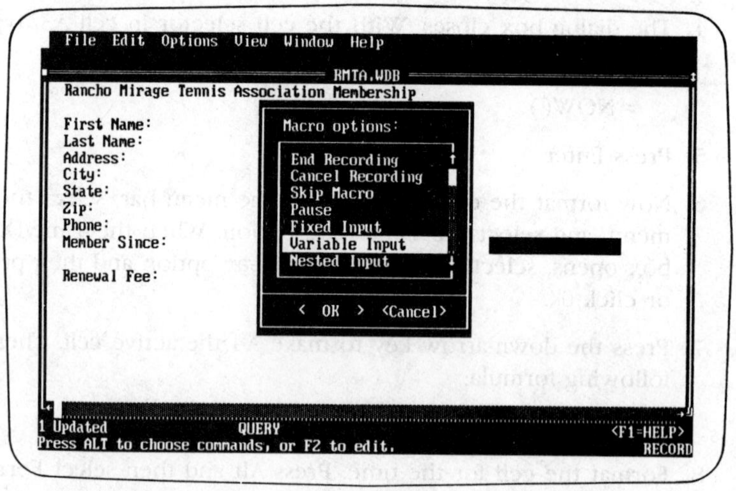

Fig. 12.6.

The End Macro Options dialog box with the `Variable Input` *option highlighted.*

4. Select the `Variable Input` option, and the next time you run the macro, it will stop and wait for you to enter the new date of renewal. The date you enter when you create the macro—or the dates you enter when playing back the macro in subsequent

months—will not become a permanent part of the macro. Every time the macro is used, it will pause for input.

5. After entering the variable as *=5/89*, don't press Enter. Press Alt-/ again and select `OK`.

Works continues recording your keystrokes. After you finish the query, have Works print a mailing label and a form letter containing the amount owed. This information can also be inserted with the variable input pause.

Use the same technique to insert a fixed input entry or a timed pause. At the point where you want the macro to stop, press Alt-/ and select the type of pause you want.

Using Nested Macros

A *nested input macro* is simply a second macro that can be run inside a macro. Create the main macro, and when you have input that is repetitious, press Alt-/ to open the Macro dialog box, select `Nested Input`, and proceed with the second macro. Because the procedure creates a separate macro, you must designate another specific keystroke and macro name.

The nested macro is also a macro in its own right, and you can play it back by pressing the designated key or keys. You can play the nested macro independently without having to play the main macro first.

Modifying Macros

Every macro you record is stored in a specific file that can be accessed by all Works tools. The file is a word processing file called MACROS.INI. Works creates and saves the file after you have created a macro. Prior to that, the file does not exist, so you cannot modify the file until you have first created a macro and then exited Works. Opening the file requires specific steps:

1. Close all open files.
2. Press Alt for the menu bar, select the File menu, and then choose the Open option.
3. Type *macros.ini* and press Enter.
4. A screen message appears indicating that you cannot use macros while this file is open. Press Enter or click `OK`.

5. The next screen offers you a choice of opening a word processor, database, or spreadsheet (see fig. 12.7).

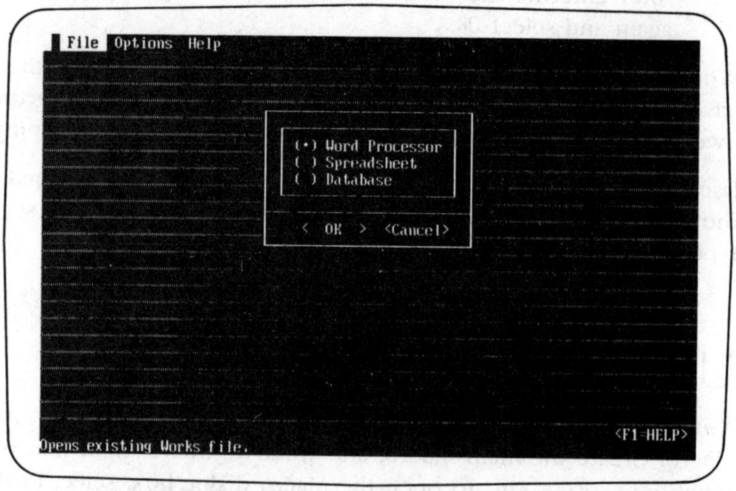

Fig. 12.7.
The file choice screen for macros.

6. Select `Word Processor`, and the file shown in figure 12.8 opens.

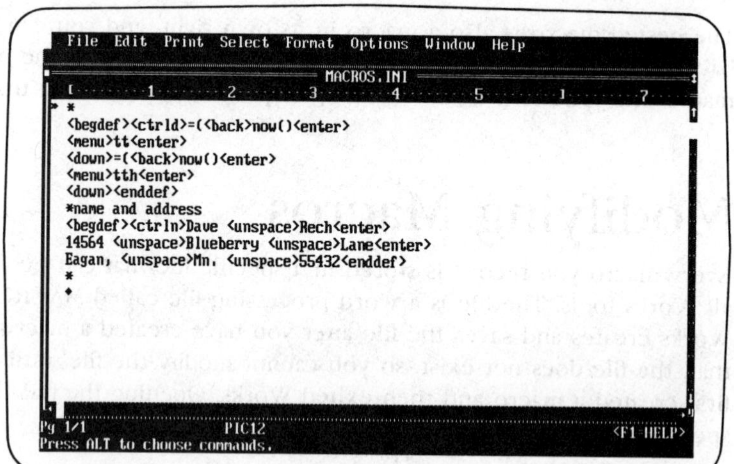

Fig. 12.8.
The MACROS.INI file screen.

Although it looks complex, the macro file contains only the recorded keystrokes with certain conventions. The asterisk (*) indicates the name of the macro. In this example, the first macro has no name. Looking closely, you can see the keystrokes that created the Time and Date macro for insertion into a spreadsheet.

The second macro is titled Name and Address. This macro types the name and address entry you specified previously. You created the macro for the word processor.

Editing a Macro

Macros are edited in the Works word processor. All the text-editing keystrokes covered in the word processing chapters will work for editing macros.

To edit or create a macro, follow the format used by the macros created and displayed in figure 12.8. The Microsoft Works manual includes an extensive listing of all the keystrokes and their individual translations into macro language.

A new macro must start with an asterisk and a title together on the same line. When you create a macro completely from the word processor, the new macro will appear in the Macro List dialog box.

One thing you cannot do when you are in the MACROS.INI file is invoke the Macro dialog box.

Changing the Playback Key or Title

To edit the playback key or the title of a macro, do the following:

1. Press Alt-/.
2. Use the highlight to select the macro you want to edit.
3. Press Alt-C to change the macro.

Turning Off Macros

At times, turning off all the macros is the easiest way to work with Works.

To turn off all macros, do the following:

1. Press Alt-/.
2. Select the option `Turn Macros Off`.

The macros will remain off until you return to the Macro dialog box and repeat the keystroke sequence. The option is a toggle and switches from on to off as it is selected.

Creating a Repeating Macro

You can create a macro that performs the same task repeatedly without you having to restart the macro every time it completes a single task. After typing in the keystrokes to make the macro work, press the same keys you designated as the macro keys. If you used the combination Ctrl-B, for example, press Ctrl-B at the end of the macro.

This procedure creates a continuous loop where the macro will continue performing. The macro may continue to invoke itself, even when all the actions desired have been completed.

At this point, simply press Alt-/ and the macro stops.

Deleting a Macro

To delete a macro, use the same dialog box you used for the other macro options. Press Alt-/ and select the `Delete Macros` option. The list of macros you have created will appear. Select the macro you want to delete.

Press Alt-L when the macro you want to delete is highlighted, and Works will delete the macro.

Chapter Summary

Macros will greatly enhance your use of Microsoft Works, particularly if the tasks you perform are repetitive and involve many keystrokes. Whenever you find yourself repeating a Works job many times, create a macro to do the job for you. With the fixed input or variable input features of macros, you can create a macro that can pause and wait for your input at any point. The macro will continue running after the information is entered.

In the next chapter, you will learn how to integrate all the Microsoft Works tools.

Part VI

Integrating Applications

Includes

13

Tying It All Together

The tremendous advantages of using an integrated program will become apparent in this chapter. You will practice integrating text, database information, and spreadsheet data. You will generate mailing labels and form letters. You also will create integrated financial reports by using copying skills that you will learn in this chapter.

Before continuing with this chapter, you may want to review the basics of file management and the concept of windows. This chapter will explain the copying and moving functions. These files allow information to be transferred from file to file or component to component. At the end of this chapter, you will learn about some Works accessories, such as the Alarm Clock. And you will learn about using templates with Works.

Prepare to integrate the four components of Works by opening three files. You may select files that you have created for your own use or select sample files used in this book. The three files used in this chapter's examples are RMTA.WDB, RENEW.WPS, and TENNIS.WKS.

Using Microsoft Works Windows

Without having to open and close files, you can work in a number of files by using windows. Works can display up to eight windows at one time, each holding a different file. The active window contains the cursor. Move the cursor to a new window, and the file in that window becomes the active file. The active window appears in a different color (on a color monitor), has a double border at the top, and has mouse scroll bars. All the information displayed on the menu bar, the status bar, and the formula bar pertain to the active window.

You can make a window smaller or larger, and you can arrange and rearrange a window by placing it in different locations on the screen. Windows also can be split. You can perform any of these features by using the keyboard or a mouse.

Take a look at the Window menu by pressing Alt to activate the menu bar and pressing W for the Window menu. The Window menu contains a list of open files (see fig. 13.1). Press the number to the left of the file you want to work with. The cursor is placed in the window containing the file you selected, and the window becomes active.

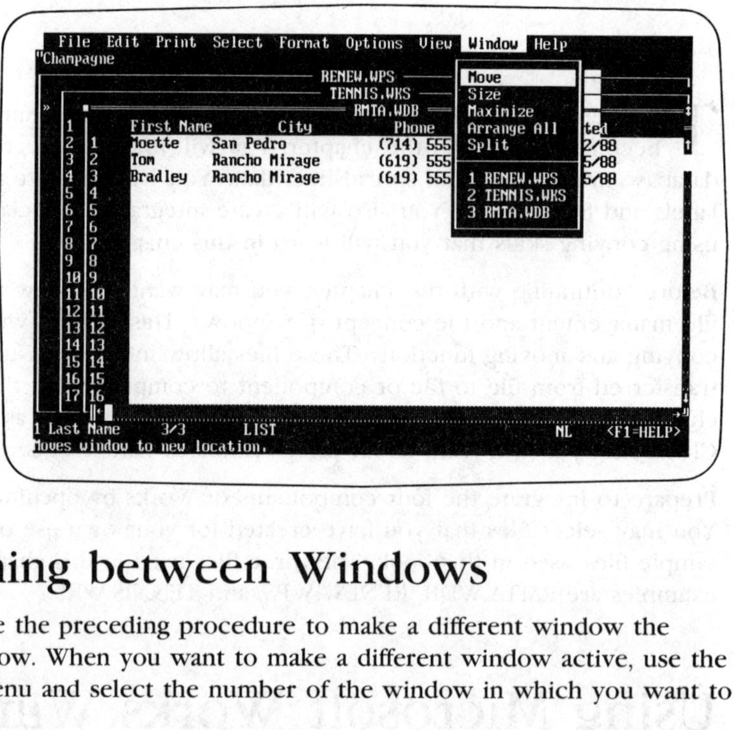

Fig. 13.1.

The Window menu.

Switching between Windows

You can use the preceding procedure to make a different window the active window. When you want to make a different window active, use the Window menu and select the number of the window in which you want to work.

Use the hot keys to accomplish the same thing. Press Ctrl-F6 to switch to the next window. Press Shift-Ctrl-F6 to move to the previous window.

The fastest method for switching windows involves using the mouse. Use the mouse to move the arrow into the window you want to be active and click the mouse button. With three newly opened files on-screen, you may not have much room in the window to place the arrow. Instead, point to the name of the file you want to become active and click the mouse button. The new active window is shown in color on your screen (if you have a color monitor). The open but inactive files are gray. (On a monochrome screen, you will notice a difference in shading between the active and inactive files.)

Moving a Window

You can move a window by using the Window menu or by using the mouse. If you want to use the menu, press Alt to activate the menu bar and then W to select the Window menu. Select Move, the first option on the menu. The active window now has a distinct border around it (see fig. 13.2).

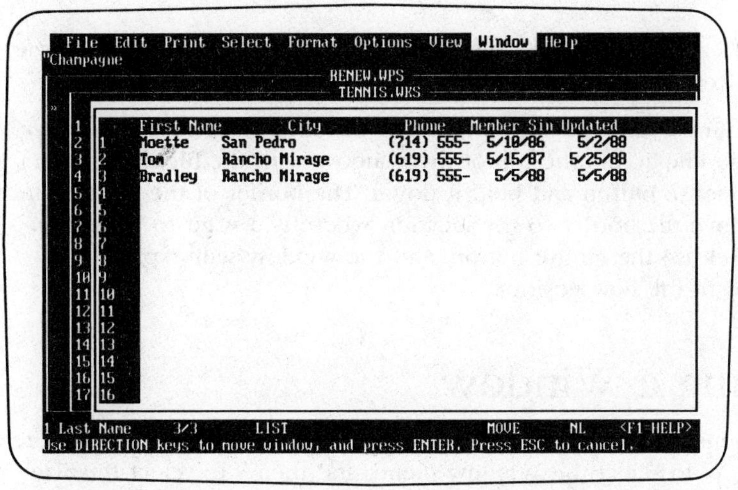

Fig. 13.2.
The active file in Move mode.

As indicated on the status line, press the cursor-movement keys to move the window to a new location and then press Enter. Press Esc if you decide you don't want to move the window and want to cancel the operation.

For this example, press the right- and down-arrow keys to move the window and then press Enter. The window is now in the lower right corner of the screen (see fig. 13.3).

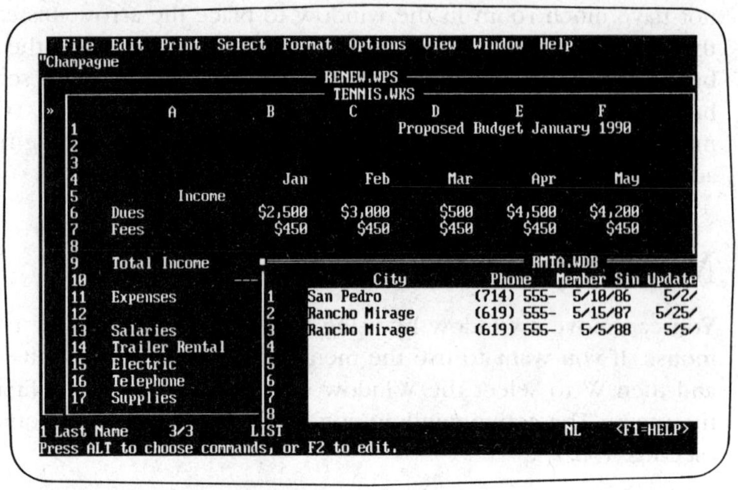

Fig. 13.3.

The window moved down and to the right.

Note: You can move the window anywhere on the screen as long as the upper left corner of the window remains on the screen.

You also can use the mouse to move the window. Point to the *title bar* (the double line across the top of the window with the file name on it). Press the mouse button and hold it down. The border of the file becomes distinct. Move the border to the location where you want to place the window. Release the mouse button, and the window will expand or contract to fit the new position.

Resizing a Window

Use the menu method to resize a window by pressing Alt to activate the menu bar, W to select the Window menu, and then S to select the Size option. The window border is highlighted. When you press the cursor-movement keys, you adjust the lower right corner of the window.

Press the up- and left-arrow keys. The window gets smaller, but the upper left corner of the window stays in the same position. Figure 13.4 shows the new border before Enter is pressed.

Press Enter and the active window becomes the size you have indicated. Remember to press Esc anytime during the process if you want to cancel the size change.

Use the mouse method to resize a window by pointing at the size box in the lower right corner of the window (see fig. 13.5). Press the mouse

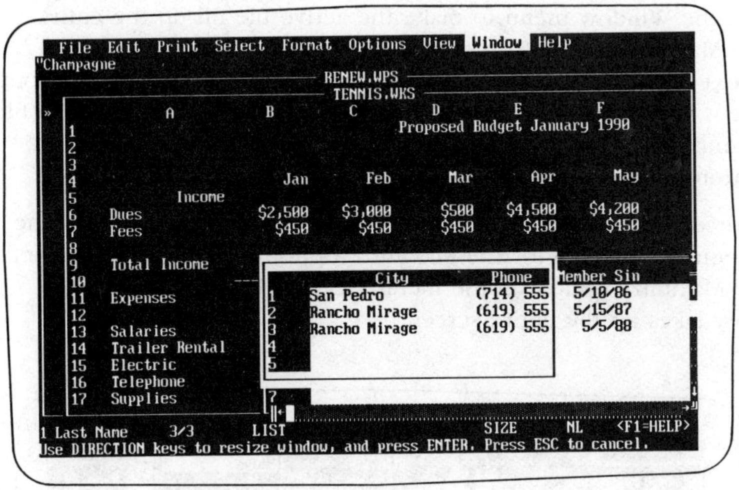

Fig. 13.4.

The new size for the window.

button and hold it down while you drag the window border until the window is the size you want. Release the mouse button, and the window expands or contracts to fit the new border.

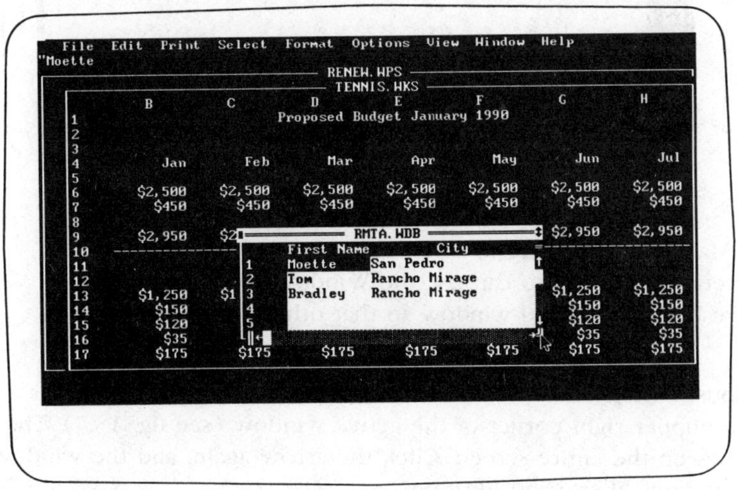

Fig. 13.5.

The mouse pointer on the size box.

Maximizing a Window

You currently have several windows showing on the screen, each containing an open file. Suppose that you decide you want to work in one file for a while without the others showing on-screen. Select the Maximize option from the Window menu to make the active file fill up the entire screen. The Maximize option is a *toggle*. Turn on the option (with the indicator next to it on the menu), and the active window is enlarged along with any new files you open. Change the active file, and the new active file also is maximized. Resize a window or select the Maximize option again, and the option is turned off.

With the cursor in a small window, press Alt for the menu bar, W for the Window menu, and then X for the Maximize option. An indicator appears next to the Maximize option on the menu (see fig. 13.6). The active window now takes up the entire screen.

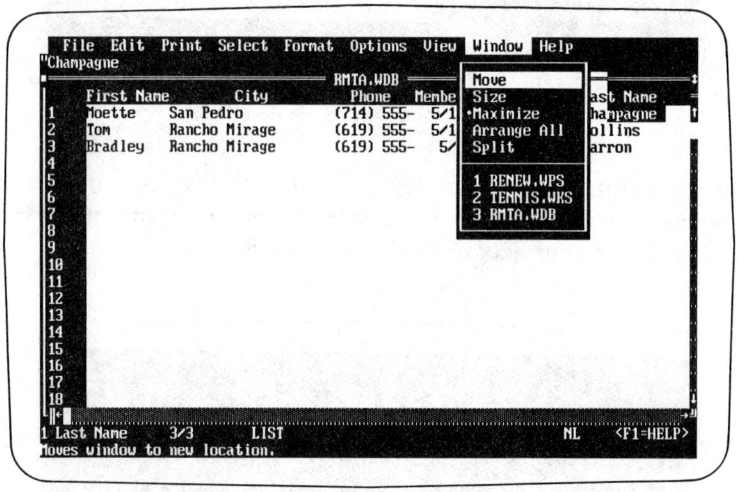

Fig. 13.6.

An indicator next to the Maximize option.

Select the Maximize option again to change the window back to the original screen size. You also can use the Window menu's Arrange All option or resize the enlarged window so that other windows become visible.

Use the mouse to maximize a window by clicking the double-headed arrow in the upper right corner of the active window (see fig. 13.7). The window takes up the entire screen. Click the arrow again, and the window returns to its original size and location.

Splitting a Window

A Microsoft Works window can be split into panes. Each pane can show a different part of the same file. This feature is a big benefit when you are

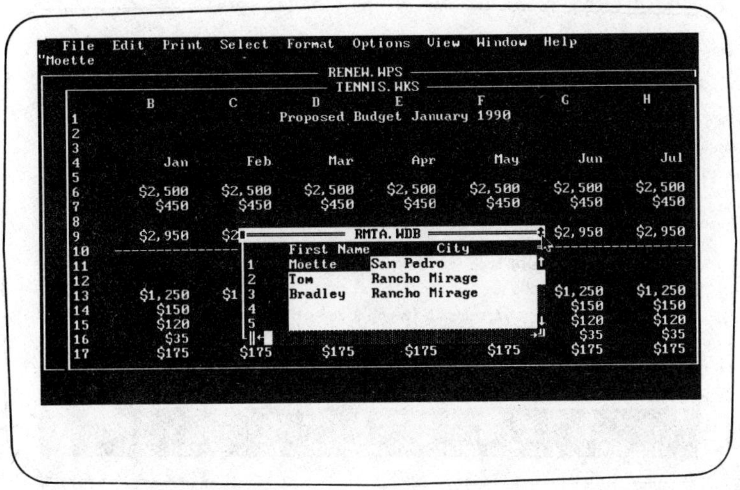

Fig. 13.7.

The pointer located on the double-headed arrow.

working with a large file and you want to see two parts of the file at the same time. In a spreadsheet, you may want to see the sales figures while you look at total revenue. In a database, you can look at the last names that start with A in one pane and the last names that start with S in the other pane.

Panes can be side by side with a vertical split or one above the other with a horizontal split. Word processor files can only be split horizontally.

Use the menu to split a window by pressing Alt for the menu bar, W for the Window menu, and T for the Split option. SPLIT appears on the status line.

With the cursor on RENEW.WPS, select the Split option from the Window menu. Horizontal split lines are inserted in place of the ruler lines (see fig. 13.8).

Press the up- or down-arrow key to move the split line and press Enter when the horizontal line is in the preferred location. In RENEW.WPS, you can see the horizontal split in the file. In the top pane, you see the date and heading of the letter; in the bottom, you see the closing of the letter (see fig. 13.9).

Remove the split by pressing Alt, W, and then T. Move the horizontal line back to the ruler line position and press Enter. As a result, you have only one pane on-screen.

While working with a database or spreadsheet file, press Alt for the menu bar, W for the Window menu, and T for the Split option. You will see a

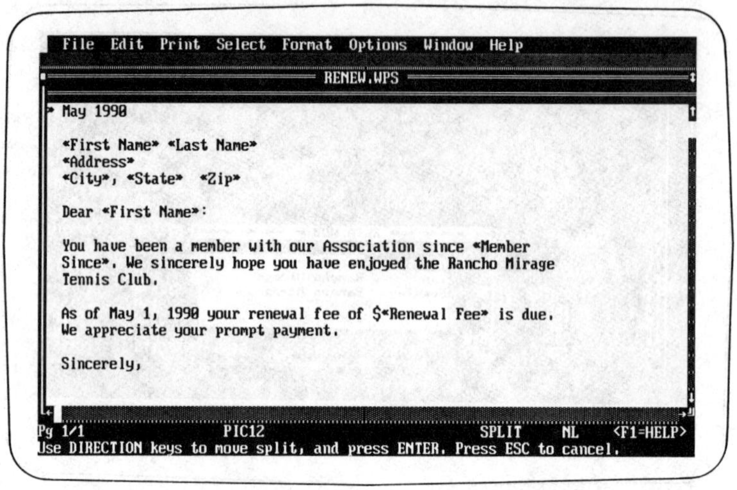

Fig. 13.8.
The horizontal split lines in the word processing file.

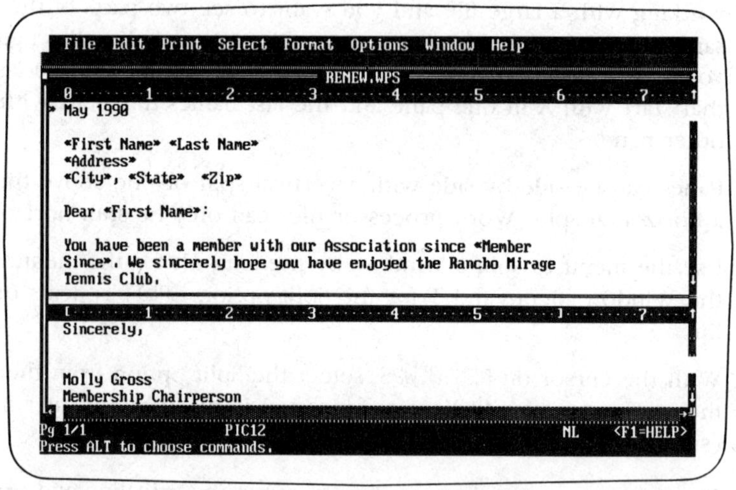

Fig. 13.9.
A horizontal split in a word processing file.

vertical and horizontal split line. Move the left- and right-arrow keys to move the vertical line. Move the up- and down-arrow keys to move the horizontal line. Press Enter when the line or lines are in the correct position. As you may have guessed, with either database or spreadsheet files, you can have up to four panes at one time. Each pane can show different parts of a file.

Figure 13.10 shows TENNIS.WKS with four panes. Move the cursor between panes by pressing F6 or Shift-F6. You can view different parts of the file in the different panes.

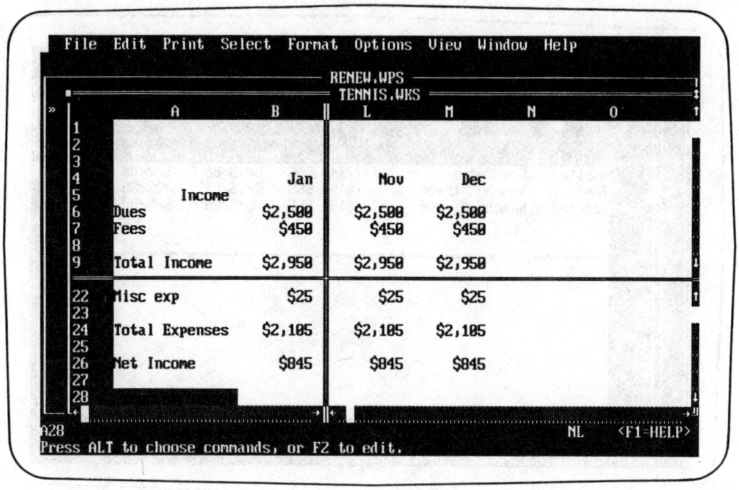

Fig. 13.10.

TENNIS.WKS with four panes.

Use the mouse to split windows into panes by pointing the cursor to the short double line at the top of the window. In the database screen, this double line is to the right of the field names (in List view). In the spreadsheet screen, this double line is to the right of the column letters. In the word processing screen, this double line is at the far right of the ruler line.

Use the mouse to place the pointer on the double line. Press the mouse button and hold it down while you drag the double line to the horizontal or vertical position. Figure 13.11 shows the pointer on the double line. Figure 13.12 shows the pane in the database file. Vertical lines also can be found in the bottom left corner of the spreadsheet and database screens.

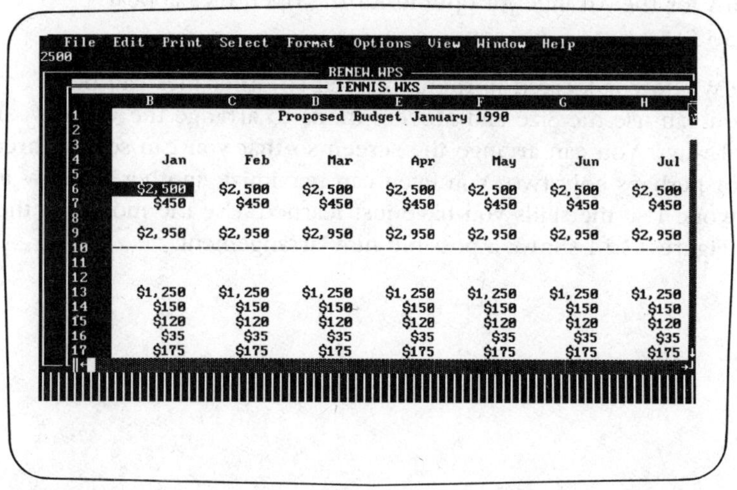

Fig. 13.11.

The pointer on the double line.

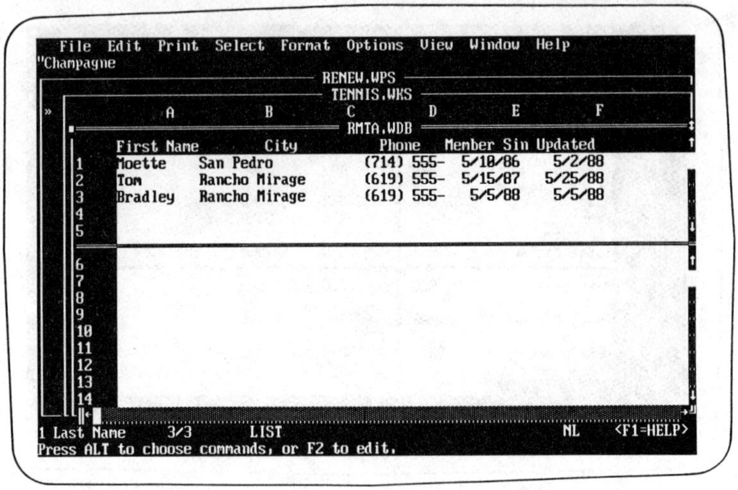

Fig. 13.12.

Horizontal panes in the database file.

Use the mouse to remove a split line from the screen by pointing at the line and then pressing and holding down the mouse button while you drag the line off the screen. Then release the mouse button.

Use the mouse to move between panes by moving the pointer to the pane you want to work in and then clicking the mouse button.

Arranging Windows on the Screen

At some point after a window has been maximized, you may again want to see all the open windows at the same time. To view all the open files through the windows, press Alt for the menu bar, W for the Window menu, and A for the Arrange All option. All the open files appear (see fig. 13.13).

The active window is located in the upper left so other files can be viewed. You can use the Size and Move options to arrange the windows in a variety of ways. You can arrange the screen so that you can see all three windows or perhaps only two. You even can maximize another window in which to work. Use the skills you have just learned. Use the mouse or the keyboard. Figure 13.14 shows a possible new arrangement.

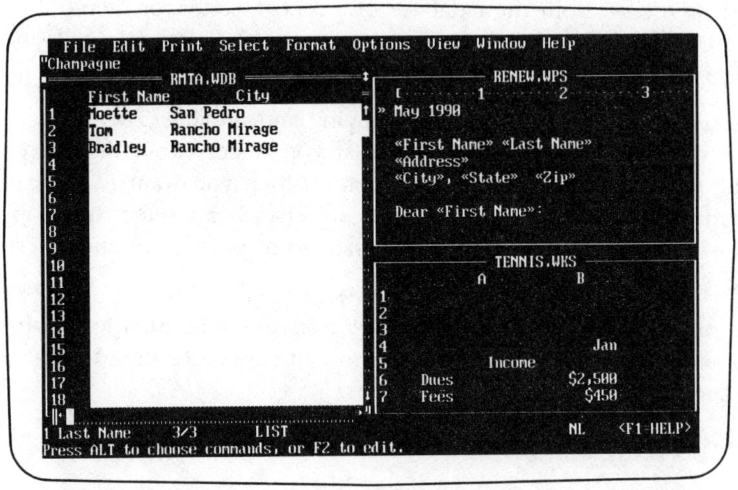

Fig. 13.13.

Windows open after Arrange All was selected.

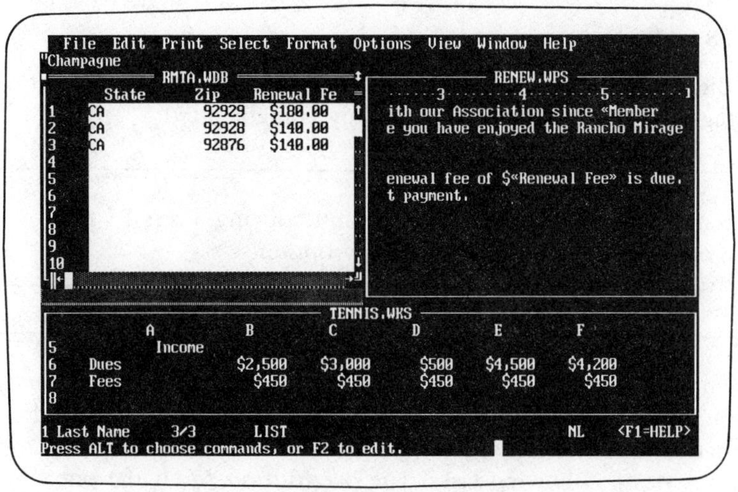

Fig. 13.14.

Three open files, rearranged.

Copying and Moving between Windows

You may have many reasons to copy from file to file. You may want to copy a group of figures from the spreadsheet to a word processing file. You can place the numbers in a report, letter, or memo. You may want to include a list or record from the database in a report, letter, or memo. You may want to copy or move numbers from the spreadsheet to data cells in the database.

The procedures are almost the same for copying and moving. The only difference between the two procedures is that you select either the Move option or the Copy option from the Edit menu. When you want to leave the original in its location and place a duplicate elsewhere, select the Copy option. When you want to remove the original from its location and insert it elsewhere, select the Move option.

Because the procedures for copying and moving are almost identical, only the copying procedure is examined here. You can substitute the Move option for the Copy option in the same steps.

Begin by indicating the text you want to copy. You can do so in many ways:

- ❑ Press and hold down the Shift key and move the cursor-movement keys until the text you want to copy is highlighted
- ❑ Press F8 multiple times
- ❑ Click the mouse at the beginning of the text you want to highlight and drag until the text you want to copy is highlighted

---

Tip: Remember the hot keys for moving and copying. Press F3 for the Move option and Shift-F3 for the Copy option.

Tip: Moving and copying text from one Works component to another will be much quicker and less cumbersome if the origination file and the destination file are both open and displayed in windows before you start any of the following tasks. The *origination file* is the one from which you are copying text or data. The *destination file* is the one in which you plan to insert text or data.

Copying from the Spreadsheet to the Word Processor

To copy material from the spreadsheet to the word processor, do the following:

1. Select the information in the spreadsheet that you want to copy.
2. Press Shift-F3. Works is now in the Copy mode.
3. Press Ctrl-F6 to move to the window in which you want to place the selected text.
4. Move the cursor to the location where you want to insert the selected text.
5. Press Enter.

Figure 13.15 shows an example in which the total income line from TENNIS.WKS is copied to RENEW.WPS.

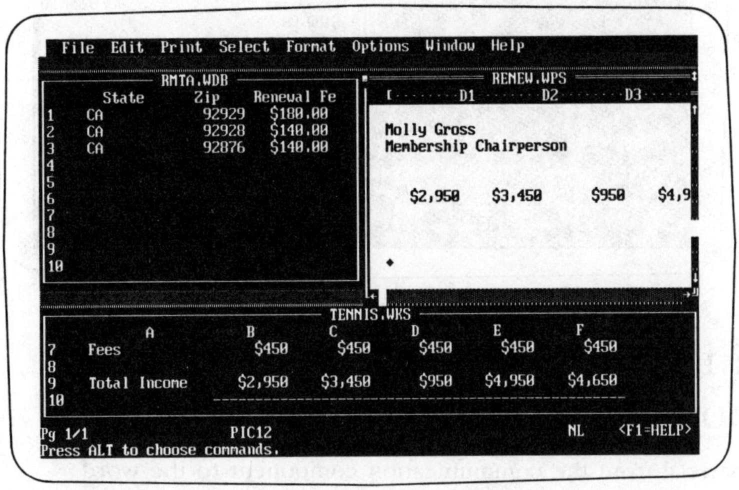

Fig. 13.15.

The total income line from TENNIS.WKS copied to RENEW.WPS.

Copying from the Database to the Word Processor

To copy material from the database to the word processor, do the following:

1. In Form view, select the record. In List view, select the record, records, field, or fields. In Report view, select a portion of a report.
2. Press Shift-F3. Works is now in the Copy mode.
3. Press Ctrl-F6 to move to the window in which you want to insert the selected text.

4. Move the cursor to the location where you want to insert the selected text.

5. Press Enter.

Figure 13.16 shows a record from the database copied to RENEW.WPS.

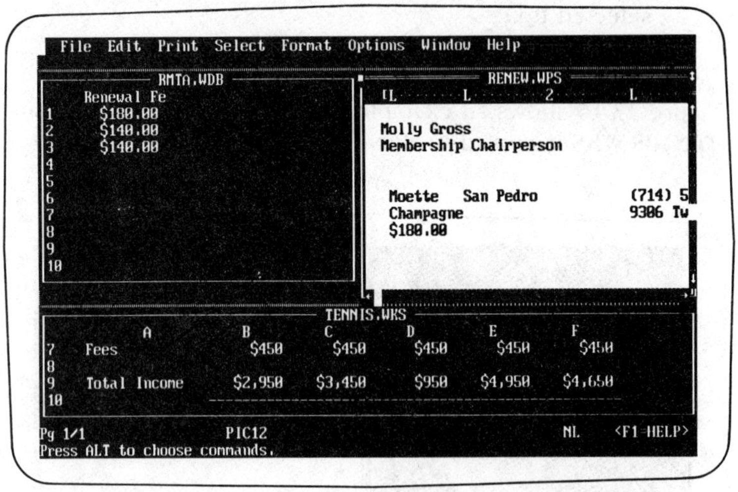

Fig. 13.16.

A record copied from the database List view to RENEW.WPS.

Copying from the Communication Component to the Word Processor

To copy material from the communication component to the word processor, do the following:

1. Select the text, table, or data displayed when you're using the communication option of Works.

2. Press Shift-F3. Works is now in the Copy mode.

3. Press Ctrl-F6 to move to the word processing window in which you want to insert the selected text.

4. Move the cursor to the location where you want to insert the selected text.

5. Press Enter.

The selected text from the communication component is inserted in the word processing component.

Copying from the Word Processor to the Spreadsheet

To copy material from the word processor to the spreadsheet, do the following:

1. Select any text, memos, or notes from the word processing component of Works.
2. Press Shift-F3. Works is now in the Copy mode.
3. Press Ctrl-F6 to move to the spreadsheet window in which you want to insert the selected text.
4. Move the cursor to the location where you want to insert the selected text.
5. Press Enter.

The word processing text is inserted into the spreadsheet.

Copying from the Database to the Spreadsheet

To copy material from the database to the spreadsheet, do the following:

1. In Form view, select a record. In List view, select records or fields. From a database, select portions of a report.
2. Press Shift-F3. Works is now in the Copy mode.
3. Press Ctrl-F6 to move to the spreadsheet window in which you want to insert the selected text.
4. Move the cursor to the location where you want to insert the selected text.
5. Press Enter.

Figure 13.17 shows data from the `Renewal Fee` field inserted into the spreadsheet.

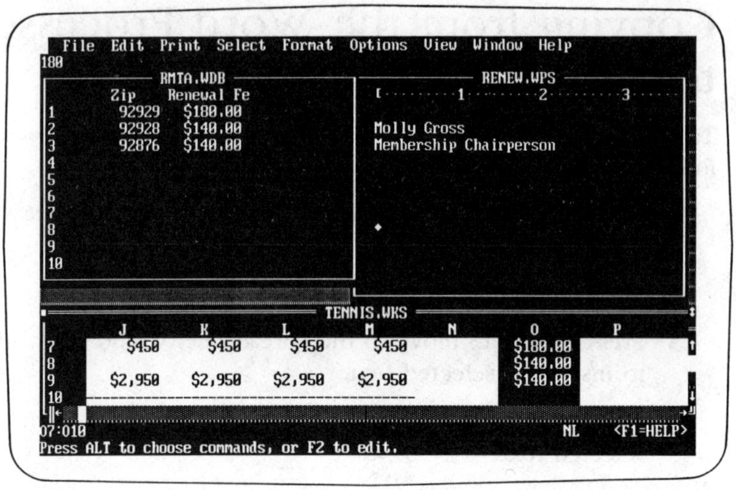

Fig. 13.17.
Database field inserted in a spreadsheet.

Copying from the Communication Component to the Spreadsheet

To copy material from the communication component to the spreadsheet, do the following:

1. Select a table, data, text, or combination of them from a communications file.
2. Press Shift-F3. Works is now in the Copy mode.
3. Press Ctrl-F6 to move to the spreadsheet window in which you want to insert the selected text.
4. Move the cursor to the location where you want to insert the selected text.
5. Press Enter.

The selected text is inserted into the spreadsheet file.

Copying from the Word Processor to the Database

To copy material from the word processor to the database, do the following:

1. Select a name, data element, or block of text from the word processing file.

2. Press Shift-F3. Works is now in the Copy mode.
3. Press Ctrl-F6 to move to the database window in which you want to insert the selected data.
4. Move the cursor to the location where you want to insert the selected text.
5. Press Enter.

In figure 13.18, a name from the word processing file is inserted in the database file under the `First Name` field. When copying the name and address of a new correspondent from the word processing file to the database file, insert the data or text one field at a time.

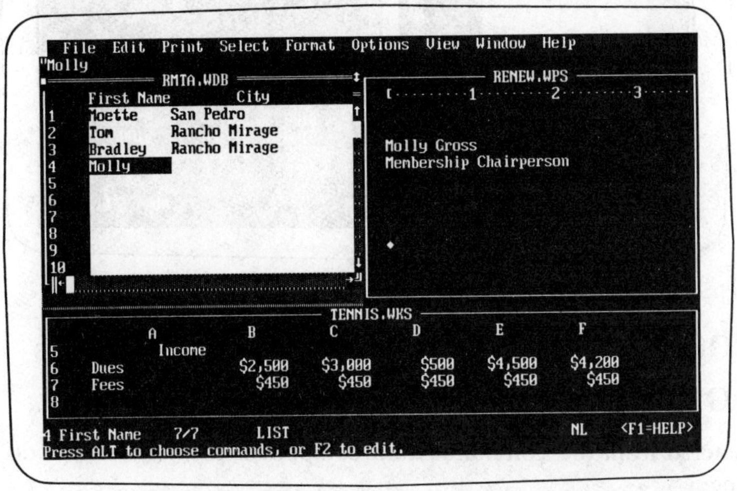

Fig. 13.18.

A first name inserted in a database file.

Copying from the Spreadsheet to the Database

To copy material from the spreadsheet to the database, do the following:

1. Select a row or column of data to be inserted in the database file. The results of the calculations will be copied. The formulas will not be copied.
2. Press Shift-F3. Works is now in the Copy mode.
3. Press Ctrl-F6 to move to the database window in which you want to insert the selected text.

4. Move the cursor to the location where you want to insert the selected data.

5. Press Enter.

Figure 13.19 shows a column of data inserted in a database field column.

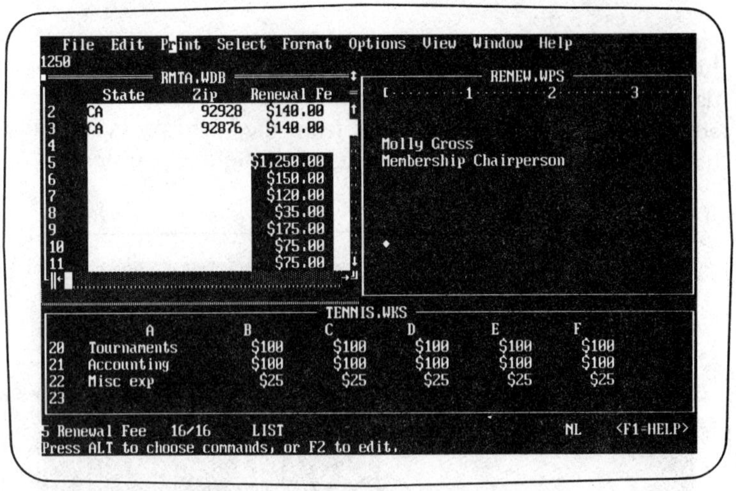

Fig. 13.19.

A column of spreadsheet data inserted.

Copying from the Communication Component to the Database

To copy material from the communication component to the database, do the following:

1. Select a table, text, or data from a communications file.

2. Press Shift-F3. Works is now in the Copy mode.

3. Press Ctrl-F6 to move to the database window in which you want to insert the selected text.

4. Move the cursor to the location where you want to insert the selected text.

5. Press Enter.

The table, text, or data is inserted in the database. Names and addresses should be inserted one field at a time.

Copying from the Word Processor to the Communication Component

To copy material from the word processor to the communication component, do the following:

1. Select the text or table from the word processing file.
2. Press Shift-F3. Works is now in the Copy mode.
3. Press Ctrl-F6 to move to the communications window in which you want to insert the selected text.
4. Move the cursor to the location where you want to insert the selected text.
5. Press Enter.

The word processing text is inserted in the communications file. The text can now be exported from your computer.

Copying from the Spreadsheet to the Communication Component

To copy material from the spreadsheet to the communication component, do the following:

1. Select the figures in rows or columns (or a range of both) that you want to be transferred to a communications file.
2. Press Shift-F3. Works is now in the Copy mode.
3. Press Ctrl-F6 to move to the window in which you want to insert the selected text.
4. Move the cursor to the location where you want to insert the selected text.
5. Press Enter.

The spreadsheet data is inserted in the communications file. The data can now be exported from your computer.

Copying from the Database to the Communication Component

To copy material from the database to the communication component, do the following:

1. In Form view, select the record or field. In List view, select the fields or records. In Report view, select sections of a report.
2. Press Shift-F3. Works is now in the Copy mode.
3. Press Ctrl-F6 to move to the communications window in which you want to insert the selected text.
4. Move the cursor to the location where you want to insert the selected text.
5. Press Enter.

The database text is inserted in the communications file. The data can now be exported from your computer.

Merging Files with Works

Use the Works merge feature to merge database and word processing files. You can use the merge feature to create personalized form letters—letters that have basically the same text but are addressed to different people. The merge feature can also be used for creating mailing labels from the records in the database. (For additional information about making a form letter and mailing labels, see Chapter 4.)

To merge two files, you need the following:

- ❑ A word processing file with place holders and/or text that will hold the position for database fields.
- ❑ A database file containing records. The data from the records will be inserted in the word processing file.

In this chapter, you will create mailing labels from the records in a database as an example of the merge feature. You can use any database you have created. For this section's example, JULY.WDB is used, and a word processing file called LABEL.WPS is created for holding the mailing labels.

JULY.WDB is already created. The file is a database containing the names, addresses (including country), and purchases of a group of customers from outside the United States. All the customers received the July mailing. This database records the response from this group.

Create a new word processing file to hold the place holders for the mailing label. Press Alt to activate the menu bar and then F to select the File menu. Press N to create a new file. With the cursor on New Word Processor, press Enter.

In this new word processing file, you are going to add place holders. These place holders will be field names taken from the existing fields in the database. Place the field names in the order you want them to appear on the mailing label.

With the cursor at the top of the file, press Alt to activate the menu bar and then E for the Edit menu. Press F for the Insert Field option. A dialog box appears. From this dialog box, select the database file you want to use for this particular mailing list. Although you may have many database files in Works, only the open database files are listed. If no database file appears under `Databases`, press Esc and open the database file you want to use.

In this example, `JULY.WDB` appears in the dialog box (see fig. 13.20). The fields of the database are listed on the right side of the dialog box under `Fields`. Press the right-arrow key to move the highlight to the field list.

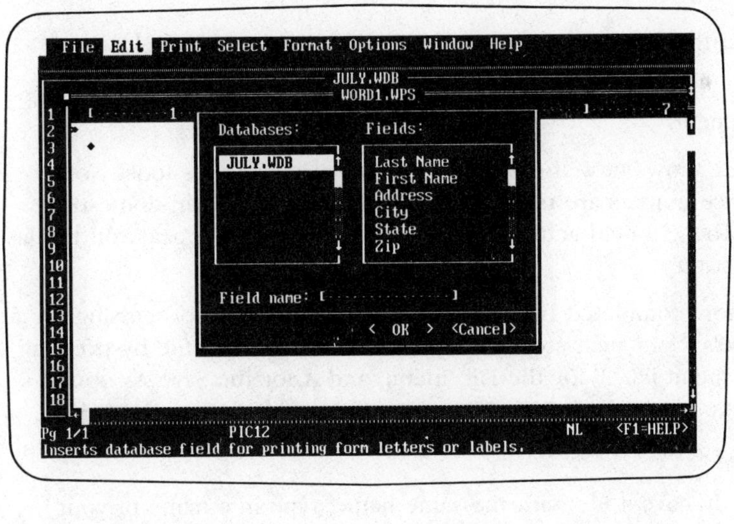

Fig. 13.20.
The Insert Field dialog box.

Press the down-arrow key to move to `First Name` and press Enter. The word processing file now has one field place holder in it (see fig. 13.21).

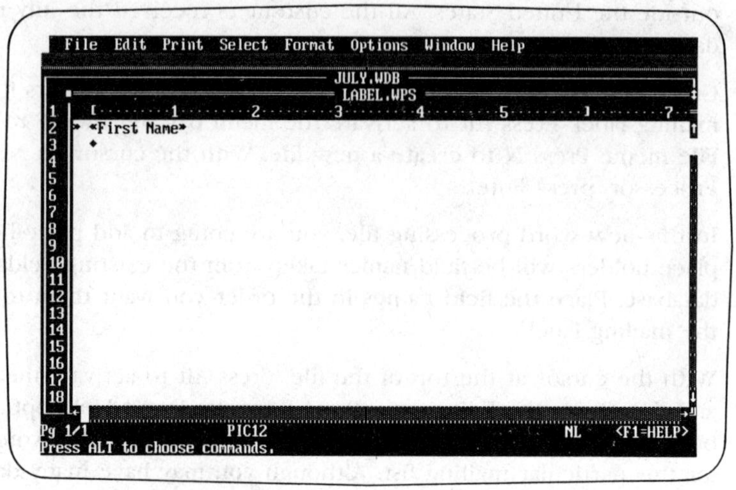

Fig. 13.21.

`First Name` *field place holder in LABEL.WPS.*

Type a space in the word processing document. Repeat the steps that follow until the entire address has place holders in the word processing document (include punctuation and spaces and press Enter to end lines):

1. Press Alt, select the Edit menu, and then select the Insert Field option.
2. Select the field name by moving the highlight to that field.
3. Press Enter to insert the field place holder in the word processing document.

Figure 13.22 shows how the completed field place holders look. Notice that the place holders are positioned a little differently than domestic addresses. The `Zip` field actually holds postal codes and appears on the last line with `Country`.

You have now completed the process of creating a word processing file for mailing labels. Your next step is to save the file. Save the file by pressing Alt for the menu bar, F for the File menu, and A for the Save As option. For the name of the file, type

LABEL.WPS

If you already have a file with the same name, type in a name of your choice. Then press Enter.

The database file and the word processing file are now ready to be merged. Before you can print the labels, however, you have to set the page size and margins for label paper.

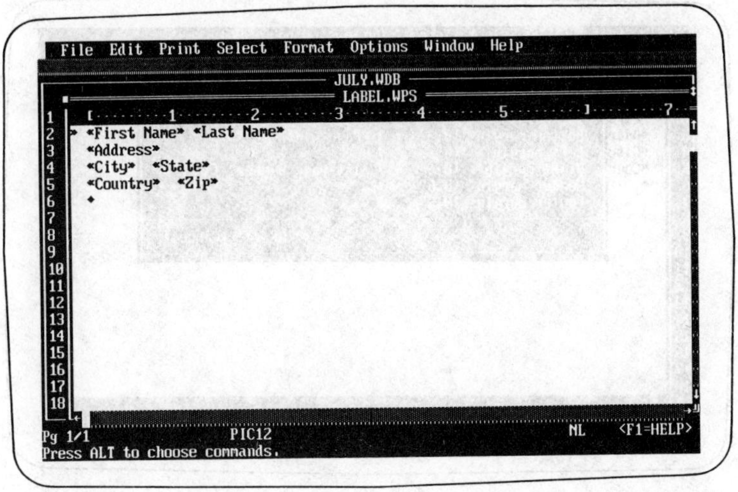

Fig. 13.22. *Field place holders in LABEL.WPS.*

Setting the Paper Size and Margins for Labels

Because this page size is different from the standard 8 1/2-by-11-inch paper, adjustments must be made. The choices you make for the page size and margins are based on the type of labels you use. The numbers entered here are for a single row of tractor-fed labels. If you are using sheets with three labels across, enter the appropriate numbers for your materials.

With the cursor in LABEL.WPS, press Alt to activate the menu bar and P for the Print menu. Then press M for the Page Setup & Margins option. The Page Setup & Margins dialog box appears.

Press Alt-L to move to the `Page length` field. Type the length of one sheet of labels. Tractor-fed labels are on 12-inch pages, so type *12"*. The measurement is from perforation to perforation.

Press Alt-W to move to the `Page width` option. Type *3.5"* for the width of one label. Go to the `Top margin`, `Bottom margin`, `Left margin`, and `Right margin` fields. Each should be at `0` for mailing labels.

Figure 13.23 shows the finished Page Setup & Margins dialog box for tractor-fed labels. Press Enter when your dialog box is set up like the one shown in the figure.

Now that the page size and margins are set, you are ready to print the labels. The database file you want to use has to be open, and your cursor has to be in the word processing file before you can print.

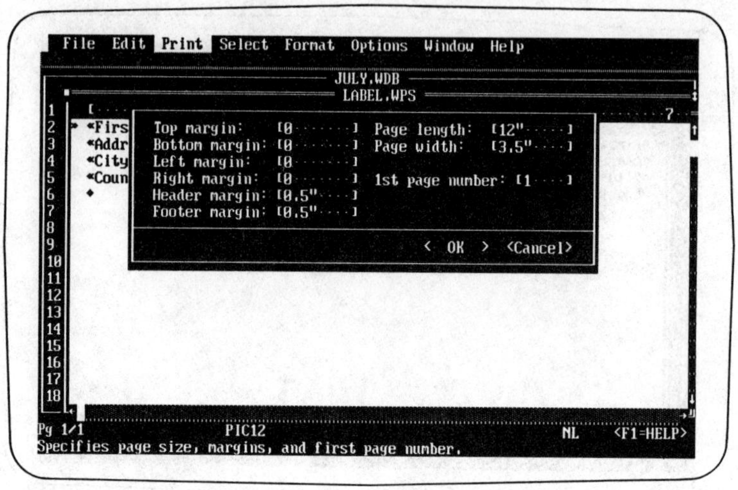

Fig. 13.23.

Page Setup & Margins dialog box for labels.

Printing the Mailing Labels

The labels must be properly positioned in the printer before you begin printing. You also have a few more choices to make before you can print the labels. Press Alt to activate the menu bar and P for the Print menu. Then press L for the Labels option. The Label dialog box appears.

Open databases are listed in the box on the left. Move the highlight to the database you want to use. Then press Alt-V to go to the `Vertical` field. Type the distance from the top of one label to the top of the next label. In this case, type *1"*. Press Alt-H to go to the `Horizontal` field. Type *3"* for the width of one label. For the `Number of labels across page` field, leave the value at `1` because there is only one label across the page. Before you press Enter, make sure that the Label dialog box looks like the one shown in figure 13.24.

Press Enter and the Page Size & Margins dialog box appears. You already have set these values, so press Enter again. The Print dialog box appears. From this dialog box, select the number of copies you want and whether you want to print any particular pages. If you want one copy of labels for the entire database, press Enter.

Your list of mailing labels is printed and ready to place on the envelopes. You have successfully merged two documents with Works. The advantages of an integrated software package like Works should be apparent.

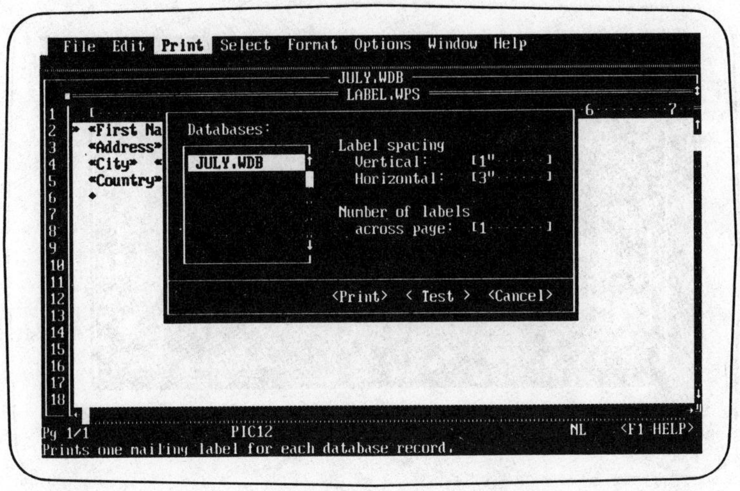

Fig. 13.24.

The Label dialog box with entries.

Using Works Accessories

Works provides accessories to make your work easy. These accessories are examined in this section along with examples of how to use them. Become familiar with these added features. They can increase your efficiency and keep you working smart.

Using the Works Alarm Clock

Have you ever been so engrossed in your spreadsheet—analyzing every twist and nuance in the data—that you forgot to look at your clock and ended up missing a lunch appointment or other engagement? The Works alarm clock can help ensure that this situation never happens again. You just have to remember to set the alarm!

Press Alt to activate the menu bar and O for the Options menu. Then press A to select the Alarm Clock option. The Alarm Clock dialog box appears (see fig. 13.25). A description of the elements of the Alarm Clock dialog box follows:

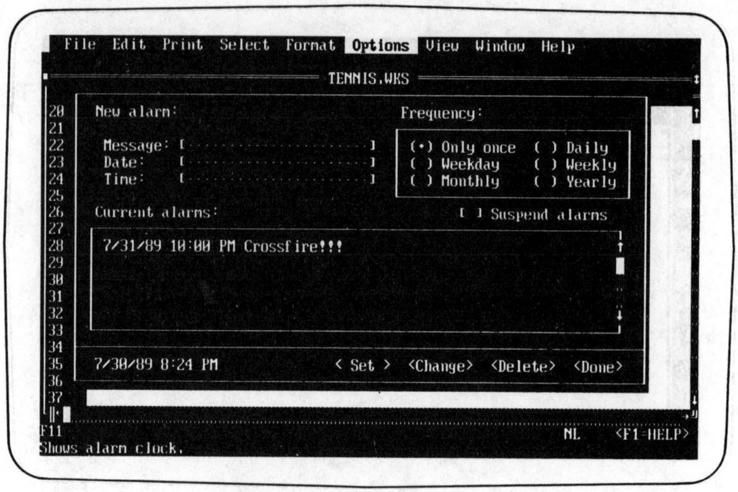

Fig. 13.25.

The Alarm Clock dialog box.

`Message` In this field, enter any message up to 60 characters long. An example is *Lunch with Vice President of Finance*. Press Alt-G to reach this field in order to enter a message.

`Date` Works accepts the date in these formats: 12/28/90; December 28, 1990; or Dec 28, 1990. Enter the date you want the alarm to sound. If you don't include a date, the alarm sounds at the next occurrence of the specified time. For regular daily appointments, leave the date box blank and the alarm will go off every day at the specified time. Press Alt-A to set the date.

`Time` Works accepts the time in these formats: 10:30 AM; 10:30 PM (or 22:30); or 10:30. With no time entered in the box, the alarm goes off at midnight.

`Frequency` In this box, select the interval you want for the alarm. Select Alt-O if you want the alarm to go off one time only, select Alt-W for weekdays only, select Alt-M for a monthly alarm, select Alt-L for a daily alarm, select Alt-K for a weekly alarm, and select Alt-Y for an annual alarm.

`Current alarms` This box lists the alarms now set, including the date, time, and message.

`Suspend alarms`	Press Alt-P to toggle this option on or off. When this option is on, alarms will not go off (but they are not deleted). Turn off this option to reactivate the alarms that already have been set.
`Set`	Press Alt-S to add a new alarm to the list.
`Change`	This option allows you to change the settings for a particular alarm.
`Delete`	Use this option to delete an alarm setting.
`Done`	Select this option when you are done in the Alarm Clock dialog box.

Set a new alarm by following these steps:

1. Press Alt to activate the menu bar, O for the Options menu, and A for the Alarm Clock option.
2. Type a message to remind you why you set the alarm.
3. In the appropriate boxes, enter the date and time you want the alarm to sound.
4. Move to the `Frequency` box to select how often you want the alarm sound.
5. Press Alt-S to set the alarm. You can set another alarm now or press Alt-D to leave the Alarm Clock dialog box.

Change an existing alarm by following these steps:

1. Press Alt-U to get to the `Current alarms` box and then move the highlight to select the alarm you want to change.
2. Press Alt-A or Alt-I to go to the `Date` and `Time` fields and type in the changes you want to make.
3. When you are done, press Alt-C for the `Change` option.
4. If you want, you can set, change, or delete another alarm. Press Alt-D when you are done.

Delete an alarm that you already have set by following these steps:

1. Press Alt-U to go to the `Current alarms` box and then move the highlight to select the alarm you want to delete.
2. Press Alt-T and that alarm is eliminated.

Suppose that you have several alarms set to go off on a daily basis, but today you have no meetings and are working intensely on a special project. Select the Suspend alarms option so that you will not be bothered by alarms beeping at you. Press Alt for the menu bar, O for the Options menu, and A for the Alarm Clock option. At the Alarm Clock dialog box, press Alt-P to turn on the Suspend alarms option. An X appears beside this option when it is toggled on. Repeat the same steps to toggle Suspend alarms off. With this option in the off position, previously set alarms will go off as expected.

When the alarm goes off, the Alarm dialog box appears on-screen. This box shows the date, time, and message. Three options are on this dialog box. Your first option is to press Alt-S for the Snooze option. The alarm goes off again in 10 minutes. Your second option is to press Alt-R for the Alarm Clock dialog box so you can reset the date and time. Your third option is to press Enter with OK highlighted. The dialog box closes, and the alarm goes off again the next time it is scheduled.

Using the Works Calculator

Whether you are in a spreadsheet, database, word processor, or communications window, you can access the Works calculator when you need it. Press Alt to activate the menu bar, O for the Options menu, and C for the Calculator option. The calculator appears (see fig. 13.26).

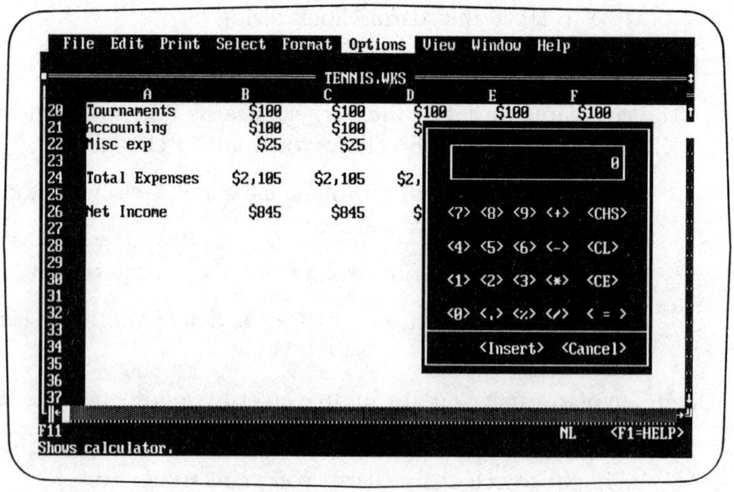

Fig. 13.26.

The calculator on-screen.

With the keyboard, press the number or corresponding symbol of the calculation you want to make. For example, multiply 899 by 0.05 by typing

899*.05=

The number 899 appears on-screen. When you press the asterisk (*), the number remains. When you type *.05*, that number replaces 899. Press the equal sign (=), and the answer 44.95 appears on the calculator answer box.

Use the mouse to do the same calculation by pointing to the number or symbol on the screen. Point to numbers or symbols in the same sequence used with the keyboard.

You can add (+), subtract (−), multiply (*), divide (/), and calculate percentages (%) using the calculator. Some of the other features are the CHS key, CL key, and CE key. CHS changes the sign of the number displayed in the calculator answer box. CL clears the entire calculator. CE clears the last entry only.

While you are working in a file, you may need to insert the result of your calculation into the file. Start by placing the cursor in the cell in which you want the resulting number inserted. Press Alt for the menu bar, O for the Options menu, and C for the Calculator option. Make the desired calculation. When the calculation is completed, press Alt-I to insert the answer in the previously selected cell.

Using the Works Settings Dialog Box

When you want to customize settings like the colors in the screen display, the number of lines on the screen, the language used, or the units for measuring input, you can use the Works Settings dialog box. Press Alt for the menu bar, O for the Options menu, and then W for the Works Settings option. The Works Settings dialog box appears (see fig. 13.27).

Note: Your Works Settings dialog box may not look like the one shown in figure 13.27. The dialog box displayed is specific to your video card and your equipment.

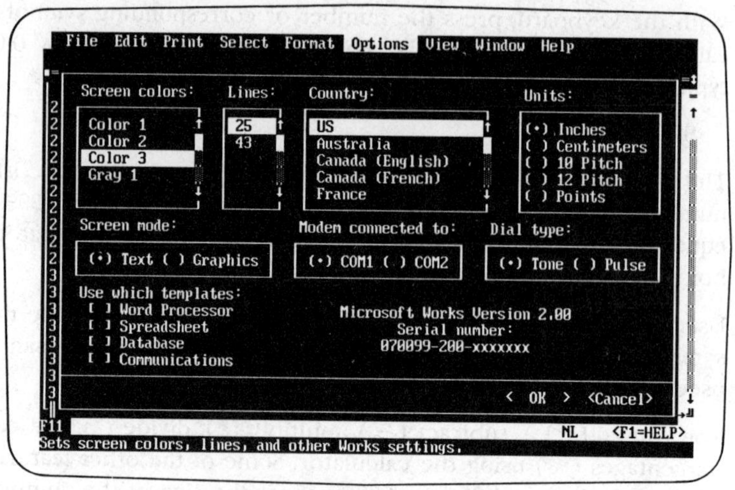

Fig. 13.27.
The Works Settings dialog box.

A description of the options on this dialog box follows:

`Screen colors` — If you have a color monitor, select from the combinations of colors available to find the easiest to work with.

`Lines` — Select from the options for the number of lines displayed. The standard is 25 lines. Individual lines will be compressed considerably if you select a higher number.

`Country` — Select the setting that reflects your location or the work you are doing. When the option is changed, the preset items listed here change to fit the standard in the country selected. The default setting is `US`.

The page size is adjusted to the standard in the selected country. The default values in the Page Setup & Margins dialog box are affected.

The standard currency symbol and display format is adjusted to the country in the spreadsheet and database.

Wherever Works prints or displays the date and time, the order and format is adjusted to the selected country standard.

	Other miscellaneous items are adjusted, including column width for the spreadsheet and database and separator characters for the date and time settings. If you select a country with another language, some of the characters will change using the selected language.
`Units`	`Inches` is the default for most numbers that have units. Works assumes that you mean one-half inch when you type *.5* in the Tab dialog box. If you type numbers with other dimensions, Works converts them to inches. If you type *2 cm*, for example, Works converts the measurement to .787 inches. If you want to work with a unit other than inches, select the unit you prefer from the `Units` section of the Works Settings dialog box. The unit you select becomes the default. If you select `Points` and then type *2*, Works assumes that you mean 2 points.
`Screen mode`	Your choices are `Text` or `Graphics`. Select `Graphics` and the mouse pointer appears as an arrow. The character styles appear (the character style bold appears bold, for example), and some formatting lines are visible. Select `Text` and the mouse pointer appears as a rectangle. The character styles appear in different colors (providing that you have a color monitor). Some editing functions are faster in Text mode than in Graphics mode. You may prefer to create a document in Text mode and then put the finishing touches on the document in Graphics mode. Press Alt-G for the Graphics mode or Alt-X for the Text mode.
`Modem connected to`	This item identifies the port to which your modem is connected.
`Dial type`	Select the type of dialing used by your phone. The choices are `Pulse` or `Tone` (see Chapter 11 for more information on setting up the modem).
`Use which templates`	When you select the Create New File option from the File menu, you can tell Works to open a template file rather than a standard Works file. The next section provides more information on setting up template files.

Creating Templates

Suppose that you are running a business with two divisions, and each of these divisions has a management department. You are in the process of setting up each department with a budget. Instead of having each department develop its own budget format, create a template for the budget so that both departments will use the same format. Only the numbers will change from department to department.

Use a template in a word processing file to establish a format for certain documents. For example, all reports to the shareholders can have a consistent header, footer, font, and format. Instead of creating these special settings every time you send a report to the shareholders, use a template that contains the settings. A template file can be created for any Works component to gain consistency.

Set up a template file by pressing Alt to activate the menu bar and F for the File menu. Press N to create a new file. Select the type of file you want to create from one of the four components. Set up the format for the template file exactly as you want it for each use.

In a spreadsheet, you may list income and expenses that will be consistent throughout your organization. In a database, you may create an invoice format that will be used in every division. After the file is created, press Alt for the menu bar, F for the File menu, and A for the Save As option. While in the Save As dialog box, press Alt-A. An `X` is placed next to the `Save as template` option, indicating that the option is turned on. Select `OK` and press Enter.

When you are ready to enter text in the template to create a document, make sure that the Works Settings dialog box is turned on for templates for any types of files in which you have a template developed. If you have a spreadsheet and word processing template developed, these two options in the Works Settings dialog box should be marked with an `X`. (To reach the Works Settings dialog box, press Alt for the menu bar, O for the Options menu, and W for the Works Settings option.)

Return to the File menu by pressing Alt and then F. Press N to create a new file. Select the component of Works in which you want to create a new file. If you have templates for the spreadsheet and word processor, select either one of these components. When you create a new file, Works will open a file with the template you have created.

Enter the data or document you want, and it will be entered according to your established template.

If you find that you want to change a template file, open the existing template file by pressing Alt for the menu bar, F for the File menu, and then O. The template files are named as follows:

TEMPLATE.PS	Word processor
TEMPLATE.KS	Spreadsheet
TEMPLATE.DB	Database
TEMPLATE.CM	Communications

Select the template you want to change and press Enter. Make the necessary changes and save the file again with the same file name.

You may find that your needs for a template have changed dramatically. In that case, you can create a new template by following the procedures for creating a template. Using this method, you may add entirely new formats, titles, headers, and footers.

See Appendix A for information about templates that are already created. Appendix A lists sources for these templates. Purchasing templates can save you time because you will not have to create the template.

Chapter Summary

In this chapter, you took advantage of Works' integrated environment. You began by learning how to size, move, and arrange Works windows. With your window skills sharpened, you learned the tips and tricks for copying between windows. The steps for copying were listed for every copy option. You explored the techniques of merging a word processing and database file to create mailing labels (see Chapter 4 for more information on this topic).

The last section of the chapter explored the Works accessories. You examined how the accessories work and how you can use them to your advantage. The options with the alarm clock, calculator, Works settings, and templates were explained.

You are now an accomplished Works user and are able to take advantage of all the features.

A

Using Works with Other Programs and Services

This appendix covers several useful topics. You will receive information on using Works with other programs and will learn how to save files to be transmitted electronically. You also will examine a list enhancement resources, including templates and electronic databases.

Using Works with Other Programs

Due to the great number of other software programs, the folks at Microsoft included in Microsoft Works the capacity to share the information in Works files with other popular programs. In addition, the information in other programs can be imported into Works.

1-2-3 Spreadsheets

The best-selling spreadsheet (as of this writing) is Lotus 1-2-3. Works will work with files created by Releases 1A and 2.0 directly—no conversion needed. Works spreadsheets also will perform without any converting of file formats in 1-2-3. The reason is that the file format used by 1-2-3 Release 1A is also used by Works.

The key parts of the spreadsheet file are recognized. The key parts are the formulas, formats, values, and range names.

Learning What Does Not Work

Because Microsoft Works and 1-2-3 spreadsheet features are not identical, you can lose minor information if you do the following:

1. Create and save a file in Microsoft Works.
2. Open the same file in Lotus 1-2-3 and then save it in Lotus 1-2-3.

The information that can be lost are Works- or Lotus-specific attributes. These attributes represent capabilities unique to Works or 1-2-3. The reverse of the preceding sequence also can result in lost information. Lotus-created files opened in Works and then saved can lose information.

1-2-3 Release 2.0 uses a string-combination operator, the & sign, which Works does not support. In addition, several Release 2.0 functions are not recognized by Works:

- ❑ All string functions
- ❑ All database statistical functions
- ❑ The date and time functions: @DATEVALUE and @TIMEVALUE
- ❑ The logical functions: @ISNUMBER and @ISSTRING
- ❑ The special functions: @@, @CELL, and @CELLPOINTER

Using a 1-2-3 file with these functions results in the values being retained, not the formulas.

Opening a 1-2-3 File

To open a 1-2-3 file in Works, use the same procedure you would use to open a Works file. Press Alt, select File, and then select Open. Select the file name and press Enter.

Other Spreadsheets or Databases

A popular database program is dBASE. To transfer files from Works to dBASE or to spreadsheets that are not compatible with 1-2-3, you must convert the Works files to ASCII (or text) files that can be loaded by other programs.

Converting a spreadsheet file to an ASCII file makes fundamental changes in the structure of the file. Formulas are not going to be retained—only the values that the formula produced.

As an example, if a cell contains the formula C1+C2, which results in the value 10, only the value 10 will be converted in the ASCII file.

ASCII files use commas as delimiters. *Delimiters* are the symbols that separate the data in the text file that come from cells.

When Works converts the spreadsheet or database file to text, the end of a row or the end of a record is separated by a carriage return and a line feed.

Saving a File as an ASCII File

To save a file as an ASCII text file, follow these steps:

1. Press the Alt key and select the Files menu. From that menu, select the Save As option.
2. A dialog box appears (see fig. A.1). Type a unique name for the file.

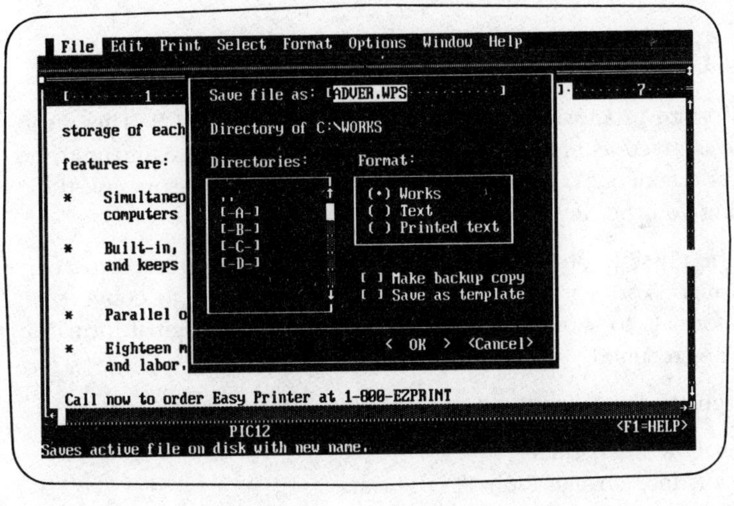

Fig. A.1.

The Save As dialog box.

3. Select the text format and then press Enter. Works responds with a dialog box informing you that saving the file this way will result in the loss of formatting. Press Enter to proceed.

The original file you have been working with remains on the screen, and the new ASCII file is saved on disk.

Opening Database and Spreadsheet Files from Other Programs

In order for Works to open a file from another spreadsheet or database, the file must first be saved as an ASCII text file (with the exception of 1-2-3 files).

Individual pieces of information in text files are delimited (separated) either by commas (for spreadsheet files) or tab marks (for database files). A spreadsheet row is separated by a carriage return. An entire database record is also separated by a carriage return.

After a file from another program has been saved as an ASCII text file, the file can be used in Works. In Works, press Alt, select File, and then select Open. Type the name of the file to open. Works will recognize that the file is not in Works format. A dialog box asks you to select the tool (the Works word processor, database, or spreadsheet, for example) into which the file should be opened.

Word Processing Files

Virtually all word processing programs can save files as ASCII. This means that the file is saved as text only. When a file is saved in this manner, no formatting is retained. To use files from other word processors, ask the person giving you the file to save it as ASCII.

It may not be possible or practical to have all the files you need to access in ASCII format. Works provides you with a limited ability to convert several file formats to Works format. In doing so, many original formatting commands are retained.

Works recognizes the following word processing formats:

- ❑ Microsoft Word Format
- ❑ Microsoft Interchange Rich Text Format
- ❑ IBM Document Content Architecture Format

As an example, if you create a file in Borland's Sprint, you can use the Sprint conversion facility to convert the file to Microsoft Word format, which Works can then interpret.

You can convert a Works word-processed file to one of three other types of files. The three types are Microsoft Word, Microsoft Interchange Rich Text Format, and IBM Document Content Architecture Format.

To convert a Works word-processed file to another format, press Alt and select the File menu. From the menu, select the Convert option. Type the file name of the file you want to convert and press Enter, or point and then click OK.

Works responds with the dialog box asking for the file to convert to. If you want, type a new file name and extension. If you type only the file name and no extension, Works will add the proper extension for you (appropriate to the type of file).

Press Enter and the file is converted and saved under the new name.

Electronic Information Services

If you have a modem, the following electronic services are available to you. Simply contact the vendor.

CompuServe
5000 Arlington Centre Blvd.
Columbus, OH 43220
800-848-8990

Official Airline Guide
2000 Clearwater Drive
Oak Brook, IL 60521
800-323-4000

Templates

Two companies offer prebuilt templates ready for your use in Microsoft Works. If you write to these companies, you can get a free catalog of products.

Heizer Software
P.O. Box 232019
Pleasant Hill, CA 94523

ATE
P.O. Box 160
Poway, CA 92064

Newsletters

To receive a newsletter that focuses on using the attributes of Microsoft Works, contact

The Cobb Group
The Workshop
9420 Bunsen Parkway #300
Louisville, KY 40220
800-223-8720

Index

D

E

F

G

H

I

K

L

M

S

T

U

V

Free Catalog!

Mail us this registration form today, and we'll send you a free catalog featuring Que's complete line of best-selling books.

Name of Book ______

Name ______

Title ______

Phone ( ) ______

Company ______

Address ______

City ______

State ______ ZIP ______

Please check the appropriate answers:

1. Where did you buy your Que book?
   - ☐ Bookstore (name: ______)
   - ☐ Computer store (name: ______)
   - ☐ Catalog (name: ______)
   - ☐ Direct from Que
   - ☐ Other: ______
2. How many computer books do you buy a year?
   - ☐ 1 or less
   - ☐ 2-5
   - ☐ 6-10
   - ☐ More than 10
3. How many Que books do you own?
   - ☐ 1
   - ☐ 2-5
   - ☐ 6-10
   - ☐ More than 10
4. How long have you been using this software?
   - ☐ Less than 6 months
   - ☐ 6 months to 1 year
   - ☐ 1-3 years
   - ☐ More than 3 years
5. What influenced your purchase of this Que book?
   - ☐ Personal recommendation
   - ☐ Advertisement
   - ☐ In-store display
   - ☐ Price
   - ☐ Que catalog
   - ☐ Que mailing
   - ☐ Que's reputation
   - ☐ Other: ______
6. How would you rate the overall content of the book?
   - ☐ Very good
   - ☐ Good
   - ☐ Satisfactory
   - ☐ Poor
7. What do you like *best* about this Que book?

   ______

   ______
8. What do you like *least* about this Que book?

   ______

   ______
9. Did you buy this book with your personal funds?
   - ☐ Yes ☐ No
10. Please feel free to list any other comments you may have about this Que book.

    ______

    ______

    ______

QUE

Order Your Que Books Today!

Name ______

Title ______

Company ______

City ______

State ______ ZIP ______

Phone No. ( ) ______

Method of Payment:

Check ☐ (Please enclose in envelope.)

Charge My: VISA ☐ MasterCard ☐

American Express ☐

Charge # ______

Expiration Date ______

Order No.	Title	Qty.	Price	Total

You can **FAX** your order to **1-317-573-2583.** Or call **1-800-428-5331, ext. ORDR** to order direct.

Please add $2.50 per title for shipping and handling.

Subtotal	
Shipping & Handling	
Total	

QUE

NO POSTAGE
NECESSARY
IF MAILED
IN THE
UNITED STATES

BUSINESS REPLY MAIL
First Class Permit No. 9918 Indianapolis, IN

Postage will be paid by addressee

QUE®

11711 N. College
Carmel, IN 46032

NO POSTAGE
NECESSARY
IF MAILED
IN THE
UNITED STATES

BUSINESS REPLY MAIL
First Class Permit No. 9918 Indianapolis, IN

Postage will be paid by addressee

QUE®

11711 N. College
Carmel, IN 46032